FIRST IN VIETNAM

FIRST IN VIETNAM

AN EXERCISE IN EXCESS OF 30 DAYS
The U.S. Army 57th Transportation Helicopter Company
(Light Helicopter) (CH-21)
1961-1962

Colonel Emmett F. Knight
U.S. Army Retired

Cover Design by: LTC Charles R. (Rich) Bryant

MAAG VIET-NAM
WORK-HORSES
57

Dedicated to Sergeant James D. McAndrew and all those Transportation Corps Aviators and Enlisted men that served in the early days of the Vietnam War;

And to my daughter Karen who waited for my return;

And to my wife Margie who has put up with the many days and the frustrations of my writing this historical memoir.

57TH HELICOPTER COMPANY
AREA OF OPERATIONS

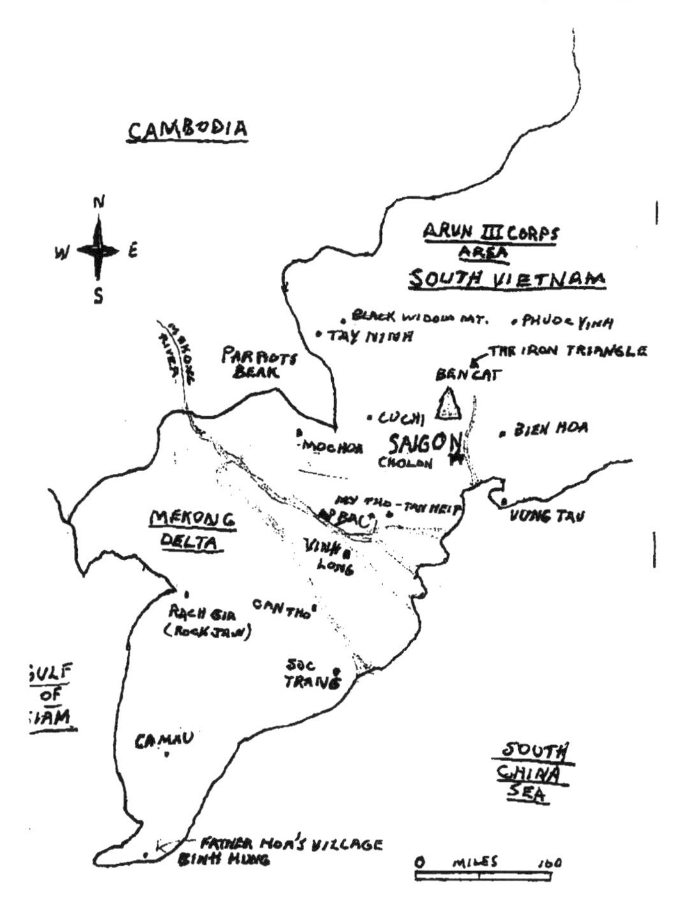

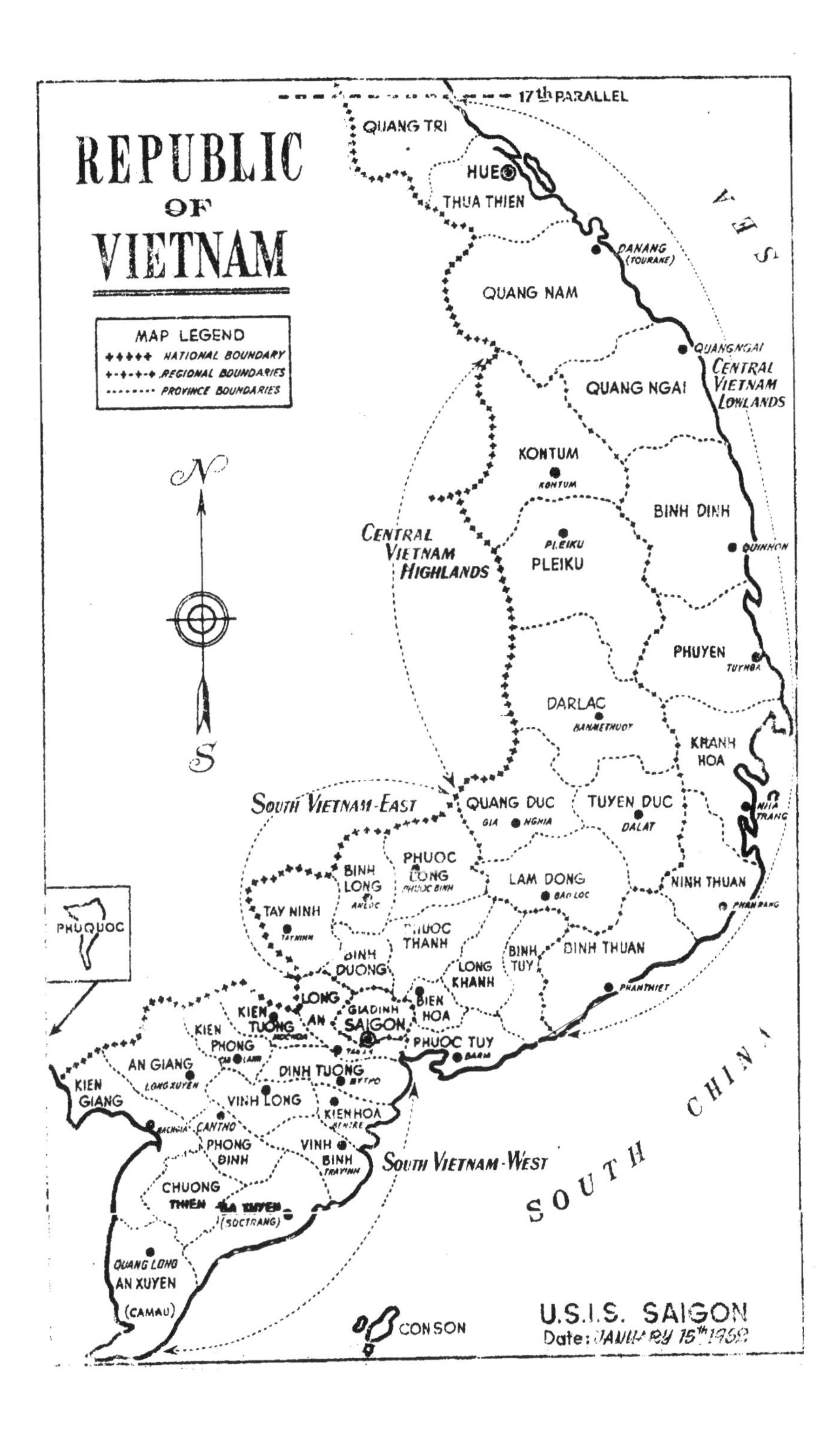

REPUBLIC OF VIETNAM
MAP LEGEND
NATIONAL BOUNDARY
REGIONAL BOUNDARIES
PROVINCE BOUNDARIES
17th PARALLEL
QUANG TRI
HUE
THUA THIEN
DANANG (TOURANE)
QUANG NAM
QUANGNGAI
QUANG NGAI
CENTRAL VIETNAM LOWLANDS
KONTUM
BINH DINH
PLEIKU
CENTRAL VIETNAM HIGHLANDS
QUINHON
PHUYEN
DARLAC
BANMETHUOT
KHANH HOA
QUANG DUC
GIA NGHIA
TUYEN DUC
DALAT
NHA TRANG
SOUTH VIETNAM-EAST
PHUOC LONG
BINH LONG
LAM DONG
NINH THUAN
TAY NINH
PHUOC THANH
BINH TUY
BINH THUAN
BINH DUONG
LONG KHANH
PHANTHIET
LONG AN
GIADINH
SAIGON
BIEN HOA
KIEN TUONG
KIEN PHONG
PHUOC TUY
AN GIANG
DINH TUONG
KIEN GIANG
VINH LONG
KIEN HOA
CANTHO
PHONG DINH
VINH BINH
SOUTH VIETNAM-WEST
CHUONG THIEN
(SOCTRANG)
QUANG LONG
AN XUYEN
(CAMAU)
CONSON
PHUQUOC
SEA
SOUTH CHINA
N
S
U.S.I.S. SAIGON

Contents

ACKNOWLEDGMENTS

This book is a military memoir so the tales that I tell are from my own mental attic, but I must recognize the members of the 57th and the 98th as well as our other detachments for they provided the main actors in the events of 1961 and 1962. I have checked occasional facts at our reunions over the years and I thank you all for the input. Some information has been gleaned from the few official documents I have retained. The places where I have relied on written sources are identified in the text and as references. Rod Magie sent along some stories and took a look at a chapter. Bill Brethour sent an early photograph of a gathering in the hanger at Tan Son Nuht which I had not previously seen. And I thank them both. Jim Tarrant and Al Causseaux dug up some copies of our old unit patches, mine I had lost over the years, so thank you much. Bill Hinds corrected my mixed-up memory of the events surrounding an early engine failure and his second time of being shot down. I am happy for the opportunity to get that about right now. The cover photograph was taken by U.S. Army Master Sergeant Al Chang. Some stories were augmented by conversation with other members of the 57th and its attachments at or near the time of the events. That was a long time ago so only the author can be held responsible for these contents.

My wife Margie was invaluable in proof reading and providing editorial advice.

PREFACE

The Vietnam Joke Book

Perhaps this story should have started on one dark night in late November 1961 with a small group of men, officers and pilots of the 57th Helicopter Company, who were standing on the deck of an old World War II "jeep carrier" as she eased out of San Francisco Bay. The comment of one of them suited the moment and it wasn't too far off for years to come either. As the Golden Gate arched high into the darkness above, my thoughts were "now that is an unusual view" and as we craned our necks and swiveled to watch the shadow of the span slip silently overhead, someone said in a totally unconvinced tone of voice "Okay. Okay; when are they going to call this freaking thing off?" (Well, that was not exactly the word he used.) That question reminded me of a silly joke that was making the rounds in those days about the child who asked "Daddy, Daddy, when may I wear a brassiere?" The answer to that question was "possibly never Bruce." And that was my answer to that querulous voice in the night.

With those comments, the 57th and the 8th Transportation Helicopter Companies went to war. We didn't know it then, though I'm sure we all felt it in our collective guts. The United States of America went to war as well that night, but the body politic didn't feel a thing for years. No one had any idea of the magnitude of the adventure that we embarked upon, with those two helicopter companies, now over fifty years ago. I have been saying for a long time that "one of these days I'm going to write a book about my outfit, the 57th, and that first helicopter year in Vietnam." That thought remained, as the war stories dwindled off in the night after the telling. And I always said: "I'm going to name it the '*Vietnam Joke Book*' because we always knew that it was a joke, even though we were never completely sure, just who the joke was on." That suspicious feeling was there, even before we got that whale's eye view of the backside of the Golden Gate Bridge. It started when we read those orders at Fort Lewis Washington which said in gist: "to proceed to an overseas destination to participate in an exercise in excess of thirty days."

History may eventually vindicate our exercise in Southeast Asia. The Cold War was still in full swing back then and our effort may well have helped to stem the communist tide. But even if that turns out to be true, there is no longer much doubt that Vietnam was a joke all right, and that we and a couple of million others like us, were the butt of it. The joke was perpetrated at the national level and was embellished on over and over again by the strategic geniuses and the self serving politicians. The military did indeed kick a lot of ass but to what end?

Anyway, for this story I eventually settled on a different title, because in spite of the larger geopolitical situation, those of us in the junior ranks operated at the tactical level. We flew missions. The missions were tough and unforgiving of mistakes. It took concentration on the task at hand. We helicopter guys had to pretty much ignore the big picture and scramble every day just to do a creditable job without worrying about the big picture. And helicopter guys did the job for years. Most flew repeated combat tours and many fine men were lost, until the rug finally got pulled out from under us, when public apathy turned to open revolt in the early seventies. Eventually, there were many units and many individuals involved with helicopters in Vietnam, but this story is about the 57th and its attached units, during that first year. We went out on that thirty day exercise in November 1961 and our first piece of it lasted a year.

CHAPTER 1

HELIBORNE COMBAT ASSAULT

"It is apparent that the communist attempt to take over Vietnam is only part of a larger plan for bringing the entire area of Southeast Asia under their domination"—John F. Kennedy, Dec 1961 (Public Papers of the Presidents of the United States. Washington, D. C. 1962)[*1]

"Chalk One commo check," "Chalk Two up," "Three to Four," "Four up," and so on through the flight of thirty helicopters. We weren't much for unnecessary radio communications in the 57th or 8th Transportation Helicopter Companies, so that's the way the first heliborne assault of the Vietnam conflict began. The next radio call was "Chalk One rolling" for takeoff. The date was the 23rd of December 1961. We were flying CH-21C light cargo helicopters which the U. S. Army had named the "Shawnee" and which were powered by R-1820 dash 103 radial engines. This was a derivative of the same reciprocating engine which two decades earlier had powered the famous B-17s of World War II. The aircraft was something like 86 feet long from rotor tip to rotor tip and was shaped with a fuselage, angled in the middle. It sported six wooden rotor blades wrapped around titanium spars and it would prove to be significantly under-powered for the hot and humid conditions of Southeast Asia.

Commanding the 57th, and the combined flight of helicopters from both companies, was Major Robert J. Dillard. I was the 57th operations officer, and with Chief Warrant Officer (CWO) Bennie B. Potts in the other seat, was flying "Chalk One", the lead chopper. We were hauling troops of the Republic of Vietnam (RVN) Airborne Brigade. The brigade objective was a suspected Viet Cong (VC) headquarters, which was located about ten miles west of Saigon in a village strung along the Kinh Xang canal, just southeast of the market town of Duc Hoa. Our assault landing area was to be along a series of pineapple fields adjacent to the village. If you had one of those old French 1940 era, one over 50000 meter maps, you would see this complex represented on the east edge of the Plain of Reeds where the "Parrots Beak" border of Cambodia reaches down into South Vietnam.

A VC radio had been monitored broadcasting in the vicinity. Army of the Republic of Vietnam (ARVN) intelligence officers, supported by U. S. advisors, figured this to be the main enemy command post for the Saigon Region and believed that a battalion sized force was operating in the area. They expected that a VC company, carrying weapons up to at least one .50 caliber machine gun, would be protecting the radio and the headquarters itself. Since the radio was known to move often, routinely transmitting from different locations, an intel patrol had been positioned nearby to report on enemy movements into or out of the area. A blocking river force was being placed where the canal emptied into the Vam Co Dong River to the southwest of the assault landing zone.

The previous day we had flown a practice lift to the Cu Chi training base being used by the 5th ARVN Division. It was located only a short distance north of our objective. Air traffic into and out of the place was routine. It provided an excellent rehearsal area. At dawn everything was ready for the ARVN to try out this new helicopter support capability in a tactical operation. The mission of the ground force was to capture the radio and destroy the unit located with it. Our job was to assault land the troops from the northeast where they would be deployed along both sides of the canal. There was little need to worry about chopper crews shooting into each other as we were carrying only hand held weapons and we had been ordered to not shoot those. The troops were to move through the village and drive the enemy into the blocking force on the river. We, in the lead helicopter, had a secondary mission. After off-loading our soldiers, we were to reverse direction and land again near the assault area, to evacuate the ARVN intelligence team waiting there.

The flight crews had completed all pre-flight inspections by 0530 on the 24 hour clock; Beginning Nautical Morning Twilight (BNMT) or "Oh Dark Hundred" in soldier language. As the sun began to rise, we taxied from the ramp beside the old French hanger that we had appropriated at the Tan Son Nhut airbase. Cockpit checks continued as we rolled out and lined up on runway 25 for takeoffto the west. Yesterdays practice lift had purposely been flown along our planned route, so we again angled northwest along the highway from Saigon toward Cu Chi to give the impression that we were just making another training run. This time however, we were loaded
with over 300 anxious troops about to experience their first actual heliborne assault.

Due to the short distance between our takeoff and landing points, we climbed to an altitude of only 500 feet in a staggered trail formation. That is with each aircraft offset slightly to right or left so as to avoid flying in the turbulent-air rotorwash of the helicopter just ahead. About halfway toward Cu Chi, the flight turned 100 degrees to the southwest aiming straight for the objective. Our release point (RP) was a major canal intersection near the market town of Duc Hoa. We reached it in a few short minutes. Radio silence had been maintained until that point but now we began a rapid letdown by announcing "RP" and dropping the collective pitch to initiate a 500 foot-per-minute rate-of-descent approach to landing. Chalk One would be at the ground in one minute. We did not plan to touch all the way down however, but would shoot to a hover and off-load the troops from just above the ground.

The pineapple fields of our assault landing area were laid out in parallel rows with plants growing along ridges. These ridges were about three feet higher then the muddy ditches between. They were spaced at intervals which were approximately the width of a CH-21C Shawnee landing gear and were aligned in the direction of our flight and planned termination. These conditions dictated an approach to a hover. We would debark troops, touching down, lightly if at all, on one wheel. Each Shawnee would need all the power it could muster as it neared the ground. The approach to hover would be a critical and exacting procedure, requiring considerable pilot skill.

At this early time of direct U. S. Army support in the Vietnam conflict, we had no supporting air cover, no armed escort, and no onboard guns other than our personal weapons. In fact, even though we fully expected to be shot at, we had been specifically told not to fire even those meager weapons. The danger, however, was limited because of the short time we would be in the assault area and by the surprise we expected to achieve. The ARVN Airborne Brigade troops we were hauling were totally unfamiliar with the Shawnee and with heliborne operations in general. They were however, airborne soldiers, who were used to getting rapidly organized after a drop. We hoped that our practice run had at least trained the soldiers to jump quickly off the aircraft, get into a fighting formation and then move rapidly into the ground assault facing directly away from the helicopters. Each Shawnee would be in the assault area for less than a minute. I might add here, that a minute in an assault area can be a hell of a long time and we always managed to do much better then that.

Things seemed to be going as planned when we completed our approach in the lead ship. Although we couldn't see behind us, we knew that the entire flight would be down and unloading as we finished dropping off our own load of troops. We heard no weapons firing until after we had completed a hovering turn for takeoff to go back for the ARVN intelligence patrol. At that point things started to look bad. As we completed our turn we saw one of our helicopters, about number eight in the flight, heave up and roll over with its rotors turning at high RPM. Those blades then bit into the ground and the helicopter was beating itself to death as we flew by. And now there was plenty of noise and lots of shooting. The crew from the downed aircraft was already being evacuated, as we returned past the wreckage on our way to complete the secondary mission, and that was just the start of what turned out to be a long day for us. We delivered the intel team back to join the main body on the ground. Then we flew over to join MAJ Dillard and his crew at the crash site. Over the next few hours, both helicopters made several round trips from the assault zone to the airbase to evacuate injured soldiers and complete other tasks supporting the mission.

As soon as things quieted down a little, the 57th maintenance team flew in to begin the recovery of radios and as much other equipment as they could bring from the downed helicopter. Back on the ramp at Tan Son Nhut, an officer temporarily assigned to the U. S. Military Assistance Advisory Group-Vietnam (MAAG-V), and one who should have known better, was already talking to the press. That was Lieutenant Colonel, John B. Stockton, who was the leader of a small team of officers that had been sent to assist the MAAG in planning for helicopter employment. He was also one of the pilots that had just been evacuated from the downed helicopter. This "expert" was quoted in the next issue of a weekly news magazine as "a highly reliable source" who said that: "It was just like World War II out there." Well, none of the rest of us felt that way, but the damage was done, and so began the typically distorted news reporting that we all witnessed during the Vietnam War.

After the initial assault action, which appeared to have been short lived, the ARVN soldiers progressed to meet the blocking force, boarded river boats and floated back to Saigon, probably with little additional enemy contact. As was to become frustratingly usual, we in the helicopter companies heard little concerning the results of the ground operation. We were told that the radio had been put out of business and it did appear that we had achieved the surprise intended. Considering the level of gunfire, we had at least disrupted the enemy activity in the area. It is unlikely however, that any lasting advantage was achieved, since the ARVN did not occupy the ground.

It is interesting to note here, that the first soldier to die in this iteration of the war in Vietnam was reported to be Specialist Four James T. Davis. ("50th Anniversary: First U. S. KIA in Vietnam" VFW Magazine, November/December 2011) He was killed on 22 December 1961 while with an ARVN unit which was trying to find a radio operating near Duc Hoa."*2 This was the same area in which our operation took place the next day. We didn't hear about Davis at the time but one can guess that this was the same elusive transmitter we were after.

VC tunnels were later discovered just a little north of Duc Hoa, in the Cu Chi area, and that might help explain why this radio was hard to eliminate. It kept coming back, but we kept trying. I participated in another heliborne assault into the same line of pineapple fields on a subsequent tour five years later. That assault didn't rely on surprise however. It followed an intensive high altitude B-52 bombing raid which was intended to soften the target, and keep enemy heads down, during the helicopter landing phase of the operation. Again, no friendly troops occupied the ground for any length of time. The results, therefore, were probably very similar to those of that first assault in 1961.

CHAPTER 2

FIRST TO DEPLOY

*"War is not an independent phenomenon, but the continuation of politics by other means" Major General Karl von Clausewitz ("On War" first published in Germany, 1832)**

The 57th Transportation Helicopter Company from Fort Lewis, Washington, and a sister company, the 8th from Fort Bragg, North Carolina, deployed to Vietnam in November of 1961. Each was also assigned a field maintenance unit, and newly constituted medical and signal detachments. Our aircraft were "cocooned" (think: shrink wrapped) in white plastic and deck loaded aboard the USNS Core. We sailed into the Republic of Vietnam and docked at Saigon on the 11th of December. The Core was an old World War II "jeep" carrier, so named for it's smaller size and it's primary mission of aircraft transport rather than aircraft flight operations. Its hanger deck was loaded with a variety of aircraft being shipped to the RVN and the flight deck was white with our ghostly looking helicopters. The 57th achieved operational readiness 10 days after arrival. The 8th Helicopter Company had had to ship some equipment and aircraft separately by cargo ship, so they had to wait for that shipment to arrive before they could be officially deemed fully ready for operations. They did however; provide their share of the aircraft and crews to join us in the first heliborne combat assaults of the war.

There were MAAG advisors down to division level and there had been some specialized advisory detachments and Special Forces teams operating in South Vietnam before we arrived. The identity of several classified outfits are still a mystery to me as well, but the 57th and the 8th Transportation Corps helicopter companies were the first

U. S. Army company sized units to deploy and the 57th was the first to become fully operational in the Vietnam War. Someone is always claiming to have been the "first" of everything, but there sure didn't appear to be anyone else, except the MAAG headquarters and advisors, around when we got there. The advisory buildup had started however, so several other units were already on the way. The port stayed busy and airplane loads of people began to appear at Tan Son Nuht daily. Officers were stepping off commercial flights with no idea where they were going or what was in store for them when they got there.

Most of the people assigned to the 57th and our detachments, were deployed with all aircraft and equipment, aboard the Core. A team, however, remained behind to close us out at Fort Lewis and then air deployed to Saigon. This group was led by company executive officer (XO), Captain Milton P. Cherne'. They were able to stop in Hawaii for liaison with the Headquarters U. S. Army Pacific and still serve as the advance party into Vietnam; air travel being a somewhat quicker way to cross the Pacific then steaming aboard that ancient tub we were on.

This team made the initial arrangements for facilities and support. They commandeered the old French steel-arch hanger from which we were to operate at Tan Son Nuht. They made the initial contacts at MAAG Headquarters and scouted out possible billeting arrangements. CPT Cherne' then welcomed our ship to Vietnam, circling overhead in a borrowed MAAG airplane, as we approached the coast from the South China Sea. Cherne' was there to greet us again at the foot of Saigon's Tudo Street, when the Core docked in the stream of the Saigon River, three days later. Three days to get just a few miles up the river? Yep; we spent those three days orbiting around in tight little circles, several miles out to sea, awaiting diplomatic clearance to enter the country; just the first of the many amusing little glitches to come.

Even before we docked, the hard working maintenance teams began stripping cocoons and reassembling the helicopters. These teams were led by 57th company maintenance officer, CWO James R. (Big Jim) Eakins, along with CWO Clarence R. Nobles, of the supporting 98th Cargo Helicopter Field Maintenance (CHFM) Detachment. CPTs William C. Rudd and Kenneth L Klippel were not there to help since they were on the advance party, but they had made sure that the tools were on board, and combat loaded, to allow that early start. The USNS Core resembled a snow storm as strips and bits of the white plastic cocooning material hit the deck. Then the engines were pre-oiled, the rotor blades reattached and many other tasks were completed before each ship was rolled to take-off position for engine run-up.

Bill Rudd and Big Jim Eakins test flew the first Shawnee over Saigon on the way to the airfield. That was not much distance in which to establish any kind of altitude so the population must have looked on in amazement as they, and the others that followed, blasted their way across town about 100 feet over their heads. MAJ Wayne Triggs, commander of the MAAG flight detachment, had provided maps and orientation information for the local flight area and, as we worked to establish the company on the ground, the pilots began familiarizing themselves with the surrounding area. We defined our local flying area pretty closely around Tan Son Nuht. Our primarily task, while bringing helicopters from the Core, was to be sure that we could all find our way around the metropolitan area of Saigon/Cholon. We located possible forced landing areas on the various approaches to the airfield, and we began to get familiar with the Vietnamese manning the control tower at Tan Son Nuht. The tower operators spoke English, but very rapidly, in a high pitched voice, and with an accent. We had to get used to that.

The command group had to handle all the myriad details of establishing us in our new, and we hoped, temporary, home. This primarily meant dealing with the MAAG staff and wading through all the bureaucratic, Vietnamese style, governmental red tape. Just staying up with the status of all of our people, the physically able, and the sick, lame and lazy, and where they all were, so that the required morning report could be completed, was difficult enough, without all the other worries of stepping, with very short notice, into a completely foreign environment.

Our mission was less than clearly stated. The MAAG staff appeared to have only a vague idea concerning how we should be employed. "To provide helicopter transportation" must have seemed like a pretty benign role; fine for supporting the advisory effort and I don't think the senior U. S. chain of command expected us to get into too much trouble doing that. It was politically expedient to support our South Vietnamese friends against the Communist bullies from the north. Just the beginning of the "continuation of politics by other means" as von Claus would say.

The first translation into English of Carl von Clausewitz' "*On War*" was published by N. Triibnew, London, during 1873 and ever since then, it has been treated as a basic text for military forces around the world. It didn't seem to occur to those in charge during 1961 that Clauses' idea of "war as a continuation of politics by other means" might no longer be viable for us; that winning such a "limited" war might not work any more. It did not seem to be well understood by our leaders, that the limitations imposed by the threat of war with China and/or Russia, let alone a possible nuclear war, would inhibit our efforts very much. We pilots didn't worry about it at the time either. Hey, that kind of strategic thinking was not on our plate. I think that, at first, we all just bought off on the idea of a limited mission to help out our strategically located ally without any deeper thought.

Closer to the action, others had more definite ideas about how to use helicopters. No time was wasted by the ARVN Airborne Brigade, as they began considering our employment. They had an immediate target of opportunity and we began detailed planning for the combat assault that was to take place as soon as possible. The brigade commander, aided by his staff and his U. S. advisors, provided overall planning for the mission and controlled the ground operation. The helicopter company commander and his operations staff planned and controlled the heliborne phase. Note the difference between U. S. Army doctrine and this arrangement. It is general doctrine for all elements of a U. S. Army operation to fall under the control of the senior U. S. ground commander. That was to include any supporting aviation elements. Since we were directly supporting the Vietnamese, and because they, and the MAAG advisory staff, had limited experience with this mode of operation, we kept a full measure of control over the helicopter piece, in this and our subsequent employment, during that first year in Vietnam.

We were a long way from Fort Lewis and the comforts of home but I think we were all too busy to worry very much about that. Nor did we think deeply about where the tide was taking us. We were also too busy to worry about von Clausewitz's view of war. The nuclear stance of the Cold War was familiar to us and we knew that the Cold War stand-off in Korea had been fought under the restrictions that the threat of a nuclear war imposed. The Korean conflict ended in a stalemate, but everyone now seemed to discount that. If we thought about it at all, most of us probably thought that this little jungle squabble would surely be fought on a much more limited scale.

What the hell, it was their war anyway and we were just there to provide a little help. So while planning for the big job, the combat assault, we dispatched a six aircraft flight to deliver rice to a village near the tip of the Ca Mau peninsula. That was about as far South as you could go in Vietnam. It was the home for a small ethnic Chinese force, friendly to the Saigon government, led by Catholic Father Nguyen Lac Hao. The alleged purpose, or cover story, for our deployment to Vietnam, was to aid the South Vietnamese in flood relief. The Mekong River and its tributaries in the Delta had delivered a little more water then usual I guess, so we delivered some rice.

CHAPTER 3

STRAF VIII

The beginning of the sixties—we are set to fight a tactical nuclear war in Central Europe. Russian armies are aimed down the Fulda Gap. The world grasps a tenuous cold war peace—no one lights the fuse. It is still a peacetime Army.

One would need to go way back to begin to tell the story of Vietnam and Southeast Asia, but we only need to go back to about mid 1960 to start this helicopter story. At that time the 57th Transportation Company (Lt Hel) (CH-21C), with its attached 98th Cargo Helicopter Field Maintenance (CHFM) team, was assigned to the Sixth United States Army with headquarters at the Presidio of California in San Francisco. Our headquarters was in California, but we were actually stationed adjacent to the Puget Sound at Fort Lewis, Washington, in direct support of the 4th Infantry Division (ID). Our home base was Gray Army Airfield (AAF). Although Fort Lewis is a large post, the airfield is closely adjacent to the main post area with snow capped Mount Rainier looming just off the end of the runway.

The 4th ID was a high priority outfit designated as part of the Strategic Army Corps (STRAC). We flew training missions at Fort Lewis and supported the 4th ID during its major training exercises at the Yakima Firing Range in Eastern Washington. We in the 57th had the comfortable feeling that our destiny was closely tied to that of the division. We weren't going anywhere if the STRAC 4th ID didn't. The 57th was identified in a lower category, as a part of the Strategic Army Force (STRAF) with a priority eight designation. That meant that our deployment priority was low enough to be almost ignored and the requirements for that STRAF VIII designation could be completed easily. No big deal, but we also knew that the 57th was on somebody's list up there in the big house. Unlike General Halftrack, the Pentagon had not forgotten us.

The 57th was a "TO&E" outfit. That designation indicates an organization that is staffed and equipped by a U. S. Army published Table of Organization and Equipment; in other words, a mature, formally established, component of the United States Army. We were equipped with twenty Piasecki designed CH-21C "Shawnee" light cargo helicopters, two Bell OH-13E "Sioux" observation helicopters for liaison flights, and a full compliment of other supplies and equipment ranging from trucks, jeeps, and radios, to gas masks, and mess gear.*

Soldiers are always proud of unit patches; due to Army regulations these were worn only on flight gear, not on other uniforms. Ours was designed by CWO Larry Kelley with the nickname "Work-Horses" written at the bottom of the patch, which showed a mulish looking cayuse pawing the air over an aircraft carrier sailing against choppy seas in front of a white peaked mountain. The presence of the aircraft carrier represented the USN ship Thetis Bay and the 57th participation in the 1958 joint Army-Navy amphibious exercise "Rocky Shoals" which had been held off the coast of California. That was a unique experience for a helicopter company because flying from a carrier deck was new to Army guys. The mountain, of course, was Mt. Rainier.

We had an authorized strength of 147 men, including 44 pilots. This was augmented by the direct support maintenance team which kicked our combined strength up to just over 200 people. Our main business in 1960 was training. Pilots flew to achieve and maintain a high level of flight proficiency, which then was routinely demonstrated in both independent operations and in support of the 4th ID. Both flight crews and mechanics had to work hard to excel in the care and handling of the CH-21C. This required that daily flights be scheduled to accomplish the transition training of newly assigned pilots into the Shawnee along with practice and skill training for the rest of our crews. Flight platoon and company exercises were flown all over the Fort Lewis reservation. There was always some administrative flying around the Puget Sound and there were regular deployments to the field. This, of course, took place along with the usual demands of the Army training schedule such as weapons qualification, annual tours through the gas chamber, and some classroom work. That sounds like a fairly full schedule maybe, but there was still plenty of time for card games and trips to the coffee shop. This stateside tour was as close as most of us ever came to being in a "Peacetime Army" during the "Cold War."

It was a normal day, five days a week, schedule. We took the weekend off like normal people. You would find about six out of twenty-two helicopters in the air at any one time, with two or three of them in the "idiot circle," as we called the traffic pattern, around the airfield. These would be practicing take-offs, landings and auto-rotations. The Shawnee sported two large rotor systems, but had just one engine to keep them both turning. Auto-rotations were therefore, a handy thing to know how to do well. Things get really quiet when your only engine fails. Auto-rotations were practiced to keep skill levels high enough to offset the immediate anxiety, induced by the silence in the cockpit, when that occurs. Making about one third of the assigned aircraft available for flight each morning kept the maintenance platoon busy but not overly stressed. The backup 98th CHFM team worked on the bigger jobs, like engine and rotor blade changes. Both groups also scheduled their work to provide the maximum possible number of "flyables" in support of the 4th ID during their field training exercises at Yakima and for other exercises.

The 57th had originally been formed at Fort Riley, Kansas in 1957, MAJ Maurice C. (Mo) Bone, Commanding. It was filled up there with helicopters straight from the production line, and with personnel from flight school, aviation maintenance schools, and by reassignment from other aviation units. Many of these people later moved with the unit from Fort Riley to Fort Lewis, and since the standard stateside tour was three years, they were still assigned in 1960. Tours, however, were up for all of them by the middle of that year. Most of the old time officers were gone by the end of the year and the remaining pilots were soon on their way. I reported in at the end of 1959.

The summer of 1960 was a turbulent period for the unit, what with all the comings and goings, but that didn't keep us from moving to Yakima for the annual division exercise. MAJ Mo Bone was still in charge but getting short. LT, soon to be CPT, Bill Rudd had reported in to replace company maintenance officer, CPT James R. Harris. Therein lays a story which is illustrative of the personnel turbulence we were experiencing and some quick thinking by Jim Harris. With all our helicopters roaring up and down dusty Yakima canyons at the firing range, and landing troops amongst big rocks and thick sagebrush, we wore out some rotor blades. A call was made to Harris back at home station, where he was busy getting ready to leave for his new assignment, asking him to send over some replacements blades before he departed. A Shawnee was dispatched to pick them up, but Jim was in a hurry or something, and he wasn't watching closely while those blades were loaded up for transport. Someone decided to ship them over on the rope cradles that were used for storage in the hanger. This was not good because, on the somewhat rough flight back over the mountain, the ropes sawed into the blades which put them in worse shape then the ones that needed replacement. The boss was not pleased! When the departing maintenance officer got that word he hastened to send over a "please forgive me" note encased in a box of premium cigars. Mo Bone passed some cigars around and relented. He didn't change a fine efficiency report, as a relieved Jim Harris got the hell out of town.

MAJ Bone left the company shortly thereafter and CPT Cherne' held the reins for about six months until MAJ Dillard took command. It is funny now to think of captains as senior officers, but the ones leaving were way senior to us lieutenants coming in, and they were leaving in droves. The original commander of the 98th CHFM, and later 57th Company XO, CPT Herman R. (Dick) Orrell, was already gone when I got to Fort Lewis, but I got to know him later when he showed up once or twice in Saigon. He would occasionally fly a U-8 executive transport down from the US Army Ryukus Islands (USARYIS) headquarters in Okinawa. We were still officially TDY from Sixth Army, but the 57th reported through that headquarters for a while. We used to call that fixed wing, multi engine, flying duty, "dress blues and tennis shoes flying," because those pilots were flying way up there in nice clean air while we helicopter jocks were way down in the mud and the blood and the beer. We were all a little jealous I guess.

Another departing officer was CPT Arthur K. Kinney. His legacy to us was his manner of flying his favorite helicopter. Art tried to always fly good old tail number 055 and he believed in really babying his engine. He would only carry loads that didn't require the maximum power of fifty-one and one-half inches of manifold pressure to achieve a normal hovering take-off. And he liked to land without straining the engine either. As a result we had a strong engine in 055 because it had a history of lots of gentle use. Whether it came from watching Art baby his helicopter, or from somewhere else, it had became company policy to not use a hovering take-off with any load that required more than fifty inches of manifold pressure to maintain a three foot hover. Heavier loads were flown where a rolling takeoff from a runway or other hard surface could be used. This would allow us to burn off some of that heavy fuel before landing, thereby reducing the possibility of over-boosting the engine.

As a result of this policy, we had very few engine failures while flying in cool, sea-level, Washington State. You could get red line power in hot and dry Yakima, but pilots were careful to avoid it there too, unless it was really needed. Later, when we hit the hot and very high humidity situation in Vietnam, it was not even possible to achieve maximum manifold pressure. No matter how hard you pulled up on the collective pitch stick, 50 inches of power or less was all you could get. Still, pilots respected the care that Art had demonstrated in flying his favorite airplane and that careful attitude carried over into our Vietnam flying. That is not to say that we didn't have problems in Vietnam. Because we had to routinely pull all the power we could get, we had eight in-flight engine failures in the first six weeks of operation there. It is a credit to our pilots that they all went in on their wheels and to our maintenance crews that they were all recovered and returned to flyable status.

Paths do cross repeatedly in the United States Army. The officer I replaced in operations was CPT Leon W. Curry and we had met before, if memory still serves, in a poker game at Schwabish Hall, Germany. We played the game nightly during that Seventh Army Field Training Exercise. The cards were dealt in a large canvas army tent placed in the middle of a muddy field near the runway. I think that Leon relieved me of some of my hard earned cash during those few games of skill and chance. CPT Curry ran flight operations with an iron hand at Gray AAF, with the able assistance of CWOs Walter H. Koehler, Lawrence D. (Larry) Kelly Jr., and Warren D. (Big T) Tinseth. We heard of Curry not long after he left the 57th when he arrived with the 93rd Helicopter Company at Soc Trang, in the Mekong Delta of Vietnam. The 93rd had originally been stationed at Da Nang, on the ocean but near the mountains, in the northern portion of South Vietnam and they had already captured a tiger cub as a mascot. The mascot came with them when they moved south, so they naturally called themselves the "Soc Trang Tigers" and I remember seeing a picture of Curry posing with the company mascot, which was by then a pretty big tiger cub. I'm not sure what became of the kitten, after it became a full scale cat, but I've a vague idea that it ended up in a stateside zoo.

The commander of the 98th CHFM was CPT Lawrence J. Herman when I joined the unit. Larry reappeared on my path years later too, in 1975, as a manager with Bell Helicopter International in Teheran, Iran. We attended his wedding there, a couple of years before the country failed in 1979. Shala was a beautiful member of, what was known to us, as the first thousand Iranian families in wealth, power and prestige. That was some wedding. It was held in a veritable palace. The main furnishings were immense valuable Persian carpets spread on marble floors. Shala gave up any claim to the family wealth when she moved to Arizona with her American husband. Larry died from an unexpected cancer a few years later and Shala claimed that his exposure to the chemical Agent Orange, used to kill the jungle in Vietnam, had been the cause of that cancer. That was before our government had decided to honor most connections between exposure to that defoliant and cancer, but I hope she was eventually successful in her claim.

1LT Donald E. Youngpeter had been standing by for the CHFM job but Don didn't keep the 98th very long. His three years were also up and he was soon on orders to leave. He now lives near Fort Rucker, Alabama, the home of Army Aviation, and handles much of the on-site arrangements for our tri-annual reunions at the adjoining town of Ozark. CPT Ken Klippel took over the 98th when Larry and Don left the unit, and soon CWO "Gus" Nobles came in to help out.

The platoon and flight section commanders all rotated out during 1960/61. CPT Richard I. Gillingham was another 57th alumnus that I got to know better while he worked for Bell in Iran. 1LT Leighton O. Markley was a particularly notable character among the officers leaving, because he was our resident instrument instructor pilot, and sang a mean version of *"On the Wings of a Snow White Dove"*. CPT Forrest L. Jorgenson left the army in 1960, but I remember an unexpected visit with him later. I was returning from instrument school at Oakland, California, driving a brand new Studebaker Lark. It was around midnight, so I was making up for lost time, when I was pulled over by the Washington State Patrol, just south of Olympia. Speeding in a Studebaker Lark; how do you like that? And it was Forrest Jorgenson in a brand new state highway patrolman's uniform that walked up to my window and yeah, he gave me a pass.

1LT Vernon (Woody) Woodward was an old bridge playing buddy, so we stayed in touch for many years after the rest of those officers scattered. We still see, then 1LT, James R. Tarrant every three years or so because Jim has held the unit together with periodic company reunions in Alabama. With the help of CWO Carl R. Vertrees (Ret.) and LTC Don Youngpeter (Ret) and others, he has managed to organize those gatherings for the past thirty years or more. All of our assigned chief warrant officers, along with all of their CH-21 Shawnee flight experience, also departed during this time. Real old timers like CWOs Jack M. Crich, Charles F. (Chuck) Hungerford and my main Shawnee instructor pilot, Wiley K. Westbrook, were soon on their way. These guys did not deploy to South Vietnam with us, but they did remain with us in spirit. They had shown us the ropes. They had given the 57th its character and had checked many of us out in the Shawnee.

The officers joining us in 1960 and 1961, were a varied lot ranging from those with combat service in Korea to "new-boys" just coming into the Army. MAJ Bob Dillard can be found in the saga of one of those battle scared Korean hills, where he was awarded a Silver Star for heroism, as a young Artillery forward observer. XO, Milt Cherne' came to us as a captain with extensive background as an Armored Cavalry officer. Ken Klippel came in to command the 98th maintenance detachment with a logistics background and was soon promoted to captain. Dillard and Cherne' had both been in the combat arms and so had I. My service started as a ground pounder in the Infantry, then later I was flying L-19 Birddogs with a 280mm Gun Battalion (Atomic Cannon) in Germany. Although I started flying fixed wing airplanes in1955, my assignment to the 57th was straight out of rotary wing flight school. I was not alone though, because not only was it the first rotary wing assignment for our new boss, MAJ Dillard, it was also his first aviation assignment of any kind.

It should be noted that many combat arms (Infantry, Artillery or Armored Corps) officers found their way into the Transportation Corps (TC) during the late fifties, as that branch of service began the major expansion of Army Aviation. A full compliment of both fixed and rotary wing aircraft, ranging from light scout to heavy transport aircraft, were being acquired during that time. The incoming pilots and aircraft were intended to fill requirements toward the establishment of a planned Army intra-theater Air Line of Communications (ALOC). Even though Army aircraft still carry a lot of stuff for the Field Army, the ALOC concept was dropped after a few years, when the Army fixed wing transport aircraft were transferred to the USAF, in a trade-off between services. I never really understood exactly what that trade was. I think the Army got screwed. An ALOC was a fine concept then and would still be today—but that's another story.

It was, no doubt unintended, but one result of the massive personnel turnover in the 57th, was that almost all of the commissioned officers that departed were very senior to the ones coming in. I arrived just before the 1960 turnover really got started and I was initially moved through flight platoon assignments until January 1961, when I was promoted to captain. Because of the exodus, I was soon the third ranking officer remaining in the 57th and so assumed duties as the Operations Platoon Commander and Flight Operations Officer for the company. I had been in grade for less than a year when we deployed to Southeast Asia.

The younger officers were all commissioned in the TC branch from the start. Some of them had gone directly into Army Aviation from university Reserve Officer Training (ROTC) programs. One officer, Second Lieutenant John L. Garner, was so new that he came out of college and went straight on to flight school, before joining us, arriving just as we were on the way to Vietnam. He helped ferry our helicopters to port and then did his first operational flying in combat. 1LTs William H. (Bill) Hinds and John W. (Bill) Smith became our new platoon commanders. 2LTs William H. (Bill) Brethour, Salvatore E. (Sal) Formica, Roderick G. (Rod) Magie, and John Garner, were assigned as flight leaders. This was indeed a junior bunch of officers. We leaned on the old timers, the Chief Warrant Officers, but as time would prove, we were quick learners when it came to operating helicopters in groups over South Vietnam.

Then there were the Olsen twins; 2LTs Donald R. and Richard J. Olsen. These young second lieutenant aviators passed through the company for a short period, before they moved on to the 33rd Helicopter Company at Fort Ord, CA. To say that they were somewhat naïve might be an understatement. It was almost standard operating procedure (SOP) for our pilots to noticeably pass gas when near a 2nd LT and then state loudly; "And another second lieutenant is released for active duty." For awhile there, the chief warrant officers had the Olsen boys convinced that since they were only young, brand new, "Two Johns" and the warrants were obviously older, much more experienced "Chiefs," with many years in the Army, that they, as second lieutenants, should salute them when passing each other on the way to the coffee shop. This went on until I witnessed it myself, on my way over for coffee one day, when I reoriented those young aviators. To finish the story though, the twins arrived in Vietnam with the 33rd that summer of 62' and from all reports did a fine job of flying there.

Let me digress here and tell you a little story about commissioned officer promotions in the 1950s and1960s. The politicians will always try to take that "peace dividend" and the public generally goes along. At the end of WWII, in 1945, the drawdown of personnel was rapid and extreme; then came the Korean imbroglio five years later. Many officers were called back in, to fight again, as the Army expanded its strength to handle that. By 1954, the Korean War was over and the Army again shrank precipitously. Because of this contraction, the time in grade needed for promotion was also extended. The normal time from second to first lieutenant was eighteen months. By the beginning of the sixties, the time in grade from first lieutenant to captain had increased to another five years. Promotions were so few that the Army published four outcomes for selection boards. An officer was very rarely selected for promotion "before his peers," or he could make it on time "with his peers." He could be found "qualified but not-selected" or just "non-selected", that is passed over.

It was not unusual, in those days, for officers coming out of WWII and the Korean War to be planning to retire, with twenty years of service, in the grade of captain. Many were also "reverting" back to a previous enlisted rank or were being offered an even lower enlisted grade so that they could "get their twenty." These guys were being replaced by brand new lieutenants from West Point, ROTC and Officers Candidate Schools (OCS). There were even some officers, who had gotten battlefield commissions, still around to remind folks just how quickly things can change in the Army. Just to add to the confusion, there were also a few non-commissioned officers (NCOs) that managed to go the other way, regaining their commissioned rank in critically needed skills. There was an old Field Artillery saying that I learned while serving with the 867th 280mm Gun Battalion. It still reflects that era well. It went "don't crap on your gun corporal; he may be your battery commander next week." Well, I never saw anything quite that specific, as I spent those many years as a first lieutenant, but the Korean War was not that far behind us then and I did see some things that came close enough.

I didn't miss any "on time" promotions, but I managed to hit the absolute peak of sixty-one months in grade before my promotion to captain. Obviously, by 1961, it was time for another war and sure enough, time in grade from lieutenant to captain shortened considerably after the last half of that year. Within a year of my pinning on the new bars, due to a rapid expansion in Army strength, the time required for promotion went down to about thirty-six months in grade. Bill Smith got the benefit of this rapid decline in time needed, so he was promoted to captain on the boat to Vietnam, when he was delighted to say "move over Knight; I'm going to pass you up!"

That 2nd LT Garner, I mentioned earlier, was so new to the Army when he joined us, that it reminds me of an old Army story about a senior officer who ran into an obviously young and confused second lieutenant who needed some guidance. The senior officer said "damn it soldier, how long have you been in the Army?" As he took a brace and held his salute, the shave-tail replied "All day sir!" That was about how green John was when he joined us. The time in grade compression was hitting all officer ranks, so I didn't spend much time in the grade of captain. Even so, one day, about three years after John Garner had joined the 57th as a brand new second lieutenant, and we had all gone our separate ways, we crossed paths again. It was during a practice alert at Fliegerhorst Kaserne in Germany. We were all dressed up to go play war, Seventh Army style; with cold weather gear and combat equipment dangling off of our web belts. I started to pass by this soldier when I recognized that it was Garner. I was still a captain and so was he! I threw my steel pot on the ground and yelled "Goddam it Garner, I've been a captain longer than you've been in the Army." And it was true. Both of us had been promoted on time, "with our contemporaries," but such is the Army!

The warrant officers had a different problem. Although the Army offered more promotion levels later, they only had three grades to worry about at the time: warrant officer one and chief warrant officer two or three. The aviation warrant officer program was still fairly new then, so all of ours were chief warrant two (CW-2) except Bennie Potts, the "grand old man" of the outfit who was a CW-3. Unlike most of the commissioned officers, all of those joining the 57th had had several years of helicopter flying service before joining us. They rotated in from either Korea or Europe where they had been flying cargo helicopters for some time. The policy at that time was to assign CH-21 helicopters to units in the United States and in Pacific commands, while the CH-34 helicopters were sent to Europe. Those pilots coming in from Korea had already been flying Shawnees over there, so they needed only local area orientation when they arrived at Fort Lewis.

Although one might think otherwise, the CH-34 drivers from Europe needed only a few hours of training to be signed off. Even though these two helicopters were significantly different in appearance, in that the CH-34 was configured with a single main rotor and a small, vertical tail rotor, while the CH-21 was a tandem, the flight characteristics were actually fairly similar. The tandem configuration of the CH-21 obviated the need for an anti-torque (tail) rotor, but the flight controls were essentially the same for both types so pilot transition was easily accomplished. Of more importance in transitioning from one to the other, was the fact that both were cargo helicopters. Cargo handling and sling operations were similar. The density altitude condition was a critical external factor to be considered in each case. The importance of RPM and engine manifold pressure control was also the same for both those old reciprocating engine equipped helicopters.

Not only were these guys familiar with cargo helicopter flying, but the flying warrants of the US Army were different back then. They were recognized throughout the Army as a "special breed." Only successful Non-Commissioned Officers were being selected for flight training in the early days of the flying warrant officer program, so all of those that came to us had useful military background and experience as sergeants. Most of them had completed overseas assignments. Many of them had combat experience dating from the Korean War and all were stable, mature soldiers. We had a number of highly qualified maintenance guys, several former administrative sergeants, and others with skills ranging from ordnance to combat medics.

These experienced individuals rapidly became the backbone of the company, not only as pilots, but in holding down responsible positions throughout the organization. They performed duties as administrative, supply, and mess officers. They backed up all of the commissioned officer positions as assistants—except for the commander and executive officer—we all "assisted" them. The warrants also had those good old army additional duties. You know the ones like document disposal, or vector control. The main jobs were always well done by our pilots, but it was sometimes a little difficult to get an additional duty actually accomplished quickly, if one had to break up the pinochle game in the pilot ready room, for some immediate requirement.

Since my primary concern was in the flying operations of the company, my interaction with the maintenance soldiers at Fort Lewis was pretty much limited to those who flew as crew members. There was a crew chief assigned to each Shawnee by tail number and he had the major responsibility for the airworthiness of that helicopter. The crew chief became dedicated to his assigned helicopter, so when you walked out to the ramp, you always found the chief proudly standing by and ready to fly. By the time the pilot got there, he would have performed a post flight inspection after the previous flight, completed or supervised any needed repair work that could be quickly accomplished, and finished a preflight inspection. The pilot would, of course, do his own preflight, but a pilot flew whatever aircraft was assigned to him for a particular flight, while the crew chief knew his ship in detail, because he always flew the same one. It was his ship. As the "owner" he felt responsible for its condition and whatever happened to it.

To us pilots, the crew chief seemed to be an integral part of the helicopter to which he was assigned. We knew them all, and we got to know the maintenance sergeants as well in Vietnam, because most of them volunteered to fly as gunners, in addition to their supervisory duties in the shops. The maintenance personnel were assigned duties and supervised by the Service Platoon Commander; the maintenance officer. He scheduled the work necessary to support our preplanned flying program. Variations in this program were common of course, so coordination between the maintenance and operations office was often needed to ensure that the required number of helicopters would be available for flight. The Shawnee always took a lot of help from its friends; lots of work to get it in the air and to be sure it stayed there. When Bill Rudd told us what he could "get up" that is how many we would schedule to fly. Oh we might try to squeeze out "one more" from time to time, but the maintenance boss always had the final word. This was the same kind of teamwork we would later use in Vietnam.

CHAPTER 4

AMBLING ANNIE

Cargo Helicopter, Army Series 21, Model C (CH-21C) manufactured and delivered by the Piasecki Helicopter Company in 1955 and nicknamed the Shawnee according to the US Army policy of naming helicopters after our native Indian tribes.

With the tandem rotor arrangement, Frank Piasecki invented one of the first commercially successful modern helicopter configurations. The CH-21 Shawnee was proceeded in the US armed forces by the Piasecki built, chain driven, H-25 "Flying Mule," and the tandem rotor configuration is represented today, in the USMC and the USN, by the Boeing built, turbine powered CH-46, and in the US Army, by the CH-47 Chinook. The Chinook is also used by our special forces and operates with foreign armed forces around the world. It is the world's preeminent medium cargo helicopter and it is again into another life extension and modernization program. The tandem configuration is well proven today. I got to know Mr. Piasecki in later years and he would probably argue the point, but looking back, we can now see that the Shawnee was really a work in progress.

The CH-21 had a long angled fuselage with two main rotors fore and aft. It had a sort of ungainly stance with rotor disks tilted slightly in opposite directions. This allowed the whole thing to proceed, in a fairly straightforward manner, through the air. All helicopters have unique flying characteristics, but the Shawnee was special. Someone has described all helicopters as "a large collection of moving parts, flying in fairly close formation, in the same general direction." Others have said that the Shawnee must have been designed by the maker of Chinese mixmasters. That's carrying it a little far, but with all those rotor blades flailing around, old fixed wing pilots are said to have thought that it was out there trying to beat the air into a state of submission, so that it could take off. We were still obeying Army regulations, so we never did christen our choppers with personal slogans or flashy emblems, although I'm sure we could have come up with some very good ones. Later, in Vietnam, when the Army was not so worried about non-standard equipment markings, one crew chief named his helicopter "Frank Piasecki's Practical Joke"; yeah, right, but the name that I think best describes it was emblazoned on the Shawnee that made the first helicopter non-stop US transcontinental flight in August 1956. They called it "Ambling Annie" and that seems a perfect fit because the Shawnee flew with a kind of a circular/up/down/sidewise shuffle. That doesn't mean it was all bad, the motion got to be kind of soothing after awhile and so restful you could go right to sleep, as long as no one was shooting at you.

The two OH-13 Sioux observation helicopters that we had are easier to describe then the Shawnee. They were built by Bell Helicopter Company and were intended for reconnaissance and command and control missions. These little jobs consisted of a Plexiglas bubble and an open truss tail boom which enclosed a small horizontally opposed reciprocating engine. It had two "saddle" gas tanks strapped to its back. The engine drove a two bladed main rotor and a small anti-torque rotor at the tail. It is now remembered principally for its role as a helicopter medical evacuation vehicle during the Korean conflict. To refresh your memory, just watch the choppers come in during the next showing of the old MASH series on TV. That's an OH-13. The Sioux however, was slower than the Shawnee and did not have the necessary range to support airmobile operations in Vietnam. We took them with us, but we eventually traded them for fixed wing aircraft that could more efficiently do reconnaissance and could keep up with us during assault missions. The Cessna built O-1A Birddog filled this bill.

Although not so noticeable in the sea-level, moderate humidity and temperature conditions of Washington state, the Shawnee was under-powered and required careful pilotage even there. It was heavy. In order to achieve the separation needed for the two horizontal main rotors it had an elongated fuselage. Although atmospheric conditions rarely allowed all the seats to be filled with troops, there were 20 of them. The work area behind the cargo compartment included the central transmission, engine, fuel and oil tanks, and the rear rotor transmission. It was this area which produced the "banana look" that became familiar to television viewers in the early days of the Vietnam War.

With two large, three bladed, main rotors it was necessary to carry around three heavy transmissions, one under each rotor with a combiner box in the middle. The forward transmission was, by necessity, mounted right over the cockpit and its high pitched whine is probably the main reason why many old Shawnee pilots don't hear so good. The rotor blades were made mostly of what a modern engineer might call the original composite material. They were a wood lay-up around a titanium spar with metal leading and trailing edges applied. In a word, the CH-21 was obsolete shortly after it came off the production line. But that is the nature of military airplanes. Technology usually matures faster then the lengthy governmental development, decision, budgeting and procurement process. It takes years to move through the process before action is taken to modernize the old ones or to buy new aircraft.

During 1960 however, the new turbine powered, utility UH-1A Iroquois helicopters were already being provided to the 4th ID at Fort Lewis. The UH-1 started its history with the US Army as a "Helicopter Utility" HU-1, therefore was familiarly called the "Huey." This nickname stuck with it, in spite of the later change to "Utility Helicopter" UH-1. The acquisition of these new helicopters was peacetime slow and we were not in line to get any of them anyway because, although they could lift almost the same load as a Shawnee, the Huey was classified as "utility" rather then "light cargo." The light cargo classification would disappear entirely when all the CH-21C helicopter companies in Vietnam were equipped with Hueys and redesignated as airmobile companies in the mid 1960s. The 57th pilots could only look with envy on those who got to fly these modern turbine powered machines. The Huey went on to became the most famous helicopter of the Vietnam conflict but the old Shawnee helicopter is what we were flying at Fort Lewis, so that is what we ultimately took to war.

Once you start a turbine, which is comparatively easy, you can almost forget about the engine unless everything suddenly goes real quiet. In flying the Shawnee, besides aircraft handling, one had to manage that cranky old reciprocating engine. Just learning to properly start the beast was a challenge. After the engine was started, one had to get the rotors up to speed using a friction driven transmission clutch and when the proper RPM was reached that clutch had to be released and a positive "jaw" clutch engaged to bring the rotors and the engine on up to operating RPM. This could be easily mis-managed by the novice pilot, where the jaw would not catch and the whole thing had to be started over, or a much worse possibility was to attempt to engage the jaw before the friction clutch had finished its job. This could result in the gnashing of transmission teeth or main rotor blades being slung all over the ramp. Assuming one was successful in getting everything up and running properly, the next problem was to taxi. You might wonder why words are necessary regarding such a mundane subject as how to taxi, but to get it right was a critical part of learning to fly this airplane.

Of course, it is not my intention to teach anyone to fly helicopters here, but a little description might be helpful in understanding the rest of the story. The helicopter pilot has two main controls in addition to the throttle, anti torque pedals and toe brakes. These are the collective and cyclic pitch sticks. The collective stick is used to put more or less pitch in all the rotor blades at the same time for increased or decreased vertical lift. At the same time, the throttle is used to maintain the operating rotor RPM. The throttle is mounted on the collective stick and is twisted as on a motorcycle. Constant throttle adjustment is required on all helicopters equipped with reciprocating engines when power is added or reduced by raising or lowering the collective. The cyclic is used to variably control blade pitch, and therefore the lift, of individual blades as they pass around the rotor disc. This allows the aircraft to achieve turns and changes in flight attitude by moving the nose up or down. The pedals are used to keep the fuselage aligned for coordinated flight as more or less torque is applied through power changes. Used together, these controls affect flight attitude, speed, direction, climb and decent. That's easy enough in the air, just a little coordination needed. A monkey could do it, right? Well not exactly and pilot finesse was required to even get the dang thing moving on the ground.

The proper technique to taxi the CH-21C was to lift the collective stick, roll on a very little throttle to get power enough to be able to move slightly back on the cyclic, thereby feeding additional lift to the forward rotor, thus getting light on the nose gear. When this was achieved, without moving the helicopter, the cyclic would then be moved slightly forward, tipping the rotor disc in the direction of desired travel, so that the whole thing would begin to move forward all at the same time. There was a lot of helicopter behind the pilot so it was important, when moving out of a parking place, to get out a ways before beginning a turn. Now the interesting part here is that the Shawnee nose gear was mounted on a single, fairly long strut. It was braced, but with the main gear way back behind the center of the fuselage, too little collective and too much cyclic in the beginning of a turn could cause problems. This was usually just a little skidding feeling if you got it just a little wrong, but it was conceivable that if the nose gear was not held light enough to allow it to begin to swivel as cyclic was applied, there was enough power up there in that forward rotor to snap the nose gear strut right off the helicopter.

You could also back one up on the ground to get out of a parking space. That was a fairly "straight forward" maneuver. You just added power, lifted the nose and pulled gently back on the cyclic. Of course it was a little worrisome to not be able to see exactly where those 86 feet of helicopter were going. Most of the helicopter was behind you and you had to rely on the eyes of the crew chief to be sure that you didn't run into something.

Once out of the parking spot, into the turn and with a little forward speed, everything got a lot easier and often as not it was necessary to slow her down so as to not exceed the maximum taxi speed as you rolled out. This was no faster then that of a rapidly walking man on the ramp and taxiways at Fort Lewis. Once off the ramp you could either lift off to a hover in the infield area between taxiways or roll on to the runway for takeoff. The 57th was primarily in a training mode at Fort Lewis, so most of the flying was conducted by students being instructed by our Sixth Army designated Instructor Pilots (IP).

These IPs were generally those with the most experience flying cargo helicopters, mostly Warrant Officers and usually the most senior of those. Some of them had been instructing long enough to have gained considerable reputation among Army Aviators everywhere. These "gray beards" had individual peculiarities of course, but they also shared some of the same characteristics. None of them seemed to talk very much while in the helicopter. They didn't participate to any real degree in the paperwork or preflight phase. They usually didn't even touch the controls during the flight except to demonstrate some new maneuver or to initiate an unexpected forced landing. Their primary intent was to not allow any damage to the aircraft, crewmembers, or anything on the ground while the student learned to handle the aircraft under a variety of conditions. When they did get on the controls it was like the helicopter took on a new life of its own. It took me the better part of three years to get that feeling of wearing the Shawnee like a second set of clothes, but our experienced IPs handled the machine like that when I first knew them. That is, of course, when they deigned to actually get on the controls and fly it at all. The IPs that I flew with most of the time during my checkout were CWOs Wiley Westbrook and Bob Ziegler. Wiley was later lost in a white out crash in Alaska but Bob made it through Vietnam with us.

The IPs might ride through some exciting maneuvers when brand new students were practicing to hover. After all, most accidents occur when the aircraft meets the ground in an unplanned way. The first time someone tries to hover, without moving from the lift-off spot or changing the alignment of the helicopter, it does not appear that a football field will be big enough to allow all the gyrations that seem to happen. It feels like you are trying to balance on top of a beach ball sized ball bearing. Say the helicopter starts to move off one way, and in a helicopter that is side-to-side, forward, backward or any other direction, so the student pilot moves the cyclic stick to go the other way. While doing that, he often not only over-controls in the intended direction, but throws in some other sideward, forward or rearward component, so that the helicopter begins to go in the opposite direction or maybe a new direction entirely. Each time the pilot over-controls, the helicopter tries to do what it has been told to do and always just a little faster. Obviously this can't go on very long and eventually one learns to barely move the cyclic stick at all. In fact when you lift off to a hover, you can almost just think about the direction in which you want to go and the helicopter will begin to move in that direction and you can stop that travel with the same slight application of cyclic.

There is more to this, but you get the idea. The pilot must also control the alignment of the fuselage. That is he must keep it pointed in the desired direction and he has to maintain the required height above the ground. Alignment is controlled by what would be called rudder pedals in a fixed wing airplane. Height is controlled by the collective stick, and the throttle in a reciprocating engine equipped helicopter. Besides the cyclic stick, all of these can be mismanaged. To further aggravate the situation, the engine could quit at any time forcing a hovering auto-rotation. Our student pilots were not new to helicopters, of course, so this phase of training was concerned with the unique characteristics of the Shawnee. We would practice holding a spot under the nose and turning the helicopter around that spot while maintaining a three foot hover. The three feet were beneath the main landing gear located way back of the cockpit and lower down, under the center of gravity of the Shawnee banana shaped fuselage, so that wasn't as easy as it might sound. We practiced turning around the main gear too and just to round it out we held hovering turns around the aft rotor pylon.

There were essentially three ways to take off in the Shawnee. Because it had wheels you could line up on a flat, smooth surface like a runway and take off like a fixed wing airplane. You could smoothly bring in full power and RPM for a maximum vertical takeoff from the ground or you could do a hovering takeoff with a normal application of power. Each of these had its drawbacks and advantages. Each was used under certain circumstances. You could get much heavier loads off the ground with a running takeoff and usually do a hovering landing at the completion of the flight as you would have burned off fuel. In a confined area, it might be necessary to achieve a near vertical takeoff to clear trees or other obstacles; a takeoff from the ground with full power might be called for. A normal hovering takeoff required less power and was easier on the engine. We practiced them all, but the one we rarely used in Vietnam was the "normal" takeoff. Even if initiated from a hover, it was usually anything but normal.

Landing, of course, could be looked at as the obverse of the various kinds of takeoffs possible. You might sometimes use a running landing for a heavy load where a hard surface was available but usually landings were made to a hover or to a spot touch down, and sometimes an auto-rotation was called for; the fastest way down. Running landings in the Shawnee were fun. It was just like landing a fixed wing airplane. In addition to other types of training we practiced instrument approaches under the hood. While the instructor stayed visual, the student had reference only to the instruments until near touch down. It was always a relief to roll out down the runway after being cooped up under that hood. Landings to either a hover or straight to the ground required the coordinated use of power and RPM. After loping down the approach at lower power settings, near the end of the decent, collective pitch, throttle and cyclic had to be applied in a coordinated way to stop the decent smoothly while not exceeding the allowable engine manifold pressure or RPM. The approved method was to bring in maximum, red line, RPM while using only as much engine power as needed so as to avoid the risk of over-boosting the engine with too much manifold pressure.

Fort Lewis sits near sea level just inland from the Puget Sound. Temperature and humidity conditions there are almost always close to 29.92 inches of mercury so that the density altitude remains at or near a "sea level standard day." The Shawnee was red lined at 2700 RPM and 51.5 inches of manifold pressure. If those limits were exceeded by an over-boost of manifold pressure or an over-rev of RPM, maintenance action was required because some damage to the engine, or other components, may have occurred. Because of the optimum atmospheric conditions at Ft Lewis, it was possible to pull more then 51.5 inches of manifold pressure but even that red line power was rarely needed. We practiced pulling to the red line in training but we generally stayed just below that for normal takeoff and landings. This was exactly reversed in Vietnam where the density altitude was always high due to high temperatures and humidity. You could not get to the maximum manifold pressure and you could easily over-rev by exceeding the red line RPM. Pilots could baby the helicopters at Fort Lewis and as a general rule we would plan the amount of weight we would load aboard based on our ability to achieve a three foot hover while using manifold pressure two inches below the maximum available for take off. As a result, in the two years I flew with the 57th at Fort Lewis, we experienced only one engine failure that I recall. This changed quickly when we began to fly in the stringent conditions of Vietnam. Engine failures quickly became a major concern.

A large part of the flight instruction in the idiot circle at Fort Lewis was for practicing auto-rotation. Things have to happen real quick in a helicopter when that engine quits pumping. It is almost as bad when an IP decides to roll the throttle off to idle while you are trying to learn how to fly the damn thing. All of a sudden there are several things to do. The first thing is to drop collective in order to reduce the pitch in the blades so that rotor RPM will not decay. Then push the nose over to maintain a suitable approach airspeed while at the same time looking outside to pick your landing spot. The rate of decent is so rapid that as soon as you are stabilized at the top, you are half way down, and it is time to start managing the bottom. The old Shawnee had some endearing characteristics in auto-rotation. Because of the large rotor disc area, it was possible to either pull collective pitch back into all the blades, or pull back on the cyclic to use the forward rotor disc as a kind of brake in the decent and to thereby cushion the touchdown. If the pilot did both in a coordinated fashion, the landing was very gentle. Unlike most other helicopters, it was sometimes even possible to move from spot to spot, a very short distance, before final touch down.

Practicing this maneuver in the idiot circle gave us the advantage of shooting to a runway of course, so just to keep it interesting, we also practiced all over the training area. That usually happened, naturally, whenever and wherever the IP thought he'd caught us napping. Most IPs waited for the time when things seemed to be going smoothly and you were just trying to get a little rest, then he would chop the throttle. After that the spot for landing became a really critical thing. You had to find the right spot while still trying to fly the helicopter, and then you had to hit the chosen spot, at the same time as you did everything else. And that had better be the best spot around too. Often, the best place to put her down was directly behind you. You were supposed to have seen that when you flew past it of course, so that you would be expected to immediately initiate a 180 degree auto-rotation.

Now a 180 degree auto-rotation may be about the most exciting peacetime maneuver one can do in a helicopter, so we also practiced doing that in the idiot circle. You've got to move like a cat to keep up with everything that's going on in a one-eighty. First, drop the collective and this time horse back on the cyclic and kick pedal to initiate a tight, nose up, 180 degree turn. Airspeed and rotor RPM decay rapidly while the nose is up and the turn is in progress, so as soon as you can, roll out and push over the nose with cyclic to regain the lost airspeed and RPM. Because you have dumped a lot of lift in the turn, the rate of decent is also much faster than in a relatively straight ahead auto-rotation, so you are at the bottom almost before you get there. We got proficient over the runway, demonstrated it in the training area, then proved it in Vietnam.

In addition to improving basic flying skills, it was also necessary to practice operating under different conditions of weather, terrain and mission. Night and instrument flying, confined area operations, and the peculiarities of mountain flying were some of these. Practice in multi-helicopter troop lift was obtained during maneuvers with the 4th ID. For us, as it turned out, the landings in the confined areas at Fort Lewis and the troop lifts at Yakima were the most useful training we practiced. The terrain at Fort Lewis is very suitable for the confined area work. The reservation is flat and gravelly, with vegetation ranging from dense to sparse, under a canopy of Douglas fir and pine trees. The Yakima Firing Range, east of the mountains, is a totally different environment. It consists of a series of ridge-lines leading down to the Columbia River. These are covered with rocks, sage brush and little else. There are few confined areas, but there are also very few spots where you can actually touch down with a multi helicopter troop lift. In addition to the military reservations, the Cascade Mountains, the Columbia River Gorge, the Puget Sound and the San Juan Islands in the Straits of Juan de Fuca, provided a variety of operating conditions upon which to hone our skills.

A typical training flight, outside of the idiot circle at Fort Lewis, would include the selection of various holes in the trees into which one might fit a Shawnee with a great deal of care and planning. Contrary to popular belief most helicopter landings are not completed at the end of a vertical approach. To do so would put you in the "dead mans curve" too long. That is where both your airspeed and your altitude are too low to allow a successful auto-rotation if the engine were to quit. Things have changed a lot now for those helicopters equipped with dual turbine engines, but a proper approach is to visualize the angle of decent which will allow clearance of all obstacles to a spot on the ground, while maintaining enough forward airspeed to stay out of the dead mans curve until, just briefly, passing through it at the end of the approach. In a single reciprocating engined helicopter like the Shawnee, getting it right was critical.

Once you got into the confined area, the next problem was to get out. That meant figuring out where the wind was coming from, where the low spots in the trees were, then estimating how to gain the most distance over the ground in a take-off run that would take advantage of the best average of the three. Sometimes, at Fort Lewis, this meant backing the helicopter almost into the trees and it usually demanded a maximum power take-off. There were many places to practice variations, and if you ever got comfortable in the confined areas you were working, the IPs could always find some new and more challenging ones. The IPs had other ideas too. As a demonstration in coordination for example, CWO Danny Hendrickson liked to take a low level run at maximum forward airspeed toward the tallest Douglas fir he could find in the open. Then very near to the base of the tree, he would pull back on the cyclic while adding power as needed, to come to a zero airspeed hover just over the top of the tree; after a brief stop, then rolling down the other side to resume low level high speed flight. This didn't compare to 180 degree auto-rotations, but it was fairly exciting.

The Army was organized in "pentomic" divisions in 1960. This was the form adopted, following the triangular divisions of World War II, as offering more flexibility in the conditions of possible nuclear conflict. Units, weapons and equipment had to be widely dispersed to have the best chance of surviving a tactical nuclear strike. As an example of the dispersion required for division exercises at Yakima, I recall once noting that seven miles were logged on the truck to get to all of the helicopters on one refueling operation. Troop lift was the main work at Yakima. This usually involved as many helicopters as we could get flyable for moving troops from one ridge line to another.

Ground troops like to take the high ground and it was desirable if no one saw them do it. We would stay below the hills, running up and down the valleys to slip over draws so that we could approach the desired landing area, usually just under a ridge crest, without being detected. The landing area was rarely level, and usually very broken, with large rocks obscured by sage brush. That meant that troops usually had to be off-loaded at the hover, or perhaps holding light on one gear, if the direction of landing was parallel to the ridge line.

Sometimes we had to land vertical to the slope; then it might be necessary to carefully pick your spot, before planting the helicopter firmly on the ground. One time I remember CWO Charley Wilhite doing that when I was in the co-pilots seat. Charley had a bad habit of sneaking into his seat wearing unauthorized cowboy boots, and it was just like watching a rodeo rider, when he slapped that machine onto the slope. The density altitude is considerably higher on the Yakima plateau than it is at Fort Lewis, so planning and flying skills were put to the test there. Although these maneuvers were not assaults, as we were to fly them in Vietnam, the practice gained at Yakima provided a solid basis for later combat operations.

CHAPTER 5

FLYING HELICOPTERS IS DIFFERENT

Having Remained Motionless In Space; Flown Backward, Forward, Sideways and Vertically in U. S. ARMY HELICOPTERS, this individual is Hereby Designated a Genuine U. S. ARMY HOVERBUG[*1]*

The statement above is from a card they gave to everyone that graduated from helicopter flight school at Fort Wolters, TX when I went through; maybe a little trite but accurate about the kinds of things that one can do in a rotary wing aircraft. There are many other statements about flying that are equally descriptive. Things like: "There are old pilots and there are bold pilots but there are no old bold pilots." Probably the most descriptive of these sayings is: "Flying is hours and hours of boredom followed by moments of sheer terror." Even the lyrical writings about "Jonathan Livingston Seagull" will seem familiar to any pilot. Although flying helicopters in the 57th at Fort Lewis hit all of that on the edges, it was mostly just plain fun. In Vietnam the "boring" part was cut way down.

Before we get into that though, I guess that I should give you a little of my background; particularly since I was kicked out of helicopter school. Well, I was damn near kicked out. Eventually the powers-that-be relented and let myself, and the six of my classmates that were involved, graduate. If you were to take a look at my class graduation picture you won't find any of us in it and all the guys that are in the picture look pretty grim. This unpleasant episode happened in spite of the fact that I was ranked number one in the class on academics, number three overall and had been flying fixed wing aircraft for nearly five years. Maybe the story is too long to tell here, but it illustrates the kind of Army we had in those days and like any good short story there is a twist in the end.

I was commissioned in the Infantry from ROTC at the University of Washington (UW) in December of 1953, then served for six months in the reserve forces as a battalion assistant S-2 at Fort Lawton, WA, and was called to active duty the following July. It doesn't have anything to do with this particular tale of woe but note that this placed us citizen soldiers just behind the West Point class graduating that year. They came on active duty during June ensuring that they all had a date of rank that was senior to all the entering ROTC second lieutenants in that year group; just coincidental I guess. Anyway, while I was attending the Infantry Basic Course at Fort Benning, I applied for airborne, ranger and aviation training. Although West Pointers routinely did that and got all of them in series, my tactical instructors said that I could only have one of them so I chose flight school. That was approved but I was sent to lead an infantry platoon in the 47th Infantry Division in the meantime. There was still a high degree of turbulence after the Korean War and soon the 47th ID flag was retired and we were marching under 3rd ID colors.

Infantry soldiers have a peculiar sense of humor and sometimes they like to use descriptive phrases to describe their division shoulder patches. For example; the 47th ID, a reserve outfit, came on active duty from Minnesota so their patch was a stylized Viking helmet which the soldiers called "an upside down flying piss pot." The 3rd ID is a famed division from both world wars, and most of the others, and its patch is composed of three diagonal white bands on a dark blue background. The troops call it a "blowout patch for a zebra." Those were fun days but after participating in a major division exercise called "Follow Me" and wearing out a couple of sets of combat boots running around playing war on the Fort Benning reservation they finally let me proceed to flight school in the spring of 1955.

We pinned on our new wings on 3 December 1955 and my next assignment was to the 867th Field Artillery (280 Gun) Battalion in Germany where I flew L-19 (0-1) light observation and L-20

(U-6) utility airplanes for three years. During that time I applied for a Regular Army Commission. My first choice of branch was Infantry; second Artillery and third Transportation. They gave it to me in the Transportation Corps (TC). Go figure! So I rotated back from Germany to Fort Eustis, the home of the TC, to attend the intermediate level Company Officers Course. Near the end of the course my class standing was high enough that they let me depart early. My orders were for temporary duty at Fort Wolters, TX to learn how to fly helicopters then to proceed to Seattle to finish up a degree at the UW and then finally for assignment to the 57th Transportation Company at Fort Lewis. This was a highly unusual set of orders covering two separate temporary duties and one permanent change of station. It took some coordination to arrange it but I was soon on my way.

Helicopter school didn't even start out well for me. I got a screamer for an IP. Now I don't react well to constant yelling in the ear. Good airplane instructors never raise their voice and I had a tendency to just tune him out while I tried to manage the machine. This just made him madder and he yelled louder. The helicopter flight instruction at Wolters was conducted under a Southern Airways Corporation contract and it didn't take long before I went to the boss and told him that this guy either had to stop yelling or I wanted a new IP. He stopped yelling and I quickly learned how to fly the OH-23. The ground instruction was finished. All of the students had been cleared to fly solo. We were all within a couple of hours from having the required amount of flying time needed to graduate. That is when I got embroiled in the situation which nearly got me expelled.

The class had been divided into several sections which were to be launched separately to match the number of helicopters available and so as to not overcrowd the training area. Everyone was flying solo; no instructors were flying. Some students had already departed the ready room while the rest of us waited our turn. Fort Wolters is situated close to a lake called Possum Kingdom and while we waited, someone got a bright idea. He asked if we could fly up to the lake. The Southern Airways manager didn't much like the suggestion but it was well within the local flying area so he decided on a compromise and said "okay, but sign out with an XC by your name if you want to do that." (XC is an abbreviation for cross country.) He then lined out a route to be followed. I had more than enough time to burn off and that trip would take up a good piece of it so I thought why not? I put an XC by my name on the local sign out sheet. After takeoff I shot a couple of approaches in the training area until it was the right time to go around the prescribed route and get back to land with my time just used up.

All went as planned, although I saw many more helicopters dashing at low level over the water then should have been out there, as I flew around the lake. It was a beautiful day and I was happy to get back to the ramp at the end of my flight. The class was over. All that was left to do was to pick up the course completion document, have a party and depart station. Although I didn't realize it at the time, it was right there that things started to get ugly. The Brazos River leads up to Possum Kingdom and one of the guys had decided to do a little low level flying up it. He hit a wire in the process. He landed back at the parking ramp and looked over his helicopter carefully but could find no evidence of the strike; not even a scratch to the bird, but being an honorable soldier, he decided that he had to report it anyway.

I knew nothing about this incident and headed home to celebrate the end of the class with my family. The school secretary had already called by the time I got there to instruct me to be at a certain building by 0800 in the morning; that I was being called as a witness in a board action against one of our classmates that had hit a wire. Okay, I knew the officer involved, and my answer to the board that morning was that I didn't know anything about the wire strike but I thought him to be a good officer. Well that evening I got another phone call telling me to report again; that I would be appearing before the board in my own defense this time. Now what the hell was this? I found out when I saw the others that had been ordered to report. The pilot that hit the wire had signed out with an XC by his name. The board decided that all of us that had done so should come back in to defend ourselves against a charge that we had all violated regulations by flying at low level up the river. I thought that the command had probably stepped in and decided that we all must have been playing tag, following each other up the river, and that the board should "get 'em all."

Now it was possibly the case that some of the XC group had flown at low level up the river. I don't know about that, but if so, I was not one of them and I never heard any one of them admit that they had done so either. The first couple of guys that came out after their time before the board had been instructed to not talk with those of us waiting our turn but they really looked downcast. It didn't take long, when it came my turn, to confirm my feeling that the decision had already been made to "hang the guilty bastards." I have seldom completely lost my temper in the Army, but as the derogatory and irrelevant questioning continued, I did.

There were some military instructors at Wolters and the senior of these, along with some school staff members, composed the board. I described my flight which included a few minutes of local flying before going around the lake. Then the stupid questions and comments began. Just a few examples follow. One of the board members asked what I was doing shooting approaches solo; "didn't I know that that was dangerous?" That was the guy that I had once seen back a helicopter up into the air for another approach to a pinnacle after a student had missed it. I couldn't think of any more dangerous maneuver for one to demonstrate on purpose, in a helicopter. They had just taught us about the "dead mans zone." He had been in it all the way; too slow and too low to auto-rotate successfully if the engine were to quit. Another asked if I had had a map of the area with me; "you could have been lost!" Now the only way to use a map in a solo helicopter with the doors removed would have been to land and study it. The area was by then quite familiar to me and it don't take a genius to fly around a lake and back along a major highway to home base. No one had a map. None had been offered. I said "no, maybe you would have gotten lost but I wouldn't have." The obvious kangaroo court just kept getting worse. I kept getting angrier and my answers just kept getting shorter.

Up to this time I had tried to be responsive to their idiotic questions but I was loosing it. I am just quoting some examples from memory but this event has stayed with me pretty well and it clearly reflects the tenor of the interrogation if not the exact words. When someone said that I should have flown the route suggested and not done anything else I said "look I had time to burn up and that wouldn't have done it. I was never more than a mile off the centerline of the route which is satisfactory even when flying an airway and besides, as far as I know, you can fly any goddamn place you please within a local flying area when you sign out on a local flight plan." Well that response was called "cussing at the board" in the final report. At the end of the day, I knew for sure that we were about to be boarded out.

There was another TC aviator; an old friend of mine from Germany named Vern Beinke, who was also involved in this. We repaired to my place and had a few drinks while discussing our options. We decided that we would go to see the Inspector General (IG) if we were to be kicked out. Sure enough the school secretary called us in the next morning and informed us that we would not graduate. We went to see the IG and anyone else we could think of to state our case. That was no help. They said the school could "board" anyone they wanted to; that it was not a legal action and there was nothing we could do. We decided that we would call the Chief of Transportation at the Department of the Army in Washington DC. In those days you had to make an appointment to speak to the Chief and we did so. Then we went back to see the school secretary. We told him that we had a phone appointment to present our case to the Chief and we requested a meeting with Colonel Inskeep, the school commandant. This finally got their attention and we were granted an interview.

The Colonel started the conversation with me by saying that "your conduct before the board was reprehensible." That's an exact quote. I'll never forget it. I answered that it was obvious that the board was just a formality; that we were going to be kicked out no matter what and, since I was not guilty of anything, I got angry. He actually said that it wouldn't be so bad "you can always go back to the Artillery." I said "no; if I don't graduate I am out of the Army." Before the discussion was over, I mentioned that when I had flown around the lake there were helicopters skimming the water all over the place and that there had been absolutely no control over the flying. The Southern Airways manager was also in the room and Inskeep asked him if that was true. Fortunately for us he acknowledged that it was.

All of this resulted in another call to report very early in the morning where the school secretary, a LTC Briggs, who seemed to be the one pushing things, again showed his style by saying "we know you are all guilty as hell but we are going to let you graduate." He went on to say that we were not to attend the graduation party. We were also told to leave post immediately. We were not to talk to anybody. (It was an instruction that I chose to disobey. I talked loudly to several of my classmates.) At the end of this meeting Briggs said that he was sending a copy of the board report to our next commanders and that he would send another copy of mine to DA where it would be made a permanent part of my record. That resulted in the bad side of my file being almost as thick as the good side for a while. I have got to say though, that I don't regret it. I am convinced that if I had not fought hard we would not have made it. I am fairly sure that the rest of them, except for Vern Beinke, just knuckled under.

That board report was waiting for me when I reported in to the 57th but a supporting word had arrived before me. Our class leader at Fort Wolters was a senior captain and he was assigned to Fort Lewis. He took it upon himself to go see MAJ Bone and tell him that it had been a put-up job. He said that a group of warrant officer candidates had been caught flying races down the known distance firing ranges and making quick stops at the butts (the target end of the range). Somehow, before board action could be taken on this errant behavior, all the tail numbers had been changed and they had nothing to go on. The XC on our sign-out sheet had given them an excuse. He felt we were just scape-goats and that our board action was intended to set an example for future warrant officer classes.

The captain told MAJ Bone that he was sure that it had never happened as alleged and even if it were true it was making a "mountain out of a molehill." When I showed up at Fort Lewis, MAJ Bone said that he had already heard that there was nothing to it; that he would file the report in the company safe, and as long as I performed my duties well, he would forget about it. No one ever mentioned it in the unit and I took that copy out of the safe about a year later. The pilot that did strike the wire was sent home without graduating, but in one of those inexplicable Army ways, he was later sent back to re-do the entire course and was qualified to fly helicopters.

As Paul Harvey would say, "now here is the rest of the story." After my tour with the 57th in Vietnam, I was recognized for planning, leading and developing tactics for helicopter employment there. This was a national level award. Vern Beinke got wind of it and he sent me a post card. It only had one line on it. It said "not bad for a cull."

Needless to say, it was a treat to get back to respectable flying with the 57th. The IPs were always calm and professional; they never yelled. The leadership was the same; they never went off half cocked. The flying was great. Some of our best trips were those annual runs to the Yakima Firing Range in Eastern Washington. When the weather permitted we would fly directly over Mount Rainier National Park. The height of the Cascades there would push you to fly at very high altitudes, sometimes near the operating ceiling of the CH-21C, just to get over the hills. On clear days you could see all the way from Mount Baker near Canada to Mount Hood in Oregon; five snow capped peaks from left to right. Mount Adams would emerge from its usual hidden position southeast of Rainier; and Mount St Helens, when its lid was still on, framed the sparkling jewel of Spirit Lake.

We also did mountain training flights over the Cascades and at Ranger Creek in the foothills where we practiced approach and landing at this higher elevation. This is careful work because flight controls are sluggish at high altitude and the margin for pilot error is slim. While we trained we also carefully noted those fields which offered the best forced landing possibilities. This was the most direct flight route to Yakima but the rough terrain offered very few clear landing areas so we were careful to note those that were there. That habitual planning for forced landings really paid off one day when CWOs Leonard R. Wilson and Robert L. Eastland's helicopter suffered a complete engine failure high over the mountain. Len was one of our instructor pilots and they put that helicopter down; way-way-down, autorotating into a very small lake that must have looked like a postage stamp from the height they had been flying.

That little lake turned out to be good practice for our maintenance team too. It was shallow and marshy with little or no dry ground but the helicopter stayed upright on what there was. It rested on its wheels which were buried in the mud on that patch of tundra. The maintenance guys made a little work platform upon which they dropped the engine from the aircraft. This was then hauled out by another Shawnee and a replacement engine was slung in and installed. Our maintenance test pilots flew the repaired helicopter out and performed a test flight on the way home. This effort took a couple of days but they got to be much faster with these kinds of recoveries in Vietnam.

I well remember one particular flight where we managed to climb above 14000 feet and made a shallow approach to the top of Mount Rainier. There ain't enough air up there to come to a complete hover so we just zeroed the airspeed and kinda slid off the other side. Now pilots are not supposed to feel apprehensive about heights but it gave me a little bit of a queasy sensation to be near stopped three feet over the snow capped crest of Mount Rainier before being dumped off into clean air-nose down to collect airspeed quickly—off the other side; felt sorta like you had just stepped off of a very tall building.

Often the weather forced us to take the round-about route to the firing range; ducking under the Pacific Northwest overcast south to Portland, then up the Columbia River Gorge past Multnomah Falls, the Bonneville Dam and The Dalles to turn the corner north, with the river, toward Yakima. Of course if you had taken a break at the Troutdale Airport, near Portland, you actually looked out the side window at Multnomah and the other waterfalls along the way as you climbed sedately out above the river to legal altitudes. Besides Multnomah, there were Latourell, Shepperd's Dell, Bridal Veil, Coopely, Mist, Wahkeena, Oneota, Horsetail and McCord Creek Falls, coursing down from the snow covered slopes of Mount Hood and spilling into the river. The mountain hovered nicely in the background as we flew up the river and we picked up Mount Adams and, of course the east side of Mount Rainier as we proceeded north along the Columbia River.

While exercises at Yakima were still full of fun flying, they were not without plenty of excitement and even the occasional edge of "sheer terror." I remember two of those kinds of incidents in particular. One of those was on the ground; when a suspicious vibration caused a crew to abort their take-off from the parking area and then quickly shut down for some additional pre-flight inspection. That revealed a near separation between sections of the drive shaft leading to the aft rotor system. This would have undoubtedly caused a disastrous in-flight disintegration of the helicopter were the vibration to have been ignored and take-off initiated. Scary! And our pre-flight inspections immediately got much more detailed.

It can be very risky flying when a medical evacuation is required, even during peacetime; especially during bad weather or at night. I went out one night with Bob Ziegler when a ¾ ton truck had driven off the road into a very deep canyon on the firing range. Since there were serious injuries involved we had a doctor aboard. We saw, as we arrived over the area, that we would have to make a zero airspeed vertical decent into the canyon aiming only at a set of vehicle headlights on the ground. Climb out would also be straight up; inside the dead man's curve all the way.

There is also a condition called settling with power that one can get into if you let the rate of decent get too high on the way down. The way out of that is to lower the nose to gain airspeed in forward flight. We obviously had no room for forward flight so expert flight control was essential on the way down. Bob handled that with his usual aplomb but he had to keep much of his attention inside the cockpit monitoring the instruments while at the same time he had to stay oriented on those pin-point headlights. My job was to stay focused outside the helicopter, straining to see the cliffs all around us so that I could let Bob know before we clipped any of those rocks with our rotor blades. We got the thing done alright but it was a little tense until we were up out of that gorge and on our way to the hospital. That experience, and some other med-evacs we did early in Vietnam made me really respect the guys who came in later to do that job as a full time mission.

There are two other situations that seem to me to be particularly risky for helicopter crews whether anybody is shooting at you or not. Flying demonstrations is one of them and close formation flying the other. They both require careful planning and control or very bad things can happen. There are teams of military flyers that demonstrate close precision flying routinely of course, but the pilots are carefully selected based on proven skill and then are specifically trained and kept current in that kind of flying. Think of the USAF Thunderbirds or the USN Blue Angels. The Army had its demonstration team flying helicopters too. These pilots are great, and demonstration flying is a full time job for those teams, but even so, bad things happen now and then.

We did some formation flying at Fort Lewis and in Yakima but normally only when it was required for a mission; those that we did fly were very carefully planned and controlled. Later, in Vietnam, we flew only an occasional close formation. We sometimes joined up and peeled off to land from an echelon when we were showing off to the USAF there, but we never found any reason to fly extremely close formations. Some leaders thought that overlapping rotor blades was good training. I thought it was stupid. As an example of how dangerous it can be; I'll not forget the result of one unnecessarily close formation that I witnessed on my second tour in Vietnam.

I was flying an aircraft recovery ship accompanying a combat assault. I don't remember the helicopter unit now, but I knew the company commander who was leading the flight. He was a well respected Army Aviator. After the tactical operation was over, he called his flight to form up into a tight formation to return to base; totally unnecessary. The mission was complete. They were just going home but he called for them to tighten it up. I was not part of his flight but was flying fairly closely alongside since I was also headed home. I watched until it looked to me like the rotor blades along the whole flight were overlapping and then I saw the blades of number two bite into the blades of number one. They both fell directly into a village of straw huts where a violent conflagration of fire and explosions erupted. Of course we went in immediately to see if there was anything we could do. Not much; our crew worked to get people away from the fires and we evacuated some wounded villagers but the two crews were gone.

Anyway, it was not our job to test the limits and we generally avoided doing so in our stateside flying. There were however, times when we just did what some would call "goofing off" but we called training; like flying out over North Fort Lewis then along the Tacoma Narrows and over the bridge to Gig Harbor and across to Case Inlet and my old home town of Allyn. We might fly on over to the Hood

Canal then up to Shelton where I went to high school. More than once we made a short stop at the airfield there for a cup of coffee, after this strenuous bit of work, before heading back down to Olympia and over the Nisqually River as we returned to base.

We would go out sometimes to drop weekend paratroopers at Yakima and some "sporting" sites around Fort Lewis. They liked to jump from the Shawnee because there was little airstream drag at very low airspeed and no tail section to worry about crashing into as you exited the helicopter. We weren't too excited about these missions because it tended to ruin the weekend but we scheduled them because the division's parachutists loved to jump and we always tried to support the division in any way they asked. Of course us helicopter drivers always questioned the sanity of anyone who would chose to voluntarily jump out of a perfectly good airplane of any kind, but especially one that could auto-rotate safely to the ground.

That reminds me of another story about paratroopers. Part of my job in Germany back in the 50s had been to run a small forward air observers school where young Artillery officers practiced adjusting fire from the O-1. I would also let them fly from the back seat a little and I even let them make some approaches and follow me on the controls through the landing. The idea was that they would then be able to maybe fumble through a landing if something were to happen to the pilot on an actual mission. One day I was finishing up training with an officer of Swiss extraction who was a master parachutist. As a sort of graduation exercise, I pulled back on the throttle and collapsed forward in my seat. Nothing happened, except the O-1 began to circle in a dead-mans spiral, so I said "okay John, what are you going to do?" He thought about it for a minute and then he answered in his Swiss accent "well damn Knight, I hate to be a dirty guy but I'm going to pin a note on your back and jump out of this son-of-a-bitch!"

There were other diversions as well. The Shawnee was supposedly designed to stay afloat in a water landing; read properly handled wet crash. The design criterion for the CH-21C required that it would float for a few moments, so that at least some of the crew and passengers might get out, after a forced landing on water. We always wondered about that and practiced occasionally; always quite close to shore and never without maintaining enough power to get back off again after the experiment. It was fun to see the rooster tail we could put up when the main landing gear and then the fuselage sliced into the surface with even a little forward "water" speed.

Then there was the day that my brother Jim, out on Vashon Island, needed a new pair of boots and thought that good old army boots would fit the bill. You couldn't land just anywhere of course, but the neighbors were probably a little surprised to see a big Shawnee hit a high hover over his backyard, then issue a new set of combat boots out the door. I was a little reluctant to show off by buzzing Allyn, out on the Case Inlet of Puget Sound, where my younger brother was running the volunteer fire department, so our passes there were sedately flown just off shore at 500 feet, or thereabouts, above the water.

I had a very good friend serving in the Oregon National Guard in those days. We had served together in Germany when I was a lowly lieutenant, and he was an exalted captain; the Battalion Surgeon. We got to be good friends anyway and when I became the ops officer of the 57th Doc Lahti was traveling to Fort Lewis each summer during the Guard's annual field training exercises. He was promoting helicopter rides for his troops. It seemed like a fine idea to me. The Army sanctioned the use of what were called "dollar rides" for both familiarization and as a recruiting tool. We would load up a box of troops and give them a ride around Puget Sound. For those who could get to a window, and weren't air sick, it was a hell of a fine tour.

To start with we would issue instructions about personal conduct during the flight.*2 Our pilots rotating in from Germany had brought back with them a Saturday Evening Post style "German" set of instructions: *"Achtenshun! Das Machinen ist nodt for gerfingerpoken und mittengrabben. Ist ezy for brekken das schpringenwerks, blowenfuzen mit loadish popen und spitzensparken. Ist nix gerworken by dumkoffs! Das rubbernecken sighdtseeren und stupidisch goofoffers bast relaxen, kipp hends in pockets, und vatch das schenry!"*

I'm sure this went over better with the troops in Seventh Army, Germany, but the Oregon National Guard troops seemed to enjoy it too and just to close the loop we handed out a set of instructions in

English. Needless to say the author, or authors, of these words hide in well deserved obscurity:

INSTRUCTION FOR PASSENGERS IN ARMY AIRCRAFT: If you will kindly observe the following rules, it will be a "hell-of-a-lot" easier and more comfortable for the crew.

-After all whose chopper is it anyway?
-Keep your goddam feet off the seats.
-Don't get snotty with the crew. Remember your pilot is still learning to fly and is more scared than you.
-If a fellow passenger becomes too nervous, belt him over the head with an empty booze bottle.
-Keep your goddam feet off the seats.
-If the pilots get into a fight over who's to fly the chopper, do not interfere. GI insurance does not cover fist fights of passengers.
-Leave each crew member a healthy tip.
-Do not ask embarrassing questions, such as; "who made that landing?" "Where are we?" etc.
-Keep your goddam feet off the seats.
-If you don't like the noise you can go plumb to hell.
-Only one person is allowed to use the relief tube at any one time, and then only when one of the crew is not using it.
-Do not touch the first aid kits. These are for use by crew members only.
-Keep your goddam feet off the seats.
-Stay out of the crew's crap game, it's strictly private.
-Always let the crew leave first, after all the dam chopper may be on fire.
-Do not leave the chopper in a wild-eyed, screaming, clawing rush; it may have an adverse affect on new passengers about to board the helicopter.
-Keep your goddam feet off the seats.
-Don't snuff your cigarette-buts on the floor, use ash cans provided. After all your pilots are butt shooters.
-Don't be inconsiderate as to ask for magazines, papers and playing cards before the crew has had a chance at them first.
-If the engine stops or a blade falls off, don't show any fear, it may frighten the crew.

-In bad choppy weather always share your grog with the crew; it may be the "hair of the dog" that he needs to put him to sleep.
-Keep your goddam feet off the seats.

There was, of course, no time for, or interest in, this kind of sophomoric humor in Vietnam. For one thing we usually kept our troop seats stored against the fuselage so that the ARVN soldiers would not get their weapons, or themselves, entangled in the webbing during rapid off-loading. For combat assaults we just placed the troops on the floor in squad order so there were no seats to put their feet on anyway. But I have included this doggerel here to illustrate another point. Most of our pilots then, were still fairly young. They had been around for a while but were still full of youthful enthusiasm. At thirty in 1961, I was among the younger guys but as the war progressed, flight crews got ever younger and younger.

Anyway, our dollar ride for the National Guard troops was made by flying out of Fort Lewis toward Mount Rainier, turning north over the Port of Tacoma while flying at about 500 feet. We would then fly westward over the water along the Elliot Bay shore. This route took us right across the Seattle waterfront to view the city skyline. From there we flew north over Whidbey Island to Anacortes and the Deception Pass where we would begin a lazy turn over the San Juan Islands before heading back to Fort Lewis along the eastern side of the Olympic Peninsula. Maybe it should have been at least a ten dollar ride.

My friendship with Doc Lahti generated another story from the summer of 1960. One of his kids was about to be born down in Cottage Grove, Oregon. When things got imminent, Doc asked if I could fly him home in time for the new arrival. Well it was a little far for a Shawnee, but why not? I borrowed a U-6 from the 4th ID and flew him down there for the big event. Doc was just in time for the delivery. Before I took off for the trip home he slipped me a nice bottle of Johnny Walker Black Label which I wrapped up in my helmet carrying bag. Now here comes the unprintable part. I parked the airplane right in front of base operations at Gray AAF. When I reached for the package, I grabbed only one strap of the bag so the scotch rolled right out and hit the concrete. You could hear my scream all the way to headquarters before I quickly got busy to remove the evidence.

I don't want to leave any impression here that it was all fun and games. By far, the most of our time was spent on the serious matters. We worked hard to gain and maintain proficiency in flying the Shawnee and we practiced flying them in groups to achieve particular missions. It was a good change to get in some fixed wing flying on occasion but flying cargo helicopters was what it was all about. Our job was to stay current in procedures and to sharpen our skills in handling the CH-21C Shawnee. We soon learned the importance of that when, in May of 1961, our nice comfortable peacetime training situation was disrupted by orders redesignating us from Strategic Army Force, STRAF VIII, to Strategic Army Corps STRAC II. Sure enough, the Pentagon had found us.

CHAPTER 6

STRAC II

"The strategic doctrine which I would propose to replace Massive Retaliation is called herein the Strategy of Flexible Response . . . for coping with anything from general atomic war to infiltrations and aggressions such as threaten Laos and Berlin in 1959."
General Maxwell D. Taylor "The Uncertain Trumpet" 1960[*1]

While the STRAF VIII designation was a comfortable one for the 57th and the supporting 98th, the STRAC II priority was another matter entirely. It was necessary to continue all of our previous activities while at the same time completing a full range of measures to allow the unit to be ready to deploy with only seventy two hours warning. Seventy two hours! That is the same as just three days. Three days! You have got to be kidding me! With twenty-two helicopters and all kinds of people, trucks, radios, tents, shop equipment, mess gear, supplies and individual weapons and equipment, the question was how does one get ready to do that? I certainly had no idea, but they gave me a copy of an Army Regulation (AR) and the additional duty of finding out anyway. Shortly after the May 1960 change in our deployment status, as an additional duty, I became the STRAC Control Officer.

A review of the AR, and some additional Army guidance on the subject, made it clear that we were faced with a major task. We were given only a few weeks to comply with all of the requirements contained in these documents and behind all the detailed guidance was the overall objective of getting ready to go somewhere, anywhere, anytime. It would be a learning process for all of us. The boss, Bob Dillard and his XO Milt Cherne', immediately began coordination with higher headquarters to gain as much insight as possible so that they could then provide guidance to the rest of us. I began to get really worried about full qualification of all of our pilots. The maintenance officers knew that their main problem would be to achieve a much higher level of equipment readiness than had been previously required. Not only the aircraft, but all of the vehicles and other items requiring maintenance, would have to be brought into top condition. The helicopters were, of course, the central problem. Spare parts and maintenance supplies would have to be beefed up if all the helicopters were to be brought to a flyable status in short order. And then a high percentage the helicopters had to be kept ready to fly so that all could be deployed within the very short timeframe allowed.

In spite of the fact that very few helicopter engines ever reached the planned replacement time; none in my memory, ARs prohibited units from building up engine Quick Change Assemblies (QCA) ahead of the by-the-book scheduled engine changes. The reason for this was to keep the demand for engines and sub-assemblies to a minimum, but everyone in the business knew that, if you wanted to stay ahead of the game, you needed to have QCAs ready well ahead of time. This was necessary because, although not recognized by the system, most engines had to be replaced early; that is, most engine changes were non-scheduled. I don't know what maintenance officers Bill Rudd and Ken Klippel called them. Maybe they weren't QCAs. Maybe they called them "engine changes in progress" or something but that key aircraft maintenance task had to go smoothly because with our new deployment priority the required aircraft readiness improvement had to be accomplished while continuing to support an increased tempo of training flights and the transition flying needed to bring newly assigned pilots up to deployment status as well.

The regulations dictated that detailed loading plans had to be created. That would be necessary if we planned to get all of our authorized Table of Organization & Equipment (TO&E) property properly loaded aboard our trucks and trailers or in shipping containers. TO&E is Army talk for all the people and stuff an organization owns. Plans would have to be made to move all of our personnel and equipment plus all of the government issued items and a limited amount of the personal property of our individual soldiers as well as the supplies that would be needed to sustain everything. So, get all the aircraft ready to fly; get all the pilots signed off to carry passengers as first pilots; get everything ready to roll down the road or be loaded aboard rail cars for movement to port; then publish it all in a Standard Operating Procedure (SOP). In short, those were our orders.

I have always been a firm advocate of learning everything you can from anyone who has been there before. We had, in essence, traded places with the 33rd Helicopter Company stationed at Ft Ord, California. They had gone from STRAC II to STRAF VIII while we went the other way. One of my first moves as the STRAC Control Officer was to fly down to Ft Ord to learn what they had done as a STRAC II unit and to borrow a copy of any plans or procedures they might have published. The pressure had apparently not been on them however, because whereas they had worked to meet the basic requirements of the number two deployment priority, they had published very little that would help us. We did hold useful discussions about what they had learned in the process and we came away ready to go it alone.

It was obviously necessary to get all the people ready to deploy with up to date shot records, wills, powers of attorney, allotments and all the myriad details of moving large numbers of individuals rapidly while also planning for the families that would be left behind. The company headquarters managed the personnel aspects of rapid deployment, while the supply officer took steps to fill all the shortages in individual equipment that were called for by Army regulations. This was all going on as people of all grades were rotating in and out of the unit at a rapid pace. Of course, these are precisely the conditions that bring to light all the problems that individuals tend to bring with them. There was no way to "finish" this job. Eventually, troops were still rotating in and out and other problems erupting as we flew to port.

Naturally, the families got a little nervous with all this activity. They were just as up to date as we were at the time. That meant that they knew that our deployment priority had been raised and that we were trying to get ready to move out quickly if called upon. It still seemed unlikely however, that we were going to go anywhere without the 4th ID and the Division wasn't planning to move. The prevalent feeling seemed to be that this was just another typical Army exercise; hurry up and wait; practice to be miserable; get ready for another footlocker inspection; fill in all the blanks. The old saying is that there is "a right way, a wrong way, and the Army way." This was probably just the Army way!

That was the general feeling alright; but some of us started keeping a much closer eye on the newspapers. If anyone happened to be serious about this new priority we might find ourselves on the way without much time for reflection about world events or where we might be going in response to those events. One important book which we read about this time was General Maxwell Taylor's "*The Uncertain Trumpet*" It was important because it heralded the US Army move from the "massive retaliation" strategy of the cold war toward the "flexible response" strategy which was gaining credence in military circles. President John F. Kennedy had already directed more emphasis on Army Special Forces and we in the 57th took this as fair warning of things to come. Needless to say we paid close attention when GEN Taylor took his trip to South Vietnam in October 1961.

While searching for information, I picked up a book that was then making the rounds entitled "*The Ugly American*" by William J. Lederer and Eugene Burdick. Published in 1958, and although only a book of short stories set in the fictional country of Sarkhan, it was a fair representation of about any Southeast Asian country that had been part of the old French colonies there. Although fiction, it purported to be based on fact and included a documentary epilogue. The book was presented as a series of vignettes and it seemed to make two central points. First, that before any attempt was made to aid any country in Southeast Asia, it was necessary to understand the culture of its citizens and that the United States of America had generally failed to do that. The second major point for me was that large scale efforts failed miserably and only those small efforts of highly motivated individuals produced any measurable progress and that even those tended to be transitory.*[2] Another book, although just another story of expatriate romance in the Far East, was Graham Green's "*The Quiet American*." It was set against a background of conflict in Southeast Asia and it shed a little more light on what was happening there;*[3] yes, but this was pretty soft stuff compared with the real touchy feely we all got a few months later. Meanwhile, we continued to put the pieces together so that we could move out smartly to somewhere.

For the Operations Officer also detailed as the STRAC Control Officer, the central task was to complete the detailed planning required for the loading and movement of supplies and equipment. This is not to say that the STRAC guy did it, but he had to document loading plans and schedule practice load out exercises. The platoons that "owned" the property had to get it ready and do the physical work. Each truck was assigned to a particular element of the outfit and that truck was to be the prime mover for its stuff. Each truck had an assigned driver and assistants were identified. Then the property assigned to each element was combat loaded on their assigned trucks and lashed down. Combat loading entails making sure that the equipment which would be needed first at destination, be loaded so that it could be gotten off first.

When the load was judged to be within gross weight limitations, balanced, properly combat loaded and as tight as possible, it was spread out on the ramp behind each truck in the order it was to be loaded aboard. Diagrams were made and pictures were taken and everything was given identifying marks. Practice load outs were conducted and adjustments were made as necessary. While all this was going on I think that the STRAC officer became the most heartily disliked individual in the organization. I was the STRAC officer. Everybody knew it had to be done, but everybody had other things that also needed to be done. Nevertheless, we practiced until we got it right and properly recorded so that it would all be old hat when and if the gong rang for real.

The full utilization of available space and weight distribution on our organic vehicles was important, but combat loading was the most critical and the most challenging problem. It took careful planning and repeated practice to ensure that the one item you always seemed to need to get at first, when you got to wherever you were going, would not be the one item that was loaded underneath or behind everything else. This requirement caused the most rework in planning, but was also the most valuable upon our arrival in the South China Sea.

Maintenance crews were able to find the tools and parts they needed quickly. They were "on top" when we began to prepare our helicopters for flight. Work began while we were still at sea.

We also soon found that it was not possible to get everything stowed aboard our assigned vehicles and we had to order CONEX containers for the overflow. Of course a part of the problem was that we could guess, but we really didn't know, where we might be going. So we had to pack up all the heaters and cold weather gear, which it turned out we didn't need, while we were not authorized and did not have the "jungle gear" or a long carriage typewriter or many other items which we did need. Several required reports were to be done "army style" on long paper which called for the special typewriter. Certain adjustments were made in the last days before deployment to rectify these anomalies and to provide a little cushion over that which was authorized by our TO&E. In the end, we couldn't solve the problem concerning appropriate climatic clothing and other gear; we took along a bunch of the wrong stuff because we didn't really know where the hell we were headed. And we didn't steal it exactly, but that long carriage typewriter was on temporary hand receipt from Fort Lewis for a long time after we cleared the post. Who knows, maybe it became another combat loss.

When the time came, we used a pretty effective vacuum cleaner approach at Fort Lewis, and from other helicopter outfits around the country, as we filled up a few extra CONEX containers for shipment. The aircraft were also weighted down with items which were considered by the Army to be part of the helicopter although not integral to it. The worst of this equipment were the armor kits which had been designed to fit under the transmissions to protect against vertical hits. This stuff was heavy and if installed would severely limit our troop lift capacity. It also appeared likely to be of little value since we didn't visualize giving anyone the opportunity to shoot straight up at us for very long. We carried it with us but it was far too heavy to be used in combat. We sure liked the idea of armored seats though and several pilots used field expedients under their posteriors as soon as the shooting started.

Another STRAC II requirement was that we have all the necessary chocking, blocking and tie-down devices needed to restrain everything for movement by truck, train or airplane and the loading and tie-down also had to be practiced. Practice alerts were held to be sure we could get all the people back to post quickly to load out all our property and secure it for transportation on our trucks and then on railroad flatcars. There were a lot of bruised knuckles, grease stained fatigues and not a little cussing by aircraft mechanics as they learned this new railroading trade. All of this learning had to be organized into a book of course because these actions had to become Standard Operating Procedure; "S. O. P." in Army talk.

Our first real test came in April 1961 when we were alerted to prepare for movement. Our heightened interest in world events had warned us that things did not look good in the old French Indo-China, particularly in Laos, but no word came concerning where, for how long, or even if, we were on the way anywhere. Our best guess was that somebody up there was trying to figure out what to do about the fact that Pathet-Lao communist forces had been joined by the neutralist forces led by Captain Kong-Le and the combined force was in the process of defeating the American advised Royal Lao government forces of General Phoumi Nosavan. Now we really started reading the newspapers.

Our practice alerts had prepared us well for these go-anywhere-anytime uncertainties. If we were headed for Laos okay and we wasted no time in packing out and loading up on the flatcars which had been spotted on a nearby railroad siding. The aircraft were made ready to fly; people were put on a very short string and then we waited. There was plenty of grousing about the old army game of hurry up and wait for about a week until we received word to stand down and prepare to move to Yakima where we would support the 4th ID in their annual maneuver at the firing range. One result of this exercise was a lost bet. Milt Cherne had bet that Bill Rudd would not be able to get everything up—all aircraft flyable—for any deployment and that if Bill did make that happen that he would wear his dress blues on the ramp for all to see. We have a picture of that event.

Looking back, it is still hard to say if the US Army really had immediate plans for us or just wanted to keep us on our toes. Whatever the plan, the result was an even more careful attention to world news and to our readiness for actual deployment. Training and aircraft maintenance began again with even more urgency. Morale in the unit got higher. Soldiers internalized the goal by creating a new noun for themselves, as in “I’m STRAC” or “You better get STRAC buddy.” Some of the wives got more nervous and there may even have been a little of that other ancient soldier reaction of “how do I get out of this chicken-shit outfit” but most everybody settled in to wait patiently for the next one and it wasn’t long in coming.

Five months later, we loaded up again and this time the 57th departed and never came back. There was plenty of confusion when that alert hit in early November 1961. To start with, the alert orders were classified Top Secret (TS). That was not a clearance level that many of our troopers carried and our first indication of the impending deployment was a flurry of activity by Dillard and Cherne’, as they began coordination with higher headquarters to clarify how these orders were to actually be implemented when they could only tell a few people about them.

But the kick-off within the company was initiated anyway, with a normal alert followed by broad hints to myself and the maintenance officers that this might be for real and we were to act like it was. I carried a TS clearance but the boss didn’t even clue me in totally. No one knew more as the command group reacted to the highly classified messages coming down through Sixth Army and the 4th ID operations center at Fort Lewis. Not the least of the problems was how to draft the orders to actually move the enlisted soldiers. Most of them had no clearance at all or were cleared to receive information only up to the confidential level. Another problem was that no one in the Division believed that the Army would send us anywhere on our own. If the 4th ID wasn’t going, we couldn’t be going. As an example, one of the items of equipment on our property book was a machine to allow receipt of crypto classified message traffic. That equipment was always kept in a secure location at 4th Division Headquarters and even after the Official Use Only movement orders were finally issued, the Division was very reluctant to let us have that machine. As the commo officer, that became another one of my problems.

After much coordination, those Official Use Only orders were published on 8 November 1961 and the salient points read: "Movement Order Number 3 . . . from Fort Lewis, Washington to Overseas Exercise Area . . . through Oakland Army Terminal . . . This is a temporary Change of station (TCS) for a period in excess of 30 days . . . ."

CHAPTER 7

PORT CALL

Picture a crystal clear cold November day when frozen lakes reflect the brilliant sun amid fresh snowfalls that blanket the fields and cling to the jagged peaks of the Sierra Nevadas . . . Smooth flying at one hundred miles per hour and one thousand feet above the ground.

This time things moved rapidly. Based on the 3 November alert warning message we moved out smartly. You might even say that we got a little ahead of ourselves. The Department of Army message dirccting our move was dated November seventh and was amended on the eighth. Sixth Army implemented the move by issuing a port call on the eighth. Fort Lewis published the movement orders on the eighth but we had already departed that station. For the second time in 1961, all our aircraft had been brought to flyable condition. Then, at ten hundred hours on that sunny Sunday morning of 6 November, twenty Shawnee helicopters rattled the windows over the 4th Infantry Division headquarters building at Fort Lewis. We did a low pass to be sure they knew that we were really leaving without them. Pilots had been rotating out a little faster then they were coming in during 1961. We were still short a few at the time. So we borrowed twelve officers from the 4th ID to fill the seats with ferry pilots.

The company was broken down into two flights of ten each. Dillard led the first group and I led the second. The port from which we would depart had been identified as the Alameda Naval Air Station, California, with personnel to be processed through the Oakland Army Terminal. The aircraft were to be prepared for shipment at the Stockton Army Depot where they would be cocooned in plastic for deck loading aboard the USNS Core. The weather in

November can be a little dicey over the Cascade Siskiyou Mountains of Western Oregon so we planned a route south to Portland turning east, up the Columbia River Gorge to The Dalles. This part of the route was familiar to us from our many flights to the Yakima Firing Range but this time we would turn south at The Dalles instead of north and head down the east side of the Sierra Nevada Mountains to Stead Air Force Base (AFB), Reno, NV where we would take the old Donner Pass over the mountains to Stockton CA.

No move of that magnitude can be expected to go off without a hitch and ours was no exception. Although minor in the scheme of things, we were presented problems that had to be solved on the run so to speak. Our first refueling stop was to be at Troutdale, Oregon, a small commercial airfield beside the Columbia River just upriver from Portland. This was a familiar field for us. When the weather precluded flight directly over Mount Rainier, we had often stopped there on our way to Yakima. We had, however, never descended on that little airfield with twenty gas guzzling Shawnees all at one time, each one ready to take on about a hundred gallons of fuel. On those flights to Yakima we had been in no particular hurry. We usually stopped for coffee or lunch and often, when the winds were behind us, we did not need to top off with gas. So I had never noticed that there was only a single three-inch hose available for refueling. This time we all had to be fully topped off for the next leg of our flight over the east Oregon plateau.

Our instructions specified an arrival time at Stockton on 7 November and included directions to avoid flying at night. As the painfully slow process of refueling continued, it became apparent that we had to do something or there would be no way to comply with both of those instructions. Because we had landed behind the other flight and so were closer to the gas pump, my second flight was refueled first. The boss decided that we should go on immediately and his flight would follow as soon as possible. We were to fly until just before dark and land at the closest airport where refueling was available. We did that, landing at the town of Redmond just before dark. In order to not crowd the gas pumps again, Dillard took his flight just a little further down the road, landing at Bend Oregon for the night. There was no good reason not to enjoy the evening so instructions for my flight crews were to get a good meal, stay sober and be ready for a dawn takeoff. The night was cool but clear and the restaurant at the motel served an excellent sirloin steak. After eating, we gathered in lawn chairs outside the rooms passing jokes and telling tales. Since we were still operating under classified orders and we didn't know much anyway, there was little if any, discussion about the flight we were then on.

It was my intention to be just arriving overhead of the Bend airfield about when I expected the other flight to be completing takeoff. We all turned in early. As it turned out we took-off a little too early because there was no activity at Bend when we flew over. The helicopters were lined up with the morning frost still coating their Plexiglas cockpits and there were no rotors turning as we flew by. We attempted radio contact but could raise no one so I decided that we would continue on our planned route. We could join up at the next stop where we would expedite the refueling process and cut down on the ground time at Reno. Time would be critical to avoid night flight over the mountain pass to the Stockton Depot.

One of the extras that had been laid on for this long ferry flight was a U-1 Otter, a fixed wing utility aircraft, piloted by MAJ Ralph Quigley commander of the Fort Lewis general support aircraft maintenance company. The Otter crew was supposed to act as a communication relay between flights and was intended to assist in the event of any helicopter mechanical problems. In Army communications protocol each unit is issued a call-sign. Ours in the 57th, was a kind of embarrassing one to us macho aviators. Our call-sign was "Ladybird." The numeral six always indicates the commander of a unit so the boss was "Ladybird 6." As the operations guy, I was "Ladybird 3." Needless to say we normally figured out a way to not use that call-sign at all. Usually we would just work our way around it with a chalk number or an aircraft tail number. Anyway, the radio traffic between the Otter and Ladybird 6 had been very frequent between Fort Lewis and Troutdale and there had also been considerable radio talk initiated by the boss back to my flight. Most pilots are habitually very sparing with radio use so the extra communication had been a little annoying that first morning. The afternoon after the flights got separated turned out to be very peaceful without the constant chatter.

We had parked side by side at Redmond that evening, so I could see when the whole flight was turning up and ready to go in the morning. There was no need for even a commo check so the only radio call for us that morning was "chalk one rolling." After trying to raise somebody on the ground while passing Bend, my flight continued smoothly and quietly onward until I eventually contacted the Otter to let them know our position. After that we flew for miles along the base of the mountains over Nevada, silent except for one more transmission. As we passed by a large group of Canadian Geese flying south in an impeccable vee formation, an unknown voice announced "look at those flocking geese." (At least that might have been the word he used.) That was the only radio call to break the air for the rest the trip that morning until a landing call was made at Stead AFB outside of Reno. No, I never did discover the origin of that important communication. Our flights were rejoined at Stead, and the boss may even have been a little irritated that we had gotten out ahead of him. Although we had finished refueling when the first flight arrived his words were a little short. "Wait, we'll take the lead from here!"

It was discovered on landing that one of the Shawnees had experienced an auxiliary fuel pump failure on this leg but that was to be the only mechanical problem for the entire flight; quite an accomplishment for our maintainers. Because a spare was not available, and because the aux fuel pump is not needed for normal flight, the decision was made to continue to Stockton before replacing it. Take-off was initiated well on toward the late afternoon. We would be able to get over the mountain before nightfall, but our run into the Stockton Depot would be chasing the shades of darkness.

The distance from start-up at Stead to the top of the Donner Pass is only a few miles and the ground elevation increases rapidly. Those heavily loaded Shawnees had to be held at a steady maximum climb to make the grade. Danny Hendrickson, in my flight, seemed to be having the most trouble getting his machine to climb. He called several times to say that he didn't think he would be able to clear the pass. Danny was one of our more experienced pilots, and an IP, so my response each time he called was a "roger" and maybe a "let us know." I figured that he would do whatever he could do to make it over the hump without my advice. He certainly knew enough to put in some more pedal to throw the aft rotor out into clean air for a little added lift or to take whatever action might help gain additional lift. Eventually I told him to do the best he could and if necessary to leave himself enough room to do a 180 degree turn and return to Stead. We would come back later for part of his load and try it again tomorrow.

This whole exercise got to be a bit much though because Dillard, in the lead helicopter, could not understand what was going on. He could hear garbled transmissions and my brief responses but that was all. So he would call back, through the Otter relay, and I would explain the latest distress call from Danny. We would fly a little further and then repeat the whole process. I suppose he thought that I should be offering more encouragement or something because every once in a while he would pass back some advise. Bennie Potts, who had been Dillard's instructor during transition training, was flying with him so I'm sure the advice was offered after consultation with Bennie. He was the respected old man of our Chief Warrant Officers. He was a grade senior to the others and was the unit standardization pilot so that was okay, but none of his advice seemed to be of much help to the crew working to milk that old Shawnee over the hill. It all worked out at the top though when Danny slipped over the crest with about three feet to spare.

The next radio call was from the pilots in the Otter. They had been relaying transmissions through the whole thing and now said "look at that beautiful sunset." That was not the most useful radio communication, but one with which we all agreed as we eased on down the other side of the mountain. The flight was relatively quiet after that sunset call but we may have bent the rule on darkness a tad as we touched down around 1900 hours at the Stockton California Army Depot. Our pilots always kept a sense of humor and they also had a fairly long collective memory. This was evidenced by the baseball hat that someone found and gave to MAJ Dillard shortly after our arrival in Saigon. They had taken the cap downtown and had it embroidered with a radio talk button and the slogan "Mike Button 6."

We had just completed a historic flight, but at the same time one of our sister companies was engaged in another notable effort. Led by Major Charles D. Hardesty, the 8th Helicopter Company was making a transcontinental flight from Fort Bragg, NC to Stockton, CA. Although we didn't know it until we saw them coming, they would deploy with us. Most of their aircraft arrived in good shape but two or three dropped out on the trip and were shipped later. We were also surprised to learn that each company would be joined by an avionics repair detachment and by a medical team. The arrival of the "Doc" should have been fair warning that we were headed into something more than just an "exercise" but we were too busy to give it much notice at the time. It was not clear exactly what would happen next, at least not to me, but the boss went right to work. After finding out that processing our aircraft for carrier deck loading would take several days, he set about lining up a USAF transport aircraft so that most of our pilots could return to Fort Lewis. Only a couple of maintenance supervisors and the crew chiefs were needed to assist in preparing the helicopters for shipment. The rest of us could have a few days at home to repack for a more graceful departure.

We still didn't know where we were headed, but it was becoming ever more clear that we were about to go *somewhere.* We hadn't missed GEN Taylor's recent visit to Vietnam and after the Laos exercise our interest level was quite high. We found slight detail in the published reports concerning his trip and nothing about any decisions that were made. Several of us however, using GI guesswork, had grabbed up the October copy of *National Geographic* that had hit the streets. It had a story entitled "*South Viet Nam fights the Red Tide*" which, although not very informative about the war, did give a concise history of the country, including the conflict in the region and it sure had some great pictures. The article provided another glimpse of what the place might look like and reminded us about what was going on over there.*[1] It was also at about this juncture that I read Bernard Fall's "*The Street Without Joy.*" First published in April 1961, that book turned out to be a very scary picture of the French Indochina war. Not a comforting read at that particular moment. Fall had reported from Indochina during the war of the 1950s and the book covered the last days of the French Expeditionary Mobile Force 100 which ended in the battles around An Khe;*[2] a name that would later become all too well known by the soldiers of the U.S. 1st Cavalry Division when they established what would become the largest helipad in the world there in 1965.

Mr. Fall put out an updated third edition of his book in 1963 in which he makes the point that we Americans appeared to have learned little from the French experience in Vietnam. We in the 57th, had already finished our first tours by then and my reaction when I read that revision was "situation normal." The third edition apparently did not get any more attention then the first one. Obviously, us Americans knew that we could easily whip any enemy as unsubstantial as the Viet Cong, even if the French couldn't. All we had to do was train the South Vietnamese in our superior methods; give them some modern weaponry and lots of money. And, oh yeah, provide some improved transportation. That's where we came in. If we lower ranking soldiers thought about it at all, I suppose that we felt about the same way as our leaders did at the time. In the context of the world politics of 1961 this seemed likely to be just an extension of our efforts in Thailand and Laos; efforts which were intended to stem the tide of communist aggression by drawing some kind of a line across Southeast Asia.

A load sucking noise should have been heard as we followed the French down the slippery slope in Southeast Asia. The body politic however was diverted by the very real threat of international communism and a belief in the Eisenhower era "domino" theory. There was, at the time, little opposition to this idea which had been promulgated by President Eisenhower and was still influencing the Kennedy administration. That theory held that when one country fell under communist domination the next in line was sure to go, right on down to Australia I guess. The idea was to bolster friendly governments by providing support, advice and training which, it was believed, would stop or at least slow down this communist expansion. There is no evidence that anyone at the time thought that it would be necessary for the United States to commit large numbers of combat troops to achieve this goal. History may show later ages if the Vietnam War was a true course, or not, but the recent French experience should have given a warning signal and if anyone had been listening carefully they should have heard it.

The flying officers and men about to be deployed were, however, somewhat oblivious to the overlying strategy or the history of Southeast Asia. There was a fair amount of anxiety evident as we prepared to leave the comfort of our homes, but it was the kind that is normally associated with heading off into the unknown not anything more prescient. At our level, down where the rubber meets the road, or maybe we Shawnee drivers should say where the wheels hit the ground, there was nothing more then perhaps a very small feeling of uncertainty. We read the papers and the books, but we were soldiers and we would go where we were ordered and do what was expected of us. The big picture was out there somewhere where the big thinkers were able to see it all and besides, we were the U.S. Army; the best in the world; able to stand up to the Russian Bear anywhere. Just because the French had failed was no reason to suspect that we couldn't prevail in a little squabble like Southeast Asia. Right?

At that moment, when history was beginning to overtake us, we boarded a C-47 Goony Bird; one that would take some of us back up to Fort Lewis. We had been unexpectedly given a very few days where we could rejoin our families and repack our bags. Unfortunately, the crew chiefs had to stay with their aircraft and our maintenance officers headed up teams as they learned a new trade at Oakland: the proper way to cocoon a helicopter. It seems to me that departing home after this short stay was harder than it had been the first time. My wife Emily was left holding the bag; living off base with our five year old daughter Karen. We owned a fifty foot long, ten foot wide, Spartan house trailer. It was parked on a rented lot just off Mt Tacoma Drive near the fort. The families that lived on base at Fort Lewis were allowed to retain their quarters and so the family community that had developed around the unit was maintained. The senior officer's wives led by Millie Dillard looked after those families for the next year. They held things together until our individual soldiers were rotated home and they were moving out to their next assignments.

CHAPTER 8

PACIFIC CRUISE

Numerous Maritime Commission hulls were converted into Escort Carriers during WWII . . . A converted C-3 Cargo Ship, the U.S.S Core was launched at Tacoma WA on 5-15-42. "The Ships and Aircraft of the U.S. Fleet—Second War Edition" Copyright 1944 by James C. Fahey.[*1]

We were gathered at the Oakland Army Terminal when more of the big picture unfolded. The 8th Helicopter Company flew in and the newly activated avionics repair and medical detachments joined us. These were small teams, numbering around twenty men each, commanded by captains. They would prove to be indispensable in Vietnam. The 255th Signal Detachment was headed up by CPT Ray A. Houts and the 129th Medical Detachment by CPT "Doc" Mielke. (We knew him by no other first name). Ray was an experienced fixed wing aviator. While he was not a qualified helicopter pilot, he was able to provide fixed wing support on operations and his team kept our radios working. Doc Mielke, however, was brand new to the Army. He proved to be a great doctor, and ran a first class team of medical technicians, but his feel for the peculiarities of Army life seemed to be one of open amazement. Again, we need to revert to TV; MASH and Hawkeye, to get a true picture of our doctor. He didn't fight the system like Hawkeye did though. He just seemed to be mystified by it.

The 8th Helicopter Company had completed a history making coast to coast flight to join us, but of necessity, had arrived at the port still short of much of their equipment. Some of their CH-21C helicopters and most of their other equipment had to be shipped out later by cargo vessel. Except for small rear and advance parties, all personnel were aboard the USNS Core on 21 November to begin the trip through San Francisco Bay. We still did not know where we were going; our orders were classified and sealed. The boss was not to open them until we were well across the Pacific. This however, did not stop a San Francisco Chronicle columnist by the name of Herb Caen. Although our movement orders were highly classified the ships sailing orders were not. Caen reported that he didn't know where the helicopter companies were going, but the ship was headed for Bangkok and would stop at Saigon along the way.[*2]

MAJ Dillard was the senior officer aboard and therefore was designated commander of all Army troops for the duration of the shipboard deployment, and it was here that I began to realize just how junior I was. Most, if not all, of the captains assigned to the 8th Helicopter Company were senior to me. Because Cherne' was leading the advance party, Dillard had no XO aboard so he wanted me close at hand during the trip. I ended up being billeted on the upper deck with some of those older 8th company captains. The troops were bunked six high in hot confined lower decks and so were the warrants and most of the junior officers. This led to the really weird situation where some of the 8th guys, senior to me, were below decks while I resided in relative splendor on an upper bunk in an air conditioned compartment with only about six or seven others. One of those officers down below was then Captain, future Major General, Aaron Lilley who in later years would be one of my post commanders and a retirement friend. He has never mentioned this incident. Although I have always wondered what he thought about it, I have not had the courage to ask.

The Core was loaded full and down as sailors say. Cocooned helicopters filled the flight deck, and the hanger deck was full of more helicopters and fixed wing aircraft. Here were the North American T-28 trainers that would double in Vietnam as ground support attack planes. All of our vehicles with their combat loaded equipment were also downstairs. The merchant sailors were busy as we left port, but after the story in the San Francisco Chronicle got around, the troops wouldn't leave them alone. They began badgering them about Saigon and they heard about Vung Tau, or as the crew knew of it, Cap St Jacques. It had also been reported that the Core would be going on to Bangkok, and since no one was sure of our eventual destination, they plied them with more questions about Bangkok. This quest for information lasted for the entire trip but was, of course, limited in scope since the sailors could shed little light on anything beyond the bars and nightclubs near the waterfronts of those places. Of course that may have been quite enough for some of our soldiers but after we passed a couple of weeks at sea we still didn't know much about anything.

The troops were pretty restless as they settled in for that first winter night on San Francisco Bay. No activities had yet been organized to keep them busy. Army troops wrestled with the unfamiliar Navy style bunk hammocks downstairs. (Belay that; "below decks.") Groups hung around talking in hushed tones punctuated with occasional gales of laughter when somebody got off a good one. The mood however was defintly subdued. Several of us stood on the flight deck among helicopters, turned ghostly white by their plastic wraps, as the night darkened and the Core slid out of the bay beneath the Golden Gate Bridge and we began a twenty-one day pleasure cruise (Army style) across the Pacific, crossing the international dateline, before steaming into the South China Sea and up the Saigon River.

It was sunshine and a smooth cruise all the way. The USNS Core was a comparatively big ship. It was not as big as a regular full sized aircraft carrier in WWII, but it did have a flight deck, a hanger deck and several decks lower down. The Core was classed as an aircraft transporter rather than an aircraft carrier and picked up its nickname "Jeep Carrier" because of the job it was designed to do. Regular flight operations were not intended. Its primary mission during the big war was to carry Army aircraft overseas for delivery to the Army Air Forces airfields which were being established on pacific islands. One take off for each airplane was all that would be necessary. For those of you who may be somewhat uneducated on Navy stuff, the USNS abbreviation identifies a United States Naval Ship that is manned by merchant seaman employees of the Navy department, versus a USS designation which stands for a United States Navy vessel manned by US Navy sailors. The Core had been redesignated for merchant seaman manning after WWII.

The USNS Core was big enough to handle the long rolling swells of the Pacific with ease so that made for a fairly stable ride. This came as a relief for me because the last time I had shipped out was about the same time of year but on a smaller troopship, the USNS Taylor, headed across the North Atlantic. Although I managed to keep my cookies then, a lot of folks didn't on that December 1955 voyage. On that trip I had a much different row to hoe then I did occupying my top bunk on the Core. The Taylor was transporting a bunch of dependant families and about 2300 airborne troops to Europe. I was one of seven Army Aviators, just out of flight school, being sent "unaccompanied by families" to join various units around U. S. Army Europe and I was a second lieutenant. Not only that, but of us seven officers, I was the most junior so they naturally made me the mess officer. I had daily duties on the Core, but they were nothing like watching those 2300 seasick troops get fed on the Taylor.

There were also some families aboard the Taylor and they were in no better shape than the troops. It's a diversion from our story here, but one particular scene from that 1955 voyage still remains in my mind. We were already a few days out on the North Atlantic sea before just a few of the families began to show up for meals. The officers and the families ate in a top deck compartment, on long tables arrayed out both sides of a central aisle. This was much nicer then the large mess halls below decks. It started to look like the kids and ladies were getting their sea legs and our table was almost full of tentative diners at meal time after about a week at sea. Everything seemed to be going nicely until one day when, during the noon meal, an orange appeared rolling slowly through the compartment door. It proceeded straight down the center aisle until the ship rolled sharply and then it turned 90 degrees and slowly rolled down between the tables to the hull. When the ship caught the back roll, the orange reversed direction and headed back the way it had come at the same deliberate rate of speed and when it disappeared back out through the compartment door about three quarters of our new diners left with it.

We won't even talk about the troop mess hall on that trip aboard the Taylor. I don't even want to think about it. But at least I wasn't the mess officer for our pacific cruise aboard the Core. It was a smooth ride and the mess facilities on the Core were much better than those on the Taylor. The dining areas were fairly small so meal times and numbers had to be precisely controlled but the chow served there was not bad.

In fact, it became fairly standard for us, on later tours in Vietnam, to barter with the civilian crews on USNS ships. We could trade rapid helicopter transport from ship to shore in exchange for some of the large supply of T-bone steaks they always seemed to carry.

There is not a hell of a lot to do on an "Army" cruise. There are no swimming pools, no bars, no gaming saloons, no waitresses or swinging singles as shown on prime time TV. While the chow was good, they weren't seven course meals and wine was not served. Sunning on the flight deck was permitted and there was plenty of room for exercise too, but I don't recall any volley ball or tennis courts up there. The ship carried a fair number of books in a trading library for us lay-abouts. They were mostly of the light reading variety, westerns, mystery and adventure stories, but that was fine with me. After reading "*Street Without Joy*," that kind of escapism was about right.

The crew showed movies most nights but there were two things wrong with that. The first was that they didn't have many films on hand; no way near enough for twenty-one days at sea. The favorite one was, without a doubt, "*Tora Tora Tora*". I must have watched the Japs strafing Pearl Harbor in this old WWII film at least a half a dozen times; great movie for those heading toward an unknown and maybe hazardous destination. The other problem was the seats. Just folding chairs, but after about an hour those things get pretty hard. You would think this would not bother a pilot because there ain't nothin harder then a helicopter seat after a few hours, but at least in a helicopter you got to watch the rice paddies go by, not just be watching the same old movies over and over. I always wondered why helicopter seats had to be so hard until a few years ago when I got an education on crash injury causes. In a crash, each inch of kopeck in a seat cushion allows for that much more stroking and acceleration of the pilots butt until it hits hard structure and the more of that, the worse the spinal injury is likely to be. So we suffered flying, but I'll never forget those hard folding chairs on the Core.

Soldiers, of course, are nothing if not resourceful. When they are out in the field they are known to be constantly improving their foxholes and when not so engaged they will often spread the 100%

wool, olive drab, GI blanket for a little game of dealers' choice. There weren't any foxholes aboard ship to keep the troops busy and no Army blankets, but there were plenty of gray Navy blankets to serve the purpose. In the pilots ready room at Fort Lewis the game had been pinochle, usually double deck; well that game continued on the Core but the game of choice was poker. There were two games going on at all times, one among the pilots and the other among the enlisted men, and others would pop up now and then.

I really enjoy a good game of poker myself, but my duties precluded joining into these. In fact it was my unpleasant job to be sure that nothing ever got out of hand in these contests and to even break them up occasionally, so that some of the more serious players would get some rest, or at least make up their bunks and clean up around them. Gambling is frowned on in the Army, particularly if anyone even thought of playing for money. But in my experience, it is a rule that is mostly ignored unless something starts to go awry. There were only a couple of problems to emerge on the Core. I had to pull one sergeant out of a continuous game in the enlisted area because he couldn't seem to lose and I broke up another game permanently where the enlisted and officers had decided to play together because some of them couldn't find seats at the other tables.

I was not able to participate directly on the Core, therefore I have no specific memories from those games, but any discussion of poker always reminds me of CWO Huey R. Nelson and a 57th game we played out at the Yakima Firing Range. It was five card draw and the draw had been made. Huey was sweating his hand; carefully exposing just one card at a time and he seemed to lose track of what was going on around him until it was his turn to make a move. He didn't realize that we were all sitting around waiting for him until someone finally said "damn it Huey are you going to fold or bet?" Huey came awake and raised to the max. Then when all the bettin and raisin got done he laid down four deuces. This would have been the big winner of course, except that when he spread his hand out on the GI blanket, there were six cards instead of five. Everyone knows that's one too many but Huey had not seen the extra one because when he spread four deuces he quit looking at any more cards. Now that is exactly the kind of thing that can cause a game to get out of hand. Huey was a little upset, you might say, but he was a gentleman and after being unable to admit the problem for awhile, he gave in gracefully. There ain't no misdeal in poker, but I have seen grown men throw the table and all the cards and money across the room for less then that.

Pocket book reading, movies and card games; those were about the extent of the entertainment available to us on this three week army pleasure cruise. I guess we all spent some time thinking, and there was some discussion, about where we might be headed and what we were going to do when we got there. I don't think there was much further doubt that we were likely to get shot at. There were, as always, duties for some of us though. As the acting XO, there were certain reports that I had to get out and announcements that had to be made. Dillard coordinated daily with MAJ Hardesty and with Buck Haskell, the Captain of the Core. He was also on the radio to Sixth Army and back to Fort Lewis fairly often. MAJ Dillard was an experienced company commander and his first concern was always for the welfare of the men under his command. He made daily trips downstairs to check on the troops and made sure that I did also. In any outfit it is important to let people blow off steam and that seems to be particularly so in the Army. Bitch, bitch, bitch, but that seems to be a basic need for soldiers. So I swung through the troop decks several times daily and mostly just let them ramble. Sometimes there was a minor problem to help solve, but mostly just a little housekeeping and a lot of talk.

We crossed the international dateline on 29 November at 32 degrees North latitude. That figures out to be about nine days out of San Francisco and about half way across the Pacific. We passed just north of Midway Island but we would never have known that if Captain Haskell hadn't told us. We hadn't seen land since losing sight of California and we didn't see Midway go by either. The ship's crew had certificates for the event though and with a small ceremony, we were each awarded a green and gold, dragon enhanced, document entitled "Domain of the Golden Dragon" which designated us all as "Rulers of the 180th Meridian."

It really started to get hot as we approached the Tropic of Cancer a couple of days later and it remained hot for the rest of the trip. Shirts off became the rule on deck and for some, even less than that below decks, where the bunks were stacked six high and the humidity rode right on up there with the rise in temperature. Hot and sticky is an understatement. The boss had instructions to open our sealed orders when we passed through the Philippines. I don't remember how the word went out to the troops, whether by announcement, memorandum or word of mouth, but it doesn't matter. The grapevine was never as healthy as it was aboard the Core and so the news went out quickly. We would debark at Saigon, South Vietnam.

The journey was not yet over though. This was not a voyage where the passengers were apprised of exactly where we were at any time, but my memory is that we left the Straights of Mindanao and sailed through the Sulu and into the South China Seas. It was like entering into another world. Here there were no longer the long rolling swells of the Pacific. The water was unusually flat and glassy with a greasy, almost oily look about it and the sunsets began to take on vivid colors. I'll not forget the first time that we saw a bunch of flying fish startle into the air and fly for an unbelievably long distance. I had always suspicioned that flying fish were just the embroidery on old sea tales. Fish don't fly. And besides what do you call them when they're in the air? Is a bunch of flying fish a school, a covey or a flock? Anyway, hundreds of fish took to the air in silver clouds on all sides of the ship and sometimes you even thought that you saw the Barracuda or whatever it was that was chasing them.

As we approached the mainland off the coast of Vietnam the sea seemed to take on an even more bilious character. We passed through floating islands of sea snakes. These clumps were several yards in diameter and I wouldn't have believed about them either without seeing them. We had one officer aboard that was already fearful enough of the snakes we were likely to find in the jungle without seeing these writhing masses go by. Bill Smith didn't talk about anything else for the rest of the way. We all got to see more of the South China Sea than we had expected as the ship slowed to a crawl and began to travel in circles. We orbited out there for three days awaiting diplomatic clearance to enter South Vietnamese waters. After the way we had hurried to get there they didn't even seem to want us, but this kind of thing turned out to be characteristic of the problems we would run into for the first several weeks in country.

A U-6A Beaver from the U.S. MAAG flight detachment came out and circled over us while we orbited the sea about three miles out. Cherne' was flying, and I think it was Major Cherne' by then. He was promoted either on the way over with the advance party or right after arrival and he waggled his wings to welcome us into country. Things were still getting sorted out between the Diem government and the U.S. advisory group but eventually we started wending our way up the narrow twisting channel of the Saigon River. The word was passed that the troops should stay off the flight deck as we moved up river because someone might decide to shoot at any exposed personnel. So we kept our heads down until the ship came abreast of the city and even then no one wandered around topside.

The next maneuver was another new experience for me as we chugged a little way up the river past the city then swung completely around in the middle of the stream to head back down. It seemed to me that the ship had overlapped the shore at both bow and stern during the turn. This expert handling continued as the Captain smoothly brought her in to tie up along the wharf at the foot of Tudo Street. Picture this; a big gray naval vessel lying beside an ancient scared up wooden wharf stretched along the river immediately adjacent to the old French downtown section of the city. The ship seemed to dwarf the whole town.

From the deck we could look for several blocks right up the main street of Saigon. This is the street the French had called the Rue Catinat and the South Vietnamese had renamed Tudo which translates as Liberty or Freedom Street. Now, it is called Dong Khoi or Street of the General Uprising; a thing that never happened but it fits right in with Ho Chi Minh City I guess. We pulled up right behind the famous floating restaurant of Saigon. (I'll bet the folks still call it Saigon.) and people were sitting just across the street from us enjoying drinks in the patio bar of the Majestic Hotel. Naturally, after twenty-one completely sober days at sea, our troops were ready to jump ship into that little bar or hit that brightly lit street without further delay. We had to get the full visitor treatment first of course, so the troops were gathered on the hanger deck for a short speech by Major General Charles Timmes, the Chief of the MAAG Army Section.

CHAPTER 9

THE PARIS OF THE ORIENT

*"There was nothing secret last week about the arrival of the aircraft carrier USS Core. Belching clouds of black smoke from its single stack, Core moved 45 miles up a tributary of the Mekong River to President Ngo Dinh Diem's capital city of Saigon and docked at a wharf directly in front of the Hotel Majestic and the Café Terraces" Time, December 22, 1961**

Like I said, MAJ Dillard was an experienced commander who always kept the welfare of his troops on top in his thinking and he took action accordingly. In addition, he was properly jealous of his prerogatives as the 57th commander. He was our boss and therefore felt responsible for all that we did and for all that which was done to us. Having already been warned of possible hostilities, the troops were assembled on the hanger deck, instead of on the flight deck, as we approached Saigon. There our commander outlined what little he knew about the situation we were likely to face in Vietnam. The hanger deck was crowded with aircraft so the approximately 450 soldiers of both companies were drawn up in loose formation below a platform on a "ladder" leading topside. As soon as the gangplank went down our newly minted Major, Milt Cherne', hurried aboard and among other things, reported that the MAAG had been told that the helicopter crews could stay aboard ship until their equipment was unloaded and then they could live in their aircraft until tents were erected at the airfield.

For that reason, when the welcoming party came aboard, Dillard's first concern was to show MG Timmes the miserable conditions in which the troops were living below decks in order to gain his support for moving us rapidly into some kind of facility ashore. Captain Haskell was also anxious to get us off his ship so he could move on out of there. After Timmes' short welcome speech, Dillard invited the general to view the ship's accommodations and as they started down the ladder, a slick wing lieutenant colonel Army Aviator, an import from Korea, stepped forward to speak to the assembled companies. Any aviator can tell you that the term "slick wing", when applied to a fairly senior officer, means one who has only recently graduated from flight school and has not been a pilot for very long. Although it had been his recommendation that we could live in our helicopters, this was our first direct exposure to LTC John B. Stockton.

It had apparently been somewhat of a surprise to the MAAG staff, when they got word that they were going to receive additional US Army "advisory" support in the form of some transport helicopter companies. It was surely on short notice and they apparently had no one in the group who was well versed in the employment of such assets. There was a small flight detachment with fixed wing aircraft supporting the headquarters, but these officers had little or no helicopter experience. In any event, the decision was made to have some "experts" flown down from the Eighth US Army in Korea. You can guess how that went. I'm sure that Eighth Army did not carefully select its best officers to send down to this small advisory team way down in Indochina. The senior officer dispatched was Stockton. He led a team of three officers, none of whom appeared to have had any special background or experience in the management of cargo helicopters or troop transport operations, but all were Army Aviators. They would act as a MAAG aviation staff. They did not lack for enthusiasm but we ignored them as best we could.

The Eighth Army team had only been in country for a maybe a week when we first saw Stockton that day on the Core. He was already dressed in camouflage fatigues and a Jungle Jim hat, which costume he had purchased on the local market. He looked like a real warrior, ready for jungle combat. The first and only words from the lieutenant colonel that day were somewhat of a surprise to all of us. He started right out with the shock treatment by saying "there's a war going on over here and some of you are going to get killed!" That statement stopped our boss MAJ Dillard in his tracks and he turned back to the platform where he told LTC Stockton to stop right there and informed him that no one talked to his troops like that except himself and that Stockton should leave the platform. Maybe he told him to get the hell off the boat. I don't know but he was sure mad enough. Whatever was said, MG Timmes waited without a word as this short discussion took place. Then the major and the general continued on their tour of the troop compartment.

After this introductory performance, the maintenance crews continued to ready the aircraft for flight, and all of us waited anxiously for word about getting onto dry land for a night on the town. The troops had gained all the intelligence they could get from the merchant seamen who had been to Saigon on previous trips and most of them had already picked a favorite sounding bar to head for. The discussion in the command group centered around what time a curfew should be applied. Possibilities ranged from 2000 hours, eight PM for civilian readers, to 2300. I thought that a more reasonable figure, after nearly a month at sea, was 0100 hours and I was able to persuade the boss to my point of view after noting that we hadn't had to administer an Article 15, non-judicial punishment, or any other kind of military justice for a month and if we were to impose too strict a curfew we would probably break our fine record that very night. Well he eventually relented and established one A.M. as the report back time. But it cost me, because I was told to be back at the head of the gangplank well before midnight to count the others back aboard the ship.

Just before dark, the word was passed that we should travel in groups of at least two and no more then four and that we should cross over no bridges because these all led to the less secure outskirts of town. I led the parade down the gangplank. On the dock I ran into an old U.S. Army TC friend who was already serving with the MAAG in Saigon and acting as an advisor to the port operation. We paused only briefly to exchange greetings. Even so, before I could get across the street, CWO Jack J. Carey, who was then my assistant operations officer, was sitting in that outside bar at the Majestic Hotel with a big glass of cold beer saying "where the hell have you been?"

Saigon appeared to be a cross between Europe and the Orient. Some called it the Paris and others the Pearl of the Orient. It was a city of about two million people in 1961, including the mostly ethnic Chinese district of Cholon. It spread way out to the West and Northwest from the banks of the river and reached toward the south along the intersecting canals and wharves of the Ben Luc River. For all that population, even then swollen by war refugees, it seemed like a rather small place from our perch on the Core. We were tied up right next to the heart of the town and three main tree lined streets ran out parallel before us. This downtown section of maybe ten square blocks contained most of the larger office buildings and western style hotels. Beyond the westernized center and the waterfront warehouses, the buildings were much smaller and appeared to be mostly residential. We were to discover later that this was not really true because there were substantial buildups in Cholon, Dacau and around the Doc Lap presidential palace where there was also a large Catholic church, a central post office and other major buildings. The U.S. Embassy was located near the waterfront but when it eventually became very familiar to television viewers it had been relocated in the central area near the palace.

These outlying districts would have to wait to be discovered though, because our attention was directed pretty close-in that first night. And it was a memorable night for many reasons, as we sort of rolled up Tudo Street. Some paused to more closely investigate each inviting bar before they passed on by to try the next one. The Capital Bar, for instance, seemed to get plenty of attention and the highest recommendation from the ship's crew was for a night club called the Tudo just a few blocks up the main drag. The strength of the MAAG in Saigon was then around 400 strong so our additional 400 plus Americans must have seemed like a real flood to the citizens along those main streets that night and the price of everything no doubt doubled instantly. Some things surely tripled.

Very few of us had any experience with the "exotic" orient, and Saigon with its "Pearl" or "Paris of the Orient" title (take your choice) was certainly exotic enough for us. About our first new taste was the beer. We later discovered other brands, but the main drink on Tudo Street was Beire 33. Thirty Three sounded like Bam e' Bam to us when the locals spoke. We were told that formaldehyde was used in the manufacture to "cure" this bitter brew, and many learned to their regret, that it didn't take too much of it to create a major morning headache; one that might even last all the day after. Even so, "Bam e' Bam and Formaldehyde" made a hit that first night and some even acquired a taste for it.

This was also our introduction to cyclos and the ubiquitous little blue and white Renault taxis. The cyclos were bicycle driven rickshaws. They had a two passenger basket arrangement in front and the drivers seemed to have legs like iron as they pedaled their loads of slightly inebriated soldiers between downtown destinations. The taxis were for longer trips, as one adventurous soul discovered to his surprise when his vehicle headed unexpectedly over a "forbidden" bridge. The only injuries of the night were the scratches and the bruises he acquired from bailing out of that taxi before he got any further astray.

The bars pumped music onto Tudo Street. The hotels, Hong Kong tailors, money changers, sidewalk soup kitchens and other shops and sidewalk merchants added flavor to the scene. A few Frenchmen still sat in the corner cafes. We noticed them in the lobby of the Hotel Catinat, and they lounged in the street level open air bar of the Continental Hotel. They reminded us of our Caucasian predecessors in this little corner of the world. All sorts of conveyances crowded the tree lined avenue as we wove our way along from bar to bar. Each time you reached a corner, a taxi would screech to a halt right in front of you and fling a door open. You had to stop abruptly to avoid a collision with these little Renaults and then you had to walk around them to get across the street. It didn't take long for some happy GIs to just climb into the open door of the cab instead and then go right on out the other side, sometimes several guys at a time, one after another, while the cabbie looked back in consternation. The downtown portion of Tudo Street only runs for about three blocks so it didn't take long to fill all the bars to capacity along that stretch. As the night progressed, people started to check out the side streets.

There were apparently rules prohibiting sidewalk merchants from peddling their wares right on Tudo Street, but there were little soup kitchen carts just around every corner. We soon dubbed them as either "Roach Coaches" or "Sidewalk Howard Johnsons." Scattered among the soup kitchens were other handcarts with souvenirs and a wide variety of small items for sale. Sidewalk vehicle repair shops were also strewn along the way. Each one of these floating establishments seemed to have its own crew of small boys with their hands out and tugging at your pockets for Piasters. We tried traveling in small numbers but the groups tended to coagulate at various places along the way that night. The Peacock restaurant was a half block off the main street and, although we were warned about the local cuisine and "Uncle Ho's revenge" some guys couldn't wait to try the local cuisine. It wasn't bad and it would later become hard to resist an occasional meal there.

A little bar called The Blue Moon had no particular credentials, but quickly became so well patronized by our pilots that it became known as the 57th downtown officer's club. I have no idea how the Blue Moon became the favorite bar for the pilots. It had no particular distinguishing features except that it was just off the Tudo main drag where the troops tended to gather. It was a calm little place where you could get quietly inebriated without attracting attention and we never had any kind of a problem there or anywhere else on the strauss for that matter; that is until the Army decided to bring in the military police (MP) later that year. We policed our own before they came in.

I have some particular memories of the Blue though. One was when I witnessed one of our more senior pilots late in the evening just outside the place. With both arms wrapped around it, he looked like he was trying to climb a telephone pole from the base up while trying to call "Roooy" or maybe it was "Newwww Yooork". There were other memorable incidents too, but one of them really sticks in my mind! That was the time, later on, when an off-duty MP got upset and placed a .45 caliber round through the back bar at the Blue Moon. Glass showered the serving gals behind the bar but no major injuries occurred. Still, someone had to reason with the drunken MP about this. I was the senior guy in the bar and so it fell to me to suggest that he place his firearm in protective custody so to speak.

Those hardy souls that managed to make it all three blocks up Tudo Street found themselves at the corner between the Caravelle and Continental hotels. The street level veranda bar at the Continental would later be a favorite hangout for war correspondents and visiting celebrities. I saw a couple of movie stars there over the next year. From the rooftop bar at the Caravelle, the war correspondents could often watch and report on the rice paddy war around Saigon in style and comfort. Among these western multi-floor style hotels was the Brink Hotel; a Batchelor Officers Quarters (BOQ) occupied by senior MAAG officers and across from that was a small restaurant which the MAAG guys recommended and we called "Cheap Charlie's." Great chicken soup—at least it tasted just like chicken. Back a block across Tudo was the brand new Rex Hotel which was also planned as billets for the growing number of officers being assigned to the MAAG Headquarters.

For some reason, a major memory for me, was hearing the American singing group "The Animals" version of "*The House of the Rising Sun*" which was emerging from an alleyway as I started walking back to the Core. That version still has an oriental sound to me. So does the sound of a helicopter overhead or a Lambretta scooter in the street for that matter. I can still hear the laughter floating out of the bars and the beeps of the taxies submerged in the wet heat of the night. That midnight walk back down those few blocks to the ship is a more vivid memory than it has any reason to be. Go figure!

Anyway, I was posted at the head of the gangplank as ordered when the others started to filter back aboard. Having put worries behind them for one night at least, without exception, this was one happy crew. The largest flock of our street commandos hit the boat about five minutes before one AM of course and there were few strays after that—none that I recall. We did have one soldier though, one of our senior sergeants, who shall remain nameless, that had to come aboard twice. On his first trip he was really happy when he went past me, but he decided that he was going to be sick shortly thereafter. So he proceeded straight across the deck to puke and whoops; off the other side. Now I think that would be about like falling off a four story building, but you know about god protecting fools and drunks; he was picked up, along with a dead pig floating down the Saigon River, by the RVN patrol boat that was stationed out there to watch our flanks. He was wet but still singing on his second try up the gangplank and he made curfew.

The dockside routine continued for several days with work going on steadily aboard ship. Preparations were also being made to house the units on shore, organize office and work space and to move the helicopters to the airbase. The advance party had made preliminary arrangements for us to work out of an old, French built, Quonset-hut style, steel hanger at the west end of the main taxiway which ran parallel to the east/west runway. This was a very large structure with adequate room to work on several helicopters under cover at the same time. The ends of the hanger were without doors and both were open to sizable ramps. Parking space was available for all the aircraft and there was enough room near the hanger to position the mobile shops belonging to the 98th Field Maintenance team and the Avionics Repair Detachment.

A very basic "office" structure was positioned along the side of the hanger away from the parking ramp and a similar structure was just across the road which led into the facility. The place was a mess; just open bays with garage style doors and concrete floors but we got busy cleaning things up and organizing the space for work. One of these bays was used as the operations office and a briefing room was established in another one. The Medical Detachment took most of the building across the street, with the Petroleum, Oil & Lubricants (POL) Section also occupying a bay at one end of that building. Vehicle maintenance could be performed on the adjacent ramp. There were no "offices" available for the aircraft maintenance guys. They just put some two-by-four fences around two areas in the hanger and held them up with the filing cabinets or whatever. It is amazing how fast things got done. The whole establishment was up and running in no time at all. People just set off in all directions to do those things that needed to be done. When the "must be done" was finished the "nice to have" began. I remember that on about the second day of the setup Bennie Potts had organized a crew to go out and cut the grass around the buildings and Len Wilson had identified an area for the volleyball court

As people worked with Jack Carey to dung out our operation shop and set up the planning and briefing space, I began the coordination necessary to allow us to begin flying. The first job was to acquire maps of the local flying area so that we could plot a suitable route from the Core to the airfield; one which would allow flight test along the way and provide some kind of open ground for possible emergency landings in this heavily populated section. The route turned out to be fairly direct, but we identified soccer fields, a golf course, and other openings along the way and altered the course to fly over them. We also began to assemble map coverage for the full area of operations. The MAAG flight detachment and CPT Wayne Triggs, who was the senior officer at the airfield then, quickly provided all the assistance we needed to begin flight operations.

Bill Rudd and Big-Jim Eakins flew the first combination maintenance test and ferry flight from the Core to Tan Son Nuht and those continued over the next several days until the ramp was full of CH-21C helicopters. Another hanger had been provided for the 8th and their preparation for operations proceeded apace. The Vietnamese Airforce (VNAF) was flying a company of CH-34 helicopters at the time so the local population knew about helicopters, but those big tandem rotor choppers blasting at low level over the center of town must have gotten a lot of attention. Planning for the first mission was already well under way by day three.

We got somewhat of a surprise on the 20th of December:

THE CHIEF OF THE GENERAL STAFF
ARMED FORCES OF THE REPUBLIC OF VIET-NAM
AND Mrs LE-VAN-TY
REQUEST THE PLEASURE OF THE COMPANY OF
Capt. Emmett F. Knight
AT Reception ON Wednesday 20.12.61
AT 37 Cuong-De Saigon
From 18,H30 to 20,H30
TENUE White Uniform R.S.V.P. 21.642 or 30.109

The senior officers from the helicopter companies had been invited by the RVN Chief of Staff to a formal multi-course welcoming feast. Junior army captains were considered senior for this purpose, since there were only a couple of majors along, so we were included. Our deployment instructions had included no expectation of such a thing as a formal dinner so none of us had either a class "A" uniform or suitable civilian attire. We did each have one set of Class "B" khakis, without ties, which we had packed along by local exception to our orders.

We were still aboard the Core and our gear was still stuffed in footlockers and so, of course, they were badly wrinkled from travel and hardly ready for wear anywhere. Someone had taken pity on us though and the invitation had a handwritten note on it to the effect that "worsted" would be okay. We had no warning time for laundry, cleaners or Hong Kong tailors either, so we policed ourselves up as well as we could and went to dinner. The RVN generals were in formal white uniforms, sporting all their medals and campaign ribbons, and the US MAAG officers in attendance were similarly attired. Even so, they treated us as the guests of honor, seating one or two of us between senior RVN officers at large round 10 man tables.

Now the fun began. We had watched the street urchins downtown when they would step on a large flying beetle, that we would call a cockroach, then pick it up, pull the wings off, and down the hatch with it. We were still innocent, but that should have given us a hint of what was to come. The first course arrived with an assortment of fermented vegetables arrayed in an equally fermented fish sauce. We later came to know this dish as a kind of kim chi smothered in "nuoc maum". That is phonetic spelling for really smelly stuff that we found out later would quickly corrode control cables when a clay jug of it broke on the cargo floor of a helicopter. Its pungent odor warned us off of that delicacy, but you had to be polite so we gagged down carefully chosen pieces.

The next course featured a good sized round slice of something that looked like a mushroom swimming in what appeared to be a nice yellow hollandaise sauce. Okay that might be eatable but cautious now; we tried to discover what this delicacy might be. I decided to forgo the pleasure when I finally understood the mushroom to be a slice of ancient egg. The Vietnamese called this a "bluot." That is another bit of phonetic spelling but the spoken sound of it did nothing to improve our appetites either. One hundred year old egg just didn't appeal to me, especially when it was immersed in a plate of what turned out to be rotten egg sauce. We poked and prodded that dish around for awhile.

Well hell, the main course had to be better right? It was chicken. What can you do to chicken to make it inedible? We slid our plates aside with most of the rotten egg still aboard thinking sure we would get new plates with the main course. Wrong; the plate was left before us when a large bowl of chicken was placed in the middle of the table. I don't know how it was prepared but it sure wasn't fried. Our table hosts assured us that it was only the guest of honor that got the head of the chicken; which they then served to us in the middle of the rotten egg sauce alongside of the ancient egg which was still floating there.

The banquet was held at a major RVN joint forces command facility somewhere in Cholon and there were only two things besides intestinal fortitude that helped me make it through those seven courses. Yes there were seven; some that I can't describe. It was a large open hall with a stage at one end. A series of performers held the stage. My table was way down range, far from the entertainment, but I would never have made it except for the girl singers that paraded up front and the warm beer that kept my glass full at my far-far-back VIP table.

We survived that festive night out with no ill effects, but we soon found that the problem of where to house the troops was not going smoothly. We were all still sweating our nights away in the hot, humid bowels of the Core. Remember that statement by the good experts from Korea that we could live in our helicopters. Stockton thought that was a good idea I guess, but we sure didn't. So after several days, we were still crammed into the Core and looking for a place to live ashore. The helicopters, and maintenance shops were at the airfield, but we appeared to be stuck on board the ship. Captain Buck Haskell was ready to resume his journey but there we were; still using the Core as billets. The brand new Rex hotel, was vacant and was under lease or something to the MAAG. It was located on the Street of Flowers in downtown Saigon, with a U. S. Information Service facility and the Rex Movie Theater as part of the building. These were up and running. The hotel was just a shell but the major construction was almost complete. The MAAG seemed determined to hang on to the Rex, so the advance party had tried to find anything else that would be suitable until something could be erected for us at Tan Son Nuht.

MAJ Dillard got right into this but soon found himself caught in the middle between the Core's captain and the MAAG colonel in charge of such things. One day, as frustration began to hit heavy, the

XO and myself were riding with the boss when he decided to go see the Colonel-In-Charge to try to work something out. That officer was unpleasant and definite that he was not going to allow us to defile his nice new place. He had it all planned to house about 100 MAAG officers and he would not consider even temporarily putting our 400 plus troops therein. Dillard tried reasoning with him: The ship needed to get underway. It would only be for a couple of weeks. We would not get in the way of final preparations for MAAG occupancy. Etc., Etc. Nothing seemed to work until finally in complete exasperation, the major said to the colonel "Okay, we are moving into the Rex on Monday" or words to that effect. That is when Milt Cherne and I left the room because it was apparent that the conversation was going to degenerate from there. It didn't last long though and we moved in on Monday.

CHAPTER 10

PROFESSIONAL EXECUTION BUT ERRANT EXPERT

"The purpose of transport aviation is to provide air transport to expedite tactical operations and logistical support in the combat zone"
*School Text 55-156, U. S. Army Transportation School, July 1961.**

Heliborne assaults weren't new in 1961, but they weren't old either. Transport doctrine then did not really envision the use of cargo helicopters in either a direct combat support or counter insurgency role. In spite of President Kennedy's attempts to move the U. S. military toward that kind of low intensity warfare, the Army was still primarily aimed at the Russian coming down the Fulda Gap into West Germany. Even so, our experience with the 4th ID at Yakima had taught us that tactical troop haul would be a normal use for supporting cargo helicopters. Transportation helicopter companies stationed around the United States, Korea and Europe were learning that troop lift in combat assault would, in fact, be our primary employment. We practiced at Yakima and we exercised the concept on actual missions in Vietnam starting in December 1961.

We also demonstrated a corollary; that inexperienced hands on the controls of a helicopter during such an assault was asking for trouble. We trained the troops. We participated in the tactical planning to ensure that our aircraft were used properly and with consideration of the capabilities and limitations of the CH-21C. We took a careful look at the ground. We ran a full-up rehearsal. We flew the first US Army helicopter combat assault in Vietnam on the 23rd of December. We lost a helicopter.

Getting shot at for the first time is one of those most memorable of events and it didn't take long for that to happen either. From the time we dropped anchor at the foot of Tudo Street until our first combat assault was about twelve days, depending on how you are counting, and in any event it seemed like a lot fewer days than that. The big project was in getting enough aircraft reassembled, test flown and signed-off to properly support the operation. Getting all the pilots up for a local flying area orientation was another required milestone and we started familiarizing the ARVN Airborne Brigade troops with the Shawnee as soon as possible. That training also began for other units during the first few weeks, but the brigade was our first priority since they acted as the only real reserve for the entire Vietnamese Army and they had already been chosen to initiate the first heliborne assault. The brigade headquarters was located at Tan Son Nuht, just down the way from where we were moving in and that was handy for the planning and coordination process which got underway within just a few hours after we stepped off the boat.

The Airborne Brigade was easy to work with. They were the elite force for the ARVN. They were trained in airborne employment and so were at least familiar with fixed wing aircraft. They also knew how to get organized to fight after a parachute drop so they could adapt quickly to heliborne operations. The brigade staff and their American advisors, with whom we did the planning, were also the best. We were moving so fast that we had no interference from the US MAAG headquarters downtown during the planning process. Even the media had yet to catch up to the game so we didn't have to carry them into the war with us, as we usually had to do later. Since the 8th was still at Tan Son Nuht with fourteen of their aircraft, we were able to count thirty helicopters for the mission. It was to be a joint mission and the cooperation between our units was practically seamless.

The planning sessions were mostly concerned with the ground portion of the mission. Dillard and I attended each meeting so that we could adapt the helicopter planning to the ground effort and brief it back to the planning group. LTC Stockton also attended but he didn't have much to say, probably because he didn't know anything about running helicopters in groups. It certainly wasn't because he didn't know how to pontify. Maybe that first run-in with Bob Dillard had cooled his ardor a little. The primary planner was the ARVN Airborne Brigade S-3 operations, MAJ An, working closely with U.S. Army advisor MAJ John Goodson. A LTC Philips was the senior U.S. advisor to the brigade, as I recall, and he also attended but he stayed mostly in the background along with the ARVN Colonel who commanded the brigade. I am sure these senior officers influenced the planning more directly while everyone else went to work ironing out the nuts and bolts.

Map reconnaissance is fine and sometimes it is all you can get during planning, but I was able to negotiate a flight in the MAAG U-6 Beaver to go out and take a real look at the terrain. This fixed wing airplane had been flown regularly over the area so we thought it would not be regarded as anything unusual in the fly-by. Even so, we didn't tarry over the objective area but simply made a one time flight over, out a ways, and back by a different route. It was enough though, to show us the configuration of the proposed landing area and the layout of the pineapple fields which would complicate the landing of the assault force. We would have to off-load the troops at a hover. We would not be able to touch all the way down.

On 22 December, the day before the actual mission, we flew a rehearsal. We loaded up the troops and flew east-northeast to Cu Chi where we shot our landings to a hover and off loaded the troops. We then conducted a brief critique with the ARVN staff and their US advisors where we reemphasized the need for speed in getting into their combat formation upon disembarking from the helicopters. It was important to us that they get quickly into their formation and then move directly away from the helicopters to begin their business. This would help keep any bad guy heads down as we rapidly got out of town.

Although not critical to the mission, I got one of my first lessons from the top that day. As mentioned before, Dillard was a by-the-book kind of guy and he had only recently finished reading the book on helicopter flying. Whereas my CH-21C instructor pilots were not too worried about following tightly to the book, his flight instructors probably kept close to the written word as they checked out the number one boss. The Shawnee cruised at eighty knots by the book. My time in the bird was also somewhat limited, but I knew that the old Shawnee would step out a good bit faster than that when not loaded down with troops or cargo.

I was flying right seat in the lead aircraft and I had the controls. Since we had off-loaded our troops, the box was empty and we were light. We were on the way back to Tan Son Nuht. I dropped the nose a little, pulled in a little more power to maintain altitude, and we stepped right out at about one hundred and ten. Well we were headed home I thought, so why diddle around here over contested area? I hadn't briefed a change in speed, but I thought that it might make sense to get on back over friendly terrain as soon as possible and that the flight behind me would just hang right in there. For the most part they did just that too.

But the boss had elected to fly towards the rear of the flight so he could watch how things were going. It wasn't long before he was slipping behind, out of formation, while still holding eighty knots. I soon got a call telling me to slow down. I tried to ignore it thinking that the IP flying with him would urge him forward so that they would close up, but Dillard's tone of voice in the next transmission told me that this was not to be: "God damn it Chalk One slow down!" We didn't discuss it any further. I had little choice but to honk the nose back up and proceed in what seemed to me to be the leisurely pace prescribed by the book. The funny thing is that I had his main IP, Bennie Potts, flying left seat with me in the lead aircraft. He didn't say a word.

The 8th guys were going through the same process we were. They were hangered at a different location on the field. They knew that they would be moving to another operating area soon and they did not yet have all of their aircraft so they were not considered to be fully operational. I think it was six of their helicopters that were still on the high seas. None the less, they were just as anxious as we were to get going and they participated in this mission with everything they had. We put thirty out of the total of thirty-four aircraft available at both units in the air for this mission.

The town was very quiet the evening before the operation. The flight crews stayed pretty close to the Rex and out of the bars that night. Any close observer might have guessed that something was up by our absence on the street. Anyway, as we learned in spades later, that didn't matter much because ARVN security functioned much like a sieve. Nothing stayed secret for long. We were ignorant of that at the time though, and we kept a low profile. Our maintenance crews worked overtime as usual and the airborne troops were lined up by chalk number well before daylight. Everybody was up and moving before dawn. Crew chiefs had finished final aircraft preflight inspections. Pilots had carefully completed their walk-around inspections and were beginning cockpit start up procedures. There always seemed to be last minute details to handle, so I was still in the operations shack trying to take care of those, as helicopters began to crank up. It was at about this time that the senior expert from Korea, with the aid of MG Timmies, threw shit in the game.

Stockton had been leaning on us, saying that as the senior Army Aviator in the country, he should pilot a helicopter on this historic mission. He was not qualified to do so, having experience only in fixed wing and in light observation helicopters; specifically the OH-13. Here he was, a fairly senior officer wearing basic Army Aviator wings. He had no training to fly any kind of cargo helicopter. He had not participated in the rehearsal and besides had been a general pain in the ass for us. Each time he approached me at flight operations, I just referred him to Dillard who said absolutely not. Well not much is absolute I guess because at the last minute Stockton appeared, with approval in hand from MG Timmes, that he would fly as a crew member on this mission. Dillard had no time to straighten it out with the General; no time and no choice.

This, of course, was highly irregular and pretty high on the stupid curve. And the word that he would fly did not reach my flight operations section until crews were already assigned and starting their engines. As operations officer it was my job to replace a fully qualified pilot with Stockton. I did that in about Chalk Eight. At least I could put him with an instructor pilot for his first CH-21C flight. CWO Robert P. Sword was chosen for this dubious honor.

I remember thinking, as I was running out to my helicopter, that this was a very bad situation. Bob Sword was, and still is, a very nice guy. He was a highly qualified and proficient instructor but this "student" proved to be more than he or anyone else could have handled that day. He had rammed his way through MG Timmes to get around me and Dillard and into a cockpit where he had absolutely no right to be. In retrospect, I should have selected the toughest, meanest, hardass instructor in the outfit for this one but even that probably would not have made much difference. Stockton had too much ego and was way too dumb to just ride along once he had finagled a seat up front. He remained on the controls, trying to fly the aircraft, during the whole flight. This necessarily kept much of Bob's attention inside the cockpit. He had to be on the flight controls fighting this inexperienced warrior for control of the aircraft, instead of being able to concentrate outside of the aircraft on his position in the formation.

Start-up was smooth. Nobody found a problem with their assigned helicopter so, with a brief commo check, we were on our way. We didn't try for much altitude as the distance was short and we settled in at 500 feet above the ground. As the flight progressed the ship being flown by Sword and Stockton slipped back, increasing the distance between themselves and the helicopter ahead of them. By the time we in the lead had reached the release point (RP) and had begun our descent, they were hurrying to close up. The result of this was that, when the flight started down, they had to hold a nose high attitude and throttle back to dissipate their excess speed. The attitude adjustment was necessary to keep them from overrunning the helicopter ahead of them and it caused a very high rate of descent as they tried to maintain their position for landing. And finally, the result of that was that they had insufficient power at the bottom to stop the descent at the required hover to off-load the troops.

It was necessary for each helicopter to terminate the approach at a three foot hover. The direction of landing was dictated by the tactical situation. We needed to place the assault troops along both sides of a small tree lined canal. The plan was to trap the enemy between these two attacking groups which would force their egress down the canal into a blocking force located at the nearby intersection with a major waterway. The pineapple fields, running parallel to our direction of landing, would not allow any helicopter in the flight to touch down.

The fields were so configured that any attempt to do so would probably cause the helicopter to lean excessively and perhaps roll over.

Sword knew all this and he was fighting to regain full control of the helicopter but to do so he had to overpower Stockton on the directional pedals, collective and cyclic sticks. It's enough to make you want to puke even thinking about it. When they pulled collective pitch into the rotor blades and flared for landing it was too little and too late to overcome the excessive rate of descent. They had run clean out of pitch, power and experience and they hit hard. That is known as "falling through the bottom." One landing gear was high on a relatively hard mound and the other one was way down in the soft furrow. Those pineapple rows were just right to have the Shawnee end up with one main landing gear down in the mud three or four feet lower than the other one. That degree of tilt was too much for the helicopter. It far exceeded the design characteristics that Frank Piasecki had engineered into the CH-21C.

The helicopter was still upright and the rotors were spinning fast. Maybe they could have saved it by shutting down at that point, but that probably wouldn't have worked either, because as rotor RPM decreases the blade tips begin to drop too and they probably would have struck the ground. And that would likely have resulted in flipping the helicopter over in the other direction. Even that might have been better because the development of the roll might have been slower and the disintegration of the helicopter blades might have been away from the departing troops. That, of course, is all guesswork. Only Bob Sword who was actually in the cockpit trying to solve the problem is really qualified to comment. Instead they tried to pull her out by adding take-off power. This caused it to roll in the direction of lean while the blades beat themselves to death amongst pineapple plants, departing troops and the ground.

They did manage to hold it together long enough for the troops to get off but I was never told how many, if any, were killed or wounded by the flying shards of the disintegrating helicopter rotor blades. The whole thing may have been aggravated by increased ground fire as the wounded duck, became the biggest target in the area. We did evacuate a number of injured troops but the source of their wounds was not disclosed. In my view, enemy action had little to do with the loss of this aircraft. There is no doubt in my mind that Stockton had set us up for this catastrophe and was totally responsible for the crash. This description is based on my own analysis. It was not taken from any official report. If there was one, I never saw it anyway. It was a difficult landing area and there had surely been some shootin' going on out there too, but it seems probable that two fully qualified pilots working together would not have fallen into this trap. Bob Sword has said that he was fighting Stockton for control of the helicopter all the way to the end.

We are talking about an event that took place when we were officially not in combat. The fact that we were even in Vietnam, in any kind of ARVN support role, was not officially "recognized." We carried only personal weapons, with orders not to fire them for any reason, and we could not yet even enter combat support time in our log books. Stockton however, was old Army. He had the ear of the MAAG command group. He was out looking for trouble and he wanted to be in the fight. Much to my amazement, this helicopter was written off as the first combat loss in Vietnam.

The crew was evacuated. Wounded were hauled out. The shooting soon died down and the maintenance crew went in to pull the radios and complete other salvage. The mission continued as planned. We hauled back the intelligence team and the ARVN began their walk downstream. The mission was deemed a success by the powers-that-be. The sequence of events leading to the crash was never officially determined as far as I know and the description above is only how I saw it. Stockton got off clean. We were involved in a fight, that's true, and maybe that alone accounted for the designation of combat loss, but I can't help but believe that there was also a large element of cover-your-ass involved. Well okay, at least we wouldn't have to worry about an accident investigation and a report if another one went down. It soon became apparent though that we were into something pretty far removed from a peaceful operation since our aircraft were being shot at daily and hit routinely. This became just the first of many helicopter combat loses in Vietnam.

That should be the end of the story, but it is not. John B. struck again that day as he was often to do in the future. It has always seemed to me that the very guy that you would not want to have interviewed by the media, is the one who turns out to be the most available to them. He is always the one standing on the ramp, with nothing to do, when everyone else is busy. In this case it was Stockton of course, who had been quickly deposited on the ramp after the "combat loss." When he was quoted in the next issue of a weekly news magazine as saying that "it was just like World War Two out there" most of us had to get on the phone right away to reassure our wives that it wasn't really that bad. Getting on the phone, by the way, was another no-easy-deal. You had to go out near the presidential palace in Saigon, to the Pacific Telephone and Telegraph building, where they would place your radio-telephone call. After an all morning wait they might get through and call you to the phone. If you continued to be lucky, you might even get in a few words before the radio connection broke down.

Young pilots don't worry much about the "Big Picture" of course. Troop lift was the name of the game so we provided it, but someone should have realized that placing an improperly trained aviator in a pilot's seat was the wrong thing to do at any time, let alone during a difficult operation. There should have been a rigorous examination of the details around the loss of a helicopter at that early stage but of course the MAAG had contributed to it so they had senior reputations to consider. Even the press, and surely the U. S. Army, should have questioned any comparison to WWII and wondered just what kind of a deal we had going here. Someone should have called time out. No one did. Perhaps I have gone into this unfortunate accident more than it deserves. After all, that first heliborne assault was accepted by the Army as having been very successful, and from the standpoint of Army thinking at the time, it indeed was. It was the beginning for all that followed in our "helicopter" war in Vietnam.

Stockton will appear again and again in this narrative, but another interesting thing happened in connection with this mission. Almost two years later, while I was stationed in Germany, I received a request for an eye-witness statement to back up a recommendation for award of the Air Medal to Stockton for his participation in this historic mission. I had already read in the Army Times that he had been awarded the Purple Heart for getting his knee in the way of the cyclic stick while crashing that helicopter. He claimed to have injured his knee when the cyclic stick wiped out the cockpit during the crash of the "shot down" helicopter. I do recall that he had limped around for a half a day with his bruised knee. I don't recall that anyone else got medals for their bruises. When they asked me about an Air Medal, I replied that in no way could I support any kind of award for Stockton and included a brief description of why not. Dillard and Cherne were also queried and probably answered in the same way. I never heard anything further on that request, but this being the Army, he probably got the medal and maybe Jungle John Stockton eventually turned out to be the hero of the exercise after all.

CHAPTER 11

THE CANADIAN, THE PRIVATE AND THE CHINESE SYNDICATE

"Oh, East is East and West is West, and never the twain shall meet . . ."
*The Ballad of East and West—Rudyard Kipling 1889**

It was during this time that one of the most improbable characters among the 57th soldiers began to gain the limelight. I had inherited a SGT Watt as my operations sergeant at Ft Lewis. He was born in Canada, and although we never saw the official records to prove it, he claimed to have been a Canadian Flight Lieutenant. When we were alerted and began to get a feel for where we might be going, he claimed to have served in Vietnam during the French Indochina War. He wore seemingly appropriate ribbons, including a Canadian Distinguished Flying Cross, but we were never convinced about the validity of those; particularly the Flying Cross. Neither the paper he produced, nor any flight knowledge he demonstrated, made the claim easy to believe. In addition, we found him distinctly afraid to fly in our helicopters. Watt was known to drastically stretch the truth on occasion, but because it might be as he claimed, that he had some familiarity with Saigon from having served there with the Canadian Forces, he was made a part of the advance party.

It came as some surprise, that he seemed to know his way around town by the time the main body was getting off the boat. As we were moving into the Rex, he became the de-facto downtown jack-of-all-trades and scrounger-in-chief. SGT Watt had some peculiarities besides the missing personal history records. When he got excited he stuttered so badly as to become unintelligible. At the same time he was likely to try to head off in several directions at once, all the while yelling at his assisting Private First Class to do something; almost anything. Because of considerable frustration at these times I would often have to say something uncharitable like "goddamn it Watt, stop talking Canadian and listen to me." Only after he settled down might something useful get done.

As evidence of the elusive nature of this soldier, is the fact that I can't remember his first name. My memory is weak, for one thing, because we never called him anything but Watt. After a thorough search of all the records in my files, which I admit are not extensive, I can find no indication that he ever fired a weapon, went to the gas chamber, performed any additional duty, went anywhere or did anything else to indicate, on orders, that he had ever been in the unit. He deployed as a member of our advance party which means that his full name, rank and serial number must have been recorded, but I have never seen a copy of those orders. One of the company clerks that served with us later in Vietnam was Specialist Jerry D. Head. Jerry has provided me with all the personnel documents in his files and personnel was his business. He also has a phenomenal memory of the people that were assigned to the unit while he was there. SGT Watt appears nowhere in his records or his memory. There is no doubt however, that SGT Watt was with us in Fort Lewis and in Saigon. He is one individual that is inscribed on my memory. I'll never forget him.

So there we were ensconced in the shell of the magnificent new Rex Hotel right in the heart of the city and preparing to operate from that perch. Of course, we had to continue to set up housekeeping, scrounge food & water, arrange with the authorities to even be there, with new passports, licenses, ground transport, communications and all the other necessities of life in a strange place. This kept the command group really busy. That's when I volunteered (read fought to give up) my operations sergeant so he could continue assisting, full time, in the downtown effort. This was not a great loss to the operations platoon since Watt required a lot of watching and we didn't have much time for it. We had responsibility for company communications in addition to handling flight operations and Watt was also the commo sergeant. As a result of his efforts, the commo section was a mess and I always felt like my backside was exposed when I was too busy to keep an eye on him.

Besides his tendency to get excited and run around in tight little circles, stuttering, SGT Watt was expert at ducking any duty he didn't like. I'll give you an example of this character's attempts to look out for himself at all times. We were headed out to a field exercise at Fort Lewis. Watt had been told to get his communication section loaded up and ready to move out. There was a ¾ ton truck assigned to the commo section for that purpose. PFC James D. McAndrew, who assisted Watt in the operations job, was my assigned jeep driver. But when I emerged from the hanger to head for the field, I found the operations jeep piled to the brim with commo gear with Watt in the driver's seat. You should have heard the Canadian talk, when I told him to get out of the jeep and get McAndrew who would drive. "Bbbbuuuttt sir ttthhee cccommo ttrrruuucckkk wwoonnn'tt run!" I told him to either get it running, or he could walk to the exercise and that I wanted his commo gear out of my jeep either way. Then I left him and his stuff standing by the side of the road. There could not have been much wrong with the commo truck, because he wasn't long in joining up to the tail end of the convoy. You figure it out. I never did.

Watt had another characteristic which was very irritating. He just had to have someone that he could order around. He couldn't handle more than one, but he did need a single soldier that he could sorta keep in his hip pocket and tell what to do. PFC McAndrew held that unenviable position in the operations platoon. It soon became clear that we could become much more efficient in the operations business, if we just removed the middle man and went straight to the private ourselves. In Vietnam, I convinced the boss to take the sergeant off my hands, so Watt continued "helping out" around the headquarters for the next year. Actually he was in Saigon for a little longer than the rest of us, because when it came time for him to rotate home he was under investigation for some alleged black market activity. He must have beaten that rap though because he managed to keep his rank

When Watt left operations, McAndrew was rapidly promoted to Specialist Fifth Class and stepped up to be our operations sergeant.

He was a fine soldier and right away lightened the load for the rest of us. Not only did he become a mainstay of things in operations but, without Watt to get in the way, he quickly straightened out the commo section. I don't know if it is true for sure because I never saw the records, but I was told that McAndrew had been a USMC non-commissioned officer (NCO) until he was court marshaled for hitting a superior officer. That being true, or not, he was a great soldier, good natured and very efficient. In fact, considering his personality, I concluded that the senior "officer" involved was probably another NCO and he very likely deserved everything he got. After Mac took over the job, I can recall very few times that I had to tell him to do anything. He just stayed very busy doing what had to be done. He was always the guy who opened and closed the place up, and in addition to the normally long duty hours, he always volunteered to man a machine gun on combat assaults. Although I didn't assign the gunners to a particular ship, I often found him behind the gun on the one I was flying.

One of the reasons that Watt was successful in producing some of the needed support around downtown Saigon was because he hung around the hotel and talked to the Chinaman at the door to the place. This man initially seemed to be just a doorman at the incomplete Hotel Rex. Watt probably learned quickly that Mr. Wong could arrange about anything. It took a little while for the rest of us to recognize that W. W. Wong was the front man for the Saigon/Cholon Chinese Syndicate, which not only had a stake in the Rex, but also owned and operated several other hotels, bars and restaurants located throughout the city. I got to know WW well myself after a short time, because one of his wives turned out to be the manager of the Capriccio, which was my favorite Saigon bar, and because of a tour-of-the-town that WW and I took one night. Olga was a middle aged motherly appearing Chinese. She was easy to talk with because she had been raised in Los Angeles until the age of sixteen.

We need to mention the Capriccio in a little more detail here, because it became the scene of a fleeting time of fame for me. The Capriccio was a popular nightclub those first few weeks we were in town. And it was doing a great business until the wife of President Diem's brother, Madame Nue, also known as The Dragon Lady, proclaimed new morality laws. The club had been filled with Chinese gals, dressed in those tight fitting slit-up-the-thigh dresses dancing with GIs to a small combo that made fine danceable music. The place was romantically low lighted and Chinese lanterns glowed against thick decorative curtains which covered the expansive front windows facing the street. Somehow this must have gotten the dragon lady's attention and she obviously didn't like the idea, because she decreed that henceforth dancing in South Vietnam would be illegal and that all nightclub hostesses had to be dressed in demure white uniform clothing. In addition all the windows had to be open to the street. The troops called it the "white law" and you can guess that the GI clientele didn't take too kindly to it. They soon figured out that they could find better places to drink just down the avenue. The "nightclub" had degenerated into just another bar and the place became real quiet. The band played on, but the music seemed tepid without dancers. All the white in the place, and the unshielded windows, made it quite somber.

Well, I had already made a fair sized down payment on my chosen bar-stool at the Capriccio by that time. I hated to see my favorite bar and my friend Olga in such a state. So one night I said to the band "you guys should learn to play a little jazz and liven up your music with the kind of stuff the troops might like." They came back with something like "what do you mean?" I said "well try some jazz" Everybody in the band offered blank looks to that. So I hummed the first notes of the "*Lullaby of Birdland*" and said something like "you know like that." The piano player was quick to pick up that George Shearing style opening bar, but after a few days it became apparent that they had no idea what to do next. So I decided to go out to the small Post Exchange that the MAAG was running, to see if I could find something to illustrate. I couldn't find any Shearing, but I did find some Bill Evans with a similar version of the Lullaby. I bought it and a couple of other records that might demonstrate what I was talking about. The band learned very quickly from these records and within a short time, with the new upbeat music, a reasonable crowd began to reappear in the place. I continued to pay-down on my barstool. And over the next year, I'm sure that I paid full price for more than one of those. But my moment of fame was that, from then on, every time I stepped through the door into the Capriccio, the piano player would interrupt whatever the band was playing and hit the opening notes of *Lullaby of Birdland* as a greeting.

One evening WW Wong invited Dillard, Cherne and I, to be his guests for dinner at a Chinese place in Cholon. The boss accepted and we found our way to the Fuji Restaurant which turned out to be a really nice place. It was softly lit, with overstuffed furnishings and polished hardwood; a small intimate place, where the cooking was done in woks and on a shining hot table. We sat down and were invited to order a round of drinks before dinner. WW had them place full bottles, with great labels of the chosen booze, before each of us. Now that was tempting but after a couple of drinks we just ordered Chinese.

After dinner, WW invited us to ride along while he visited all of his six wives. Dillard and Cherne declined, but my curiosity was tweaked, and so what the hell, I'd take the tour. WW called up a chauffeur driven black Oldsmobile and we took off to visit wives working at back alley habachis or fine restaurants and crowded bars stretching from Cholon to Saigon. We started at a large open-air place in downtown Cholon, which was crowded with customers, where WW introduced me to the "front" gal, while the Olds idled in the street. Then we moved on to the Tour de' Ivory, a fine bar located about half way back to Saigon, where we met the bartender. We hit a couple more places before we met young wife number five, who was hunched over a hibachi in an alley behind another fine restaurant. We ended up at the Capriccio, where it was obvious that Olga was the number one wife, and after this tour, it was equally apparent to me that WW was the big man around town; in more ways than one.

Here again Watt had demonstrated his ability to find just the one guy to do his work for him. Once we learned, however, that we could handle things directly with our Chinese doorman at the Rex, SGT Watt quickly became less useful. WW almost disappeared from the scene after the hotel was completed, and up and running for the MAAG, but we would see him occasionally at the Capriccio. I had been taking a meal there sometimes and I really liked their veal scaloppini. Then I thought back on that midnight tour with WW and decided maybe I ought to have a look at the kitchen. Yep; a hibachi in the alley, but hell the veal was still good. At least that's what they said it was. On seldom occasions, I would find myself with an afternoon or early evening off and would hove in there to visit my barstool. Ray Charles was popular at the Blue Moon too, but it was during a quiet afternoon at the Capriccio that I first heard his "*Hit The Road Jack*" and now, when I hear that song, my mind does one of those snap-back-to-Saigon things. A post traumatic stress thing you think?

The "Story of Watt" is, I'm sure, still going on today if he is still around. Some time after our tour was finished Milt Cherne' sent me a copy of a letter that he said was "floating around Camp Carson in 1963." It was purportedly from Watt's commanding officer in Vietnam (that would be Cherne') to Watt's then current boss at Carson. The missive was obviously authored by Watt and it would have done Walter Mitty proud. The thing is too long to enter here but it describes Watt as far, far better then the ideal soldier; unbelievable would be a more accurate description. To quote a few very fanciful lines: "I have used Watt in every conceivable place in the unit and often at battalion staff level. . . Often times we permitted Watt to fly organic aircraft . . . While in Vietnam, Watt was Chief of Pathfinders, Aviation Section MAAG . . . Superior job working with Lt Cols and above . . . Had a little trouble because he over-rode orders of some Colonels . . . and gave hell to another Colonel . . . but he saved lives both times." You get the idea; two and one-half closely typed pages of this pathetic fantasy drivel. I would tell you more but I don't like self inflicted wounds.

I ran into Watt a couple years later in Germany. My outfit, from the 3rd Armored Division, was grading a field training exercise being conducted by the 5th Infantry Division Aviation Battalion. I was driving through the area and there, visible from the road, was Watt. He was still a sergeant and he obviously hadn't changed much since our 57th days. He was closely supervising one private who was driving a tent peg into the ground. I couldn't resist. I got out of my jeep and quietly walked up behind him, then I said, in a load and exasperated tone of voice, "Goddamn it Sergeant Watt, what the hell are you doing!" I swear that he jumped straight up, turned 180 degrees in the air and came down in a brace, saluting and talking Canadian again. Some things don't change.

Some other things do change however; on a second Vietnam tour, five years later, I eagerly looked for WW, Olga, and my favorite bar. They were nowhere to be found. I looked for the Fugi restaurant and other landmarks of the Chinese around town. These too were shuttered. I could never get any real lead, but my guess is that they had taken their money and gone to Hong Kong. And it would not surprise me to find out that Olga was running some fine restaurant and bar in downtown Los Angeles today; with WW running his stable of wives around Hollywood.

My friend the "Private," SGT James D. McAndrew, volunteered to extend his tour of duty six months beyond his normal rotation date. We had talked about it and my advice was to think twice about it. We had several discussions about it. I had decided to hang around awhile to try to help the new guys pick up the tricks of the trade. We talked, but he was enjoying the fight and he decided to stay. He was lost in a tragic helicopter crash shortly after the rest of the original members of the 57th had gone home. While flying as gunner over the delta one day, his aircraft went down; killing all aboard. I will describe what probably happened in more detail later, but the news of that January 1963 accident hit me hard. There were other friends aboard that flight as well and they all are missed, but Mac was a very great personal loss to me.

CHAPTER 12

FROM THE REX TO WAR BY TAXI

The ubiquitous taxis of Saigon . . . ancient blue and white Renault mini four doors with smoking rear mounted engines and typically aggressive big city type drivers dodging among people, animals, bicycles, cyclos and motorized conveyances of all kinds.

We fought the battle from the Rex Hotel for the next few weeks. It could hardly have been called a hotel at this point. It had no reliable electricity and few fixtures anyway. It was about a 10 story walk-up as I recall. The elevators didn't work yet. There was no running water. There was no furniture. But it was a roof and we crammed everybody under it. We put several army cots for multiple occupancy in each room. We installed a G.I. field mess on the rooftop balcony and placed canvas blister bags for water on each floor. Needless to say, there were no telephones either so we hung a jeep radio on the roof top balcony railing just outside the boss's room. This allowed us to communicate in some fashion with the airfield. We couldn't use our jeeps because they were not properly licensed to operate in Vietnam.

Diplomatic Clearance, passports, licenses, billets; for a place that apparently wanted and needed our support there sure seemed to be damn little preparation for our arrival and a lot of administrative crap to go through. But we didn't lay about waiting for it all to come together. Planning for troop familiarization training and heliborne missions started immediately. All the helicopters were made flyable. Ferry and test flights were completed. Our vehicles still could not be used by the time we became fully ready for flight operations so we would grab our flight gear and strap on our weapons then hail a taxi to go to war.

Those were some fun days there in the shell of the Rex Hotel. Naturally, the officers were placed on the top floor so daily we had to climb up all ten of those floors; useful for keeping in shape I guess. My room was on the corner of the rooftop balcony overlooking the main drag running from downtown Saigon to the ethnic Chinese district of Cholon. Five or six of us shared this space—platoon commanders, CPT Bill Smith and LT Bill Hinds with a couple of the flight leaders, LTs Bill Brethour and Sal Formica. There may have been one other guy squeezed in there too. Anyway, this was the same tight fit everywhere. There was a swimming pool located on top of our room, and since the construction of the place didn't look all that good to us, we were glad that they hadn't pumped any water into it yet.

We got all the sights and sounds drifting up from the street. Some of those seemed very exotic to our "new" in-country eyes and ears. I remember, in particular, the sticks they would beat together to advertise the sidewalk soup kitchens. They had a rhythm all their own, yet were reminiscent of the "bones" played by old time jazz minstrels. As you lay sweating in the wet night heat, and listened to those bones providing a strange rhythm to the constant beeps of the Renault taxies and the loud chanting of the cyclo drivers over the musical-vocal hubbub of the city, you knew you were in the ancient Orient for sure.

The boss was working the housing issue among many others and the rest of us also stayed plenty busy. Out at the airfield things were humming. You could get a couple helicopters inside each end the hanger for maintenance; more if you took off the main rotor blades. You didn't have to worry about the doors. There weren't any. The rest of the helicopters were parked in line abreast along the ramp leading to the taxiway. We were not faced with an air threat and we were told that neither rocket nor mortar attacks had yet been experienced at Tan Son Nuht so the kind of parking dispersion we had practiced in field exercises at Fort Lewis was not needed.

A planning map of the entire operating area, covering the ARVN III Corps zone, was pieced together and hung on the operations wall.

The area was divided into III and VI Corps later but at this time III Corps included the subordinate Fifth, Seventh and Twenty-first Divisions. It was bordered on the west by Cambodia and the Gulf of Siam. It extended from the middle of dense jungle well to the north of Saigon all the way south to the point of the Ca Mau peninsula where the country ended and from there up the east coast along the South China Sea to complete the boundary. It was a very large expanse of territory; too big for one helicopter company to cover, but this was our operating area.

While the mechanics turned wrenches through the night, work also began early and stopped late for the rest of us. We in operations were already planning missions and crews were flying them. Soon we were fully operational. We could even drive our vehicles on base at Tan Son Nuht, but it was still a little irritating that we had to take taxis between the airbase and the hotel, because our Vietnamese license plates had not yet been issued; they never were while we were at the Rex. Mission planning was completed during the day by coordination between our assigned mission flight leaders, company operations and III Corps U.S. advisors. The boss was briefed in the late evening at his room in the Rex. Very early in the morning we would organize a fleet of those "blue and whites" and head for the airfield. By planning some extra travel time, we could get all our pilots out there for a mission briefing before the always early takeoff times. By the time the sun rose in the morning, we were ready to pull pitch.

The maps we were given were old, but fairly good ones. They were published during the French/Japanese era in Vietnam during WWII. Vichy France collaborated with the Japs in Indo-China during the war and I believe that our maps were dated 1944. They were fairly detailed because of the large scale, much like a US Army tactical map would be, but still they were really sketchy for air navigation purposes. That was because of the lack of man made features outside of Saigon and the other larger towns that were widely spread over the area. My Tho and Long Binh were the towns we mostly staged from in the Delta. Muc Hoa and Tay Ninh were centered to the west and northwest near Cambodia. Cu Chi and Bien Hoa were located to our north. They provided assembly points from which we could service the Iron Triangle and from where we could follow the railroad and highways further north and east. There were roads to most of these places. There were the long canals and the squared off rice paddies of the Mekong River delta, and there were the rubber plantations tucked into the jungle, but it was still hard to locate specific points among large areas of rice paddies, jungle, mangrove swamps or the plain of reeds.

We found it necessary to triangulate from river and canal intersections, and the few man-made features, to find many of the grid coordinate locations where the ARVN wanted to go. Sometimes this method seemed a little indefinite, particularly near the western border, where we were at pains to keep out of Cambodia. Airmobile operations were new to the officers and troops we would lift into battle. The troops needed helicopter and air assault training. We combined that with pilot area familiarization flying. ARVN soldiers were briefed through an interpreter then they were loaded on and off the helicopter under pilot supervision. They had to be able to get aboard quickly and off-load in seconds before we were satisfied. Proper loading was also essential to keep them from entangling themselves in the seats or with each other, and to have them in fighting formation upon debarking in a combat zone.

This training was soon expanded to each of the Divisions located in the Corps area. We committed a team of two helicopters and crews to this unglamorous, but critical, training job daily for the first few weeks. While concentration was on training after the first combat assault, several other missions were already being scheduled and "ash & trash" hauls were being requested daily. You know what those things are; they ranged from resupply missions out to the widely scattered advisory teams or jungle outposts, to hauling RVN tax collectors or U.S. VIPs somewhere, and there was of course every other conceivable mission in between.

We began committing six aircraft, in pairs, daily. Because of the lack of flight following and the poor or non-existing communications, we did not fly single aircraft missions. It was obvious that if a single helicopter were to go down, nobody was likely to know about it and therefore nobody would be able to respond in a timely fashion. We knew that by continuously operating in the adverse weather, high density altitude, conditions of the area we were putting unusually high strains on our engines and could expect some failures. If a single helicopter were to go down in contested territory, we felt that we would have little chance of evacuating the crew before the VC got to them. It was no surprise to us when our prediction of engine failures proved only too true, but soon we were conducting flights over the entire operating area anyway. U.S. Army advisers were anxious to show off their new toys I guess because they sure kept us busy.

Meanwhile, back at the Rex in the evenings, we ate our GI "home cooked" meals, drank our blister bag water, took our medic prescribed anti-malaria pills, answered any incoming mail, conducted our beside-the-army-folding-cot briefings and then usually "hit the strauss" (sorry, a little German hangover there I guess) downtown for a couple of beers. Just before dark one night we got to witness a great side show. It was a real Chinese fire drill. Everyone has heard about those, but it is rare to actually get to see one. It was a genuine Chinese fire drill even if it was carried out by Vietnamese. The Rex Theater, adjoining the Rex Hotel, began to smolder and soon there were little people crawling all over the thing; up the sides, in and out of the windows and racing across the roof. There was considerable activity down in the street as well, but evidently no fire engines were available because we saw no big equipment. Even so, the air was filled with bells and whistles and screaming and yelling. It was pandemonium there for awhile. I guess they eventually managed to put out the fire by smothering it with their bare hands because eventually the smoke cleared and everything went quiet just as quickly as it had started.

The Mekong River was at flood stage and the cover story for our deployment to Vietnam was to provide air transport for flood relief efforts. In keeping with that, we sent out a six aircraft flight to carry rice to a village near the tip of the Ca Mau peninsula. This was Binh Hung, about as far south as you could get in Vietnam. It was mostly populated by Chinese refugees led by Catholic priest, Nguyen Lac Hoa. Father Hoa had been driven ever further south as communist governments took over in China and then North Vietnam. He led a very small and isolated army fighting the communists down there. He was highly respected by the South Vietnamese and he badly needed the relief flight. This was the first logistics support flight for the 57th and we were to make repeated trips to Father Hoa's village over the next few weeks, but this first mission was a learning experience. Binh Hung was a long way from Saigon over territory that was completely new to us. Bill Smith was the senior of our two flight platoon commanders and so was placed in charge of the mission. An experienced Chief Warrant Officer flew with him in the lead helicopter.

We completed the mission planning with the III Corps headquarters and its US advisors. They made the necessary arrangements with Father Hoa. We planned the flight carefully and the only real order that was given to Smith was to get back to Saigon before dark. There would be no communication with the flight from soon after take-off until they got back within radio transmission distance from Tan Son Nuht; and our radios had very limited range. You can imagine our concern when darkness fell with no sign of those six helicopters on the horizon. Through the dark of evening you could see the color creep up on the boss's face as he became more worried and more angry. Me too! Those guys had been given plenty of leeway but still managed to miss the one definite order they had been given. The flight finally checked in about an hour after the sun went down. I know that Dillard had a hard time not cussing out the whole bunch, but after telling me to let him know what went wrong, he just left the area. It's a good thing he did too, because as the crews began to come into the operations office, many were seen to be toting a great variety of strange automatic weapons. That would have really set him off.

Army pilots had never been particularly fond of the standard .45 caliber Colt automatic pistols that were issued to them. Some of our pilots had shot so badly at the Fort Lewis firing range that that they were now a little concerned about it. They complained that if they ever really had to use that pistol it would already be too late. The enemy would have to be so close before they could hit him with the .45, that they might just as well throw it at him, as to try to shoot him with it. One of the pilots had even come into the operations office waving his sidearm in the air and yelling for our attention. Then he extracted the clip from his .45 and showed us that it was full of those little packaged prophylactic rubbers and he said "Hell, I can't hit anything with this thing anyway, so I'll just screw em." (It is even possible that he used stronger words than that to make his joke.) That was just a preview of the problems to come. Some of the guys on this mission decided it would be a good idea to trade out that disaster-relief rice they were hauling for a better choice of weapons from Father Hoa's army. They came dragging in with everything from Swedish-Ks to U.S. Army grease guns. There were Thompson sub-machine guns and several others kinds, but the favorite upgrade appeared to be to the Israelite Uzi. Before they left the flight line I relieved them of that entire ill-gotten arsenal and locked it inside a recently emptied CONEX container.

Things were a little tense at the morning briefing. First it was explained to all aircrews that it was poor manners to exchange relief supplies for anything, let alone the weapons that the reliefee just might need sometime. I was still pissed and reminded them again that the primary job for all of them was to fly the airplane. They were not there to shoot up the jungle on approach or engage in shooting out of cockpit windows at any time. Their U.S. Army issued weapons were designed for close in protection only. Combat conditions required that all of their effort be given to flying the helicopter, particularly while landing or taking-off. They would have to concentrate all of their attention between inside the cockpit and outside just to properly manage the aircraft. They could not be looking out the side windows for bad guys. They would have to rely on other crew members to look out for enemy guns.

All of our pilots had been cleared, and signed off on orders to carry passengers, but this was before the Army started designating "Aircraft Commanders." We were still manning the cockpit with pilots and copilots. The guy in the pilot's seat was in command of the aircraft and everyone knew it. Even when an IP was along, he might offer words on how to best fly the machine, but that is as far as he would go. I again reminded them that crew members were not allowed to shoot anyway. Those were our orders. When and if we were ever authorized to shoot, it would be only after the guns were released to fire by the mission commander at flight lead, and then each pilot would be responsible to control the guns on his own aircraft. The late arrival the night before still rankled, so it was also reiterated that an order was just that. No interpretation was necessary and no deviation was expected. This information was imparted with not a few cuss words and no other subjects were discussed at that meeting. Father Hoa's guns were returned to him on a subsequent mission, and considering the situation, our relations with him continued amazingly well.

It must be noted here that it didn't take long for things to change. Even though we were under restrictive orders, we were already designing field expedient methods to allow us to shoot back and we continuously discussed the matter with the MAAG. They were reluctant to change the rules though because it was still not officially acknowledged that we were even there and the office workers downtown couldn't really believe that anyone would actually shoot at us. There is an old army saying that "the enemy always gets a vote." As we expected, he did cast his by repeatedly firing his guns at us, and so we soon returned the favor.

We were learning important lessons, as we went, in those early days before we moved out to Tent City at the airfield and one of them was a painful one that nearly got me fired. The ARVN was interested in conducting an operation into an old French rubber plantation located near the village of Ben Cat to the northeast. The proposed landing area was represented on the map as rubber trees but the ARVN assured us that it would be no problem to land there. That seemed questionable so I borrowed a U-6 Beaver from the MAAG flight detachment to run a recon; just a simple fly-by, but enough to get a look at the proposed landing zone. A low pass showed that it was indeed a rubber plantation, but the trees were just newly planted and only stood about two feet high; no more problem for our helicopters than tall grass. The French might not like it but that was the only possible place near where the troops wanted to go. Final coordination was made with the supported unit and their US advisors. They were not concerned about any damage to the rubber trees and the plan was finalized by the early evening of the day before the mission was to be flown.

So we wrapped up things at the airfield, caught a Lambretta scooter to the gate and then a blue-and-white back to the Rex. I had been working with the ARVN on the mission for a few days but had not had time to brief the boss. I had a map and a plan outline under my arm when I went to brief Cherne' and the newly promoted LTC Dillard. It was well after dark when I unrolled the map on Dillard's bunk and pointed out the planned landing area. He said "but that's a rubber plantation." I said yes and explained that I had personally looked and the trees were no problem. He said "the map shows that rubber trees are planted there." I said yes but the trees were very small; no problem for the helicopters and it was the only place around where we could land. The ARVN and their advisors wanted to go ahead." Dillard said "we are not landing in the middle of a rubber plantation." It was late and I was beat. The mission was ready to be flown in a few hours. When he said for the second time that "we were not going to land in any goddamn rubber plantation," I completely lost my cool and said "all right goddamn it but then you plan the next mission" and stormed out of the room.

Bill Rudd, who was billeted in the same room, heard that comment loud and clear and told me that he thought I would be relieved on the spot. Dillard must have exercised great restraint. I got on the horn to the ARVN and scrubbed the mission. He never brought the subject up again and I sure didn't either. It is no excuse but I had been working dawn to dark for several days and I was worn out. The fact that I didn't lose my job still amazes me.

CHAPTER 13

THE LEARNING PROCESS REALLY BEGINS

The learning process can be greatly accelerated when someone begins to shoot at you.

There was only one guy in the MAAG who had the necessary credentials to sign for and take possession of our crypto machine. That is the devise which is intended for use in transmitting and receiving highly classified messages. This individual was the MAAG Top Secret Control Sergeant; actually a Specialist (Spec 4). One day, shortly after our arrival, he went to see his girl friend up in Bien Hoa. The Viet Cong scarfd him right off his bicycle and carted him away to their jungle lair. I don't think they did that because of his duty assignment, but more likely, just because he was peddling along in contested territory where he was easy prey. But how stupid can you get? Even at this early stage in the festivities how dumb was that? The Cong were now leading this guy away through heavy jungle. The MAAG was understandably concerned and they were anxious to get him back. So that led to our next major mission. This one was supposed to be a real coup.

It was envisioned by the U.S. intelligence wienies (read CIA), our resident Eighth Army Aviation expert, and the U.S. advisors to the Airborne Brigade who went along with it, that we would make a recapture by helicopter. When we went over to the brigade headquarters to begin putting our piece of planning together, we found that the intelligence concerning the whereabouts of this guy was at least two day old, and it would be three days gone, before we could get there. If that sounds like a farce, it surely was. We asked if they really thought that would be good enough. Wouldn't they keep moving him? The area just north of Bien Hoa is fairly heavily covered with jungle so there were only scattered places where we might be able to land the kind of large flight they were talking about. We argued that we would need much more timely information before we could locate a landing area close to where they were likely to be. We tried to tell 'em, but nobody cared much about what us helicopter jockeys thought. They were intent on moving quickly while there was a chance that the specialist was still fairly close to Bien Hoa.

Okay, but it was already two days after the capture before we were able to spend just a short time in planning with the Airborne Brigade. Their plan was to lift troops into a hole in the jungle a few miles north of Bien Hoa. The forty-eight hour old information had led them to believe that the Cong was holding the specialist near there. In spite of our misgivings, that the intelligence would be three days old by the time we could mount a heliborne assault, we followed our leaders and planned to put thirty helicopters into that small jungle clearing.

When you are going to lead thirty helicopters into any jungle landing area, it will probably be the only one anywhere around, and it will always seem to be too small. This one was indeed pretty tight. The same good people were planning this mission that had planned the first combat assault, with the important addition of the nameless guy from the CIA, upon whose word the whole caper was predicated. Stockton considered himself to be a true helicopter warrior by then, so he too contributed words of nonsense to the discussion. The 8th was still at Tan Son Nuht, so they were to provide about half the helicopters needed to further the grand design, but they felt no need to contribute their expertise to the planning. They felt, and rightfully so, that anything they might offer to this rarified crowd would likely be ignored anyway.

There was little time for much more then a map recon and a quick fly-by before mission launch the next morning. The brigade felt like they would need to deploy an entire reinforced battalion (1036 troops) to have any chance of success in an area where "friendly troops had never been before." (We were to hear this "never been there before" refrain often over the course of the next year, but soon came to disbelieve it.) It would require a total of four lifts to get the battalion on the ground so we plotted several doglegs, in and out, to avoid using the same flight route over and over again. We had to limit our flight time so that all the lifts could be completed without a refueling delay. That meant that the routes could not be very widely separated. At least, the MAAG had learned its lesson and Stockton was not scheduled to fly a troop carrying CH-21C this time. Not to be dissuaded however, he would borrow an OH-13 from the 8th so that he could observe the mission.

We flew to Bien Hoa to pick up our first lift near dawn and headed for the assault area. You would have noticed some real consternation in chalk one when we had to lead the flight into an assault landing, over an OH-13 which was parked with its rotor still turning, right in the middle of the touchdown area. I'll never understand it, but Stockton had already landed and was out on foot investigating the supposedly hot, enemy controlled tree line. The distance from the pick-up site to the landing area was short so we were flying at tree top level and we had popped out right at the edge of the clearing. Stockton had landed just ahead of us and we were way down the approach and committed to land before we first saw him. When an old recip helicopter, like a CH-21C, has been committed to land, with a gaggle of similarly engaged helicopters behind it, you are truly committed. Any attempt to change much by the time we saw that little aircraft parked in our way would have led to mass confusion and probably serious error. It could easily have ended in another major accident, so I just hollered "look out for the H-13," terminated as far forward as I could get, and hoped for the best.

Some of the crews, about halfway back in the flight, had to do some tight evasive maneuvers to avoid hitting that OH-13. They had to slip to the side to find new places to land and there was a still a good possibility that rotor downwash would flip over that very small helicopter with its still turning rotor. Fortunately that didn't happen and we managed to convey the word, through the U.S. advisor on the ground, to Stockton, to get that damn helicopter out of there before we got back with the next lift. Captains, no matter what their training and experience, are not equipped to confront idiotic behavior from

Lieutenant Colonels. Dillard had no such reticence and Stockton had no further direct dealings with us. That is not to say that he would stay clear out of the picture. He was a substantial pain in the ass until he was forced out of the country.

I saw two more helicopter related incidents within a couple of weeks that involved this expensively trained, senior ranking aviator which I might as well cover now. Dillard had made it clear to Stockton that he should stay the hell away from us and our helicopters. The 8th did, however, loan him an OH-13 on at least two more occasions before they left town for their new duty station up country. I was at the Airborne Brigade coordinating a mission one day when Stockton was also in the headquarters. While leaving the meeting I noticed an OH-13 sitting by the flag pole outside. We had just seen Stockton depart by sedan for MAAG headquarters downtown, so I called the 8th and asked if they would like me to bring the helicopter back for them. They said sure so I hopped in and fired it up.

Before taking-off I checked that the magnetos were operating properly but I found that there was a 300 RPM Mag drop on one side and a 150 drop on the other. These were serious discrepancies. The helicopter should have been grounded until they were corrected. Still I decided to take it home where it would be easier for them to work on. The engine was running rough enough that I just hovered the helicopter around buildings and over obstacles to return the thing to their hanger. They were located clear down toward the other end of the airfield and all the while I was hoping that the engine didn't quit. I was careful to have somewhere to go if it did. I went into their operations shack when I got there and said "What the hell are you guys doing? That helicopter should have been grounded!" Somebody said "well we tried to tell that dumb son-of-a-bitch but he was in such a goddamn hurry he couldn't wait and if that asshole wants to kill himself its okay with us."

I'm sure I was not witness to all the rest of Stockton's capers but I happened to be at the MAAG flight detachment one day when he flew onto their parking ramp in an OH-13. He was late for a rest and recuperation (R&R) flight to Bangkok I guess, because he scrambled out of the helicopter and left it running on the ramp as he ran to catch the MAAG U-8 twin engined airplane that was turning up and ready to go. I couldn't believe it. I stood there and watched it churn. The OH-13 was running at idle speed and had been left that way. This time I said "to hell with it, somebody will shut it down or it'll run out of gas" and I jumped back in my jeep and drove away. I was plenty fed up with Stockton by this time and it is probably a good thing for me that he and his team had pretty much retreated to the MAAG downtown. It is possible that I might have said or done something regrettable.

Stockton be damned; it's time to get back to chasing captured Spec 4s through the jungle by helicopter. After narrowly avoiding the parked OH-13, the mission proceeded as planned with three more lifts but there was another minor complication. The distance between the pickup site at Bien Hoa and the hole in the jungle was so short that we did not have time to gain altitude but instead stayed at low level. Even though the lead helicopter tried to fly a different route each time, as we neared Bien Hoa on the return leg, at least one aircraft in the flight flew over an old gutted French colonial house with no roof and a machine gun in the basement. The gun would cut loose and we found holes in some of our helicopters. That was getting irritating, so on the next trip out of the assault area I purposely diverted slightly to fly over that place and I had my crew chief deliver a few rounds in reply. We were still being told that we couldn't even shoot back if we came under fire but enough is enough. We probably only scared the guy but we didn't get shot at from that house any more and no one said anything to me about it. Soon the rule was changed to "its okay to shoot back if someone is shooting at you."

My memory is unclear about where my leaders, Dillard and Cherne, were on this mission. They were not along and probably had urgent business downtown. I was leading the flight and the decision to take that machine gun under fire was mine. This illustrates a point about how things can escalate in the very early stages of conflict. It was the comparatively junior officers making many, if not most, of the decisions on or near the ground at the point of enemy contact. The chain of command then had to decide to back up the action and modify the rules or heads would roll. This circumstance happened repeatedly in the early days of the Vietnam War and the rules of engagement changed accordingly. It is easy to see how this kind of action and reaction creep can alter the overall level of conflict intensity. Sometimes it seems to me that we just kind of backed into that particular war.

This is just a short story about one hundred and twenty helicopter loads of combat troops flying into the jungle to "rescue" one errant Spec 4 in a place where we were told no ARVN had ever gone before. It was based on the best intel the ARVN and the CIA could provide but it was just a little bit old by the time the troops hit the ground. The American soldier and his captors were long gone by then of course. It is unlikely that they had ever been there in the first place. It is hard to believe, but what the Brigade really found around that hole in the jungle was a friendly ARVN ranger company. They had been in the area for some time apparently, but nobody seemed to know it.

We gathered at the Airborne Brigade every day for a while as reports came in of sightings of a naked white man being herded through the forest and shown off in successive villages until he disappeared across the Cambodian border. But the big thinkers had learned by then that three day old intelligence was like none at all, and fewer possible landing areas appeared as the jungle deepened, so we didn't try any more helicopter recaptures. It was several weeks later when the VC actually released this guy, at the edge of the jungle, not too far from where they had picked him up in the first place. No, I don't have any idea why they did that; never heard of anything happening like that ever again and we didn't hear anything more about this situation either. The Spec 4 just disappeared back into the (I'm sure) friendly fold.

When we reported to the MAAG that we had been shot at and hit again on this mission, they didn't believe us. The prevalent feeling at the time was that the insurgents were purposely trying to avoid American casualties to lesson the probability of more American involvement; so if we got hit at all, it was probably some kind of mistake. We were advised to not worry about it and just fly our missions. After that, we began to take Polaroid pictures of the holes that were regularly appearing in our helicopters and we would attach these to the after mission reports we sent downtown.

It was at about this time that we got to working seriously on our lack of armaments. It had quickly become obvious to us that we needed some kind of protective firepower and we began employing our crew chiefs and volunteer mechanics as gunners. They had only light hand held automatic rifles but that at least gave us one guy looking out for trouble at each of the cargo doors; one on each side of the helicopter. This was only minimally satisfactory so a further field expedient solution was soon tried. This consisted of an M1918A1 .30-caliber machine gun mounted in the forward cargo door, while the crew chief was stationed at the rear cargo door with his hand held automatic weapon. Although crude, this system did provide some firepower for protection at the landing zone. Like most improvisations, this one went through a few changes before a satisfactory configuration was established.

The basic installation for this old WWII machine gun was arrived at by removing the pintle from a triangular ground mount and welding it to an iron bar which was then secured to the door frame with a hinge and locking pin arrangement. This allowed fairly good movement in traverse and elevation when the gun was mounted. I don't remember anyone shooting up those door frames or rotor blade tips so maybe we had some kind of stops too, or maybe it was all luck and skill.

The same arrangement was initially used in both the fore and aft doors with a bungee cord tied to the bar at the aft door so that the machine gun could be swung inboard, out of the way for troop entry and exit. This seemed like a good idea at the time, but it sure didn't work out in practice. When that aft gun was swung inboard it was difficult to get the troops to leave the aircraft, or do anything else for that matter, because the business end was then pointed straight up the troop compartment. Besides, if the troops did manage to overcome their fear and sidle past that ominous barrel, it became of obvious concern to the pilot and copilot that they were sitting at the wrong end of a shooting gallery. There would be a serious problem in the cockpit should there be any little nervous mistake on the part of the crew chief. Change one was instituted immediately and the crew chief returned to his hand held light automatic weapon.

Ammunition feed to the forward gun was another problem. With the belt feeding directly from an ammo box on the floor, stoppages due to belt twisting were common. The only immediate practical solution was to mount the ammo box directly on top of the gun to ensure smooth untwisted entry of the rounds into the breach. That part worked fine but, of course, the solution brought its own set of problems. The main problem was that the gunner had to peer over the box and aim by pointing the weapon parallel to his line of sight which was about two feet over the barrel. There were no aerial trigger components available either, so with the standard ground pistol grip in one hand and the ammo box in the other to help steady things up, successful gunnery was largely a matter of practiced guesswork.

Many of our volunteer gunners became quite proficient in spite of these limitations, although they were inclined to gripe about it. "Why don't we get some real aerial guns anyway?" was the standard beef. Cherne' was working the problem hard. He did try to get us the proper aerial guns but those were all in the USAF supply chain and the interservice aviation roles-and-missions dispute took precedent over our minor combat requirements. Prying aerial armament off the Air Force was impossible. We were not too worried about it though because we were not into target shooting anyway. If our guns were accurate enough to hose down a tree line, that was generally all that we needed for suppressive fire in the LZ. This field expedient, with minor modifications, did the job even after some relief was provided by the arrival of the Utility Tactical Transport Company (UTT) with its armed UH-1As beginning in mid 1962.

We were working with the 7th and 21st ARVN divisions in the Mekong Delta and with the 5th Division around Cu Chi, Tay Ninh and in the jungle area around Ben Cat, which had been known since the French were around as the Iron Triangle. During an early mission out of Soc Trang, with the 7th Division, we saw how inadequate our close air support was going to be. The senior advisor to this division was LTC Frank Clay, a son of GEN Lucius Clay of WWII and Berlin Air Lift fame. In my opinion, Clay was one of the best of the senior advisors we worked with but COL Cao, the division commander, was not an aggressive fighter at all. The division plan was weak this day and Clay knew it, but the division commander was unfamiliar with heliborne operations, was unwilling to sustain casualties, and he was also very resistant to advise.

The plan included a Vietnam Air Force (VNAF) attack to suppress any fire from the perimeter of the assault landing area. The air attack was to lift just before we dropped off the friendly troops. They got it just a little wrong and blasted the place while we were still in it unloading our passengers; that makes for an exciting few minutes. These were North American T-28s being flown by USAF "round eyes" with VNAF trainees aboard. The T-28 might have been a great trainer, but it wasn't worth a damn as a ground support aircraft. It couldn't carry either enough armament or fuel and with a VNAF pilot-in-training you would get about two ineffective passes and then they were flying off to refuel. It didn't take long for the round eyes to get more serious. You could always tell when they were on the controls because the support got a great deal closer and more accurate. Still when the close air support was a T-28, you had to hope that another one was arriving on station before the first one ran out of ammo or gas. That however, was not the usual case and when that "fighter cap" left, the bad guys just stood up and took aim at the rest of us.

The late arrival of the Air Force was some disconcerting to us that day. They didn't see any reason to lift their fires just because there were a bunch of helicopters next to the tree line. They missed us anyway and the operation continued in what would become a familiar way. The ARVN didn't seem too worried about the Viet Cong because they just hunkered down in the LZ to eat their lunch and wait for the subsequent lifts to arrive. After lunch they formed up for the attack and wandered off the field. The assault area was an island in the South China Sea just off the mouth of one of the Mekong River tributaries. The "attack" continued as we watched many people abandon the island and swim for shore. We think that they might have been the enemy because eventually the ARVN captured a VC sewing machine to prove it. That's all they captured but at least they didn't sustain any casualties.

Sometimes the close air support that was provided in the early days was by an old WWII B-26 light bomber. This was really neat. That aircraft would turn into the target area like a commercial airliner, way off and straight in. They carried plenty of gas and ammo but by the time they got lined up for attack it must have been pretty obvious to the "target." The VC had plenty of time to bury themselves or even go elsewhere. Later, when some USAF pilots tried to fly that light bomber like an attack fighter, with tight turns and climbs, the wings fell off.

We were quick to note some other peculiarities of the war at this point. Seems like every time, when we first flew over the villages and along the canals and rice paddies of the delta, we would find the blue and red banner of the Viet Cong flying everywhere; from houses and rice paddies. Even some red and yellow hammer and sickles were among them, but nobody was shooting at us. By the second flight over the same area, lots of those VC flags would be gone and a few yellow and red striped Republic of Vietnam flags would have been run up. On this trip we would start receiving a little fire. By the third flight, all the VC flags would be gone, RVN flags would be flying everywhere and everybody was shooting at us.

Things got a little tight on this mission when one of our helicopters hit a dry rice paddy dike at the pick up site. They striped a gear which flew up through the rear rotor disc. Then the helicopter rolled over and started to burn. We had one very experienced and capable pilot flying with one very weak pilot on that ship. Guess who was on the controls? Anyway we learned then, that a rice paddy dike was as hard as a brick shithouse when it was dry. Some of us were already on the ground before the accident happened. There was a lot of ducking and scrambling for new territory when pieces of the rotor blades started to fly. Then just as everyone was tentatively regaining their feet, the fire got going good and the ammo started cooking off. Now everyone started running in a fast, low-moving crouch to get further away from the heat and noise. To add insult to injury, the weak pilot was flying the right seat and the helicopter rolled to the right which placed him on the bottom when it came time to get out. This didn't slow him down at all as he just stepped on the other guy's head to bail out of the left hand cockpit window.

The crew chief, SP6 Donald W. Cline, sustained the only injury, with a bad back burn, but there were a number of extremely pissed-off people around after this example of flying skill; especially after ducking for cover not once but twice. A further contributing factor to our general irritation was the casual nature of the ARVN "assault," the miss-timed "close air support" and the fact that a red & blue VC flag could be seen flying over a haystack right next to the troop pick-up/crash site. One of our pilots, CWO Jerry Bishop, had had about enough of diving for the ground and he and another guy started out to "tear down that goddamn flag." Jerry was a young two time Silver Star winner from the Korean War so he didn't lack for guts, but both of those guys must have suffered a momentary lack of brains. We managed to dissuade them from this personal attack when someone reminded them of the well known VC habit of booby trapping just that kind of display.

LTC Clay was certainly upset as well, but he was more concerned with the failure of the mission itself. As more information arrived at the command post about that ARVN walk in the woods he got very quiet. We flew a few more missions with the 7th over the next couple of weeks but they did not appear to be much improved. Eventually the U. S. Army senior advisor told the ARVN division commander that he had to learn to use the helicopters to gain better results or he would be unable to provide that support any more. This turned out to be fine with that ARVN hero and we didn't fly any more missions in support of the 7th Division for a number of weeks. That doesn't mean we could relax though. The other divisions picked up the slack but with the same tepid results I'm afraid. Clay eventually prevailed, the planning got a bit tighter in the 7th and the results were a little better the next time we went out with that division. Better maybe; but everything is relative.

There was no doubt left in any of our minds that things were going to get progressively worse and that the USAF was ill prepared to help out much. Our flight crews were getting a little tense. The sound that a .30 caliber round makes when it enters and exits the helicopter is much like a can under pressure being loudly opened twice and that ain't too bad as long as it doesn't hit anything critical on the way. We began to hear that sound fairly often. We kept taking our pictures. The headquarters guys still held the position that it couldn't be that bad and besides officially we weren't really there anyway. It wasn't until after U.S. Army Captain Don York was blown up on the road to Ben Cat in the Iron Triangle that the MAAG began to believe our reports.

We aviators had been led to believe that normally the VC would explode their mines under the lead vehicle of a convoy unless a U.S. advisor was in that jeep. If an advisor were in the jeep they would let it go by and key their ambush under a following vehicle; they seemed to be trying to avoid U.S. casualties. As I have said, the belief was that the enemy did not want to do anything which would be likely to result in more U.S. involvement. Something changed. Two MAAG officers had been killed in earlier ambushes riding those lead jeeps. Therefore orders had been issued to our advisors to not ride up there. This time the guerillas passed up the first jeep and hit the one back in the convoy with a tall blond American in it. MAAG headquarters concluded that the U. S. Army officer had been specifically targeted since the remotely controlled 105mm shell booby trap had been exploded right under his jeep.

Don York was a friend of mine. He was the first guy that I personally knew to get killed in Vietnam. We'd had a chance to get acquainted at the Five Oceans officers club shortly after our arrival in country. He had volunteered to "ride along" on that convoy. We went in that day with a flight load of troops to secure the ambush area and evacuate the wounded. There weren't many of them. The ambush had been so successful that the ARVN dead were stacked and hauled out in the back of 2 ½ trucks. We brought Don back on my helicopter.

CHAPTER 14

CHINESE ZODIAC

1961 the year of the OX—"Bright, patient and inspiring to others. Marry a Snake or a Cock. The Sheep will bring trouble".
*1962 the year of the Tiger—"Aggressive, courageous, candid & sensitive. Look to the Horse & Dog for happiness. Beware of the Monkey".**

Although the Rex was just a shell, it was a sorta civilized shell and we were getting used to the city life around us. They had begun construction of a tent city at the air base, and we would move soon, but we had learned some of the peculiarities of Saigon in the meantime. We discovered the outlying districts of Cholon and Dacoa. Cholon, the Chinese section of the city had its own distinctive character and Dacoa had some special attractions as well. We watched the "Street of Flowers" live up to its nickname as blossoms filled up the middle of the divided street with a vast array of color. We quickly learned that the weather changed often and rapidly; it was either very-very-hot and very-very-humid or very-very-hot and very-very-wet. That did not discourage us from occupying the little outside street-corner cafes during daylight when we got a chance. There we would sit in our sweat or rain soaked shirts watching the native population go by.

A few of us also discovered a fine French café which was far enough off the main drag to be just beyond the normal range of our GI exploration of Saigon. This was the Mayflower Café which served great food, including the best french-onion soup that I have ever tasted. It was patronized by a mix of the remaining Frenchmen in town plus Vietnamese in stylish western clothing, and a few well dressed Americans. It was a quiet place with nice décor and fine service. You could easily think that you were dining in Paris. We kept this discovery low key because we didn't want to flood the place with a large number of our compatriots; shouldn't have done that I suppose but our advantage didn't last long anyway. The 57th "word-of-mouth telegraph" always did its work extremely well. The truth will out. Our discriminating diners soon filled the place up most nights. Our troops also continued to expand their knowledge of the cocktail lounges, and after watching a few windows exploding up front, we all learned to sit far to the back of the bar.

I soon discovered that I could trade a single US Greenback dollar for a Chinese, Mexican or French silver dollar coin. There were even some old American silver trade dollars for sale in the little mobile shops set up between the soup kitchens and shade tree mechanics along the main avenue. The sellers would even take about the equivalent in piasters. This seemed like too good a deal to pass up, so I set out right away to corner the market in silver. Eventually I acquired a stack of coins that would reach from my hand to my elbow. Of course we were supposed to only use Vietnamese Piasters on the street. GI talk reduced piaster to a simple "P" right away of course. Soon after arrival we had been required to surrender our green dollars for U.S. Army issued Military Payment Certificates (MPC) at the official exchange rate. Some of us had squirreled a few bucks away anyway since we believed that a U.S. dollar might be more useful than a Vietnamese "P" or a military MPC if we were forced down in contested territory.

Piasters were supposed to be purchased at the officially pegged exchange rate. That is what we were forced to use the first time but it was an obvious imposition on us. It was soon readily apparent that no one traded at the official exchange rate of about 75 to one when Hong Kong traders were everywhere and were happy to trade at the much better rate of about 118 to one. MAAG officers led the parade to the Hong Kong traders. I wasn't too careful about what kind of money I used to buy those silver coins as long as it was about a buck U. S. Wouldn't you know it, I got my come-uppance later anyway when someone slickied my silver dollar stash out of my foot locker. We had some Vietnamese labor around the area by then. I became more careful to keep that foot locker locked after loosing my small hoard. I was able to bring a few foreign silver dollars home with me at the end of the tour, but not many, because they had been swept clean from the Saigon streets pretty quickly, and besides, we found much less time to shop after we hit the tents.

The MAAG was still very anxious to get us out of their hotel but it took a while to get the tents up at Tan Son Nuht where we could at least be close to our helicopters. In the meantime we continued to fly daily missions and things settled down to about one full scale combat flog twice a week where we used all the flyables that Bill Rudd could produce. Old timers will notice that I am not using the terminology that was foisted on us in the early days. We were told that what we were doing was "combat support" and should be recorded on our DA Form 759 Individual Flight Records as CS not C for combat. Well that was not exactly true unless the bullets that were coming our way were somehow different than those that came later. The flight category of Combat Support was invented as a way to avoid acknowledging the true nature of things. To avoid the appearance of non-compliance with the various treaties that had been signed, we were officially just there as transportation support. How do you like my choice of words; "appearance of non-compliance"? Not my words really; the lawyers and politicians got there first.

Every day, when we were not fully committed to fly combat assaults, three flights of two helicopters each were scheduled for smaller missions. At first these were mostly familiarization training for ground troops and their junior leaders. Although there were some VNAF CH-34s around, and some ARVN soldiers probably remembered a few choppers from the French era, few of them had had anything to do with helicopters. The training we had been doing with the ARVN Airborne Brigade was quickly extended to the other units of the III Corps. We eventually trained thousands of soldiers. Other kinds of two plane missions ranged from carrying government officials to isolated places to relocating families in and out of jungle outposts and there were all kinds of other requirements as well.

These missions could be interesting. For example, one day we were up in the jungle somewhere. Our mission was to evacuate casualties from an old French triangular mud fort that had been occupied by RVN Self-Defense (SD) troops and their families. The fort had been attacked by the VC on the previous night. At the same time we were to bring in a new set of troops and their families. The SD element of RVN military capability was composed of ostensibly friendly people from areas under the ostensible control of local province chiefs; similar to what we would think of as a militia. They were very poorly armed, even more poorly led, and they were dressed in what we foreigners called black pajamas; so were the Viet Cong. They were hard to tell apart without getting up close and personal. The question for us usually was "whose side were they really on?" Someone thought it was a good idea to have the SD defend isolated outposts; way out by themselves where effective command, control and communication must have been nearly impossible and support was, practically speaking, non-existent.

Whereas we had difficulty sorting out one black pajama clad farmer from another, the VC did not. Frequently, they would decide to take out one of these isolated outposts. No sweat; they were sitting ducks! The outpost where we were to make the switch that day had been completely overrun. The mud walls of this "fort" may have been comforting, but they probably offered little protection. There was rudimentary wire surrounding the place. It had gravel filled tin cans, and rattles made out of gourds, hanging on it as an early warning system. There were no heavy weapons. The VC must have had little trouble overrunning the place. There were only a few survivors for us to haul out.

On the return trip we brought in replacements. This meant the troops, their families and their stuff. Our loads included everything from howling babies to pigs and chickens. Some mothers even managed to get aboard with lunch still cooking on the hibachi. We made them put out the fire of course, but that still left us to worry about the "nuc maum" fish sauce they were carrying aboard in clay pots. We had already learned that this was very corrosive stuff. Nuc Maum; a horrible smelling concoction that would instantly corrode control cables if one of those pots broke or spilled on the cargo compartment floor. We didn't make a passenger count. They were small people. If we could get it off the ground we went; even though it seemed tragic to put these families back into such an untenable position.

One of the most critical missions we flew was to backload parachutes after the Airborne Brigade had jumped into a combat position. The brigade constituted the entire ARVN reserve force so getting their chutes back to them quickly was critical and I am reminded of one such mission. We were again called in to an isolated jungle fort that had been overrun. This time a relief force had jumped in at dawn. We had then gone in with several ships to return this airborne force to Saigon. On the next day we took a flight of two helicopters out to bring back their parachutes. It would take us several trips. On the first trip in we carried a mixed load of passengers. One was a catholic priest, another was an ARVN paymaster and there were various other, apparently important, people. Each one seemed to bring along a couple of personal guards. We had been told that the parachutes had priority over any passengers coming out and were assured that these guys were aware of that. We double checked that they understood.

Each time we loaded up we would send word to the visitors that they had better go back with us now. We would even wait a few minutes but they were too busy to leave I guess. On the last run before dark, our cargo compartment was filled with parachutes from the floor to very near the ceiling. Then, of course, all the strap-hangers decided it was finally time for them to leave. Well we could barely bring the helicopter to a hover without any passengers. The tree line was close and it was problematical whether we could clear it on take-off with the priority load we already had. With the crowd of people now stacked in behind the load of chutes there was no way we were going to be able to take-off.

On the intercom, I told the crew chief to kick some of them off. Apparently no one wanted to spend the night out there in the jungle. We were the last train out and nobody would get off. The crew chief argued and the sun descended to the horizon and we tried to pull enough power to fly. We couldn't even make the oleo struts on the landing gear extend let alone achieve a hover. Some of the pilots in the outfit used to accuse me of having a very even temper; always pissed off. This time I really lost it! I unbuckled from my cockpit seat and went over that load of parachutes screaming like a banshee. They probably didn't understand the words but they fell all over each other to get out of my way. I then motioned to the priest and the paymaster to get back aboard by curling my finger at them while holding the flat of my hand against the rest of them; no guards and nobody else. It was getting pretty dark by the time we barely cleared the tree line out of there.

Another important job was to fly teams out to place radios at outlying units where such commo capability had not previously existed. These places had often been attacked and sometimes overrun because poor commo made the ARVN response time way, way too slow. I went along on one of these radio installation missions one day when I needed to get out of the office and it was one of two times that I experienced an involuntary physical reaction to a very loud noise.

We were just outside of another triangular mud fort dating from the French colonial period. The place was way out in the western Mekong Delta and it was an obvious target for the VC who were thick in them parts. We had dropped off the radio installation team and parked just outside of the walls. Since we wanted to conserve gas and things looked secure enough we decided to shut down the Shawnee while we waited. The sun was hot. The cockpit seat was comfortable when you could slouch down in it. I went to sleep. Just when I was getting well settled the SD troops fired off a 105mm round from the mud fort. The cannon muzzle was about forty feet away and the round whistled right over our helicopter. My knees collided with my chin before I woke up. I grabbed a handful of collective and it's a good thing we were shut down or we might have met that round in the air. The place had only one artillery piece and we learned that it was normal practice for them to wheel their cannon around in 360 degrees and fire it in any direction at random times. This was intended to keep the VC loose I guess. No target; no way to know if they hit anything so of very questionable value, but it sure got my attention.

Just to finish the subject, the other time I had an immediate adverse physical reaction was while off-loading troops during an assault. The machine gun was mounted in the forward cargo door just behind the pilot's seat but I had not released the gun to fire. My attention was focused inside the helicopter. I was looking over my shoulder at the crew chief to see when the last soldier got off the aircraft. When that happened, I intended to initiate take-off immediately just as we normally did. Most of the troops had exited the aircraft when the gunner at the forward door thought he saw something directly in front of the helicopter and let off a long burst of fire. This time the muzzle of the .30 caliber machine gun was about a foot from my window and it seemed to be right in my ear. My reaction was to pull sharply up on the collective stick. Now this is supposed to be a coordinated application of power; not a spastic maneuver. The other pilot was holding down on the collective and yelling "no, no, no." We reached about a five foot hover as the crew chief helped the last troop out the door. It was a long step for him but he had a nice soft rice paddy to land in anyway. With a lot of help from the CWO flying with me, we eventually managed to fly without damaging the engine or the aircraft. This was to be just the first of several conversations that I had with a gunner about when he should, or should not, fire his machine gun.

One of the weirdest things we discovered early on was that any aviation fuel (AVGAS) we would need while operating outside of Saigon had to be delivered by ESSO. That's right, before any combat assault, the ARVN would contract with the ESSO Company to deliver gas to wherever we were staging the troop pickup. ESSO then had to drive their vulnerable trucks down the unsecured roads which they were only willing to do during daylight. It was also reasonable to assume that this could only be successful if ESSO paid their "taxes" to the VC along the way. This, of course, blew any chance of operational security. The gas would arrive in 55 gallon drums, usually at a small airstrip, the day before an operation was to take place. The whole surrounding area couldn't help but notice the activity. We bitched and moaned to the advisors at III Corps headquarters, but nothing changed. This was one of the earliest indications that we were involved in little more than a crazy game.

The 55 gallon drums also presented a problem. You had to expect that the drums might contain a little water, either from mishandling of the fuel or condensation in the drum. Not much water could be allowed to get into the helicopter fuel cells or we would increase the risk of engine failures. Refueling always took time. No matter how fast we were, a sizable delay could be expected when refueling was necessary. We only had so many helicopters to bring to the party and generally the ARVN showed no intent to fight with anything less than a reinforced company on the ground. They often wanted the whole battalion before they would move out so that usually meant at least one refueling. Of course that also meant that the VC could just go away while the ARVN waited for the rest of their troops to arrive. Although any delay seemed of little concern to the ARVN, their U.S. advisors would get upset. They knew that a successful operation depended on rapid action after the initial heliborne assault. If we took too long to finish refueling while the ARVN waited, any remaining advantage they might have had would probably have been lost. We always tried to do the job right and complete turn around flights as quickly as possible.

A quick turn-around was very difficult to achieve when you had to pump the AVGAS from drums. Our solution was to have the 55 gallon drums placed upright overnight which allowed them to sit long enough so that the water, heavier then AVGAS, would accumulate at the bottom of the drum We used 55 Gallons Per Minute (GPM) hand pumps to transfer the fuel to the aircraft. The last tree or four inches of gas would be carefully left in the bottom of the drum along with any water that might have been trapped there. The helicopters would then be left to sit for a short time; long enough to settle the gas and the aircraft fuel cells would be drained just before starting the engine. This was working fine until Dillard noticed what was going on and, after checking with his IP, ordered us to start filtering our fuel through chamois cloth as prescribed by regulations. Well it was time to talk to the boss again, but I had already been burned a couple of times, so after a brief protest along the lines of "but that ain't going to work," I retreated to try to figure out a different approach.

After consulting with Cherne' first, Bill Rudd and I decided that we would really have to try to make it work in order to demonstrate that filtering the fuel through chamois was not feasible. On the next assault mission we loaded our entire POL section along with our most senior NCOs aboard the maintenance helicopter along with pumps, chamois cloths and anything else that might conceivably help to filter the fuel. When the time came to refuel, we attacked the problem in a military manner. We tried every trick we could think of to force the AVGAS through those chamois cloths. Well we spilled a little gas and gained a little trickle into the helicopters. There was much cussing and yelling by the NCOs and much straining by the POL guys on the pumps. There was also way too much time expended in the effort. Eventually we saw that the pumps, which were unable to move much gas, were instead pumping air back into the drums, and they were beginning to swell up from the back pressure to the point that we feared that they might explode. I turned to Cherne', who had been standing back and watching all of this, and asked if we might get on with the mission. He took on the unenviable task of explaining to Dillard, who had also been observing, that he had given the go ahead.

We were still assigned to the Sixth Army at the Presidio of California and were still on temporary duty orders to Vietnam at this time. MAJ Dillard had been promoted to Lieutenant Colonel when LTC John Stacey from Sixth Army, showed up to see what we were doing and report back to that headquarters. As an additional task, he was to recommend who should remain to command the 57th now that Dillard was an LTC. Majors normally commanded aviation companies so that was probably the determining factor when, shortly after Stacey's visit, Bob Dillard was transferred to the MAAG headquarters.

We also got word that the 45th battalion headquarters, to which we would be assigned, was on the way from the states; now that sure got my attention because the 45th was full of captains, all of whom were senior to me by date of rank. I figured that I was about to get a lot of free advice or more probably just loose my job to one of these guys. Fortunately for me, that didn't turn out to be the case, for two reasons. First, only one of the officers, CPT Sam Bass, was CH-21C qualified and he preferred to fly the fixed wing U-1 Otter assigned to the headquarters. The second reason was more important. The battalion commander, LTC Howard Richardson, knew that they would be getting more companies to supervise. Even though the headquarters was to be co-located with us, he instructed his staff to leave us alone.

One of our pilots had gotten a new job when he had bitched about the food back in the Rex; Charley Larkin became the Mess Officer. The food actually improved somewhat. The meat was not quite as rainbowed with purple. Jack Carey decided he had been the Assistant Operations Officer long enough so two of the guys who had joined us from the 33rd Helicopter Company stepped up to the task. CWOs David R. Saylor and Ulyses Lamkin shared the job. Dave provided most of the humor and Lam did most of the work. Tent city was up and running before the New Year got very old and we were quickly rooted out of our cushy hotel billets. Actually the tents weren't too bad. They had wooden floors and we all purchased bamboo beds and thin mattresses from local merchants. We placed the legs of the beds in large number 10 cans hoping that the sharp edge would keep snakes and varmints from climbing into bed with us and we hung mosquito nets to slow down the flying bugs. One of the tents was designated as an officer's club and chit-books were sold to finance the purchase of a bar and small tables with plastic chairs. CWO Allen B. Causseaux signed up as the club officer. I had been told that Al, or ABC as most referred to him, had been the youngest Master Sergeant in the Army before going to flight school so he knew a good job when he saw it.

Besides the oppressive heat and the dirt streets that frequently turned to mud after each rain storm, there was one other thing I really didn't like about tent city. We had cold water, open air showers and mahogany seating in the outhouses; sounds okay doesn't it? But why did they have to paint those seats with creosote? It wasn't ring around the bathtub one had to worry about; it was ring around the butt when you tore yourself loose to get up. I'll bet the carpenter that built those things was a Viet Cong sympathizer; either that or he had a hell of a sense of humor. This situation was bad enough that we even made occasional special trips downtown in search of the "porcelain pony" which could be found at any MAAG billet.

Soon it became apparent that some of our troops were finding alternate living arrangements downtown; still unlikely to have air conditioning but the room would probably have at least a ceiling fan. It didn't help much with the toilet problem though. Remember, this is French colonial architecture we are talking about here and a porcelain stall with raised foot pads and a hole in the floor was the best you could expect. Me and the boss held out against this trend until the tents were becoming pretty empty at night. Still it was an interesting option if the rent wasn't too high. CWO Richard W. Parsons had found a nice little centrally located room downtown but then he got sick and he was soon to be evacuated home. Before he left I entered into negotiation with Dick to buy his furniture and take over his room. When I told Milt that I was thinking about abandoning my tent, he said: "okay when are we moving?" Now this was only a small, one man, room so we negotiated alternate night occupancy and we used the room when we needed private space to write our periodic reports.

Those reports eventually became a sore point for me and I'll break into this narrative to tell that story now. Various elements of the Army soon became interested in what we were doing "over there" and the Aviation Center at Fort Rucker was the principle agency concerned with the aviation piece. We spelled out our actions in quarterly reports. We noted our accomplishments and lessons learned in detail. The MAAG then classified the reports and sent them on. It was a little disconcerting to soon read them, de-classified and covered, often word for word, in the Army Aviation Magazine under a Fort Rucker officer's name. But with an old wooden bladed fan turning slowly overhead as it tried to move the sodden air over our sweating bodies and with big bugs on the floor and green lizards (Geckos) on the ceiling, Milt and I worked hard on most of the very words that were used in those early "*Vietnam Reports*."

Cherne said he would come to work in his dress blues if they got 'em all flyable. Done on 29 Mar & 6 Nov 61 CPT Rudd in front. CWO Nobles, MAJ Dillard, CPT Klippel & CPT Leon Curry, Opns Officer in March.

1st Platoon mid 1961. Huey Nelson, Knight, Bob Ziegler behind Bill Brethour, Ace Ellett, Charley Larkin, Bill Smith & CWO Jim Crabtree playing with his Yakima exercise 'stash. We all had them for a short time.

CH-21C SHAWNEE over the Nisqually Flats, Fort Lewis, Washington
29 March 1961 alerted for deployment to Laos we guessed. We rattled the windows over post headquarters.

We did it again on 6 November 1961 as we let the 4th Infantry Division know that we were indeed leaving without them and we began our "exercise in excess of thirty days."

US Information Service Library on corner, Rex Hotel & Theater with cyclo and Renault Blue & White Taxi

The most convenient bar across from the Rex

The Caravelle Hotel on Opera House Square

(Authors collection)

The Gia Long Palace government office building – at the head of the square by the Rex Hotel

The ubiquitous Renault Blue & White Taxis flock around the streets of town.

The Doc Lap Presidential Palace after the February 1962 bombing with one wing gone – from as close as they would let me get.

(Authors collection)

The Continental Palace street level open air bar under the awnings – the favorite hangout for American entertainers and other such visitors. Looking up Tudo Street from Le Loy Plaza.

The Opera House on Le Loy Plaza; then looking down the street past "Cheap Charley's" Restaurant on the corner; they served great chicken soup – at least it tasted just like chicken - and on to the river.

(Authors collection)

The Street of Flowers fills with blooms in season for several blocks from the circle by the Rex to the river.

Tudo Street shoppers and walkers

Tudo "Freedom" Street – formerly Rue Catinat

Lei Loy sidewalk with peddlers, Diners & shoppers

(Authors collection)

Although none appear to be present in this picture, the Americans called this Tudo sidewalk café the Bird Watcher's Corner. Maybe the cyclo driver is taking a break with his friends.

Sidewalk Howard Johnson soup kitchens came in all shapes and sizes – and all around the town

(Authors collection)

CWO Len Wilson, 1LT Bill Hinds, CPT Doc Meilke, The Boss MAJ Milt Cherne',
1LT Bill Brethour, CWO Big Jim Eakins, CWO Quintin Dunbar, CWO-3 Bennie Potts, just off the boat
in our old French built hanger at Tan Son Nuht with pill box hats and the creases still in their pants

CPT Ray Houts & CWO Dave Saylor scouting out the bars.
There is the infamous Bam E Bam & Formaldehyde beer.

Dave again, me and Doc Meilke at a party.
VNAF invite – don't know where we found
the white shirts. *(Authors collection)*

(U. S. Army Photograph)

Our tough looking boss. The picture that hung in the Pentagon E-ring mis-identified as a USMC pilot.

His not so near as tough looking Ops Officer, but at least I wasn't called a Marine. *(Authors collection)*

ABC in a pensive mood at our first airport mess hall in the hanger where we watched them bomb the palace. *(Authors collection)*

MAJ Cherne' tries to explain something to LT Formica at the wall map in operations. *(U. S. Army Photograph)*

Me keeping an eye on Sal Formica and others. Giff Gifford happy to see UTT. Close up of XO Bob Webb.

Me & Charley Larkin hit the streets in Muc Hoa. An intrepid advisor, Sal and me at Tan Son Nuht.

(Authors collection)

Tent City at Tan Son Nuht with Willy J. Williams shading his eyes. Several weeks here until more permanent structures were built. The wood benches out front are wash stands, Army style. We all acquired bamboo beds, foam rubber mattresses and mosquito nets. All that was missing was closets.

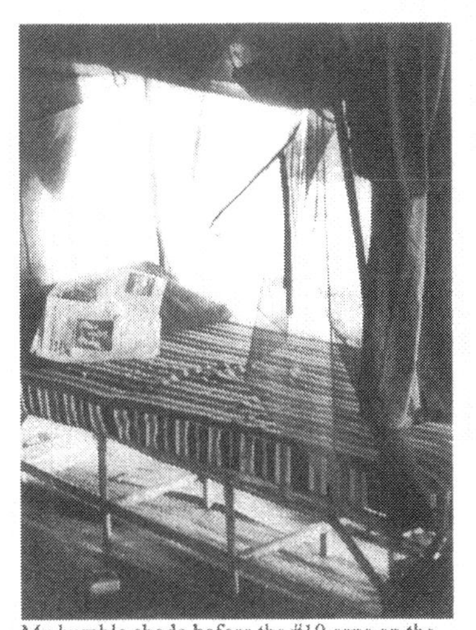

My humble abode before the #10 cans on the legs of the bed. The sharp edge was said to discourage snakes and varmints.

The first Shawnee Tepee. We had already traded something for VC flags and weapons. Everyone chipped in to Buy the tables and chairs. *(Authors collection)*

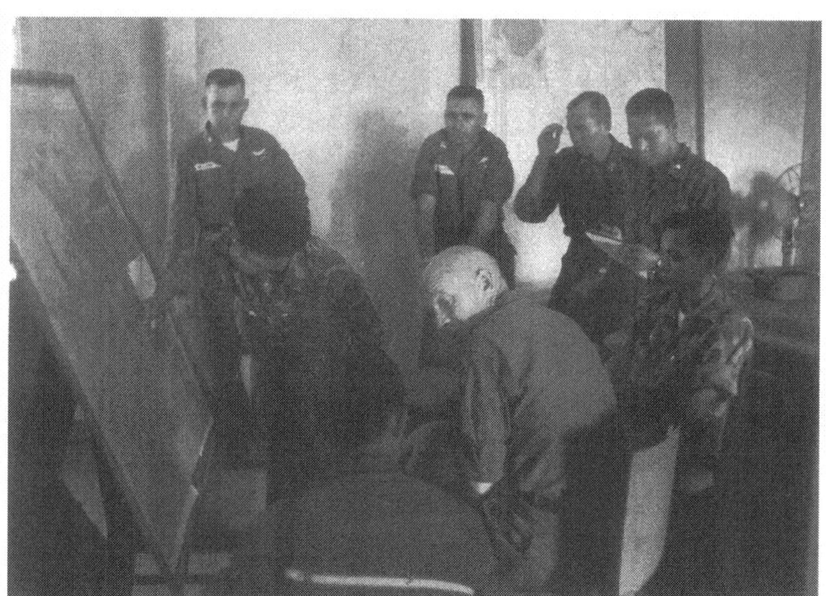

Planning Group at the RVN Airborne Brigade for the first few missions. Clockwise from top left: MAJ Dillard, me, MAJ Goodson S-3 Advisor, RVN MAJ An S-3, two unknown RVN operations officers, LTC Stockton, unnamed CIA guy.

A light load of soldiers headed out.

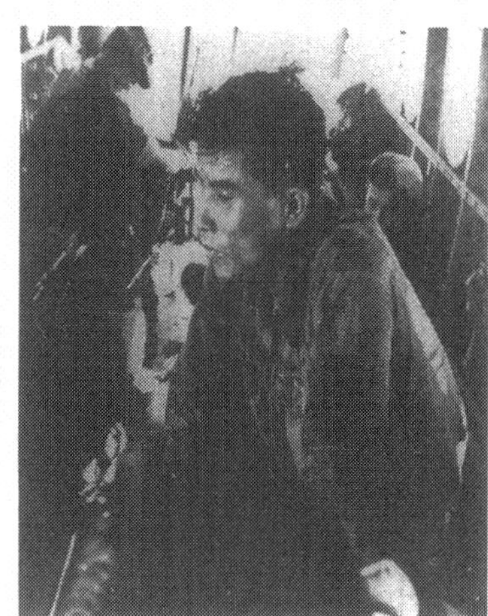

And back. *(U. S. Army Photographs)*

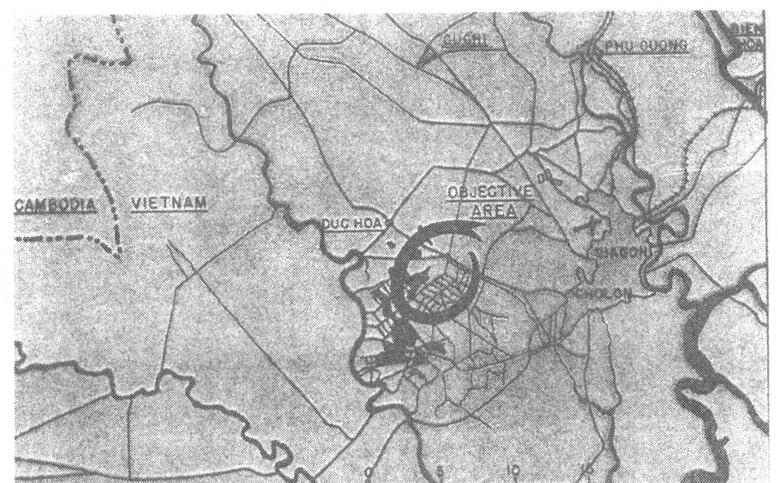

These are from the original briefing material to be used with 1: 50000 maps. Scale in miles at bottom. Objective blow up shows arrows for flight approach, landing and departure from pineapple fields The black areas indicate the river and "avoid" probable enemy positions – not to scale.

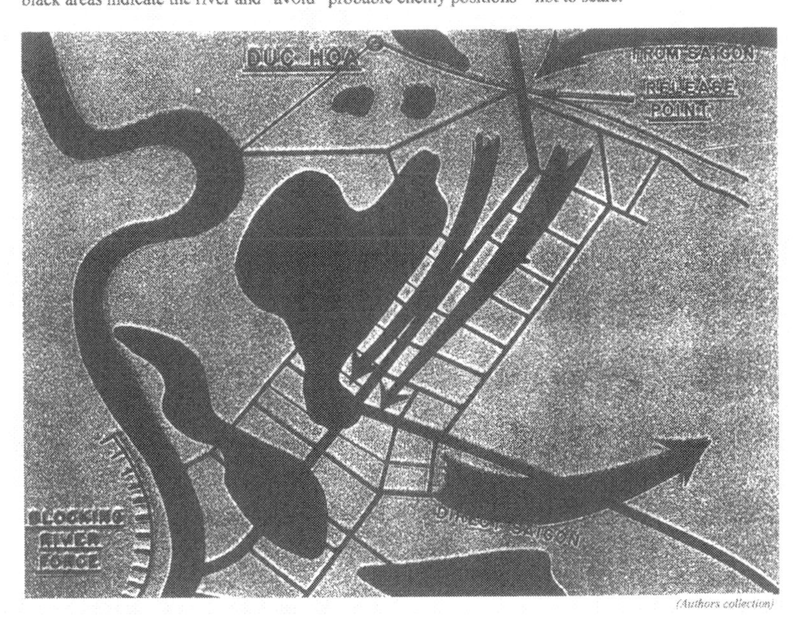

(Authors collection)

Echelon Right – eight out of ten, caught just right over the Mekong Delta. *(U. S. Army Photograph)*

We didn't wear the bush hats very long – just had To try 'em out Soon lost the crease in the trousers too.

Training RVN a first big task. CWO Dick Parsons Instructs through an interpreter. *(Authors collection)*

We started with hand held weapons at the doors, then added 1918A1 .30 caliber machine Guns at the forward door. I think this is Crew Chief SP-5 Odis D. Henley with the automatic sub machine gun.

SP-5 Leon B. Talley on the .30 caliber Gun

An Army of Vietnam soldier awaits the assault

(U. S. Army Photographs)

A composite mission.

(U. S. Army Photographs)

The boss talks with pilots. From the left: CWOs Billy J. Williams, Giff Gifford, Frank Frost, Don Beachnau Huey Nelson, Len Wilson, CPT Bill Smith, CWOs Bob Ziegler, Big Jim Eakins, Willy Williams behind Walt Sabey. From the left hunkered down: CPTs Bob Webb, Ray Houts and MAJ Milt Cherne'.

Same Discussion: Houts and Gifford now standing. CWO Bennie Pots hunkered down and Willy Williams where you can see him.

(U. S. Army Photographs)

"Ruff-Puff" ready to load up for a third lift – Crew chief with stick to get positive measure of fuel remaining.
Regional Forces & Popular Forces = Ruff Puffs in G. I. talk. SP-6 Carl Green helps them aboard

XO CPT Bob Webb marks grid coordinates with CPT Ray Houts, U. S. advisors and RVN leaders

(U. S. Army Photographs)

Another two ship mission to another jungle fort. *(Authors collection)*

The Rubber near Ben Cat with its protective trench. Friend or foe on the trail? Anybody's guess.

(Authors collection)

Lunch call: From the left: LT Rod Magie, CWOs Ken Donley, Don Youngblood, CPT T C West, Dick Smith, me and Giff Gifford in the back, CWO Charley Larkin and CPT Dick Bastion lead the parade.

Time / Life stringer Mert Perry with TC and Larkin enjoy lunch in the shade of a Shawnee.

Dick Bastion looks off as Charley and I have our Normal after mission critique. *U. S. Army Photographs)*

We were happy to see the armed UH-1 arrive and Cherne' briefed the USMC into Vietnam

CWO Bennie Potts receives the first Air Medal actually awarded in Vietnam. BG Stilwell and 45th Bn Cmdr LTC Howard Richardson discuss the design of the MAAC-V patch before the colonel lit his pipe.

(Authors collection)

The blades are still coned up as we settle old 208 into a Shawnee sized hole in an overgrown paddy. The blades have stopped without striking water or weeds. Someone was watching because we are still in the cockpit – unable to move no doubt on this my last flight in the 57th during late November 1962.

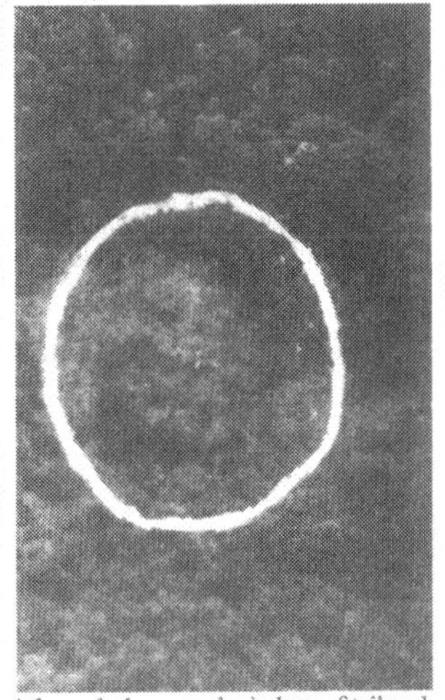

See if you can find the helicopter in the circle to the right pictured through the crazed window of tail end Charley. It is the one down in a low spot of the jungle that the B-26 destroyed for us. What fun.

(Authors collection)

(U. S. Army Photograph)

GEN Hamlett, Army Vice Chief of Staff congratulates me at the 1963 AAAA convention as Aviator of the Year for which the pilots and maintenance people standing with CPT Bill Rudd were largely responsible.

(Authors collection)

CHAPTER 15

FEBRUARY SURPRISES

The Mekong Delta . . . a vast area of rivers, overflowing canals and flooded rice paddies; with few "cities" but many small tree lined villages strung along the canals; the Plain of Reeds to the west, jungle on the far west, north and east; deep mangrove swamps lying to the southeast between the many mouths of the Mekong tributaries.

Those early flights to Father Hoa's village could be hazardous to your health. These weren't combat assaults. They were resupply runs but there was plenty of VC activity on the way. We staged operations out of Ca Mau, which had a short dirt runway and was about the last place we could refuel, as long as somebody had delivered a little AVGAS. To reduce our exposure over the flat fields, we elected to make the portion of the flight from Ca Mau to the village by contour, flying just a few feet above the ground. By doing so we saved the fuel that would have been expended to climb, at a higher power setting, to a safe altitude and it gave us an element of surprise as we approached Binh Hung. An altitude of three thousand feet was accepted as the lowest flight level needed to avoid effective small arms fire but it took a lot of gas to get there. There was no fuel to be had at Binh Hung and the round trip back to Ca Mau left little reserve, even without the climb.

Father Hoa was a striking individual. He was big even for a Chinese and he looked like the warlord that he was, with his small hardened army deep in the Mekong Delta. He was completely surrounded and cut off from the ARVN and Saigon by well organized VC units operating below Ca Mau. In addition these units were supported by a particularly large and ugly bunch of VC located in the forested U Minh Mountains near the western edge of the peninsula.

There is a town out there named Rach Gia, which oddly enough is pronounced "Rock Jaw." We left that place alone during the early going. The ARVN didn't want to go there and that was fine with us. The entire Mekong Delta from Rach Gia south was hotly contested anyway, so we were getting plenty of attention on our flights to Binh Hung. Much later, towards the end of 1962, an assault was made from Rach Gia into the U Minh Forest. The 57th lost a helicopter on that operation but at least all the helicopter crews returned okay.

Binh Hung was situated along a canal, as were most villages in the delta, and was surrounded by rice paddies; at this season flooded with water. There were few spots where one could find dry land to off-load rice or other supplies. Since we were scheduled to make repeated trips, Father Hoa decided to build a helipad for our use. This gave rise to a memorable incident. When we first landed a two ship flight on that brand new pad, it appeared to be ready. The mud had been piled up, leveled out and it looked solid. In addition to the supplies, we had carried in some RVN dignitaries. We pilots were invited to go to lunch with the group. Things looked okay so we shut down the helicopters. While we were gone, they sank slowly down in the mud. We returned from town, with the entire village in tow, to see our big old Shawnee stuck in the mud up to the belly. The other ship was still not too bad but ours was in about over the landing gear wheels.

There are a couple of ways to get a Shawnee unstuck from the mud and brought to a hover. The danger is that one gear will loosen while the other remains mired. If that happens, the helicopter can roll over on you. You can wiggle the landing gear gently, while pulling up carefully and if things work out okay, you're on your way. We tried that. It didn't work. The crowd watched and drew closer while we tried the gentle method and they could see that there was a problem.

The other way to get out of the mud is to pull straight up on the collective with full power but then there may be an even greater danger of a roll-over. I wanted the crowd out of the way before we tried that one so I leaned out the window to wave them away. They just moved closer. That wasn't going to work, so I told the crew chief to get out and have them move back; well away from the helicopter. He tried but without much success, instead the whole bunch of them raced over to the helicopter where they grabbed ahold of the landing gear and pushed up on the fuselage. About a hundred Chinamen were planning to lift that eighty-six foot of helicopter out of the mud and into the air. We had to go find an interpreter to get 'em to let go.

We shouldn't make fun of them though. A few years later, when I was flying CH-34 helicopters in Europe, I found that an American GI could be just as confused by something new to them. The CH-34 cockpit is positioned high up, and directly over, the large main landing gear. A soldier can stand on the wheel where he can talk directly to the pilot. Out on maneuvers with the 3rd Armored Division one day, a soldier on the ground beside the helicopter indicated that he wanted to talk to me. I told the crew chief to have him climb up on the wheel. The crew chief pointed to the wheel so the GI leaned down close to the hub, cupped his hands around his mouth and shouted: "hey pilot" at the wheel.

The surprise that can be achieved by contour flight can be very valuable as long as the enemy does not know exactly when you are coming or what route you will take. Even if he does have warning, low level flight lessens his ability to react even if you happen to fly right over him. When you first hear a helicopter approaching it is very difficult to tell exactly where the noise is coming from. You can get a general idea, but the direction and therefore the route of flight is hard to establish. It didn't take the VC long though, to put out a paper diagram showing their fighters how to narrow this problem down. The diagram instructed them on the proper use of terrain and how to make a rudimentary underground funnel apparatus that might help a soldier more closely identify the direction of an approaching helicopter so as to give them a shot at it. We didn't realize, at this early stage, just how crowded with VC this lower peninsula was nor how well organized they could be. They had yet to show that they were able to do us too much damage. We started learning the hard way on the fourth of February when we lost our first helicopter to proven ground fire. Chalk One, the lead helicopter in the flight, was hit.

Since there was no such thing as Search and Rescue available, one of the first rules we had established was that the ship flying immediately behind one that went down would go in to evacuate the crew. It was also ordered that all the weapons and the ammunition on the downed aircraft would come out with them. The day that Chalk One went down we had not yet picked up the ground troops. We were flying in the number two position. We immediately went in after the crew.

The flight was in a staggered trail formation which placed the lead just to our right front at eighty knots airspeed and very low level. Although we didn't know what had happened until later, chalk one had picked up a .30 caliber round, dead center through the forward pylon, where it hit and knocked off a cyclic control link. This took away most, if not all, pilot control. The forward rotor system began to climb and the helicopter began to roll. As we watched, the nose of the helicopter rose rapidly upward until it looked like the aircraft would tumble clear over on its own tail. It had also rolled hard to one side. When it reached a near upside down position, the "dog link" control rod must have fallen back into position briefly, or something else happened, because the crew was able to regain enough control to roll it upright and auto-rotate to the ground. It landed on its wheels and we touched down right beside it.

Platoon Leader, Bill Hinds and CWO Robert L. Eastland, had been flying the stricken ship. My ops sergeant, Jim McAndrew, was the assigned gunner. Although I didn't know it at the time, CPT Jack Hutchinson, from the newly arrived 45th Battalion Headquarters, was also aboard. We used to call Bob Eastland "Farmer Eastland" because of the way he managed to wear his uniform and his slow, deliberate way of moving; but he sure moved right out that time. He was the first one of the crew to climb aboard our helicopter; seems like he was leaning out of our forward cargo door urging the others to hurry-on before the rotors stopped turning on the downed ship. The "Guest" Captain, who had hitched a ride at the last minute and the crew chief didn't need any urging; they were right behind him. Just before take-off in Saigon, CPT Hutchinson had decided that he would be the gunner for the lead ship. He didn't bother to tell anybody either. He wanted to get an early start on heroism I guess but it didn't take him long to abandon ship when the time came.

The next thing we see are Hinds and McAndrew, huddled down in the long grass of the small clearing, having a conference. Now there was shootin' from the edge of the jungle going on and it seemed like a hell of a place to be discussing the weather; but then, as we watched in amazement, McAndrew high tails it back to the downed helicopter while Hinds continues to crouch in the grass. Although I didn't figure it out at the time, what with all the noise and tension, McAndrew had gone back to retrieve the machine gun. SGT McAndrew was the assigned machine gunner, but he had been ordered off the gun, after the flight was in the air, so that this uninvited officer could take his place. What could he do? This was a Captain; senior even to the pilots. But what the Captain didn't realize was that McAndrew had half loaded the machine gun. And what McAndrew didn't know was that the Captain had done it again. So the gun was fully loaded with a round in the chamber; ready to fire and nobody knew it. Since this self appointed gunner had failed to bring the gun with him, McAndrew had gone back to get it. Being naturally in a hurry, he just separated the ammo belt down a few rounds, so when he jerked the weapon out of the gun mount and turned to leave, his fingers hit the trigger. He put six rounds through the empty pilot's seat.

Now we had what sounded like a war going on out there as McAndrew dropped down beside Hinds again to explain what had happened. It seemed to me like a damned poor time for more discussion, so I got up out of my cockpit seat, went to the forward cargo door and drew my pistol! Then, leveling my forty-five well above their heads I let loose a round. When they turned startled looks in my direction, I crooked my finger in the "come hither" sign. They got the message and proceeded to get aboard. That was the first and only shot that I fired in anger during my tours in Vietnam. Once in a while though, I might have mentioned to a gunner that he should fire. I have an Air Medal for "meritorious achievement" for that little ruckus. Meritorious achievement my arse, but that was before we were judged by higher headquarters to be in combat. They weren't being shot at in downtown Saigon and they still weren't willing to believe that we were. We weren't at war and it is hard to be valorous in someone else's war.

As a result of this event and the other lessons we were learning, we cleaned up our procedures again. The boss normally elected to fly well towards the rear of the flight. This position was considered to be one of the most likely places to get hit, and it allowed him to view the flight in progress. A Maintenance officer always flew tail-end-Charley. This was so that he could land to assist an aircraft on the ground with mechanical problems without disrupting the rest of the formation. Now we also recognized that the lead helicopter might be forced down, for one reason or another, and that someone familiar with the details of the mission had to be ready to take over the flight.

That person should be someone who had been intimately involved in the planning so that he could take over the lead without hesitation. This meant that one "planner" should be leading the flight and another planner should be flying the number three helicopter. The idea being that if the lead ran into trouble, and the number two aircraft went in for the pick-up, the crew of the number three helicopter could continue the mission uninterrupted. We had known that before of course, but we just hadn't thought it clear through and actually specified the proper flight positions. As the ops officer this caused me to almost always be flying in the lead or number three position but that was okay with me. I had good officers to help with the planning and man the office, so if I wasn't hog tied by some other problem, I preferred to fly.

Proof of this arrangement was not long in coming. We had flown only a few more missions supporting Father Hoa's little army when we had another one go down near where the first one had been shot down. This time it was Don Herman who found himself unexpectedly grounded in the middle of an unfriendly rice paddy. Flying with him that day was good old instructor pilot Benny Potts. Knowing Benny as I do, I expect he was just riding along watching the scenery go by while Don did all the work. But when the engine quit, and things got quiet, Benny quickly grabbed the controls and managed to pull just enough pitch to milk the powerless ship over a tree line and onto the ground before anything more broke. Benny later got an Air Medal for that exemplary bit of flying.

The following helicopter, Chalk Two, went in to evacuate the crew. We, in Chalk Three, continued the mission while making radio arrangements to secure the downed aircraft. Tail End Charley landed on the way back to try to determine the extent of the problem. This time things worked out properly. A senior U.S. advisor to the III Corps

Headquarters in Saigon was along for the mission. He was very complimentary to us for being able to continue the assault without interuption, but he was, as usual, less than happy with the results of the ground effort because few VC were home to eventually be attacked. Almost all were gone before we could get the reinforced battalion in to the pending fight. Three VC and about ten pounds of documents were picked up; hardly seemed worth the effort.

Again a full maintenance crew had to be brought in to recover the helicopter. Helicopters were going down right and left. If quick fixes were not possible, we would arrange some kind of overnight security and teams led by either Bill Rudd or Ken Klippel would arrive in the morning to manage the emergency repairs. This usually entailed slinging in a new engine, dropping the failed one out of the downed helicopter, and then installing the new one, in the middle of the rice paddy mud. The old engine would be lifted out right away with the repaired helicopter following as soon as it could. This would all be going on while the team was under the immediate threat of enemy action; sometimes it turned out be actual action with fire from an adjacent tree line or village. Dave Saylor brought the new engine in this time and then slung the old one out. As Dave said later: "with a 2500 pound load hanging down like a yo-yo, I wasn't able to take much evasive action."* Those unglamorous maintenance tasks were not without risk.

They say that bad things always seem to happen in threes. That may be true; at least it must have felt so to Bill Hinds. His second shoot down, and the second one for the 57th, occurred while he and Blair Hileman were returning from a troop training mission. A .30 caliber round hit a rotor blade retaining cuff which caused a very heavy vibration and then a wild ride to get the helicopter on the ground. Neither of them said much to me about it at the time, or maybe I was already getting a little jaded and didn't pay enough attention, but it must have been a good landing. They walked away from it.

The third bad thing came soon for Bill Hinds, he would be there to get the next big scare for the company. One afternoon we got a call that a VNAF T-28 had gone down in the South China Sea, just off of the seaside resort of Vung Tau. As was usually the case, a

USAF "round eye" had been fying one seat. The Air Force initiated an immediate search and requested our help. We established a grid pattern search at low level while the Air Force continued their pattern at a slightly higher altitude. As evening approached, and darkness began to really inhibit the search, we reluctantly began to call things off. Unfortunately no survivors had been found.

Bill was flying one of the last helicopters to start home, while I was in the other one of the pair, when we pulled up to altitude. We had no commo with the fixed wing aircraft operating in the same area (no commo! but that is another story). We were well on our way, at about 1500 feet, when the USAF decided to give up too. At that time, one of the T-28 drivers chose to do a chandelle (high speed turning "showoff" climb) from the surface to his cruising level. The airplane was nearly inverted when it passed between our helicopters on the way up. Obviously the pilot didn't realize we were even there, but it looked to me like he had passed right through Bill's rotor disc. Close! Close to a mid-air collision. It is little wonder that Bill became a tiny bit antsy for a while, after that third close call.

We continued to fly missions and develop procedures as we went along. We didn't have "a book" as Milt would say, "we were writing the book!" The long flights to Father Hoa's village were wearing out the crews. It placed them uncomfortably close to fuel exhaustion before they could get back to a refueling source. To make things a little more interesting, all helicopters do not burn fuel at the same rate. Red lights were coming on too often. I felt it necessary to warn the pilots to be careful in their flight planning because if anyone were to run out of gas not only would it be a dangerous situation, but I might personally have to recommend that they be grounded. My timing was exceedingly bad on that one. It had become more and more clear that we would be getting shot at routinely. About a half a dozen pilots informed me that they would like to turn in their wings anyway.

Some of those pilots thought that they had been shot at enough in Korea. Others just didn't like the idea of being targets in the first place and we were all a little dubious about our support of the Republic of Vietnam in their war anyway; especially since they didn't seem to take it too seriously themselves. Well I lost it again and gathered all the pilots together for a briefing; (Some of the pilots alleged that it was really a joint and several ass chewing) where I reminded them that they had all been accepting flight pay for a number of years, without reservation about when or where they would fly, and "what the hell did they think; just because they were now getting shot at did they think that they could simply decide to quit flying?" I assured them that I would recommend disapproval of any such application, and that I'd be sure that anyone who tried to turn in their wings would get to fly as much or more than anyone else. Cherne' was silent during this tirade, but he told me later that he thought that I had always talked too quietly and that this was the first time he had really heard me use my "command voice." No one ever mentioned the subject again. No one actually tried to quit. All of our pilots went on to do a fine job of flying for the rest of the year and most of them came back for later tours. Maybe they were just testing me.

On the twenty-seventh of February 1962, we witnessed a series of large explosions downtown when a pair of unhappy VNAF pilots, flying USAF supplied AD-6 aircraft, decided to bomb the palace. We had established a temporary mess hall at a hanger over by the VNAF helipad at Tan Son Nuht, and some of us were there when the air raid started, so we climbed up on nearby trucks to watch as the two ground attack planes made repeated passes at their target. That was before they turned and aimed straight at us. Needless to say we all abandoned our elevated perches and ducked for cover. The show was soon over though. They made a couple of low passes over the airfield and then departed towards Cambodia. We learned later that the bombs they dropped had blown a large hole in one wing of the palace but had missed the ruling family almost entirely. The Dragon Lady had gotten a scratch from flying glass and it is perhaps a shame that that was all it was. Madame Nhu had been, and would continue to be, a pain in everyone's ass. She seemed to exert far too much influence over the others in the palace. She often operated loudly on her own and in contention with everyone else. Her distain for Americans was already very apparent.

As the shooting ended we all hurried back to the hanger. I headed for the operations phone. I was anxious to get on the horn with MAAG headquarters to ask a serious question; just whose side were we on anyway? And after this surprising example of Vietnamese airmanship we also decided that we had better spread out the helicopters on the parking ramp. Pilots moved some of the Shawnees into the infield, between the ramp and the runway, where at least they wouldn't get 'em all on one pass. Others were picking up weapons and getting into flight gear. We had decided we would move our aircraft to Vung Tau if necessary, so flight leaders were gathering maps and assigning crews. Soon, CWO Quintin R. Dunbar came in from the ramp. Q was holding a hot .30 caliber bullet and he was yelling loudly that the spent round had taken a gouge out of the pavement near his feet, and that it had damn near taken his head off, before it bounced again off of the ceiling of the hanger. Well, the operations office was a little busy right then so nobody paid any attention to him. He finally threw the bullet on the floor and turned around to leave saying "Screw you guys. I almost got killed and nobody gives a damn." (The words are not exact but you get the idea.)

I was still holding on to the phone trying to talk to somebody, anybody, and looking down the approach road, when a heavily armed VNAF airman started coming toward us. He was carrying a heavy automatic weapon at parade rest and had an ammo belt looped around his shoulder. As he marched steadily closer, our guys looked around and started to notice him. Now we were all were getting a little nervous. When he got close enough that I could have thrown the phone at him, I really began to wonder whose side we were on. At that point he turned around and faced back down the road the way he had come. We guessed that someone had sent him over to protect us. Later, Nguyen Cao Ky, commander of the air base, drove his jeep up to reassure us that everything was all right. Well that made us feel a little better, but it was still a long while before we were able to get anything out of the MAAG; in fact, I don't think we ever did. Needless to say, we quickly developed an evacuation plan, so that we could get ourselves and our helicopters out of harms way, were this sort of thing to become commonplace.

Q Dunbar, the guy with the near miss bullet, and I used to fly together fairly often. We got along well and made a good team in the cockpit, but Q was getting a little nervous about the arrangement. It seems like we were taking our share of hits although none of them came through the cockpit and they had missed all the people in the box. One of the American reporters we saw fairly often was Francois Sully of Newsweek. We saw all of the reporters, because if they wanted to go very far out of Saigon, they all came around looking for a ride. They were always extra passengers so we used to call them "strap hangers." One day Sully was strap hanging along with Q and me as we headed for another isolated French fort. It was out in the periphery of the jungle northeast of Saigon and we were again hauling tax collectors or something.

The first thing that went wrong was when we landed in the middle of the minefield surrounding the place. No one had mentioned this little obstacle; they never did. The SD did have people out to greet us and they had laid out panels to guide our landing. The problem was that they had no idea how much room it required to land two large Shawnee helicopters. They had placed the panels right up against the mud walls of the place, just inside of their rudimentary warning fence. We had seen these before; no sweat, but it was pretty tight inside that fence. Naturally, we had no commo available to discuss the situation with them. We elected to land outside the wire where there appeared to be a nice level open field. We touched down and lowered the collective pitch stick. We didn't get it all the way down, because right away we noticed, that our welcoming committee had started to leave the area. Actually they were stumbling all over themselves; some were even running away.

This was the first known 57th encounter with a minefield. Nobody had mentioned minefields. If we had thought about them at all, we would have expected any mines to have been laid between the warning wire and the walls of the fort; not outside. It was pretty obvious however, that something was wrong here. We initially figured that the SD soldiers must have thought that they were about to be run over by a giant praying mantis appearing helicopter, but I called the other ship, and our crew chief, and told them to not let anybody get off the helicopter, while we tried figure out what was going on.

After about thirty seconds, we saw that there were what appeared to be, fragmentation grenades hanging off the fence, which was oscillating back and forth right next to the cockpit. "Well damn!"

(That's not exactly what I said.) I thought that we must have landed in a minefield, and that the pins on those grenades were probably meant to be pulled out, if anything moved the wire. The downwash from our rotating blades was moving that fence around a lot. Now the next question was: "how do we get out of here?" It didn't seem like such a good idea to just shut it down and hope nothing exploded. We would then have to walk out of there. Pilots don't like to walk anyway, particularly in minefields. We just looked at each other, then with few words, it was agreed that we would do a max power takeoff and try to outrun any fragments. We were still holding some power and pitch in the blades. There were no loud noises under us as we lifted off. Whew! The next time we came in we scouted around to find some tight Shawnee sized spots inside the wire. Another lesson learned.

The visiting firemen got out to do their business and Sully went with them. Q and I sat around waiting for them, while we got rid of the shakes and planned the best exit route. Generally that had to be into the wind and over the lowest trees in the surrounding jungle. Some smart VC must have figured that out, or maybe he was just lucky, or maybe the bad guys were all over the place. Anyway, we picked up a round on the way out. It came up through the cargo compartment floor, peeled up the toe of Sully's right boot and grazed past his ear before exiting out the side. That was the only time that I ever saw anyone kiss the ground. When we got back to Saigon, Sully jumped out of the helicopter and did just that. He had already been kicked out of Vietnam by President Diem so this was to be his last big adventure before he left the country. Ah well! He had planned a big party to celebrate his leaving and Q and I, along with our whole crew, got an invitation. It was a hell of a party.

It is hard to believe, but after this mission, Q refused to fly with me any more. He claimed that I was a "goddamn magnate ass and every time he flew with me we got hit." It didn't seem to me that we were getting hit any more then anyone else but I did find a chunk of a frag grenade lying under my feet after that job. It was about an inch in diameter but I don't know how the hell it got into the cockpit. We couldn't find any holes and all the windows were there. Of course they were all open and so were the cargo doors. I kept this little souvenir and it is probably still around here someplace.

CHAPTER 16

ABLE, BAKER, CHARLEY, DOG

Like I said, I was going to name this the Vietnam Joke Book, because we knew it was a joke, but weren't sure just who the joke was on, but that was not the only reason. It's the ABCDs that top my memory list; the Accidents, the Buffoonery, the Comedy and the Damn-foolishness. And of course, the people involved in them; often myself included.

Things soon began to get routine; not that they all of a sudden became unexciting, but we settled down to a method of operation that made things fairly predictable. We could now allow our flight platoons and the maintenance teams to have some idea of what was planned for the morrow. We could outline what would be likely to happen on the next day and for a few days into the future. And we eventually moved into a more permanent cantonment area. The standard army canvas tents were replaced with wood and screen buildings. These were about the same size as the tents had been, but they were a little cooler and more civilized. A concrete block combination wash building and toilet facility was erected. Separate buildings became the headquarters / orderly room combo, and the mess hall. The officers club, "The Shawnee Teepee," was reopened in another one. Similar club facilities were provided for our enlisted members and a chapel was planned and opened before we finished the tour. This continued to be the base for the 57th, and when it was redesignated, the 120th Air Mobile Company, for the duration of the war. By the time we moved into these new improved digs, our leaders' characteristics were well known and various personalities in the company had begun to take more definite shape.

LTC Dillard didn't hang around long enough to get his share of CWO humor. They had gotten him with the mike button hat, and they found one more opportunity before he left. Our jeeps had finally gotten properly licensed to drive; all fixed up with official Vietnamese license plates, and Dillard was driving himself back from a meeting down at the MAAG compound one day, when he sideswiped a local bicycle rider. The main streets were always crowded with all kinds of conveyances, not just bicycles, so the accident was understandable. Fortunately, the damage to the bicycle was minor, if any, and there were not even any scratches on the jeep; no one was hurt. The boss settled the matter out of court on the spot. Some piasters changed hands and everyone went away happy. He did not, however, advertise the incident when he arrived back at the airfield. I don't remember who was riding with him that day, but whoever it was must have let the cat out, because the next morning the jeep appeared with a little red bicycle painted on the front fender.

When Dillard left, Milt Cherne' took over and he seemed to me to be a fine commander. I particularly liked that he left us subordinate leaders alone to do our jobs and his critiques were usually on target and never harshly delivered. Milt was of medium height, with outstanding military bearing, as they used to say on officers efficiency reports. His uniform was somehow always clean and pressed. He worked well with the reporters that started to hang around and he looked good in their pictures. Although Milt rarely smoked, a photo of him sitting in the cockpit with a big cigar clamped in his teeth came out looking suitably fierce, so it found a place on the "E" ring wall of the Pentagon for a number of years. The "E" ring is where the big wheels sit. You know, like the Secretary of Defense and others of that ilk. As a holdover from his cavalry days I guess, he often carried a swagger stick made from a 50 caliber shell casing which was attached by an aluminum rod to the 50 caliber bullet at the tip. He was also very weight conscious.

Our Doc, new to the army, did not exhibit these characteristics. Doc Meilke was sorta soft and rumpled. His uniform always resembled an unmade bed. He usually appeared in public with his shirt tail hanging out, his tummy hanging over his belt and his pockets unbuttoned. The pockets, in particular, used to bug Cherne'. He would use his swagger stick to flip up the pocket flaps on the Doc's shirt saying something like "better button up Doc." Well Meilke was a fine doctor. He did not intend to remain a soldier, but he always scrambled to comply each time this happened. I felt sorry for him and I had gained some insight into the boss by then. I knew that he took pride in his appearance and was always aware of his physical condition. I recommended to Meilke, that he should carry one of those little wooden tongue depressors in his pocket, and the next time Cherne' poked him with his swagger stick, he should play like a doctor; take out the depressor, tell Milt that he didn't look well and ask him to stick out his tongue. Well that seemed to do the job; the dual of the swagger stick and the tongue depressor was soon over.

That swagger stick got me in trouble once in a while too. I often had to go by III Corps Hq to get instructions from the senior operations advisor there. LTC Olsen was an easy guy to deal with. He was all business about what helicopter support was to be provided, and his group did the top level mission arrangements with the ARVN division to be supported, but he was careful to not get into the details of the helicopter piece. He understood that the matching of our capability, against the mission desires of the ARVN division and their US advisors, was ours to figure out. One of the few times I ever suffered any adverse feedback from Olsen was when Cherne' decided to go with me to make an occasional visit to III Corps Hq. He would always, of course, stop for a chat with Olsen; never anything significant to discuss, just routine business. The problem was that the boss had the unconscious habit of tapping that swagger stick on the top corner of the Colonel's desk as they talked. Cherne' never noticed the color flare-up start on Olsen's face. He didn't see the set of his mouth get grimmer as the conversation went on. Olsen never said a word about it, until the next time I was in alone to see him, then he'd let loose with a string of words like "why does that goddamn Major keep pounding on my desk with his goddamn swagger stick?"

The boss shared a "hooch" with the Doc, our 98th CHFM boss Ken Klippel, and the 255th Signal Detachment Commander, Ray Hout. One bright day, Ray and the Doc decided to play a little trick on Milt. You know how a military belt was constructed in those days, to allow various lengths to be achieved with the same belt. You could adjust it so that, when it was worn, there would always be the regulation three inches of belt protruding beyond the brass belt buckle.

This was done by clamping the belt fabric, in the rear of the buckle, at the desired length. You just cut off the unneeded length of fabric behind the buckle. Well it occurred to these two geniuses, that if they cut about one-eighth of an inch off that belt and re-clamped it every few nights, while Cherne' slept, he would never suspect a thing, while the belt just got slowly tighter and tighter. Pretty soon Milt started to look like a couple of link sausages tied in the middle and he appeared to be holding his breath all the time. Cherne' was, as I have said, very proud of his physique. He thought he was badly gaining weight, and damn near stopped eating at all, before these two jokesters pointed out that his belt looked like it was trying to strangle him and it seemed to be getting shorter all the time.

It was my habit to always try to keep the commissioned officers from flying together in the same cockpit. The CWOs had more cargo helicopter flying time and were older with more air sense then our young officers. However towards the later stages of the tour, MAJ Cherne' would occasionally decide, at the last minute, that he wanted to fly with me in the lead ship. Usually this worked out okay but I remember one flight when things didn't go as planned. We were taking off from Vinh Long when Cherne' turned out in the wrong direction after take-off. He was aimed directly for a low-lying obstacle in our way before I could react. His recovery was excellent. When I pointed out the error of his ways he just continued in a lazy 180 degree turn to get back on track. This allowed the flight to follow without a hitch. There was just a minor problem though; we had flown through a telephone wire on the turn; no problem we just trailed a long length of commo wire for awhile, but it illustrates the value of attending the briefing and reading the map before a flight. Cherne' rarely seemed to have time to do that. Wires are a constant hazard for low flying aircraft. If you were to try to fly through a power line, made of heavier wire, more tautly strung, you probably would not make it. The incident with Cherne' that day, instantly reminded me of a conflict with a telephone line that I nearly had one day while I was in fixed wing flight school.

My instructor in primary flight school at the time was a laid back, slow talkin, Texan. He used to sit back there in that animated kite we were flying, a soupped up Piper Cub, and throw as much crap in the game as he could. He never said much but, for example, he liked to get ahold of the exposed control cables and sneakily pull on them while the student pilot tried to keep the airplane from turning upside down. He would keep pulling until one of the student's feet was jammed to the wall on a rudder pedal, while the control stick was being held in place by brute force. The student always took too long figuring out what was happening before the instructor would release everything. The airplane would go into some kind of immediate, unplanned, abrupt maneuver. The student pilot then had to try to figure out how to recover from it.

He also loved to give you forced landings. He would pick the worst time and place he could find. He would have made a great Army CH-21C Chief Warrant Officer instructor pilot. One day he chopped the throttle on me. It was no problem because there was a nice forced landing field right in front of me. I just didn't see the telephone wire that was strung across it until I was way down the approach. Then I hesitated about admitting defeat, before adding power. I'll never forget that country boy Texan drawl, just before I added power to go around, when he said "Well you know Bell Telephone Company ain't gonna like this." That statement instantly crossed my mind when Milt snagged the telephone line.

It must be noted here, that Cherne' was a talented writer. Even though very few were getting approved, he pressed higher headquarters in writing, for the awards and decorations he thought we were due and he continued to do so after our "exercise" was over. It is only through his efforts that most of us eventually saw any recognition at all. Benny Potts is the one guy that I remember who actually had an Air Medal awarded to him, in a company formation at Tan Son Nuht. The rest of us waited for months and were never sure that anything was coming our way. There is no doubt in my mind that many crew members who deserved medals never did get any kind of recognition.

And that brings to mind another funny incident. My position, when Benny got his medal, was at the front right hand corner of the troop formation, so I was in just the right place to hear an exchange that took place between our 45th Battalion CO, LTC Richardson, and BG Joe Stillwell Jr., who was the Support Command Commander and

Richardson's boss. The general had pulled Richardson off to one side so he could talk to him about the new Support Command shoulder patch, which was being designed to replace the MAAG Vietnam patch. Now Richardson was a pipe smoker, so as they stood there at ease, he began to fool with his pipe as pipe smokers will do. Stilwell kept talking while Richardson got the pipe going good. Finally the general noticed what was happening; whereupon he told the LTC in no uncertain terms "colonel, I really do not appreciate people smoking a pipe while I am talking to them." What happened next is where it gets funny, because Richardson jerked to near attention as he put the burning pipe in his pocket. The conversation continued while the pocket smoldered and the colonel squirmed.

When we moved into the new cantonment area, Cherne' ordered everyone back on base; no more off post housing. He and his executive officer, CPT Ivan R. (Bob) Webb, stayed very busy establishing the company at our new location and bringing all hands back where we belonged. Bob was one of several pilots that had joined us from the 33rd Helicopter Company. These were volunteers, who climbed aboard the USNS Core in Oakland, just before she up-anchored for parts unknown. With nothing more important to do when they weren't flying, the pilots began to assign nicknames, mostly based on television cartoons, for some of the commissioned officers and for each other. Bob kept his head down in the orderly room so much that he became known as "The Shadow." He was also a very quiet guy so he seldom seemed to be around; sometimes even when he was right there.

Bob was a relatively small, lightweight, officer and he was always very soft spoken. As the XO, his place was normally in the headquarters, where he carried out the many administrative duties necessary to keep the company functioning. He was rarely out on the flight line, or hanging around operations, like the pilots normally did when they were not flying. So hence; The Shadow. Even though tied up at headquarters a good bit, he did his share of flying when he was able and he was known to be a good pilot. My own nickname, by the way, was "Boris." He was the little villainous fella in one of those famous, Rocky and Bullwinkle type, Saturday morning cartoons. Boris had beetle brows and he was always mean and angry looking.

They didn't call me that to my face but I was just like him they said, you know, real even tempered.

As I've previously mentioned, most of the guys did not like the army issued Colt .45 caliber pistol so some of them managed to arrive in country with their own favorite brand of personal weapon. The .45 was the side-arm pilots were supposed to carry. It was intended for use as close-in, self protection, if one were to be forced down in unfriendly territory. The Shadow carried a .357 Magnum, long-barreled revolver, for this purpose. He carried it in a western style holster on his hip. You get the picture: small guy with a big gun. The damn thing reached half way to his ankles. Bob soon acquired another nick name. He was called "Quick Draw McGraw" when he hit the flight line.

The most important job for any XO is to stand in for the boss when he is not around. Once in a while it is necessary for him to make important decisions; sometimes at some personal professional risk. Bob Webb found himself in that position late one night that I will never forget. Remember, at this time we were flying some pretty ragged helicopters, with no flight following of any kind. The USAF had just begun to establish an operations center at Tan Son Nuht but it was not yet up and running. That didn't matter much to us though, because our Very High Frequency (VHF) Army radios were incompatible with Air Force Ultra High Frequency (UHF) radios, so we couldn't talk to them at all anyway. We had Frequency Modulated (FM) radios for internal company air-to-ground commo but these were also of fairly short range. It didn't take but a few miles away from base, before the only commo our helicopters had was with each other, when flying in close formation. Eventually, we traded in our OH-13s for fixed wing, 0-1 Birddogs, into which we jury rigged an Air Force UHF radio. We strapped the radio onto a piece of plywood which we threw into the Birddog cargo compartment. That O-1 would then fly at altitude over the helicopter formation, so we could at least relay to our close air support, during combat assaults.

This, by the way, was the situation throughout that first year. The crew in one helicopter flying alone, either had nobody to talk to, or they were on intercom talking to themselves. It was not unusual to have one of a pair of Shawnees become unflyable. On two ship missions one of them might decide to go no further than some remote rice paddy. When that happened it was up to the crew of the sister ship to take the necessary action to evacuate the crew, protect the aircraft and get the recovery operation started. We saw no reason to expose our air crews to the added risk of single ship operations. It was not yet our war. The MAAG still had on rose colored glasses concerning ground fire, but because of other problems, they had agreed when it was established as policy, that we would not fly single ship missions.

I chose the title for this chapter in order to remind the reader just how long ago we are talking about here. Able, Baker, Charley, Dog has long since faded from use in the Army phonetic alphabet. The early 1960s are now over half a century ago. Any modern helicopter pilot who might happen to read this story would probably be unable to even identify the antique machines we were flying back then. The word primitive might come to mind for anyone thinking about those days. Using helicopters as an integral part of ground combat was just getting started in the1960s. These were not the highly computerized, heavily armed wonders of today that we were flying. You didn't exactly have to hit 'em with a rock to get them to fly, but you did have to touch 'em right to get 'em off the ground. And flying them was the easy part; it was the maintenance guys that had to work the hardest to keep 'em up.

It was usual during full scale assault missions to lose one or two helicopters either to mechanical failure or ground fire. We knew, from experience, that this would often happen, so during assault missions, we tried to lay-on at least one additional "spare" ship. We would station it at the pick up site to help ensure the combat integrity of the ground force when one went down. Our maintenance operations were taxed to the max. The six helicopters on support missions four or five days a week, interspersed with using all of our flyable ships to support combat assaults on the other two or three days per week, was soon established as the maximum amount of flying that our maintenance and supply operations could handle. And that was far more then any helicopter company had ever done before. It was a 24/7 operation to get as many helicopters up as possible for the troop carry missions, but rarely would that be as many as the ARVN ground commanders and their US advisors wanted, so we were very reluctant to waste flying hours.

It is important for troops to be inserted into a combat situation with as much unit integrity as possible. We knew that and responded as best we could, but because of the shortage of helicopter transport, it was usually necessary to make multiple flights to put a battalion on the ground. Turnaround flights had to be made as quickly as possible so that all of the fighting companies would be available in the assault area as quickly as possible. We have covered these points before, but I am mentioning them again here to explain another one of our operational policies. We always needed all of the helicopters we could get for combat assaults. Therefore, we coordinated a policy with the III Corps advisors that we would not fly administrative or logistics support missions on those days when a combat assault was to be flown.

Naturally it would happen when the boss was away. Maybe he had been called back to USARPAC or something. Anyway, he wasn't there to provide us with the usual flank protection against higher headquarters inanities. It started with a late afternoon telephone call from the III Corps advisory staff in which they tasked us to fly a single helicopter mission. We were to transport visiting American dignitaries *and their wives* out of Saigon to receive a briefing at the Bien Hoa airbase. Bien Hoa is not far out of Saigon. But a single ship? To ferry *VIPs with wives*? Over an area where ground fire could be expected, and had been experienced, by those of us who had flown over the route a few times? On a day when we were committed to support a full scale combat assault with already too few available helicopters? This would break most of the rules we had established concerning the commitment of our limited flying assets; even though the rational had been explained, and the policies agreed upon, by our seniors in the MAAG. To limit discussion, they also ordered the flight at the end of the day. The US Army Saigon Warrior staff officers were about to head home. They didn't have to explain breaking the rules which would short change the tactical mission. They obviously didn't want to recognize the added risk involved for the VIPs *with wives.* They knew that they were ignoring our agreed upon and well established policies, but they wanted no discussion with us about that.

I immediately questioned the mission. I asked them to withdraw the requirement, but soon all of the senior officers had departed for their quarters. Our reporting chain of command was still back to the

Sixth United States Army at the Presidio in San Francisco, California. We were in direct support of the MAAG Vietnam with operations primarily in the III Corps area. We got our missions through the III Corps G-3 advisory staff but this was not a command relationship. The operations officer, LTC Olsen, had passed on the mission as requested by MAAG HQ and he felt that he could not modify it. The 57th was on its own because the 45th Battalion Headquarters was not yet in country. Cherne' was gone, so my only remaining avenue was to go talk it over with our company XO, Bob Webb.

We felt that if the mission stood, we would be subject to continued violation of what we considered to be necessary policies. We decided that we could not let the matter rest. We grabbed a jeep and headed downtown to the Brink Hotel where most of the MAAG senior officers were billeted. We found Olsen at the roof-top bar but he refused to budge saying that he wouldn't even talk to us. We then asked to see COL Daniel Boone Porter, the III Corps senior advisor, (That's a hell of a good name for a combat infantry "Bull" Colonel isn't it) but Olsen said that that was impossible as the colonel had gone to bed. He then asked which of us was senior. Bob said that he was so Olsen, the staff officer, pulled him to one side and tried to give him a direct order. He ordered us to fly both the assault and VIP missions as directed. That is when the Shadow showed his true colors. I heard him say "No sir I won't order a single ship flight. Somebody will have to relieve me first and I'm sure they will have to relieve CPT Knight too. I don't know who is next in line but they will probably have to relieve him too."

That didn't end it of course. We next found COL Porter's room number and knocked, but he had obviously gotten a call from the bar, because he wouldn't answer the door. We returned to the roof, where Olsen said that we should go see Col Del Bristol. He said that he had already called him to tell him we were coming. Bristol was a very senior Army Aviator who, for some reason, was in-country for a few days. He had no direct say in the matter, but he was a very well respected officer by all concerned. We were led to believe that the MAAG would abide by whatever he recommended. It was coming up on midnight by the time we got to his hotel room and it was well into the wee hours before we left.

Since I tried to do most of the explaining, most of Bristol's remarks were aimed at my poor attitude. We explained that we generally had one or more helicopter go down for one reason or another, during every assault mission. We were advised that we should ignore that and instead "keep a positive mental attitude." After going back through our rationale in detail, including the degradation of the combat mission planned to kick off in the morning, the lack of adequate communications and the unnecessary risk to the VIP-with-wives passengers, Col Bristol finally agreed. We flew the assault and postponed the VIP flight until the following day when we could properly support it. I'll always remember CPT Webb for his actions during the boss's absence that night. Bob had one more nick name. Sometimes he was referred to as "Deputy Dog." Well he sure was no "Shadow" during that imbroglio. He was a regular Pit Bull Deputy Dog.

Ken Klippel, the 98th CHFM Commander, was also our resident Mormon. He quietly objected to flying on Sundays, but when that was necessary, he did so. He and his assistant, CWO Nobles, and their crew, worked the same long hours, seven days a week, as did all of the maintenance people. Nobles was not a rated pilot, so Ken flew the required test flights and participated in many helicopter recoveries. The remarkable thing to me was that Ken seemed to wear his long underwear at all times; hot, humid or wet, it didn't matter. I never knew that religion, of any persuasion, required such diligence. I only flew with Ken a couple of times, because we were both usually very busy going in different directions, but he was an accomplished pilot and an experienced maintenance test pilot.

He stepped up to one major problem that I especially recall. The wet flight conditions and high humidity began to cause our layed-up wooden rotor blades to de-laminate, and various other repairs were required; you know, like bullet holes. He had made arrangements with the U.S. Army maintenance officer working with Air America, a CPT Nick Stein, to evacuate our damaged blades, for exchange and replacement from the States. Well it wasn't until we were damn near out of rotor blades, that Ken discovered that Stein had just stacked the blades in their shipping cans behind the Air America hanger, where he had forgotten about them. No rotor blades were in the exchange system. Ken quickly decided that they would need to start a program of depot level blade repair immediately. Spec 6 Niles Myers made a name for himself by forming up a small team to do this depot level job. They reglued the de-laminations, and patched the holes in our rotor blades on site. As far as I know, they continued to do that for the entire next year because the supply chain never did catch up.

MAJ Nick Stein is not central to this story, except for this one screw up, but I got to know him well later. We used to run into him in downtown Saigon once in awhile and he had easily the most uncouth mouth on him of anyone I had ever met. And you might remember that I had once worked in the Alaska gold mines where most workmen were pretty crass. About every fourth word out of their mouths averaged four letters. Nick was an obvious screw-up in Saigon. Years later I was running a maintenance battalion in Savannah, GA when Nick showed up on reassignment. The brigade commander called me in and said "I understand you know this guy Nick Stein. I understand he is a nere-do-well. (Those are not exactly the words he used.) He is about to retire. What should I do with him?"

I started back peddling right away but it was too late. Nick came to work for me. We were just getting started with a project we called "shine-em-up." It was late in the war and we were beginning to transfer Hueys, from the active army flight training base, to the National Guard. We had been training Vietnamese but the war was drawing down. The helicopters had been run hard and put up wet. I just knew that any problem with an aircraft that I turned over to the Guard, would escalate up to the Chief of the National Guard, over to the Chief of Staff of the U.S. Army, and then rain down disaster all over my head. I also knew that, in spite of everything, Nick Stein was a competent maintenance officer. I turned the project over to him. I explained it to him in ding-dong-school terms; if Nick wanted to reach retirement, every helicopter we transferred had to be perfect. He did the job and retired shortly thereafter as a Major.

Bill Rudd, our 57th maintenance boss, was a prince. He did the job day in and day out. When the rest of us took a little goof-off time now and then, Bill worked. He managed the repair of our helicopters while many of his senior maintenance sergeants volunteered to fly as gunners and worked double shifts. Engine failures were getting endemic. I don't remember the number of hours before an engine was supposed to get a half life inspection, but none of them seemed to get that far before they had to be changed anyway. The rebuilt engines coming out of the Spartan Company overhaul facility were the worst. They suffered such a high rate of infant failure, that pilots were wary of flying any Spartan overhauled engine with less than 50 hours on it. If it got past 50, it would probably be okay until 85 hours; after that they were watched very carefully. Pilots would scramble to fly an engine that was within those hours of operation. It is a mystery to me how Bill, and the maintenance guys who worked for him, ever kept up. I do remember that when he got an engine overhaul out of Spartan, he didn't just pull it out of the shipping can and install it. He would first have his mechanics tear it back down then reassemble it before it went into a helicopter. So, like the 98th, Bill's guys were forced to do a little depot level work too.

Like Ken, Bill Rudd flew mostly test flights and helicopter recoveries so he didn't get out on very many assault missions. I tell a story on him, which he denies to this day, but it is a true story. For some reason, we shared a cockpit one day. We were flying at low level, out over the Plain of Reeds, heading for a troop pick up at Muc Hoa. When I say "low level," I mean we were cutting a trail through the weeds with our rotor downwash. We had had a couple of months' experience of being shot at by then, but Bill hadn't been out of the test flight pattern at Tan Son Nhut much. We had the windows open and everything was going fine, until some bad guy out there let loose with a good burst of six. Bill looked around kind of startled and said "what the hell was that?" Bill rarely cussed. I said "They're shootin at you, you dumb son of a bitch." (I did cuss on occasion.) Well Bill didn't want to hear any more of that irritating gunfire noise, so he reached up and closed the window.

CHAPTER 17

TASK FORCE SMITH

At the beginning of the Korean Police Action (a forerunner of the Vietnam non-war) there was a task force named Smith. It was named after the American officer leading one of the first small units of U. S. Army resistance to the North Korean invasion of South.

Task Force Smith was a very small outfit which was precipitously thrown into the fight. The force consisted of two infantry companies and some reinforcements which added up to about 540 men. They were equipped with rudimentary anti-tank weapons including some 75mm recoilless rifles and a few bazookas. They had 60mm mortar and .30 caliber machine gun sections. They used these meager weapons to harass the North Korean Army, including several Russian provided T-34 tanks, that was high-balling down the main highway through Seoul. The task force had very little to fight with; only light infantry weapons. They were heavily out-manned and out-gunned. So they pulled back in good order. They are now heroes in Korea because this was the first American unit to come to the aid of the South Koreans in 1950 and they slowed the enemy advance until U.S. Infantry Divisions could get to the war.*

We were early on the scene in Vietnam too, with about the same number of troops between the 8th and the 57th and our equipment that was just about as obsolete as that first U.S. Korean task force too, but the similarity ends there. Our Task Force Smith was a lot different. In our case it was just the First Platoon Commander, CPT Bill Smith, and the task was the one he presented for us. It started back at Fort Lewis, when our IPs were having trouble getting him through transition and flying well enough, to be qualified to carry passengers in the CH-21C. As the

Operations Officer, I was concerned when those deployment warning orders came in and Smith was still not signed off. I told the IPs to either fail him or qualify him! They qualified him and I gave it no further thought. On the boat to Vietnam he was promoted; he was our senior platoon commander and he led the first mission to Father Hoa's village. We have already discussed that effort, where his flight got back late and the pilots had re-armed themselves with strange guns. He flew missions for a while, doing fine until one day he put the aft set of rotor blades through the goal posts on the soccer field in the Mekong Delta town of My Tho. Bill was always good for a laugh but we thought that this was carrying it a little too far.

Bill Smith was a natural entertainer, although I'm not sure that he always meant to be taken that way. We had all heard about his dread of snakes during our recent voyage and even those doleful laments were funny. I'll never forget the morning that I had marshaled the platoon and section leaders to take a tour of our new facilities. We had just arrived at Tan Son Nuht. Our hangers and the grounds around them were a mess. It looked like the grass hadn't been cut since the French Indo-China War. We had just started walking down the road running along the side of our hanger, when a skinny snake wriggled out of the grass right beside us. He was going like hell but he was making about as much progress sidewise as he was going forward. He wasn't making very much headway. Now you have to visualize this: Bill was a tall guy, about six foot four or more. He took one long startled look at that snake as he said "well hell, if that's all the faster he can move, no sweat!" At the same time, he stretched his legs out into the longest steps I have ever seen. We all got a good laugh out of that maneuver but the accident at the soccer field was another matter entirely.

We still hadn't resolved the Stockton caused helicopter loss. As far as we knew we were still operating under regular peacetime U. S. Army Regulations. We didn't know if this one was to be called an accident, logged as a combat loss, or what. A decision had not yet been made on our first helicopter loss. Often when things went wrong, I felt that I could, or should, have been smarter. I couldn't help believing that this accident had been partly my fault. The pilot that Smith had chosen to fly with him was a fine one; that's the reason that I hadn't objected to them flying together. I knew that Bill had had difficulties back at Fort Lewis, but the crew assignment appeared to meet my instructions, that we should always try to pair strength with weakness in the cockpit. The problem was that CWO Lamkin had just joined the 57th in Oakland so he was new to the unit. He didn't know that the Captain might need help. I had neglected to warn him. Nobody told him. Bill was in command and flying the aircraft. Lamkin thought that the Captain knew what he was doing. He must have been as surprised, as anyone would have been, when they flew through the goal posts. I shadowed crew selection much more closely in the future.

The boss decided that we would have to, at least, give Smith a post accident check ride while we waited to see if an accident investigation would be necessary. He failed the check ride. The problem was that Bill was so big and so strong, that when he froze on the controls, the IPs had a very hard time overpowering him; even to save the aircraft from crashing. During auto-rotations, he was late pulling collective pitch and/or rotating the helicopter as needed to stop the rate of decent at the bottom. The IPs flying with him could barely overpower him to move the controls so it often seemed to them that the aircraft was just going to plow into the ground.

We needed every pilot we had so we stretched things and gave him another try with our standardization IP. After the ride the stan pilot still considered him to be too dangerous to carry passengers. Cherne' and I discussed our options and decided that we would give him ten more hours of instruction before another check ride. We agreed that he could choose any IP that he wanted for those ten hours, and pick any check pilot he wanted, for the final ride. Unfortunately, his chosen IP came into operations, after a few hours of trying to teach him to auto-rotate successfully, yelling "god damn it, that son of a bitch is trying to kill me." None of the instructors that Bill worked with was strong enough to overpower him when he froze on the controls. He couldn't pass a check ride, so eventually it was decided that we would be better off if he just flew our fixed wing aircraft. During the rest of the tour, he flew the Birddog over some of our troop lift flights, to provide navigation and communication assistance. He was also nominally left in charge of his platoon for awhile and, low-and-behold, he was again flying the Shawnee when he was assigned at Fort Eustis,

VA, after returning home. I guess they either found a damn strong IP or they didn't try many auto-rotations.

It was usual for me to be working on upcoming missions until late. Often it was eight PM, 2000 hours for military guys, or even later, before everything was sorted out. Often, I kept a couple of officers with me to help with pilot and aircraft assignments and with the other pieces of the planning process. It was often well past dark before we could head back to the company area. The evening briefings were held in the Shawnee Teepee officer's club. It was usually necessary to hold one platoon, and often both of them, somewhere during the afternoon so they would stand by there until the evening briefing was finished. I saw no reason why the pilots couldn't relax while they waited, so the bar was open until I got there, no matter how late.

Soon, my habit was to walk in and head straight for the bar, where ABC usually had my vodka tonic waiting. Then, while someone wrote the next day's crew assignments on the briefing board, I would order a second drink then turn around to begin the briefing. This was usually quickly and quietly completed. The two ship missions were pretty standard. The mission, grid coordinates and any special instructions were all that was needed. If there was to be a tactical assault, a more detailed briefing would be done, just before take-off in the morning. Sometimes, if we were very late for the evening briefing, one or two of the pilots might have relaxed a little more than usual. If that was the case, they might start leading the crowd into choruses of "yea" or "boo" depending upon what was said. You know, I might say something like "the second platoon will be flying tomorrow" so some of the pilots would applaud and loudly yell "yea." When that died down, I might follow with "but the first platoon will have to stand by" so then the others would boo even more loudly. Then I might follow with something else like "if nothing comes up I may be able to release you fairly early" so then they would yell "yea". There were variations on this harassment too. All of which, I was usually able to take in good humor, or at least ignore.

Late one evening I was driving my jeep back to give the evening briefing. Smith was in the front passenger seat and three lieutenants were squeezed into the back seat. I don't remember what it was, but I had told Bill earlier to take care of something that needed to be done. As we started to move, he started questioning me on exactly what he was supposed to do and how he was supposed to do it. The guys in back knew that my temper sometimes got just a little short and that Bill could easily set me off. So maybe it was a put-up-job, I don't know, but anyway I lost it, just as they knew I would, and said something like "god damn it Bill, every time I tell you to do something you ask me how to do it! I don't give a damn how you do it! Figure it out for yourself and don't ask me again!" The conversation continued in that vein for a good part of the ride back to the compound.

I was about back to my normal, even tempered self, when we pulled in to park at the Shawnee Teepee. I un-assed the jeep and headed for the bar. Soon I was beginning to mellow out over my second vodka tonic, so I turned around to begin the evening briefing. As I did so, the lieutenants-in-the-back-seat began their revenge. They had just gotten ahold of one of those brand new pocket tape recorders and they had recorded my outburst at Smith. They began playing it loudly to the assembled audience. Well, in spite of my "Boris" nickname, I had a hard time keeping a straight face and I had to laugh along with them. It's funny the way the message gets across sometimes though; after that little performance, few people asked me how to do anything; they just got on with the job.

Sometimes, when things had settled down in the evening, I would join the poker game that had been going on before the briefing. I'm not sure, but I think some of those "worthless warrant officers" even held a chair vacant for me, because they just knew that it was going to be easy money for them. Well, it wasn't really that easy, because I usually only played until I was a little ahead before leaving the game to get a different kind of rest and recuperation. That didn't stop them of course; they were sure that they could get into my wallet. Maybe the best player in the group was CWO Billy J. Williams. Billy J usually seemed to hold good cards, and when he didn't, he would often bet so high it was difficult to call him. He never seemed to run out of money. None of the rest of us was very flush, because most of our checks were paid out back home to support our families. Even so, these were table stakes / pot limit games. We just assumed, that it was because Billy J was not married, that he always seemed to have plenty of bucks. Years later ABC confessed that he had backed Billy J when he needed cash, which was probably a very rare event in any case and of course, he assured me that they never took advantage of me. Aaahuh!

Smith used to sit in on the game once in awhile; not too often because he hated to lose, and Bill just couldn't give up on a pair of aces. He was fascinated by them. You could tell that he had a pair of aces, every time, by the rigid way he held his cards when they showed up. He would draw to the aces, and even when his hand didn't improve, he was very reluctant to throw it in. When such a deal was over, we usually had to throw that deck away and bring in a new one, because Bill had held the cards so tight that he had crimped the aces. I remember one night when we were sitting around waiting for Bill to decide what to do with his pair of aces. It got to be a long time, before someone finally said "god damn it you big son-of-a-bitch either fold your hand or bet your cards!" (That's not precisely what was said; I've modified it a bit, but I am just one of seven guys that will remember that game).

The lieutenants didn't sit in at the poker table much. They either had their own thing going, or they were just too new to the game to get involved with these high rollers. Hinds may have sat in occasionally and I'm pretty sure that he was the ring leader of that lieutenants-in-the-back-seat gang. The others in the back seat were probably flight leaders, Bill Brethour and Sal Formica. I don't remember for sure, but both of them were quite capable of pulling a stunt like that. Bill and Sal were conscientious young officers who performed their duties well, although each of them had certain peculiarities.

Lieutenant Brethour had picked up two names from our ever observant CWOs back at Fort Lewis. They called him Breathless sometimes, but they usually referred to him as "The Banker." That was because Bill was always there when he was told to be there, but you had to be sure to do that if you wanted to see him much past three o'clock in the afternoon. He had no intention of making the Army his career. He knew that he would be getting out soon to go back to college. He intended to be a veterinarian, not a banker, but anyway he was really a civilian at heart. All that being said, Bill was a good pilot and a fine officer. He did become a horse and dog medic back in

Kansas, and at one of our reunions about thirty years later, he and Sal showed up in their Vietnam era flight suits. I expect that they were the only two guys still in good enough shape to do that.

Lieutenant Formica and I usually had a comfortable relationship in Vietnam. He was aimed at a career in the communication industry somewhere, so I often left it to him to handle the media types that would come in to view our operation; not just the local Saigon war correspondents, but the famous ones from the states too. He was good at it and he liked to do it. He talked to guys like Army historian, Brigadier General SLA Marshall, and the famous columnist, Joe Alsop. He was also a very good planner. He was meticulous about it and always presented a thoroughly thought out piece of work. The job always included crew and aircraft assignments, which he would have posted on the board in the operations shack ahead of the morning briefing. This is where our relationship might break down. The problem was that there would invariably be changes to make. Sal did not like changes nor did he like anyone else messing with his solid plan.

Sometimes, I would want to make one or two changes in the crew assignments; being careful to insure that strength was paired with weakness, as I saw it. Most pilots do most things well, but maybe some others, not so well. I had already been burned twice. I felt that I knew the pilots throughout the company the best to be able to balance the crews. The thing that would usually upset the apple cart though, was the late arrival of unexpected people that wanted to ride along. These ranged from war correspondents to senior staff officers from the MAAG HQ downtown. I used to call them "maggots and strap-hangers" until I got a direct order to stop doing that. These guys never seemed to realize the problems they caused for us, or for the ARVN commanders with their late arrivals, and they seldom called ahead. Our planner had to find space for them on the helicopters, and get them oriented. Of course, the ARVN commander would then find himself short of troop space; we had to kick one soldier off for each strap-hanger we added. Sal thought I should just refuse to let them aboard, but there was little that I could do to stem the tide. I had offered several suggestions along those lines already but had been told to just quit fighting the problem and make room for them.

Each time Sal was doing the detailed planning the late changes would come in, usually after everything was set to go, but before we could get off the ground. I rarely had the time, or the patience, to wait while he screwed around before doing what had to be done. All latecomers' names would have to be added to a helicopter tail number on the operations board, so that we could keep track of them. They had to be briefed, and they had to be spread out in the flight to lesson the tactical impact on the troop lift. Sal would gripe and stall. I sometimes had to take over from him to keep things moving.

One morning, after his vocal irritation had been going on too long, I said something like "look Sal just make the changes on the board and lets get on with it" but since things were continuing to go too slow for me, I probably said "alright dang it, give me the dang grease pencil (those may not be the exact words used) and I will make the changes myself." This time when I started to add the new names to the board, Sal said "god damn it, everything you touch turns to shit" (yes, those were the exact words he used). So I replied "okay Sal the next thing I'm going to touch is your efficiency report!" I did in fact, write up a pretty lousy report while I was still angry, but then I put it under my mattress and slept on it for a few days, before throwing it out. It did not reflect the fine officer that he was, most of the time.

Sal may have also thought that I was a little cavalier with some of the important correspondents that came to visit. I was always busy, and they did not appear to be central to my business, so I spent very little time worrying about them and even less time dealing with them. I know now of course, that that was a mistake, because they sure as hell had more to do with the outcome of the war than I ever did.

We inadvertly treated the internationally known, and close buddy of the Kennedy family, columnist Joe Alsop, badly one day. I was leading an assault flight into VC Village that morning with Alsop aboard my helicopter. He, along with the other strap-hangers, had been briefed to not get off the aircraft when we landed the troops, but Joe wanted to get off to take a picture or something. He told the crew chief that he would just be a minute. The crew chief said that he told him twice, to not get off the helicopter because CPT Knight would surely take off without him. We were leading a flight of helicopters.

There was no way that we could wait for Mr. Alsop. That afternoon he walked out, through the swamps and the rice paddies, with the troops.

I'm sure Sal gave me hell for that one but he was a good guy, except for his reluctance to accept that plans are usually no more than just the best basis for change. Just as he had planned though, and probably without a hitch, when he returned to civilian life, Sal Formica went on to be part of the media profession in Washington DC. One must wonder of course, how Sal handles the changes that must routinely hit in that environment.

There were three other young lieutenants with us from the start. They were, for the most part, quiet warriors. They were Second Lieutenants; they were Two Johns, or Gold Bar Shave Tails, and the Chief Warrant Officers took care of them. The Chiefs took care of me too, of course. We went through Oregon a few years ago and stopped to see one of my favorite CWOs who had retired in the area. Charley Larkin was our host and he was serving coffee in the morning. My cup ran dry and I had started to get up for a refill when Charley grabbed my cup and headed for the kitchen. My wife, Margie, said "hey wait a minute, he can get his own." Chaz said "no, that's alright; I always had to take care of him in Vietnam so I'm used to it." Well I laughed at that; no one ever got me coffee in Vietnam, but there was of course, some truth in it. I always got a lot of help from my friends.

When I was leading a flight, there was almost always a CWO flying with me, and he would be handling the aircraft much of the time. Some of the pilots were not reluctant to tell me how I had screwed up the mission planning, or the flight lead, after we had landed. Larkin was among the most straight-forward about it; he *always* let me know. Charley had joined the 57th from a CH-34 company in Germany, as had many of our pilots, but only Charley came out of there with the distinctive nickname of "Wolfgang". They called him Chaz sometimes, but Wolfgang was so ingrained among his contemporaries, that they often just shortened it to Wolf. I doubt that I will ever know how that nickname was acquired. It surely wasn't from the Saturday morning TV cartoons as most of ours were. Maybe it had to do with a specific gasthaus or maybe it was just his ability to get along so smoothly in the environment in which he had to work. It probably had nothing to do with his usually direct and sometimes contentious manner. Strange maybe, but I always appreciated his directness and his advice.

CPT Bob Webb had led the contingent, from the 33rd Helicopter Company, in to join us before we deployed from California. The group also included LT Roger P. Bailey, but I don't remember him well, because young officers were easily absorbed into the pilot group if they weren't holding flight leader positions and if they weren't normally involved in mission planning. Bailey flew his missions like everyone else until his service obligation ended and he was happy to leave and return to civilian life. I have mentioned LT John Garner before. John was a solid citizen and he performed his duties in Vietnam very well. As mentioned earlier, I saw him once later, as a Captain in Germany, so he must have stayed in the Army for a while. LT Roderic G. Magie rounds out the list of young commissioned officers who first flew with us and he was the youngest of the crew. Rod was a tall, quiet guy who went on to gain a law degree after his Vietnam service. He always did his job faultlessly and he never raised his voice, except for one time when he had to be physically restrained from attacking a senior officer, who he felt had made some bad decisions. What is that old saying about deeply running still water?

We had gotten a fill of about six or seven pilots, on ninety day temporary duty from Korea, by then. An old friend, CPT Dale Rubsamen, led them in. Besides being a friend, Dale was senior to me by date of rank. He could have stood on ceremony but he didn't. Whenever I think of Rubsamen, I visualize the baby blue, 1952 Mercedes, 220 convertible coupe that he brought back with him from Germany in 1959. That was one neat car and I have always wondered what happened to it. Unfortunately, I don't remember the names of the lieutenant and CWOs that were in the group for a couple of reasons. First because they fit right in from the start, and so when I look back on it, they don't stand out as individuals but just more helicopter seats filled with competent aviators. They all simply flew missions. The second reason is that about the only thing that I took home with me after the tour, was a footlocker full of ratty old clothes and the poorly, but freshly laundered, Class B uniform on my back. The only paper I brought out were the orders sending me home and a few pictures.

We lost some people almost as soon as we arrived in Vietnam. One of them, CWO Walter McAnerney, left us for early reassignment to Fort Bragg and Special Forces training. And although I have few records, I do remember that our first personnel casualties did not occur on the battlefield. Two of our members had to return home early. They were CWO Edison I. Roberts and a senior master sergeant. I knew neither individual well, and since this was a company headquarters administrative matter, I was not involved in the details. I have therefore, been unable to verify the name of the sergeant, but the flight that they were on did not make it home. That old four engine Lockheed Constellation went down somewhere in the Pacific Ocean without a trace. Not even an oil spot was ever reported.

I started this chapter by recording the story of our Task Force Smith. Bill finished his tour with the 57th as the administrative officer. I'm sure that by this time, he was ready to go home because he sure wasn't very interested in doing that job. A letter came back to Cherne' from CPT Don Jordon, who was the company XO after we had all returned from Vietnam. It indicated that a lot of paperwork, including efficiency reports and recommendations for awards, had been shoved, unfinished, under his mattress when he left the country. But Don said that they had fished them all out, and sent them on their way, as soon as they found them.

Bill Smith retired as a full colonel, a thing that came as a surprise to some of us, but he must have found his nitch somewhere. His troubles in the 57th did not follow him for the rest of his career. I used to run into him fairly often while he was assigned as the Inspector General at Fort Eustis, VA. The command there was quite happy with his performance of duty and he was well thought of by his contemporaries on the staff. He died several years ago of testicular cancer, but he maintained his sense of humor to the end. The last time I saw him, was just after another of his trips up to Walter Reed Hospital near Washington DC. I asked him how he was doing and he said that he "had been in the hospital so many times, and had been examined by so many doctors, that now, every time he saw someone dressed in white he automatically dropped his pants"

CHAPTER 18

ENTER THE UNITED STATES MARINE CORPS

From the halls of Montezuma to the shores of Tripoli . . .
Drum Roll please!

The Marines are a tough bunch. There is no doubt about that. Consider that individuals join the Corps in the first place, knowing what they are probably getting into. They must come in with a pretty aggressive attitude to start with. Serious training and subsequent experience reinforces a warrior ethos and leads to a very high sense of personal worth. When this type of individual is aggregated, and led by others cut from the same cloth, you will surely get an outfit with great cohesiveness, fighting spirit and a very high opinion of themselves and of their organization. The mission will get done! If that paints a picture of aggressive pride that might get somebody killed; well there is that. Of course it might also lead to feeling of superiority over others in the same business.

The United States Marine Corps Medium Helicopter Company, HMM-362, showed up at Soc Trang in the Mekong Delta during April 1962. By that time the Army's 45th Transportation Battalion (Transport Aircraft), our next higher headquarters, was sharing space with us at Tan Son Nuht. Our sister company, the 8th, was at Qui Nhon supporting the ARVN II Corps. The 93rd, another CH-21C company, was at Da Nang working with the ARVN I Corps near the border with North Vietnam. Several other Army Aviation units had also arrived. The 18th Aviation Company, flying DeHavilland U-1A Otters, was operating around the country and the 339th Transportation

Company (Aircraft Direct Support) was located half way up the coast at Nha Trang. The 3rd Radio Research Unit was flying a few, radio-direction-finding equipped, U-6 Beavers. The 57th Medical Detachment (Air Ambulance), equipped with brand new UH-1A helicopters, also arrived in April and there had been one lonely CV-2 Caribou operating in Vietnam for some time. Air America was there, piloted by not a few Army Aviators in mufti.

We wondered why. Why send in the Marines when it had appeared to be an Army show? The ARVN sported only a very few Marines, so who were these guys going to advise? Just fooling; we knew that they would be supporting the ARVN the same as we had been doing. So, at the time, we simply credited their arrival to politics. Even then, we knew that all the services would want to get a piece of the expanding action in Vietnam. The American public still knew very little about what was going on in Southeast Asia, but all of the uniformed branches of the service surely did.

We had also noted that a senior USMC colonel had recently been assigned to MAAG HQ. He was reputed to be the most senior, of the full colonels assigned to the staff and he was said to be a tough old bastard. We also heard that he had started pushing for the assignment of a Marine helicopter squadron from the word go. If there was more to it than that we didn't know it. Any deeper MAAG planning would have been highly classified, and since this was still early in the advisory stage of things, it would have been only "contingency" planning. So we figured great; jump right in, the more helicopters the better! USMC ground forces didn't arrive, in force, until 1965.

LTC Richardson, the 45th Bn Cmdr, filled up his U-1A Otter with battalion staff members and flew to Soc Trang to welcome the HMM-362 squadron into Vietnam. MAJ Cherne' and I were invited to go along to present an introductory briefing to the commander and his pilots. Cherne' did the briefing. I don't really know what I was doing there, because I just stood in the back of the room and watched. I'm sure that I was introduced as the operations guy for the 57th but nobody paid much attention to me. For my part, I stood there in open mouthed amazement to see the room packed full of USMC commissioned officers, including some quite senior ones. The squadron (about the same size as an Army helicopter company) was led by LTC Archie J. Clapp. Another LTC was going to be their base commander at Soc Trang. The operations officer was a major and all the pilots were either captains or lieutenants. They planned to have another major assigned as liaison to the ARVN III Corps Hq. We already knew that a senior full colonel had arrived at the MAAG in Saigon.

All this "rank," when we had only one LTC battalion commander, who was also the senior Army Aviator in country. A major commanded each Army helicopter company, and captains and lieutenants were in leadership positions only. The rest of our pilots were chief warrant officers. I was sure anyway, that our Army CWO pilots were better than the USMC commissioned officers at piloting cargo helicopters. Our warrants had been flying cargo helicopters, as a full time occupation for a number of years, while their young officers must have been at about the same flying experience level as were our commissioned officers; but no doubt about it, this USMC crowd sure as hell out-ranked us clear across the board.

A few days later, during one of our first joint missions, probably after some comment of mine about this rank disparity, a young lieutenant said to me "you god damn Army guys just come in and screw around, but for us Marines, this is the only war we've got." That remark stuck with me. What war? We were there, ostensibly, only to provide advice and some helicopter transport support to the RVN in *their* war effort. Even though this was way before we bought into the whole conflict, with major ground forces, the warrior attitude was alive and well in the United States Marine Corps. In spite of the high rank structure enjoyed by the Marine squadron and the aggressive talk, we planned and led joint missions for a few weeks, while the Marines got familiar with the operating area.

HMM-362 was equipped with Sikorsky S-58 helicopters. Ours in the Army were called CH-34s. The USMC version may have been a little different, because of service peculiar modifications, but not much. The S-58 helicopter was powered by the same kind of engines that we had in our CH-21 Shawnees but the S-58 was about 1000 pounds lighter and it's engine was only driving one set of main rotor blades. Its cargo compartment was smaller then ours, so they didn't carry much heavier loads then we did, but they could get off the ground, fly out of ground effect, pass through transational lift, and get into the air with that load much quicker than we could do it. That could be embarrassing on occasion.

For example, one day we were operating with the Marines from a small clearing along side of a rubber plantation, just northwest of Cu Chi, on the edge of the jungle covered Iron Triangle in War Zone "D." We were lifting troops from that location, to a spot where the ARVN thought that they could intercept some fleeing VC. Due to the peculiarities of the site, we were aligned parallel with the S-58s and both flights would be taking off at the same time. It was only a short distance to the jungle ahead of us, where there were very tall trees that faced us along the edge of the clearing.

There was one little notch in the tree line. I had to walk over to the lead S-58 and ask the Marine flight leader if he would mind holding off to the left so that we could plan to fly out through that notch. We would need it. We were in rough terrain, which would require a hovering take-off. I pulled in all the power that I could find but still couldn't achieve a hover. I told the crew chief to kick off a soldier but we still couldn't even get a bobble on the wheels. I had him kick another one off and we began to feel a little air under the tires. There was a slight mound out ahead of my helicopter; maybe a hundred yards out, but it would be all pilot technique to get over it. To my further embarrassment, I was still trying to get my lead Shawnee off the ground, when about the fifth S-58 blasted by us, well up in the air.

In addition to the power-to-weight ratio advantage of the S-58, the Marines also had "Charley" aboard. Charley was the name that everyone in Army Aviation called helicopter automatic flight controls (AFC) in those days; as in "okay let Charley do it." The Army had a few AFC installed in CH-34s stationed in Europe, but we had none in our CH-21s. I got a kick out of following the Marines around down in the Delta one day, after they had begun taking the lead down there.

We were headed home after dropping troops, when they decided to turn the navigation and aircraft handling problem over to Charley. The technology for helicopter automatic flight controls was not well advanced at the time and Charley could not hold an exact heading. The Marine flight would proceed in the correct direction for a short time, before it would drift off, so pretty soon Charley would turn them back towards the desired heading. That track would be slightly overshot, or the drift would set in again, so after a while they would turn back the other way and etc, etc. We were dutifully following along behind them as we zig zagged over the rice paddies. I finally had to call them up, to tell them "hey you guys, if you don't fly a straight line pretty soon, we are going to run out of gas back here." They didn't know if I was kidding or not I guess, so the pilots got busy and things straightened out for the remainder of the journey. Once we got up in straight and level flight though, the old Shawnee could move right out. Occasionally, on a routine ash & trash mission, our pilots might find themselves coming up behind a couple of Marines, cruising along on Charley, at 80 knots or so. It was neat to drop the nose, picking up speed to about 120 knots, while sneaking up on the S-58s, then race past them at what appeared to be twice their speed. Hell, it wasn't much of a put down, but it was fun anyway.

I was still doing the mission planning and the 57th was leading all the joint flights; continuing to show them around, when I was treated to an unforgettable tongue lashing by a USMC full colonel. We had put together a joint mission, to combat assault elements of the ARVN Airborne Brigade into a village right up against the Cambodian border. The place had been identified as a major staging area, on the enemy route back in from one of their Cambodian sanctuaries. The mission was all set to go at oh-dark-hundred in the morning.

The USAF had their Air Operations Center (AOC) fully up and running by then, so we had been given instructions that, before we flew any more assault missions, we would have to brief the Air Force Brigadier General (BG) running the place. This was so that the AOC could then tell everyone, from the ARVN Commanding General, to the province chief in the target area, what was about to happen. The idea was that any friendly troops could be warned, and if anyone on the Vietnamese side didn't like it, the mission could be altered or even cancelled. Nobody much cared what we Army Aviators thought, but we didn't like this arrangement at all. It had already become very apparent that ARVN security was incredibly bad. This procedure was bound to make it worse, if that was even possible; no way they could keep a secret. The VC would know we were coming. They would either leave the area, go to ground, or stay to fight. They would be forewarned. Not good, but our orders were to go through the AOC.

So now it was late in the evening before the mission. I was standing around ready to brief. The Marines had indicated that they would attend but they had not yet arrived. It had gotten later and later, until finally a USMC full colonel landed at Tan Son Nuht. I don't know where COL Richard E. Carey had started out from but he flew in from Soc Trang on a big tailed C-47. That old Goony Bird was being used to support the Marine helicopter squadron, from their main Far East base in Okinawa. COL Carey was obviously the man up the chain of command, in charge of HMM-362. I met him outside the AOC, introduced myself, and thinking that he would like to know the basic mission plan, before going in to see the Air Force BG, I said "Colonel if you would like a pre-brief before we go in there, I would be happy to do that."

Carey was a big guy and he stood there looking down at me for a moment. Then he said "no, that won't be necessary." He stopped speaking for another moment and then he said "and furthermore, I'm sick and god damn tired of taking orders from a freaking junior Army captain." (Well freaking is not the exact word that he used and I'll never forget the one that he did use either.) It will come as no surprise, that this response from a very senior officer, whom I had never seen before, came as somewhat of a surprise and I backed off quickly. Those two eagles on his shoulders, all of a sudden looked gigantic to me. There was no one that I could turn to for aid. The senior Army Aviator in Vietnam was LTC Richardson, and neither he nor my boss MAJ Cherne', were anywhere around. They would have been severely outranked anyway. Hey, this was just supposed to be another routine mission. I was on my own.

What happened next was even more surprising than his verbal assault on me had been, because Carey walked into the briefing room where he told that Air Force general, in no uncertain terms, that the USAF support his helicopters had been getting was totally inadequate. He went on to say that the Marine helicopter squadron would not be flying any more missions, until they had either USMC or US Navy air support. I don't remember any of that Navy high performance stuff ever flying down in the Delta, but the USMC surely got their own air support when they later moved north. In any case, Carey was right about the air/ground support deficiency, and his tirade must have gotten someone's attention, because the USAF started to bring in some AD-6 attack aircraft and eventually some A-1 gun ships. These provided improved ground support; much better than the T-28s, but as far as we helicopter guys were concerned, the Air Force was way late in deploying them.

Needless to say, much to the consternation of the ARVN Airborne Brigade, we cancelled the mission that had been scheduled for the next morning. The Brigade had already brought their troops into Tan Son Nuht, but they turned them all around and sent them home. As you can probably guess, after that dark encounter, the Marines planned and led their own damn missions in the southern part of the Delta. We began to follow them around, in what later became the ARVN IV Corps area. We led the joint missions in the III Corp northern portion, but I sure as hell didn't plan or lead any more of them down in their area.

We staged out of Soc Trang once in a while and I was always amazed at the condition of the USMC camp; it was a real mess. Wooden walkways were laid over deep mud, between hastily erected tents, and they were seemingly without much of any kind of flooring. Nothing seemed to be aligned in a dress-right-dress manner, as the Army would do it, and it looked like no improvement was planned. I wondered if they just liked it that way or what. We got the answer when HMM-362 rotated out in six months or so. We didn't know that such rotation was normal for USMC units. The first guys knew that they wouldn't be around for long anyway.

HMM-362 was replaced by HMM-163 at Soc Trang, but shortly after that the Marines switched places with the Army's 93rd Helicopter Company up in I Corps. We were led to believe at the time, that the Marine S-58s had been sent up there to take advantage of their better power to weight ratio, versus the CH-21. That made sense to us, because it would be a significant improvement for operating in that mountainous region. We can now guess however, that the real reason was because contingency plans had already been made to bring USMC ground forces into the I Corps area. They came over the beach in 1965 to counter any invasion which might occur from across the demilitarized zone between North and South Vietnam. Eventually the USMC had its hands full trying to control things in that narrow mountainous corridor between the ocean and the Laotian border.

The commander of HMM-362 was LTC Archie Clapp. That name probably lent itself to several play-on-words but the one that we heard was "Archie's Angels." It was the well known nickname of the unit. The media loved it! You can guess of course, that this nickname was derided somewhat on the Army side of the helicopter community. Some 57th wag came up with the idea of matching the first name of our boss with a similar catchy title. The ever present CWO sense of humor rose to the occasion. In a fit of typically self depreciating humor they decided to call themselves "Milt's Misfits." This didn't last long enough to qualify as an official nickname. It was just a joke; sort of a back handed slap at the Marines and their assiduous maintenance of their glamorous image. (When the 57th was redesignated as the 120th they adopted the nickname of "The Deans" reflecting our first year of learning and the passing on of our experience.)

There are numerous "Jar Head" jokes that Army troops like to tell. A favorite in the 57th was the one defining a Marine Corps squad. "Do you know the definition of a Marine Corps squad? That's one shootin', one lootin', and six takin' pictures!" Not a fair representation of the USMC I'm sure, but that single Marine helicopter squadron way down there in the Delta certainly got plenty of media attention. Toward the end of their six month deployment they were visited by Ms. Dickey Chapelle who's article "*Helicopters Over South Viet Nam*" was published in the November 1962 issue of *National Geographic*.*[1] Despite of the predominance of Army helicopter outfits in Vietnam, she spent almost all of her time with the USMC squadron. There were pictures of Army CH-21C helicopters illustrating the story, but little credit was given.

In addition, she bought off on the fiction that LTC Clapp was the developer "of bold new helicopter tactics" and supported the idea that he had originated a new tactical employment of helicopters, in what became known as "Eagle Flights." To greatly over simplify, this was a technique where you loaded up a bunch of soldiers, then flew around at low level waiting to be shot at. When that happened, you dumped off the troops so that they could quickly engage the enemy, or as an alternative, you could put a small unit on the ground and hold a larger force airborne nearby, to go in immediately if the first group became engaged.

To set the record straight, the Eagle Flight concept was really the invention of US Army CPT Richard A. Jones, a field advisor to elements of the 21st ARVN Division, and it was a tactic we in the 57th had tried on several occasions. It was a favorite of Cherne's. I am sure he covered the tactic when he briefed HMM-362 upon their arrival at Soc Trang. I even wrote an article, after my return home, which was based on the concept but enlarged to suggest a pre-planned target array, with random, last minute target selection, and a jointly trained helicopter/ground force, including a battalion sized reaction force.

I sent this to *The Infantry Journal* but they never published it; probably because they objected to the expanded decision and control aspects which, in my version, would have been exercised by the senior aviator involved. That would have been against Army doctrine. I'll never know exactly why the Journal rejected the article. They never answered the mail or returned the article, but four years later, I rewrote it from memory as a paper for the Canadian Land Forces Command and Staff College which I was attending. My paper was reviewed by a U.S. Army Infantry colonel on the college staff. His only comment was that "the ground commander had to be in charge all the way" thus confirming an ancient piece of doctrine which probably goes all the way back to BG Black Jack Pershing's punitive expedition into Mexico before WWI.

Another well known writer to visit in late 1962, was Richard Tregaskis who had written a WWII book about the USMC in the Pacific. Published in 1943, it was entitled "*Guadalcanal Diary*" and told the story of that epic battle. Tregaskis had landed on Guadalcanal with the first waves of Marines assaulting the island and he told a hell of a good story.*[2] It is no surprise that he spent much of his time with the Marine helicopter squadron, when he decided to write about

Vietnam. This one, entitled "*Vietnam Diary*," was published in 1963. Like Ms Chapelle, Tregaskis spent much of his time with the USMC, but he did a good job of balancing his account between Army and Marine units. He flew with both and named names. I'm even in the book, on page 173, where he mentions extraneous radio talk about an H-21 that was having trouble with its landing gear. That would be me; and it sure as hell wasn't extraneous to me!*3 His account, by the way, ain't quite right, but we'll tell the true story later.

My personal association with USMC helicopter squadrons ended when HMM-163 moved north, but years later I was in the official book store at the Pentagon, where I picked up a USMC publication confirming that they had invented the tactics which won the helicopter war in Vietnam. Really! It was about the early days and it outlined all of the magnificent advancements that had been made by those HMM squadrons. I didn't buy the thing and I can't name it either, because when it came to the part where the author was comparing Marine helicopter tactics with Army tactics, I threw it down in disgust. They did indeed learn and apply some new tricks over there, but nothing we hadn't been doing before, and most of which we handed down to them.

Where it got to me the worst, was where it stated that the Army helicopter units were afraid to fly at night! Afraid to fly at night; what an ignorant and arrogant statement. It is a fact that we were not flying night missions at the time, but there were several good reasons why not. The first was that no one was requesting them. The III Corps advisors were sure that, until the ARVN could find and fix the Viet Cong in the daylight, it would be futile to go after them with a night heliborne assault. The VC normally just melted away when faced with an assault in the daylight and it would be even easier for them to do so in the cover of darkness; especially after a bunch of noisy helicopters had blasted their way in near them. I will admit that the Marines were more aggressive than we were about adopting someone else's war, but I don't remember that they actually accomplished any successful night operations in the III Corps area. I doubt it. It is also interesting to note that night heliborne operations were very unusual at any later time in the war. U. S. advisors felt that at-or-near dawn attacks were likely to produce the most successful results so we usually planned our assaults to arrive at dawn.

Over the years I've had interactions with various elements and individuals in the USMC. And although those events have little to do with this story, except for maybe a continuation of one Army guy's view of Marines, a couple of them are funny enough to add here.

You probably know that much of the research, on various kinds of vertical lift air vehicles since the 1960s, has been funded and managed by the Army. NASA and the other service have had their own programs of course and there have always been a number of joint service projects underway. That includes the early XV-15 tilt rotor work, leading up to the development of the V-22 Osprey, which operates in the USMC today. The Army began the initial engineering development. They wanted to continue it but could not support the requirement against other Army needs so the USMC took over the project. And it is well that they did so, because the development would probably have died aborning if they had not. The USMC enjoyed support in the Congress of the United States that we in the Army could only envy and so as a Marine program the V-22 stayed alive. That, by the way, might also explain why media attention is so important to the Marines. The congress loves it. The USN may not be all that excited about it though, because the funding for all USMC stuff comes through the Navy budget where something else always has to give.

The Boeing Company had teamed with Bell Helicopter Textron to complete the USMC V-22 development and to begin production of the aircraft. One day I sat in a private meeting between a senior Boeing manager and the three star Vice Admiral, who was the Commander Navy Air Atlantic (COMNAVAIRLANT); boy I never did get used to those Navy acronyms. Anyway, the Boeing guy was holding forth on how great it was; the V-22 was going to solve all the problems, etc, etc. I watched as the blood started rising on the admiral's face and his expression became more explosive. The enthusiastic talker didn't notice until too late. As the Boeing executive slid ever further down in his overstuffed chair, the admiral said in loud and measured tones "the goddamn Marine Corps hasn't been over a beach in twenty five years and they are sucking up over half of our Navy aircraft budget!" Well so much for that meeting.

The other kinda funny story has to do with a tradition in the USMC. If there are more than a couple of former Marines in any location, they are likely to get together to celebrate the birth date of the United States Marine Corps. A large such birthday party is held annually in the Hampton Roads area of Virginia. Margie and I participated in some of those. One year it was attended by General Al Gray, Commandant of the Marine Corps. General Gray was not a particularly big fellow, but he was built like a spark plug, and looked like a tank. Those parties were always held in formal dress uniform and Gray's awards and decorations reached from below the pocket line of his blouse to almost over his shoulder. Gray was standing with a group of officers, discussing whatever, when he got bored. He looked around and noticed a group of wives standing over to one side talking to each other. He said "I think I should go over and greet the ladies" whereupon he headed off, full tilt, in their direction. The ladies saw this miniature armored missile headed in their direction and scattered like they had been hit with in-coming.

Well there are lots of other stories. That will do for now, but I've got to say that the *National Geographic Magazine* got to me again in March 2004, when they featured Archie Clapp in a little write-up entitled "*An Angel Gets His Wings Back*" which shows Archie sitting in the cockpit of one of the HMM-362 helicopters that had just resurfaced from a boneyard somewhere. That part of it was fine, and good on him, but the lead in sentence continued to provide misinformation in typical media / USMC fashion, where it stated that Archie Clapp had commanded Marine squadrons during the first U. S. helicopter mission in Vietnam.*[4] I wrote a letter to the magazine about that misrepresentation and received a reply which was not very satisfactory either. The misleading words were left to stand of course, so the USMC myth continues.

CHAPTER 19

AT WAR WITH THE AIR FORCE

Off we go into the wild blue yonder climbing high into the sun . . .
and very reluctantly into the mud, and the blood and the beer.

Nah; we weren't at war with the Air Force; they were on our side. Really they were. The way that I saw it, the USAF presented a different face to the Army than it did to anyone else in the 1960s. Army Aviation was caught right in the middle of the inter-service squabble. Army flyers were attuned to the needs of the ground force. We were a part of the ground force. We believed that boots-on-the-ground were necessary to achieve either tactical or strategic victory. In that regard, we tended to view the USAF as a supporting service. That was not, however, how they viewed themselves. As the situation developed during the early 60s, the Air Force was almost totally oriented on their primary missions of strategic defense and air superiority. Although little effort had been placed on the development of a modern air to ground support capability, they did recognize that support of Army ground operations was one of their missions. So when our Army aircraft began to show their stuff in Vietnam, Army Aviation was seen as a primary threat to that mission, and to the control of the air space over the battle area, which they also believed to be their responsibility.

When the USAF established its AOC, it seemed to us that this was just another attempt to control anything and everything that flew in Vietnam. The inter-service battle about who flew what kinds of aircraft, where they could fly them, and what kinds of missions they could fly, was alive and well in the Pentagon at the time. Vietnam was, of course, central to the discussion. It looked to us like the USAF was intent on making that division of responsibility as close to the ground as possible. The Army belonged on the ground! They could stomach the Army's use of little fixed wing airplanes but bigger ones should be flown by Air Force pilots. They grudgedly acknowledged that the Army could go ahead and fly their helicopters but they seemed to be worried that those helicopters might get in the way of Air Force operations. And certainly the Army should not be expending any violence from the air. That was strictly Air Force business!

Did all this high level in-fighting directly affect our operations? You bet; and USMC COL Carey had voiced a concern that we all felt about USAF ground support. The T-28 converted trainer just didn't have the armament or staying power required and the B-26, which was occasionally used, was a make-shift back stop. Even though we were flying helicopters that were already obsolete, and rapidly becoming pretty ragged, we thought that using surplus trainers, or going all the way back to WWII to find any kind of usable close air support aircraft, was a bit much.

I was at the Fort Myer officer's club in Washington DC, one night in early 1963, where I got an explanation about why this antique equipment was still being used. The explanation has stuck with me. I was a little in my cups, and I was still a freaking junior Army captain, but I started expounding about the crappy ground support the USAF was providing in Vietnam to an Air Force colonel, that happened to be sitting beside me at the bar. I questioned him, too loudly probably, about why the Air Force had not developed a modern close air support aircraft that was capable of supporting the conflict there. When the colonel got tired of my bitching, he said "the United States Air Force has had to expend all of its limited resources on the strategic cap against the Russian Bear, and if we had not done that, you couldn't even have your crummy little ground war." That may not be an exact quote, but it is close, and it was less than satisfactory, but it did lay out the rational for USAF budget priorities at the time.

The inadequate ground support was not the only issue we had with the USAF in 1962. The AOC was another. They arrived at Tan Son Nuht and got set up for business early in 1962. The first minor irritant for us was when the Air Force recognized the AOC with some kind of unit award for going in early and setting up the center under hazardous conditions or some such nonsense. By the time the AOC was ready for operation it had been established in a very large, climate controlled building at the center of the air base. It was not particularly hazardous. In fact it was barely risky at all, unless you caught a cold from the frigid air conditioning. We had our plywood quarters near the AOC at Tan Son Nuht. We figured it was about as safe a place as there was in the country. The Army never did give us, or any of the other early Army Aviation units, any recognition for going in early; hazardous or otherwise. In fact to all intents and purposes we weren't even there. We treated the news of this Air Force award as the joke we thought it to be, but all of a sudden, the AOC was open for business and they immediately tried to take control of the air; all of the air.

That air conditioned award was just a minor thing of course, but it was a major mistake, in my opinion, to have to tell the AOC ahead of time when and where our helicopters were going. As I have said, too often probably, ARVN security was incredibly bad. There was already little doubt in my mind that the enemy would always have a pretty good idea of what was about to happen anyway. This added coordination through the AOC was likely to make that security problem even worse. Also, for me, this was just another do-loop in the already convoluted trail one had to take to get a mission together.

That being said, the people inside that nicely appointed building were a great bunch of folks, as the working people always are, and they had a fine tuned sense of humor. Almost daily, I would head over there, usually with another one of our pilots, after we had spent a long hot, damp, sweaty day flying and putting the next mission together. On more than one occasion, as we walked through the front door, some Air Force joker would shout something like "hey, get out of here with those filthy stinking flight suits. You'll foul up our air conditioning!" (Well not exactly; they often used even stronger and more repetitive language than that). Sometimes there were other pleasantries aimed our way too, but they were always yelled at us in a good neighborly, sporting, manner. You couldn't help but join in on the laughter at your own expense.

Another major irritant emerged as time wore on. Often, when we were going about our business of flying over the Delta, we clearly saw the enemy grouped or running for cover where they presented an obvious target for an air strike. We would dutifully note the grid coordinate location and identify the characteristics of the target, along with the flight conditions over it. We would then report it back to the AOC along with a request for action. Nothing ever happened! We would even offer to send an O-1 birddog out to act as a forward air controller for them. Still, it was no thanks and no VNAF / USAF manned airplane would get there anytime soon!

Maybe the problem was the coordination they had to go through to take any target. Hours likely went by before they could get through the USAF-VNAF-USA-ARVN-Province Chief daisy chain. It would probably have been far too late to bring effective fire to bear on anything anyway, and everyone would have lost interest, before they could get the mission approved. We also had the sneaky feeling however, that the USAF just didn't trust us Army guys to properly identify a good target for them from the air. The proper doctrine was for a soldier on the ground to *ask, sometimes plead,* for an air strike. If the mission was eventually approved, the target would then have to be confirmed through a USAF Forward Air Controller (FAC) flying above it; not by an Army Aviator.

One day, after several weeks of this frustration, Charley Larkin came in from a flight over the Plain of Reeds. He had clearly identified a Viet Cong group out there by their red star decorated banana leaf helmets. They were out in the open, with nobody else around for miles, and they had no place to go quickly. It was a perfect target for an air strike. Charley had of course, reported it by radio to the AOC. As soon as he landed, he came into the operations shack to see what had happened. Nothing had happened! Well Larkin was getting short by then and he was getting a tad sick of this normal lack of response. We were used to it but damn!

So he talked me into going over to the AOC. He was determined that this time we should make it happen. We took our dirty smelly flight suits into that nice air conditioned building where we each sat on a corner of the operation officer's desk. Then we told the major that we weren't leaving until a strike was approved. We kept at him, even though he tried to shoo us off, until he got on the phone and stayed on it; yelling at other people. The mission was finally approved. We headed back to our flight line where I had more work to do. Charley still had no faith that they would actually attack the target, so he hopped into our Birddog and went out to watch. Maybe the coordination got more efficient in later years but I am sure that this was the only AOC approved ground attack mission that ever flew, based on our identification of a target.

The next USAF related story that I have to tell involved me and the operations officer of the "Mule Train." That was the Air Force outfit flying the old C-123 fixed wing cargo transports out of Tan Son Nuht. I'm afraid that this one does not reflect great credit on me. Anyway, a group of us were out on the town one night when I got into a physical argument with this guy. I didn't know him, but he came up beside me at the urinal in the men's room and made some derogatory remark. I didn't even understand what he had said, but I knew it was not intended to be pleasant. I got to thinking about it while I finished my business, then I followed him out to a booth where he had just taken a seat, and I said "that's all right Sonny" while I knuckled his crew cut head. We were just leaving the place, and as I went out the door, he came flying out after me.

He clubbed me on his way by and things were definitely getting serious until some of my guys and some of his guys held us apart. Now neither of us was very big, so this was not too tough a job for our buddies. CWO Don Herman had me by the collar. Don's hand was about the size of a dinner plate and he was holding me up so that my toes could barely paw the ground. Well, if we couldn't hit each other, we would just yell at each other. He was carrying on about the goddamn Army when, in the middle of his tirade, he said "the only Army people over here that are worth a shit are the helicopter pilots!" Shucks, things settled down right away and we even exchanged telephone numbers.

He wanted to fly a CH-21 and offered to trade me for a ride up front in a C-123. Both things eventually happened and I have a couple of cards that he gave me around here someplace. One is entitled "The

Air Force Prayer" and it sez "God grant me the eyes of an eagle, the stealth of a stalking tiger, and the balls of an Army helicopter pilot." The other one is the business card of one James Edward Joseph, Captain, United States Air Force. On the back of which he wrote "I put you in the left seat with Gen Harkins" (aboard) signed Jim Joseph. Well now, I don't remember the general being back there, but maybe he was. I have it on record!

As a post script to this story, let me tell you one of the reasons why I always thought that the USAF took over the Army CV-1 Caribou. Both these cargo lifters, the C-123 and the CV-1, were tail loaders, with the fuselage designed to allow straight-in loading under an elevated tail structure. When the Army's 1st Aviation Company came in, they lined up their CV-1s on the ramp next to the Air Force C-123 line. When you looked down the ramp the tallest tail sections were on the Army Caribous. With that elevated tail they appeared to dwarf the Air Force C-123s. You just know that that must have irritated hell out of the Mule Train pilots. I figured it to be only a matter of time before the USAF had to correct such an embarrassing situation. Well, I was just kidding about that, but the Air force was serious, and they got our CV-1 Caribous in 1966.

Now this next part is again not directly related to our experience with the USAF in 1962 but, as the lawyers would say, it leads to character. I was back in Vietnam running an aviation maintenance company at Vung Tau when the Army and the Air Force finally reached a new agreement cutting up the air mission between the services. In the process, among other things, we had to turn over our Caribous to the USAF. That event well illustrates one of the main conceptual differences between the services. The Army in Vietnam had been using the fixed wing CV-1 cargo airplane in a "retail" delivery system. They would fly them into short, unimproved landing areas, as near to the ultimate user as they could find space. DeHavilland had had long experience designing aircraft for the "bush" pilots of the Canadian and Alaskan North, and for the US Army. They had specifically built the Caribou to do this kind of job; get in on short fields and on rough surfaces if necessary; then to need only a short take-off run to get back into the air again. In Vietnam, they operated mostly between short hard surfaced runways but many landing fields were made of only Pierced Steel Planking (PSP) or packed dirt.

Our Caribous were doing things like delivering people, rations and mail. They were making medical air ambulance runs and providing rapid emergency resupply to units in the field. They rarely returned empty from a mission. There was always someone or something that needed to be somewhere else. Retrograde hauls were normal. One of these missions was to trade-out helicopter engines and other major items to and from my shops at the 611th Aircraft Direct Support (ADS) Company for return to the United States for repair. Helicopter engines were always in short supply and they were available only on a direct exchange basis from the 34th General Support Group at Tan Son Nuht. We would send a bad one up on a Caribou backhaul and get a new one delivered on their next retail flight to Vung Tau. There is an old Army belief that leaders should never screw around with a soldier's mail or pay because these things contribute directly to morale. Good meals are of nearly equal importance. So the delivery of the mailbag, the paymaster and the Christmas turkey, all had a direct impact on unit morale and on mission accomplishment. And helicopters need good engines to stay in the air. The Caribou companies had been efficiently carrying out these important missions since 1962.

I remember seeing an Air Force captain land an O-1 Birddog one day, when we were operating our CH-21s out of Can Tho. His name was Richard Secord, later Major General Richard Secord. It was rare to find a USAF pilot anywhere near the ground outside of a major air base. We didn't know what he was doing, actually on the ground, at a short strip so far out of Saigon and we never found out either. He attained considerable notoriety in the Iran/Contra affair years later and he must have been doing Sneaky Pete things even back then. Anyway, he came in hot. He never put any flaps down. Army pilots always put down at least 30 degrees to reduce landing speed and roll-out distance. Even 45 or 60 degrees of flap are available on an O-1 and can be used for very short fields. The Air Force captain's touchdown speed without flaps was so high that I thought he was headed for the rice paddies off the end of the field. Can Tho had plenty of runway but he used all of it up before he got that little airplane stopped. That piece of USAF demonstration flying in 1962 should have warned me about what would take place when Air Force pilots began flying the Caribous in 1966.

The first thing that happened was that most of the airfields into which the Army had been flying were declared unusable for the CV-1. They did not meet minimum USAF standards for operation. They could not land the Caribou on them because the fields were either too short, or too narrow, or the surface was not thick enough to carry the weight of the airplane, or all of the above, according to USAF regulations. Those airfields had been okay for us; and we are talking about the good ones. PSP and dirt? Forget about it!

Next we found that our retail delivery system did not fit the Air Force method of operation. They measured their effectiveness on tonnage hauled. You don't get many tons out of hauling paymasters, mail bags or hot meals; nor out of T-53 engines either. They could not adopt a retail mentality. It didn't fit USAF doctrine. Air Force operators did not get much credit for small loads of people, mail or meals. It soon became "full and down" before they would fly to, or from, even the big airfields. You know, the ones the commercial passenger airplanes use. I had to begin shipping my engines up and down the Saigon River by barge or cross country by truck convoy; the turn-around time lengthened by an order of magnitude. Helicopters on the ground are useless, but at least they didn't use much gas, while they were grounded waiting for the direct exchange parts to arrive.

The need for high speed retail delivery didn't go away of course. The Army started to fill that gap with Chinook helicopters, at probably ten times the expense of the fixed wing Caribou, and to add insult to injury the CV-1 Caribou disappeared from the USAF inventory within a short time. The Lockheed C-130 Hercules became the main cargo aircraft in Vietnam. The Herc was, and still is, a magnificent heavy cargo lifter, but the medium fixed wing cargo aircraft, and the retail mission as the Army saw it in the early 60s, did not survive.

While the Army was still flying the Caribou though, a funny thing happened. I don't know the real details; I wasn't there, but I heard about a CV-1 that had crash landed at a short dirt strip in the jungle; in the highlands around Bam Me Thuot, I think it was. It was reported that someone had managed to land a Caribou, with GEN Westmorland aboard, and the landing gear up. Now that would be hard to do because of all the red lights in the cockpit, the warning noise in the headset and the shaking of the control wheel; all of which occur when a Caribou is approaching a stall with the gear up. The crew must have been a little nervous; a really embarrassing situation for them, but no one got hurt. The news of course, traveled all around quickly and gained its share of fame. The pilot was said to be a guy named Charley Klopp and the incident became known around Vietnam as Klopp's Flop.

The Army 1st Aviation Company arrived, operating from Thailand with their Caribous, in early 1962. That roughly coincided with the assignment of USAF operators in the control towers. Much better radios were also installed at Tan Son Nuht. We had been able to talk with the VNAF controllers at the tower before the USAF arrived, but their English was not good and our Vietnamese language skill was nonexistent. That being the case, we had negotiated a deal where we kept most of our operations away from the main runway. The 57th helicopters were parked on the ramp near our hanger, which was located at the southwest corner of the air base. We were able to take-off and land over the fence, using the sod area between the taxiway and the runway. We would stay at low level until we were far enough out to not interfere with any fixed wing operations. We didn't even call the tower unless we had a flight of several helicopters lining up or landing on the runway. Naturally this had to change when blue suitors took control. We still mostly went in and out over the fence but we would at least let them know.

Even our US Air Force tower operators were not used to dealing with Army helicopters; especially in groups. This led to some amusing situations before all the wrinkles were worked out. The first story that I heard involved the Identification Friend or Foe (IFF) radio. The Air Force and Army fixed wing airplanes had these installed but we didn't have them in our helicopters. Many of our CWOs had not had an occasion to use one but of course their sense of humor remained intact. The IFF used a coded signal to paint a bright signature on the newly installed radar scope in the Saigon tower. It made a brighter "blip" then that which was returned from only the aircraft skin. Fixed wing flyers normally kept the IFF turned on. It would be on when one of them contacted the tower for landing instructions or whatever. A tower operator might want to positively establish which of several targets on his scope represented that aircraft. If so, he would have the pilot turn off the IFF momentarily so that he would see one blip on his scope blink and dim. I have found that Air Force guys like to use colorful slang now and then and they had adopted the word Parrot to identify the IFF radio. Rather then tell a pilot to turn off his IFF they would tell him to strangle it. The first time they asked one of our crews to "please strangle your Parrot" the pilots just looked at each other and, with normal CWO directness, they responded by saying "What's that tower? They ain't no birds in here with us."

The weather over there could turn on a dime and this led to the next weird interaction with the tower. We had completed a combat assault down south of the Mekong River as the ceiling began lowering and it started to rain. We had learned that there always seemed to be just a little room under the monsoon storm down where the Delta was flat. It was just about at sea-level and there were very few tall obstacles around. We also knew that you could further improve the odds by flying west to the shoreline of the South China Sea than following it up to the Saigon River before heading back in to Tan Son Nuht.

That afternoon we started out on a direct heading for home. The ceiling gave us a couple of hundred feet and the rain wasn't too bad. As we got further north though, the weather began to really sock in, so we aimed out to the ocean shore. By the time we were halfway up the Saigon River, the clouds were hanging so low that we were flying at about fifty feet over the mangrove swamp, and the rain was so heavy that forward visibility had been reduced to a quarter of a mile or less. We had reduced our airspeed to around forty knots as we approached the city. The weather was looking a little close, but we now knew that we would not have to land in contested territory or try to pick out a large backyard somewhere. So I called for landing: "Saigon tower Army 220 and flight is two miles out for landing, over." "Negative Army 220 the airfield is closed." "Roger Saigon we are a flight of helicopters. We have adequate ceiling and visibility for the approach and we don't need your runway." "No. No. No. You can't land here Army we are closed." This argument continued as I altered my heading to land directly at the main runway intersection and a flight of 12 CH-21C helicopters blasted directly over the tower at fifty feet or less. We damn near blew their roof off.

The USAF brought good radios with them, and the air traffic that Tan Son Nuht was beginning to handle made efficient tower control absolutely necessary. In fact in later years Saigon was said to be the busiest airfield in the world. We were happy to have them with us, but they needed a little training with regard to the Army and its helicopter operations. We were still talking with them after we got on the ground in that storm. We went face-to-face in the tower as I tried to explain the difference between a fixed wing airplane and a helicopter. I told them *again* of our intent to avoid landing in contested territory unless we had planned on it. We held to the agreement that we had worked out with the Vietnamese; that we would land over the fence and stay off the runway, but we were going to land when we needed to do so. They finally relented and agreed; as long as we didn't fly over the roof of the tower again.

It has never been that easy for me to get along with the Air Force. I have said, over the years, that "I felt like I had spent more time fighting with the U.S. Air Force than I had fighting against the Viet Cong." Of course the USAF was well established at Tan Son Nuht by the time I was back for my second tour there, but my problems with them continued. When I was assigned to command the 56th ADS Company in Saigon, it seemed like things would be okay. My usual business was conducted at Hotel Three, which was the main Army helipad at Tan Son Nuht. It was well away from the Air Force operation and it had its own Army control tower. My helicopter maintenance hanger was there, and that's another funny thing, it was the same hanger we had used as our first mess hall in the 57th back in 62'. That was from where we had watched the bombing of the palace. I rarely saw a 120th helicopter at Hotel Three though. Maybe they were still hopping in and out over the fence like we had done back then.

I also had a fixed wing maintenance hanger in the 56th which, of necessity, had to have access to a runway. It was located near the main runway intersection, right in the middle of USAF business, so naturally most of my problems with the Air Force, on this trip, started there. Their tower people had gotten somewhat used to dealing with the Army, but they just didn't seem to like it when one of our small, single engine airplanes got in their way. When a twin engined U-8 had to be test flown they tolerated that, but when an O-1 or U-6 rolled out, they made damn sure that it burned plenty of gas on the taxiway while awaiting its turn to fly.

When we weren't doing maintenance on the helicopter side of the airfield, we were in the aircraft recovery business. Units no longer tried to do much repair in the rice paddies or boondocks. Our job was to go out, rig any downed aircraft in our area and call in a CH-47 Chinook to sling load it out. It was usually a helicopter being recovered so, when that was the case, it was no problem to bring it in to the helipad. The typical Air Force attitude hadn't changed much over the years though. It came to a head with the tower again one day when it was a fixed wing U-1 Otter that had gone in.

The aircraft had had a complete engine failure but the crew had managed a nice forced landing on a very narrow and short dirt road out there between rice paddies. The aircraft was on its wheels and had suffered no further damage. We quickly flew out and rigged the Otter for Chinook evacuation. As usual we then led the lift back to Saigon. We called for landing, on the sod next to the main runway intersection. This would place the Otter where we needed it, beside our fixed wing hanger, but the tower responded "negative; take it to the helipad." So another round of discussion began, as we explained that we had a fairly large fixed wing airplane on the hook and if we took it into the helipad we would have to take the wings off and truck it over to where we could work on it, and from where it could take-off, when we finished. The tower was still saying no as we dropped the Otter on the infield next to the runway and our hanger. There was no further conversation this time. Maybe they had caught a little incipient anger in my tone of voice on the radio and didn't really want to hear any more of that.

One of the first things that I had noticed, upon my arrival in the 56th, was that our cantonment area was located on the same field where the 57th tent city had been erected at the beginning of festivities. Of course it was much improved, with nicely floored wood and screen buildings, clubs for the enlisted soldiers and those old mahogany, creosote cured, outhouses had been replaced with cement floored washhouses. Best of, the latrines sporting genuine porcelain ponies. Well the USAF decided that they had to have that piece of real estate and they had to have right now. We were ordered to move to new quarters; relocating to what had been the "Camp Alpha" replacement center. Those "repo-depo" buildings were just across the fence from where the 57th (by then the 120th) housing area was located. Although this was closer to our helicopter work hanger, Camp Alpha had been established to house soldiers for only a few days, when they were either moving in or out of the country. It was not well developed for long term occupancy and it was in need of repair. The Air Force insisted that we needed to be out quickly; in a matter of days. We were able to salvage very little else but you can bet that we ripped up those porcelain ponies and took them with us. The Air Force moved in behind us in a month or two and made it into a parking lot.

Our major recurring problem however, was at the fixed wing hanger. We shared a ramp with the headquarters of a USAF comm/recon outfit. That organization was commanded by a full colonel and they were equipped with some kind of specialized gear mounted on large trailers. Their parking ramp was immediately adjacent to our hanger. Those trailers were never seen to go out behind a truck anywhere, but they seemed to have the ability to move directly sideways onto my portion of the ramp. They would encroach slowly, and our guys pushed back as well as they could, but eventually it reached a point where we couldn't even get a U-8 out of the hanger to test fly it. Then I would have to get into it; *again*! Well I discovered that it was no easier for an Army major to deal with an Air Force full colonel than it had been for a freaking junior Army captain to deal with a marine bull colonel. After I would get run off, which happened most times, I would call for help from battalion headquarters and our LTC commander would arrive to chew my ass then go over to try reasoning with the United States Air Force himself. The 34th Army Group commander would be the next party to get involved if necessary. The trailers would then be reluctantly moved back over towards their own real estate before they again began their encroaching creep onto mine.

This running turf battle never really ended, and there were other aggravations as well. I always tried to handle these first with the USAF major who had the working level responsibility for running the airfield. The CWOs in the 57th would probably recognize the situation when I sometimes arrived at his office in a less than happy frame of mind. That fellow major was a good officer though and he always tried to help. I eventually found that he also had a good sense of humor. As I came storming through his door one day he took one look at me, got up from behind his desk, walked calmly over to a steel wall locker, opened the door, crawled in and closed it behind him. And that is a good a place as any to end this description of my personal war with the United States Air Force.

CHAPTER 20

A LOOSE SHOT GROUP

When firing an automatic weapon keep your finger light on the trigger. Limit fire to bursts of six rounds or the muzzle will begin to climb and your shot group will go to hell! Basic Infantry Officer Training 1954

The stories that follow will form a loose shot group of events that are apt to pop up in my memory from time to time. They are in no chronological order, nor do they fit into a very logical sequence, but together they form a mini-composite of our Vietnam experience in mid-year 1962. Often, when one starts out with a collection of events like this, one starts first with the weather. One thing we didn't have to worry about in that regard was weather forecasts. There weren't any. The weather liars hadn't arrived. We had to do the mis-calculations ourselves.

The weather; the consistently lousy weather. The place was always hot, sticky and usually wet. Even when we had brilliant sunshine we were wet with sweat. Mold and mildew were the nature of things and when the monsoons started to hit; Katie bar the door. One day we were lined up on the dirt runway out at Moc Hoa. We were waiting to lift an ARVN force back from a reconnaissance through enemy territory. It started to rain so we all scurried back to our helicopters to sit out the storm. Soon the rain began coming down so hard that we couldn't see the end of the forty foot rotor blade hanging out in front of our cockpit. It was a micro burst and it didn't last long but I had never seen rain so thick that you couldn't see forty feet through it.

I had gotten an early lesson concerning the weather one day from a couple of VNAF pilots in a U-6 Beaver. I couldn't find a U.S. plane, so I had borrowed the Vietnamese aircraft and crew to fly a recon over a planned mission area. When we got over the spot, we found it to be totally socked in. The cockpit was occupied of course, so I was trying to do my job out of the back side windows. Well it just wasn't going to work, so I told the pilots "let's go home." They turned east and flew for awhile, then without any radio contact or explanation, they dumped the nose and headed straight down through that mess. I didn't know what was going on! Were they intent on committing suicide or what? I even started to get to my feet, and I was about to yank one of them out of his seat by the back of his neck, when we broke out over the water. They knew that there would be at least a little clear air down there, but I didn't at the time. It turned out that neither of these aces was instrument rated. That was how they always got below an overcast. As a normal approach method, it sure scared the hell out of me!

Those VNAF pilots weren't the only ones that could show me neat tricks either. Each of our own pilots had unique skills. Several of them exhibited some special talent when flying the machine. CWO Dave Saylor, one of our would-be maintenance officers, had volunteered to help out with test flights when needed. He would first complete the test which cleared the helicopter for a return to flight status. After that, he loved to initiate a max takeoff, while holding one pedal to the wall, which threw the aft rotor system out to one side. The rear rotor system would then continue to circle around the forward rotor system as he held the pedal. That 86 foot long helicopter seemed to just screw itself into the sky. That didn't really have much utility, but it looked spectacular. On the other hand, maybe that helped clue us into the idea that if we held in a little extra pedal the aircraft would fly in a crab; that is very slightly sidewise. At altitude, when viewed from the ground, the long Shawnee fuselage would appear to be following its nose in one direction and yet be actually headed in a slightly different direction. If VC gunners led the helicopter when shooting up at one flying above them, as they had been instructed to do, the rounds would likely miss. At least that was the theory.

Another thing was that all of a sudden everyone became a maintenance expert. Saylor was just one of them. A pre-flight inspection, if it is thoroughly done by any pilot, is good enough to ensure safe operation. Of course you can't see into the engine or transmissions, and there are other things that can cause the aircraft to quit flying right, that you would be unlikely to catch on an external inspection. Several of our pilots were experienced maintenance officers from previous assignments. They felt that only by closely observing the work while it was actually being done, could they become familiar enough to avoid flying those aircraft which might be considered "weak sisters." Although this idea was widely held, it worked just the opposite for Big Jim Eakins and the other maintenance officers. They normally got stuck flying one of those suspect aircraft in the maintenance clean-up position as "Tail End Charley." Since the maintenance officers felt like they had to stand behind their workers, they usually volunteered to fly the weak ones anyway. But they sure didn't like a bunch of people looking over their shoulders while they supervised the work. To keep the traffic down in the hanger, an order had to be given to all of those would-be maintenance officers directing them to stay out of the hanger and out of the maintenance people's hair. They didn't get to pick the aircraft they would fly either.

Besides the maintenance experts, who were not reluctant to air their personal beliefs, there were the instructor pilots who could also be fairly opinionated. One subject was a favorite of both camps. The IPs always liked to discuss the flight characteristics of the Shawnee and how to best manage the helicopter. The maintenance guys would join them in arguing one particular subject; whether it was more likely to damage a helicopter by over-boosting the engine with too much manifold pressure or by over-revving the drive train and the engine by too much RPM. The rest of our pilots would even take sides in this critical argument from time to time. These educational talks about how best to fly the Shawnee could get quite intense.

The density altitude, at which we were operating, precluded much chance of an over-boost anyway, so the real question was: how much will it hurt the aircraft to push the RPM past the red line at the bottom of an approach if one needed to do that to keep from crashing? My judgment was that it sure couldn't help anything much and should be avoided if possible. I didn't feel qualified to really participate in the technical discussion, but I let it be known that exceeding the red line RPM did not seem like a good idea to me. There may even have been one or two in-flight demonstrations to try to prove a point on this. I have always hoped that more damage was inflicted on those pilot's egos than to the airplane when, and if, that ever happened.

We had too many instructor pilots. This was because, back at Fort Lewis, some of those pilots returning from Korea were already IPs in the CH-21 and some of those coming in from Germany were IPs in the CH-34. Since the unit had at this time, a major work load in transitioning other newly assigned pilots into cargo helicopter flying and checking them out in the Shawnee, the decision was made to put them all on Sixth Army IP orders. For a short time, while still on temporary duty from Sixth Army, we reported through the U.S. Army Ryukus headquarters in Okinawa, Japan. That group noticed the excess IP staffing and sent down instructions to reduce the number.

There was no discussion; just the edict, by name, of those who would no longer be IPs. Well there were a couple of things that bugged me about that. The first was that they had just whacked off the bottom of an alphabetical list which included our standardization IP, Bennie Potts and several of our most experienced instructors. It was directed that CWO Bob Zeigler would be the first to go, of course, and next were to be Len Wilson and Willy and Billy J. Williams and on up the list. The second irritation was that when an IP was flying, the crew was logged as first pilot and instructor pilot on the DA Form 759 flight record. Any other time we had to log first pilot and co-pilot. Nobody liked to have to record combat support co-pilot time. It just didn't seem fair to add a bunch of ex-IPs to this situation. The Army, following the USAF lead, got around this later by designating Aircraft Commanders so that most crews could log AC and first pilot; thereby avoiding the recording of co-pilot time. But that was then and this was now. I sat on the letter for a few days, but I didn't have the time or the inclination to argue about it. I just consigned the thing to the round file and never heard anything more about it.

Moc Hoa was one of those places that we staged out of often. We usually had to stand by there, after a troop haul, in case further transport was needed. We spent a lot of time "kicking rocks" along the side of the runway. Rain was not the only thing that could get thick out there either. The flies were damn near as thick. When the sun was shinning, we would sit in the shade of our helicopters to eat our lunches. It was the only shade around. Usually, our meals were just old Army "C" rations dated 1944, but sometimes the mess hall would have provided bag lunches. That was better than the Cs, I guess, but you had to be careful to wave all of the black cloud of flies off the food, so you could get a quick bite out of a sandwich, before they swarmed back all over it.

Later in the war the media liked to report on any "friendly" atrocity they could find. They did not often cover enemy atrocities. Even though there were far and again more of those, our reporters were rarely on hand to see them and I guess they weren't "news" anyway. I witnessed only one such "friendly" event, that I recall, and I personally put a stop to that one as soon as I saw what was happening. The ARVN had managed to capture some VC, and we had flown out to pick them up and bring them back to Moc Hoa, where the ARVN intended to hold them for a time. They placed the group under guard a short distance away from the runway. We were sitting in the shade of our helicopters when I noticed that an ARVN soldier had dug-in an entrenching tool, handle up, and had then seated a VC soldier on it. The ARVN soldier began to hit the VC soldier on the head with the butt of his rifle, obviously intending to jam him down on that handle. I moved! Sprinting over there, I yelled at the NCO who stood watching, to knock it off. That we couldn't stand for that kind of thing. He probably didn't understand the words, but he damn sure got the meaning and the beating stopped. I like to think, by the way, that any responsible American officer or NCO would have done the same thing.

Some time later, we were again kicking rocks at Moc Hoa, when a series of dumb things happened. This time our job was to place a battlefield assessment team at the site of a fight where the VC had suffered a large number of casualties. Most of the carnage had been the result of air strikes and the dead were scattered over a wide area. There were two complications on our mission that day. The first was that we had brought along a bunch of strap-hangers. Okay, maybe it is not fair to call this bunch of Army colonels "strap hangers". They were U.S. Army War College students and faculty on an "overseas visit." The other thing was that a newly assigned 57th aviator was with us.

Bob Corneil was a senior captain who was on the promotion list to major. He was on his initial orientation flight. CWO Benny Potts, who had been designated as his IP, was flying with him. My job was in jeopardy again, by the way, because a couple of senior captains had now joined us. Even so, I was still the ops guy and was trying to run the mission. Soon, the visiting armchair colonels wanted to go out and take a closer look at the battle area. Corneil thought that was a great idea and volunteered to fly them. With considerable reluctance I told Benny "to go ahead; take them out there but be careful." On the way back they flew over a bunch of oriental troops in those funny little banana leaf hats with the red star painted on them; obvious bad guy uniforms. The colonels wanted to take a closer look, so our new captain agreed and returned to circle over them at a nice low level. Well, the VC couldn't miss such a fine target so they shot them. Bullets came up through the cockpit and instrument panel, hitting Corneil in a leg and showering Benny with bits of flying Plexiglas, qualifying them both for Purple Heart medals. Some of the War College colonels may also have gone home as Plexiglas wounded heroes. I forget.

Corneil was soon promoted to major and he was still in a cast when he was sent north to command the 8th Helicopter Company. He was however, in my view, a slow learner. There is an old saying that if you lead with your chin you are bound to get your nose bloodied. I was not there, so I won't pretend to know exactly what happened, but it sounded to me like a repeat performance. I understand that they were again circling at low level, this time over a hole in the jungle, when their helicopter was shot down. A senior advisor wanted to take a closer look at a jungle village and, in this case, it cost him his life. They were banked over, hard in the turn, when a single bullet killed the pilot, CWO Joe Goldberg, and the helicopter just continued the roll into the trees. With a great deal of good luck and effort, MAJ Corneil was the only survivor. CWO Goldberg, the gunner and the crew chief died. This was the first Army pilot and partial crew to be lost in the war. The news was taken hard in the 57th where most of us knew some of the crew of that helicopter. Goldberg was a friend of many of our CWOs. As tragic as this loss was, it did not, of course, stop our daily missions; either exciting or mundane.

Quite often we would be called upon to deliver government functionaries to various locations around the Corps area. Father Hoa was not the only Catholic leader of some importance so higher ranking visitors also called on other Catholic villages. It was apparent that the Diem family subscribed to that religion because we never seemed to carry VIPs to any of the other types of religious centers; except maybe to try to collect taxes or well after the place had been involved with some kind of enemy action.

There was one medium sized place down below Can Tho that I happened to visit twice. The village surrounded a fair sized church and was about the only place I remember, outside of the few major towns down there, with any kind of an organized appearance. It sported a single road leading through the center of town that was long enough and wide enough to park two Shawnees in line. We parked them there the first time we flew in. The ARVN assured us that there was no risk and that they would provide security. We were invited to go to lunch with our VIP passengers and the church leaders. They introduced us to a fruit that, as best I could understand it, was called breadfruit. I don't know about the name for sure, but it was a grey blob just a little bigger around than a softball, and when you picked it up, your fingers sunk in to about the second knuckle. It smelled like a weird combination of citrus and garlic. Of course, we had to try it, so as to not offend our hosts. If you held your nose, it didn't taste too bad going down, but it was not nearly as good coming back up.

The next time that I saw that town we were carrying in an ARVN team to assess the damage from an attack that had taken place during the night before. It looked like the fight was hardly over as we approached the village. The trees along the main street were shattered and the debris of recent battle was scattered along it. Occasional rifle fire was still being heard as we picked up a load of wounded people and flew them out. We made another med evac trip before we took our original passengers back to Saigon and it was a nervous situation each time. I was amazed that the battlefield assessment team had gone in that quickly and I made the assumption that the Diem family religion had had something to do with it.

Flying about the country you saw many unusual things. What we saw one day appeared peculiar to us but we didn't think too much about it. It looked like some kind of construction project was going on in the little town as we flew past. The freshly cut planks were of bright new wood, which seemed to be out of place among the native huts, so on the way back we dropped a little lower to see what we could see. They appeared to be constructing boxes of some kind. It looked like they were making coffins. When we reported this strange behavior to our ARVN 7th Division Liaison Officer, Dai Uy (Captain) Lang, we learned that the VC often forced the villagers to build coffins just before they attacked somewhere in the vicinity. The coffins were for their own expected casualties, but the construction project was also intended as a threat to keep the village elders in line.

Dai Uy Lang was a friendly outgoing little guy who spent much of his time with us in Saigon He is hopefully alive and well in San Francisco or someplace now; he very well might be too. He was a survivor. When I was working in Vung Tau during 1966 a tire blew out on my jeep. That noise, as you might imagine, was a little disconcerting considering the circumstances, but I survived without injury. I decided to walk on to where I could call back to get my assigned "driver" to fix it. My PFC driver rarely actually drove me anywhere but he could fix a tire. Pretty soon an ARVN jeep sped by, kicking up the dust, before it slammed to a halt and backed up to me. In the back seat was Dai Uy Lang.

This was more than four years after we had first met, but Lang was still a captain. He told me that he was lucky to have survived during all the government intrigues and coups that had been going on. He said that he had even been under arrest for a while, but that he had eventually been cleared, and had been marked as "non-political." This allowed him to stay alive. He could not, however, be promoted. Even so he was filling a lieutenant colonel's position as the intelligence chief of the Vung Tau District. We talked about a few other things while we sped downtown. He told me that he now owned several properties in Saigon, including a couple of bars, and he invited me to be his guest at one of them sometime. But the funniest thing was to find out that he had spent more time in the United States than I had during the nearly five intervening years. He had been attending various U.S. Army stateside schools, while a German tour had poked a large hole in my time at home. So while I had spent but little time in the good old US of A, Dai Uy Lang was living it up in the land of the big PX.

Recounting these stories, leads me to worry that somebody might miss an important fact. You must know, that the kinds of things that happened to me in Vietnam, were happening to all of our pilots; not exactly the same things of course, but similar. Also, the tempo of action and the violence was steadily increasing. It seems inexact to say that the combat assaults had become routine; but they had. It is a hell of a note to get used to being shot at; but it happens. Many 57th stories will never be told. As noted before, we all wrote after action reports. A copy of each of those was held in my operations office at Tan Son Nuht, but damn it, they all just disappeared about the time we began to rotate home. That has always galled me, but except for dates and places, they were probably less than illuminating anyway. ABC (club manager Allen B. Causseaux) had managed to find a source for a large wheel of cheese, which he kept, centered on the officer's club bar, and the pilots always seemed to be in a hurry to get back to the Shawnee Teepee for some cheese and crackers or something. They did not seem to have much time for writing reports. I didn't have much spare time to check those reports for completeness either.

Most of our pilots were pretty phlegmatic anyway. You might say that their reports were always a little short on detail. They usually didn't have a lot to say in the evenings either. For example, Willy Williams and Bob Eastland were good friends. They could usually be found at the same table in the club; not saying much, but enjoying each others company. One night, after too many glasses of "cheese and crackers" maybe, one of them quietly reached over the table, and without even getting up, he knocked the other one on his ass. Few words had been spoken, at least not loudly. The victim got up, resumed his seat, and that was the end of the conversation. The punch was probably thrown by Willy but it could have been farmer Eastland.

Bob gave me a demonstration one night, about just how quietly explosive he could be. We were sharing a blue and white back to the base fairly late one night. Those lousy taxi drivers used to kick the price up to about double after midnight. It was a little later then that when we arrived at the Tan Son Nuht gate. We didn't like it, but we were prepared to pay the exorbitant price, and we started to hand over the piasters. The taxi driver wouldn't take the offered money. He insisted on a second doubling of the fee. We threw the money in through his window, but he kept screaming at us for more, as we started to walk away. Bob must have looked kind of menacing when he turned and headed back towards the cab, because the driver frantically rolled his driver-side window up. Unfortunately for him, he had forgotten that the window behind him was still open. The farmer reached in and slammed the taxi driver's head into his window so hard that it broke the glass. Bob never said a word. When the gate guards started to walk our way, that blue and white was out of there.

I'll tell you about an old warrant officer, who worked for me in the 56th Aircraft Direct Support Company during my next tour, which further illustrates just how hard it was to get anything out of some of these guys. Mr. Usher was a warrant officer junior grade, but he had been a mechanic and a UH-1 crew chief before he had gone to flight school, so calling him old is not an exaggeration. One of our main jobs in the 56th was the recovery of downed helicopters. Since I had participated in a number of those myself, there was no doubt in my mind, that all of the pilots in that company were deserving of at least one valorous award but Usher's after action reports were not very illuminating. His would go something like this: "Went to grid coordinates XY123456. Recovered UH-1D tail number 62-1234 and returned it to the helipad at Hotel Three."

I got him in the office one day and told him "Mr. Usher I know you are running into problems out there, so I know that you should be recommended for some kind of a medal; probably several of them, but you've got to give me something on which to base a recommendation. I need more detail. You have got to make your after action reports a little more flowery." He did. The next time he went out on a recovery it had definitely been a risky operation under enemy fire. His report was: "Went to grid coordinates XY123678. Recovered UH-1D tail number 64-2346 and returned it to Hotel Three." But there were little flowers drawn all up and down the margins of the report. We managed to get it out of him eventually and he got his medal.

Most of the 57th pilots were just like that. Their reports were not flowery and besides we weren't getting any medals anyway. Their after action reports were always as short as they could make them. I had been replaced as the ops officer, so I was no longer responsible for that safe, but when I went looking for the reports, I was flabbergasted to find them gone. I have my suspects but that is all that I have ever gotten! So my paper record is very limited. If it ain't in my memory bank all I can say is: "sing loi." That is the GI interpretation of the Vietnamese slang for: sorry about that! It is not an exaggeration to say that, by far, most of the stories of that first US Army helicopter year in Vietnam will never be told. Having said that, however, there are still some stories laying around up there in my cranium, so we'll press on.

We took some Vietnamese VIP visitors up to Ben Cat one day. This town is located in the heart of the Iron Triangle. It is surrounded by jungle but with a large rubber plantation on one side. The rubber plantation was interesting. The trunks had been chevroned so that all of the trees looked like they were wearing sergeant's sleeves but with the point of the stripes at the bottom. Attached to each at that point, was a cup to collect the rubber sap as it bled from the tree. Synthetic rubber had been around since WWII, but there was still plenty of demand for the real thing, so even with the war going on around them, the French with Vietnamese help, were still farming it. The VC also liked the rubber plantations since the ARVN usually avoided attacking while they hid inside them. Nobody wanted to damage a commercial crop that produced foreign exchange monies but we pilots already knew that "the rubber" could be a dangerous place.

The Ben Cat area had been the scene of several VC ambushes and attacks so we were familiar with it. We had been there before. We managed to squeeze our two helicopters inside the defensive perimeter where we shut them down to wait for our VIP passengers. It was not an altogether comfortable situation. We were next to the village on the inside of a ditch separating the place from the rubber plantation. The ditch was lined with bamboo spears that had been lodged into the ground with the pointy end up and aimed toward the rubber. These had been treated with bad stuff and were designed to impale the foot of any VC attacker. The trees were close to the other side of the ditch.

I spent a few minutes examining the ditch and the rubber farming before I turned to look back toward our parking place.

We had been assigned only one armed guard and I noticed that he was staring at the helicopters. He might have been quite familiar with the rubber plantation but he was obviously not at all that familiar with our helicopters. I walked over to him and said "hey, the VC are not going to jump out of the helicopters." Then I pointed out at the rubber trees. "That's where the bad guys will come from. Look out there!" He just smiled and looked at me. I guessed that he didn't understand English so I took him, gently by the elbow, turned him about, and pointed him toward the likely enemy avenue of approach. It wasn't long before he was turned back our way but at least he looked over his shoulder at the rubber trees once in a while.

These "ash and trash" missions could sometimes get a little exciting. We sort of got used to the engine failures, but I may be the only guy that rode through an in-flight, partial disintegration, of a CH-21C main rotor blade; twice. There may have been others with that experience, but if so I didn't hear about them. Both incidents were kinda scary, but are still very funny in my memory. We had been having some problems with delamination of the wood lay-up of our blades, but this was different. In each of my cases, one blade from the forward rotor disc, shed about four feet of its metal trailing edge from the trim tab to the tip of the blade. That instantly created a significant imbalance in the forward rotor system. This, in turn, caused the aircraft to start jumping up and down with each rotation of the damaged rotor blade. It made a hell of a noise when it happened. There was a very loud bang and it felt like we had been hit with a shell from a 57mm recoilless rifle or something. We were doing violent three or four foot hops with both me and the other pilot trying to hang on to the controls. I don't even like to think about what was happening to the gunner and crew chief in back. I don't know what they were hanging on to.

The first time it happened we were flying back empty from Vung Tau to Saigon. Here, and in many other places, is where my lack of any written record shows up; I don't remember who was flying with me that day, nor do I remember why the second Shawnee, that would normally have been along with us, was not there. Perhaps we had flown down to the newly arrived 611th Aircraft Direct Support Company for some assistance. But to continue the story; when that piece of blade departed, the aircraft began jumping up and down so hard that we could barely hang on to the cyclic stick. Conversation in the cockpit went something like this. Other pilot: "Oh shit, we've been hit." My response was: "yeah but we're still flying."

There was no attempt at further conversation as we wrestled the aircraft to the ground in a small clearing among the mangrove bushes. The crew was okay so we immediately set up a perimeter. Everyone got out of the helicopter quickly and got down in a defensive circle around the aircraft while we tried to figure out what to do next. We were looking up at the rotor blade with our mouths open when a column of small, fully armed, green suited people began to emerge from the surrounding bush. We held our fire (read: scared stiff) while they approached, and it's a good thing that we did too, because it turned out to be a friendly ARVN patrol. They didn't stay long though; other business to attend to I guess, because they showed us their backs way too soon.

So then we got busy with the duct tape. We called it Green Tape or 100 MPH Tape. In the old, Model A Ford days, it was a pair of pliers and a length of bailing wire and you could fix anything. Now it was duct tape. Our crew chief stripped off most of it that he had been using to hold the sound proofing together between the cargo compartment and the central transmission area. We took this and wrapped it around the "injured" blade to hold it together. At least we hoped it would do that! When we brought the helicopter to a hover, the four foot hop was still with us, but it was no longer quite so violent as long as we kept the speed down. I don't know; I just never liked the idea of spending the night out in the boonies, especially with only me and three other guys for protection. We hovered about 15 miles back to Tan Son Nuht at about 15 MPH.

The second time it happened, it was a kind of repeat in the cockpit. We had just picked up a load of troops from Tan Heip and were leading a flight out on a combat assault. The blade went. The conversation in the cockpit was again about the same. Other pilot:

"Oh shit, we've been hit." My response was the same: "yeah but we're still flying." We carefully lowered the collective stick to start down. Both of us were as tight on the controls as we could get when a big tree began to loom in front of us. I began trying to turn the helicopter slightly to the left but I couldn't move the cyclic. The other guy was convinced that any movement of the controls might have a disastrous effect. The conversation in the cockpit then was: Me: "let's turn to the left a little." Other pilot: "no! We're not moving anything." Then me again; "well we better move something or we are gonna run into that tree." Well we got it down without ramming the tree. We told Chalk Two, the helicopter that had followed us down, that we were okay so he went on to complete his mission. We were still fairly close to Tan Heip so we weren't too worried when the ARVN squad that we had been carrying wandered off and left us standing there.

CHAPTER 21

THE IDES OF MARCH

A Soothsayer: "Beware the ides of M arch."
Caesar: "Yond' Cassius has a lean and hungry look."
Antony: "Cry Havoc, and let slip the dogs of war."
A Tragedy by William Shakespeare CIRCA 1600[*1]

The reader should also beware. Although our 57th problems were not on the order of those facing Julius Caesar, this chapter will reflect poorly on some senior individuals and cover some of the gripes that still irritate me today.

As in any war, the vast majority of our citizens that served in Vietnam were among the best that our society has ever produced. It also seemed to me, however, that we were running into a lot of strange American behavior at some senior levels. That is not an unknown phenomenon either, but I thought that we were seeing more of it than should have been the case. As has been repeatedly noted, and not only in these pages, the South Vietnamese government was weak and the military leadership was poor. Leaders seemed to be far more worried about themselves, and each other, than they were about fighting either the Viet Cong insurgency or the North Vietnamese. The Republic of Vietnam never seemed to be fighting for its national life with the intensity it needed if it were to have much chance of success. This is not hindsight; it was evident to many, if not all of the actual participants from the very beginning. But our American leaders just kept following a loosing bet by piling on more people and more dollars without ever solving this basic problem.

That is not to say that we hadn't progressed some, militarily, by 1969. After many years of hard fighting, we seemed to have beaten them into near submission by weight of superior technology and firepower. By that time we could travel most major roads at night, which was some indication that we might finally have 'em whipped. During a temporary duty (TDY) trip I made in April of that year, it looked like things were well under control to me anyway. My mission took me to major headquarters all over the country where it seemed to me that tactical activity was low. The GIs were saying that the only priority requisitions leaving Vietnam were for whitewash, grass seed and floor polish. Commanders like to keep the troops busy painting rocks and polishing floors when there is not much else to do. The polish at MACV headquarters was so slick that you had to be careful to not slip on the floor. You might fall and break your butt.

But that was eight years after we had started assisting South Vietnam with U.S. Army helicopters. It was four years after we had gotten serious about it. And by 1969 it was politically too late. It took another six years to finally loose it completely; after we had withdrawn all of our military forces and the congress had withheld all monetary support for the South. That, of course, is the final thing that still pisses me off. After all those years, all those casualties and all those promises, and after we had ourselves pulled out, we wouldn't even support the South Vietnamese with enough funds or materiel to allow them a fair chance to fight for themselves. The RVN leadership and most of the top military just couldn't believe that we would do that and they lost whatever confidence that they had previously had in themselves.

It took a long time to screw that one up but we finally managed to do it. And maybe there was no way to avoid it, after we had gotten our feet firmly stuck in the quagmire, as David Halberstam had termed it in his 1965 book "*The Making of a Quagmire.*"*[2] But there were more than a few higher ranking U.S. military officers around in the early days that didn't see the future the way that Halberstam saw it. Generally, the field grade officers we worked with were excellent, but some of them seemed to be overly enthusiastic about getting fully into the fight, right from the start. There were two lieutenant colonels in particular, with which we had to deal, who typified the overly enthusiastic category. John B. Stockton was just a middle grade lieutenant colonel, but he was the first relatively senior Army Aviator that we encountered, and you have already read about some of his shenanigans. We'll cover the other one later; after we finish the Stockton story here.

American soldiers, "soldier on". For the most part they do the jobs that they are given as well as anyone could do it. Many enlisted soldiers became heroes. Officers, of course, do the same; they will normally strive for excellence and many of them will be heroes as well. Good leaders will always work to complete any mission given to them. At the same time they will do their best to *avoid casualties.* But remember; tough fighting, with lots of casualties, is what produces the heroes. Good leader try to *reduce the need* for heroism. Bad leaders seem to have little regard for the number of friendly casualties that might result from their actions. They are often fearless themselves for they are far more interested in personal aggrandizement than anything else.

One of my bosses said something during a discussion one day that well illustrates this point. It was later in the war. We were loosing far too many people and aircraft to accidents. We were also putting too many hours on our helicopters in what I thought to be unnecessary flying. My comment that accidents would be reduced, if the unnecessary flying were reduced, brought the following response: "Casualties are going to happen anyway and if I am being measured on how many hours my unit flies, we'll fly more than anyone else." How's that for effective leadership? I didn't really recognize, in the beginning, that anyone could be so self-oriented, or intent on a damn-the-torpedoes approach in fighting this kind of insurgency war, especially one in which we were as yet only advisors.

The appearance of LTC Stockton on the scene in Saigon was my first indication that we could be getting into something different; something where rational people might not always be in charge. Stockton was a problem for us from day one. And, in my view; he continued to be a problem for the U.S. Army until the day he retired. Some of the following account of the Stockton odyssey came from Bob Dillard who stayed in touch with us periodically while he was assigned to the MAAG Headquarters downtown. Stockton and his team were also flying desks down there, after we managed to get him out of our hair. Dillard had just spent some temporary duty time in Laos and was about to be reassigned state-side. He was on his way to join the Howze Board which had just been formed to identify future requirements for Army Aviation. Bob Dillard was one of the good ones. We were sorry to see him go. But before he departed, he told us that Stockton would also finally be going and we were very happy about that.

Stockton and his team had been assigned to Vietnam, on 90 day temporary orders, from Korea. Dillard told us that the other members of the team had quickly left for home, or had gone back to Eighth Army as soon as their 90 days were up, but Stockton had refused orders to go. He was than issued a second set of written orders which he ignored as well. It had never even occurred to me that an officer could do that and get away with it. This guy *was-by-god-going-to-participate* in what he must have seen as his last opportunity to be the warrior that he thought he was. Dillard told us that the third order for him to get out of country was delivered verbally, in person, by the Commander in Chief Pacific, Admiral Harry D. Felt, who was in Saigon for a meeting. Felt went out of his way to give Stockton a direct order to be on the next airplane out; one which would leave within the next twenty-four hours. He finally went. I wouldn't be surprised if a military police escort was necessary, all the way to a seat in the airplane, to ensure his compliance.

You can guess where this guy turned up next; at Department of the Army in Washington DC, of course. There, he no doubt spread his view about what was happening in Vietnam. The remark he made to the press, on the ramp that day of our first helicopter assault, was probably a good forecast of what he had to say later. Remember he had said: "it was just like World War Two out there." What a crock; and he must have been one of the first "expert returnees" from Vietnam after helicopters were being flown there. At least he was the first relatively senior Army Aviator to have spent more than a few days there. I shudder to think of the kind of misinformation he probably deposited at Headquarters DA. I hesitate to think that anyone there would have believed him.

That was the last that we in the 57th heard about this LTC Army Aviator at the time, but he stayed in the Army and he continued his gung-ho activities. Incidents were reported from wherever he was assigned. About a year or so after we saw the last of him, he was assigned to the 11th Air Assault Division; a test organization which was just forming up at Fort Benning, GA, to develop the airmobile concept. We heard that he soon took a very large "tactical" flight of helicopters (about fifty of them) from Fort Benning, GA, down into Florida without filing a flight plan. This violation of Army and FAA rules may have gotten plenty of attention from civil authorities, but the powers-that-be at Fort Benning must have thought nothing of it because he was allowed to continue his assignment as the commanding officer the 227th Assault Helicopter Battalion; one of the three major experimental aviation organizations in that division.

Being a polite person, what I would call Stockton's cavalier manner, was admired by some; probably including many of the soldiers assigned to the 227th and the 11th Division. My guess is that many of his troops would have responded well to his flamboyant, if erratic, leadership. When he later commanded the evolving division cavalry squadron, his soldiers were encouraged to wear bushy mustaches and they were outfitted in black Stetson style cavalry hats. They had a mule for a mascot. The non-standard appearance of his troops was not allowed under the uniform regulations of the time and would normally have been frowned upon by the brass; instead the 11th Air Assault Division adopted much of the non-standard appearance. I'm sure the troops loved the special treatment and reveled in the feeling that they were getting away with something. It was great for morale. The black hats are still worn by the elite 1st Calvary Division. It was however, said to be against a direct order, when Stockton shipped his mule to Vietnam with his deploying organization. I understand he got hell for that but he didn't get relieved and again it was probably great for morale.

When the 11th was redesignated as the 1st Air Cavalry Division and headed for Vietnam, Stockton was the commander of the Air Cavalry Squadron; a helicopter outfit designed to scout in front of the division, the same as armored cavalry squadrons had been doing for armored divisions in Europe since the end of WWII. The division was deployed to Vietnam in a non-tactical movement aboard ships. Even so, the accounts that I have heard, say that while they were still on the high seas, Stockton began agitating for an assault landing across the beach. That would have been very difficult because neither the Army organizations aboard, nor the ships themselves, were combat loaded and they were headed for an administrative port; no matter, he would tear the ship apart if necessary and storm the town.

Cooler heads prevailed and the 1st Cav landed at Qui Nhon, as expected, with no enemy contact. Qui Nhon was a secure port; or at least as secure as it got in Vietnam. There was no opposition. There were no casualties and no heroics were required to come ashore. That must have been a hell of a letdown for Stockton. He was unable to get the attention for which he was undoubtedly looking. The USMC stole his thunder when they came across the beach in 1965 with banners flying so that everyone would know that they had arrived; a loud announcement to the world that America was now in Vietnam for combat; good sense or treaties-be-damned.

Stockton lost no time however, in getting his nose blooded. In fact he got the whole 1st Cav Division's nose bloodied. Written accounts differ slightly but this is the gist of what I understand to have happened. Very soon after arrival, the air cavalry squadron was tasked to perform a recon of the area approaching, and into, the Ia Drang Valley. When the air cav helicopters received fire they returned it immediately. With Stockton's usual disregard for instructions, he then piled-in the rifle company which had been assigned to him to guard his helicopters; *and only for that purpose.* When the rifle company became fully engaged on the ground, the rest of the division had to come to the rescue. This set off the first large scale battle of the war between the U.S. Army and the North Vietnamese Army (NVA). Stockton reportedly received a very gentle ass chewing for committing that company without orders, but it made no difference because within three days he did it again. This time he reportedly lost his command and was transferred out of the division.

You need to understand that Stockton had been given a reconnaissance mission. Unless cornered into it, a recon mission does not normally include actively engaging the enemy in battle. A helicopter force can obviously avoid such cornering. By committing this small element of the division without orders to do so, Stockton had caused a large part of the division, and its green troops, to become fully engaged before the division was ready to fight and at a time and place of the enemy's choosing. If one believes in the generally accepted principles or war, those are *basic things-not-to-do.* His disobedience of orders and his over eagerness for battle continued a trend of behavior in 1965 that we had first seen in 1961 and early 1962.

For many years, I wondered if I had gotten the correct slant on this event. I thought maybe I was just basing my view on our earlier experience with Stockton. I recently read an account however that confirms my suspicions. The book, ("*Delta Force*" published by the Arms and Armour Press in 1983, by Col Charles A. Beckwith, US Army Retired and Donald Knox) *3 reported on a meeting between that tough, legendary, Special Forces officer, with the 1st Cav Assistant Division Commander, BG Richard Knowles. Beckwith, the commander of Delta Force, had been called in to see if Delta could do anything to assist in the fight that Stockton had just gotten them into.

Knowles had gotten Stockton on the radio when Beckwith was present. He was there when BG Knowles told Stockton that he didn't appreciate it that he had taken a rifle company out and then had used it for an unauthorized purpose; that now the division would have to mount an operation to get it out. After that mild rebuke, the general was satisfied that he had really told Stockton off and he asked Beckwith if that wasn't so. Beckwith reported that he just looked at the general, before saying that if an officer under his command had disobeyed such an order, he would start him marching East until he hit the China Sea., or words to that effect. Obviously I was pleased to read that account because it exactly confirmed my thinking concerning both Stockton and the generals who had put up with him for so long. Why wasn't Stockton relieved on the spot; the first time? How had he lasted in the U. S. Army this long?

According to the U.S. Army, the battle in the Ia Drang was a success. There was fierce fighting and great valor was exhibited by those who fought. The generals got the big set-piece battle they were looking for and the 1st Cav did kick some NVA ass. If you were convinced by the body-count logic the Army was using at the time, it could surely be called a great victory. The count was only 305 killed on our side against an estimate of 3561 killed on theirs; that's about ten to one, so it had to be a fine victory, right? I don't see it that way, and the 305 dead on our side might not see it like that either. I have no reservation about blaming those casualties on Stockton. He was so anxious to get into a fight that he couldn't wait. Some of those 1st Cav soldiers would very likely have died later anyway, soldiers do get killed in war, but later they would have at least been fighting on their own terms. They would have been much more likely to have fought when and where their really competent leaders chose; not on a battlefield where the enemy lay in wait and not before they had had a chance to get their feet on the ground and become a little more seasoned.

Stockton didn't completely disappear off the radar screen when he was finally removed from command in the 1st Cav. He was still allowed to skate and later made full colonel. Rumors continued for a number of years. It was said that he got kicked out of England after creating an international incident having to do with some lord's wife. The last thing I heard was that he was in Heidelberg and was running the liquor stores for the US Army in Europe. Rumors; I don't know what truth there is to them, but there is no doubt in my mind that this guy was extremely dangerous to himself, and anyone who happened to be around him, so I personally tend to believe just about anything concerning this particular loose cannon.

My respect for all general officers had always been high before my tour in Vietnam, but then I didn't personally know any of them at the time. I thought, like most young officers, that all the generals must have had something on the ball to get where they were. I still think that is true for the most part; but in Saigon, I started to get to know some of them better than I ever had before. For example, our first exposure to MG Timmes, Chief of the MAAG Army Section, had been fine. I was very impressed when he purposely didn't seem to notice as MAJ Dillard ran that out-of-line LTC off the USNS Core, but my regard for him lessened considerably when he later directed that that same LTC would fly as a pilot on our first mission. My respect didn't improve much either, when neither Stockton nor anyone else was held accountable for the resultant loss of a helicopter.

None of the senior officers from MAAG Headquarters came out to see us during the first few weeks we were there; in fact not many of them ever did. We did eventually get a visit from LTG Lionel McGarr, Chief of the MAAG. He wanted to see for himself the evidence that we were actually being hit. We showed him a couple of bullet holes and several patches as we walked him around the aircraft. Things were going fine until he looked up into the rear of the long Shawnee fuselage and observed that we could carve a hole back there and add a tail gunner. Maybe he thought that we could just station said gunner up tight against that R-1820 engine, with his head poked up against the rear rotor transmission, or something. Well, you could give him some leeway because of his ignorance about the CH-21C and helicopters in general. Or you could think that he was making a joke; maybe, but he wasn't smiling. We didn't consider it to be a joking matter so we weren't laughing it up either. We just stood there and let it pass. This was our top general; surely he couldn't be serious.

GEN Paul D. Harkins soon arrived to head up the new US Military Assistance Command—Vietnam (MACV) which replaced the MAAG. We saw him passing through occasionally, but he did not stop by for any briefings that I recall. Harkins was an officer whose background was in the use of armored forces. He had made his reputation in tank warfare during WWII. It seemed a little strange to see him and others of his era, with WWII background, assigned to manage our effort against this guerilla insurgency. But that is the precisely the background of the very senior officers we had in the U.S. military at the time. Our civilian leadership was also of this vintage. And it may be argued that therefore, the U.S. was essentially unprepared for any kind of a South East Asia jungle guerrilla war.

BG Joseph W. Stilwell soon arrived to head up the new Army Support Command which was to oversee the 45th Transportation Battalion and the other logistic organizations supporting MACV. He was the son of "Vinegar" Joe Stilwell of WWII fame. The troops called him "Cider" Joe. He took his job of overseeing the aviators seriously and even went so far as to take flying lesson in Vietnam. He also enjoyed flying as a gunner on our helicopters. We called him "the world's highest paid gunner" and we wondered if he didn't have more important things to do.

MG Delk Oden came to visit early on. He was the Chief of Army Aviation at the time and came from an infantry background. The visit to our hanger went fine. He didn't make any smart remarks about our old helicopters, or anything else that I remember for that matter, and soon he was off for rest and recuperation (R&R) in Bangkok. A close friend of mine, CPT Bob O'Donald, was flying with the MAAG flight detachment and he, with another pilot named Muttoni, loaded up Major Generals Oden and Timmes in a U-8D for the R & R trip. I had known Bob since primary flight school and I knew that he always told the truth and that he was not inclined to exaggerate; so when he told the following story, I believed it.

Bob said that, as they were reaching flight altitude, the generals in the back seat were discussing the advisory effort. Soon, Oden said to Timmes that "the first thing we have to do, to get this war off the ground, is to get rid of those goddamn TC aviators." He then seemed to realize that there were two young pilots aboard and leaned forward to poke one of them on the back with the question "isn't that right you guys?" Both pilots were TC aviators. Bob says that they just looked at each other and then they turned their collars around so that the generals could see the Transportation Corps insignia they were wearing.

Muttoni was a real character. His nickname was "Mutt." He acted to fit the name so everyone called him that. The U8-D was a small twin engine aircraft. It did not have a bathroom; instead it was equipped with a funnel kind of apparatus, called a relief tube, which a male passenger could use in emergency. It was hung on the back of the cockpit seats and to use it you pulled it back into position with your hand. No, I don't know what the ladies were expected to do. This was well before the modern volunteer, full gender accommodating, Army. About an hour into the flight, Oden got up to use the relief tube. Mutt said to Bob "watch this" and jerked the control wheel back and forth quickly. Then, as the general was wiping himself off, he began to apologize for hitting an air pocket. I guess you could call that a dirty trick, but those TC guys figured that he deserved it.

As far as I am concerned this story illustrates a basic fault in our approach to that war. The general had voiced an opinion that was full of crap. Number one, it seems to me that it was another small indication of just how little faith some of our military leaders had in the advisory effort, and how anxious they were to call the war their very own, even as early as 1962. Remember this was just the beginning of the expansion of what had been a small advisory effort. We helicopter guys were not even officially acknowledged to be there. We were classed as advisory support. We hadn't yet been officially allowed to shoot back. We were supposedly supporting the South Vietnamese in *their* war.

As a Transportation Corps (TC) branch aviator myself, the second issue is more personal for me. The Transportation Corps helicopter companies were redesignated in mid 1963. Instead of Transportation Corp companies they became "Airmobile" Aviation companies. This was a true reflection of the job we had been doing in Vietnam but the new title called for the "branch immaterial" assignment of commanders and key officers. That quickly resulted in "getting rid those goddamn TC aviators." Combat Arms pilots of the Infantry, Armor and Artillery took about all of those *branch immaterial* slots. This occurred, in spite of the fact that TC aviators were the most qualified officers to run those companies at the time the switch was made. If it really made any difference the fair thing to have done, would have been to send most of us back to our original combat arms branches, where we would have had an equal shot at those jobs. This is not a minor objection. This switch in assignment policy placed us all behind our combat arms contemporaries in later selection for "good" assignments, schools and promotions.

Soon after the Transportation helicopter companies were redesignated as "Airmobile" the rules for recording flying hours in Vietnam also changed. We Transportation company pilots had been told to record our time as "Combat Support (CS)" instead of "Combat (C)." The assault missions we had been flying as Transportation companies were no different than those that were later flown by the redesignated companies and recorded as "Combat." Oh things got more intense as the fighting went on, particularly after America decided to take full ownership of the war, but the holes we were collecting as TC aviators were just the same as the holes the later "combat warriors" got in their helicopters, and while fewer, the casualties were just as real. Not only did the CS designation often poorly describe the type of flying we had been doing but it also required the helicopter crews to log 15 more hours of flight time for award of the Air Medal (AM) than was to soon become the standard. It had been 40 hours of CS for each award of the AM; now it became 25 hours of C. The change of criteria was needed, but it was arbitrary and suspiciously related, closely, to the redesignating of the helicopter companies. It was not retroactive to cover the earlier Transportation Corps helicopter company flying.

Until those Transportation companies were redesignated, most combat arms pilots (Infantry, Armor & Artillery) had been flying either small fixed wing airplanes or small observation helicopters. They flew artillery forward observers in Cessna O-1s. They performed liaison flights or carried commanders around in OH-13s. They flew the U-6 Beavers in flight detachments and ferried senior officers around in twin engined aircraft. There were a few fixed wing Otter and Caribou companies, but these too were commanded and staffed with TC aviators. Twin engined OV-1 Mohawk companies were assigned to Army divisions and each division aviation company had light and utility helicopters assigned. These were flown by combat arms types, but most of the pilots that were trained and experienced in flying helicopters *in groups,* were TC aviators. The majority of officers with any experience conducting combat assaults at the time were TC aviators. I was one of them.

It is also true that almost all, if not all, of the more senior TC aviators had previously been in the combat arms branches anyway. The expansion of Army Aviation began *in the Transportation Corps* during the late fifties with the assignment of many combat arms officers. Until these pilots had been, sometimes arbitrarily reassigned to TC, they had gone to the same schools and had had the same assignments as currently serving combat arms officers. None of this made any difference. Henceforth, most TC aviators became aviation maintenance officers with the attendant limitation on their assignment and promotion opportunities. I was stripped of my operations officer primary military operational specialty (MOS) and given a maintenance officer primary. As you can probably tell that still hacks me off. This is not to say that maintenance is not important or that the officers assigned to run those airmobile units did not do a fine job. They learned quickly, but their main qualification to get command of those companies in the first place was that they wore combat arms insignia. I guess that those Armor, Infantry or Artillery guys were presumably more ready than were the TC aviators to shoot and be shot at; ready to "get this war off the ground."

But enough of that tirade. A fair number of senior officers were coming over from the various elements of the Army by the summer, to get a better idea of what was really happening in Vietnam. Of course they didn't have much to say to us pilots about their observations, but one crusty old Brigadier General, whose name escapes me, did have an interesting thing to say after a few days out in the field with the ARVN 7th Infantry Division down in the Delta. He was obviously unhappy, but he didn't say much at first, as we hauled him and the soldiers back and forth; out to a village or rice paddy and back in the afternoon after another leisurely stroll in the sun. They probably hadn't caught up with many guerillas in the processes and he seemed to be getting a little more upset as time went by. The last we saw of him, he said to me "the problem here is you guys with your goddamn helicopters. You haul everyone everywhere. What the hell has happened to the Infantry? They used to know how to walk!" There is something to that statement. The ARVN sure didn't seem to know how to walk. They didn't want to walk very far, or stay for very long, so they surely couldn't have put too much of a damper on the VC activities in the areas they visited.

There was another state-side visitor, that we got directly involved with, whose name we all knew. It was Secretary of Defense Robert S. McNamara. On this particular occasion he was flying out to see how the "strategic hamlet" program was going. That questionable program was predicated on the idea that the villagers could be uprooted from their homes and villages and placed in centrally located, government provided and protected compounds. They would be happy to do this, the planners said, because of the added protection from the VC and the much nicer houses to be built there. From the beginning this program seemed to me to be doomed to fail and in the end it was just another fraud on the United States and the citizens of South Vietnam. It of course, had very little to do with "protection" but was really all about *control*. The planners ignored lots of inconvenient facts. An obvious one was that most of the people left in the villages to be displaced were old men, women and children. Those of fighting age were already in somebody's army; mostly the VC army, so the government would usually only be protecting the villagers from their own sons, fathers and sometimes daughters.

The Vietnamese worship their ancestors and most of them have traditionally been buried near their home villages. Vietnamese country folks, like those anywhere, are strong on family and farm. They want to be near their fields. The government intended to allow them out of the strategic hamlets in the mornings to work their far-away fields during daylight but they would have to walk out and then back for lock-down before dark. The advertised rationale for these government established hamlets seemed to me to be just a smoke-screen anyway. The real reason, I figured, was to gain control of the population which had been supporting the VC in the rural areas. It was along the lines of the old saying that if you want to kill all the alligators, first you got to drain the swamp.

American funding was supposedly contingent upon an agreed-to schedule of construction and occupation but that was easy; the GVN worked the schedule fine on paper but as the dollars kept flowing, not many strategic hamlets actually got built. Well we aviators weren't taking the sophisticated view in those days, but the neat barracks like buildings that we saw lined up in military fashion, behind squared-off and fortified barbed wire with a single lockable gate, looked a lot like a concentration camp; could have fooled us.

I'm sure the program was doing just fine the day we flew Secretary McNamara and the other VIPs out for their inspection. It was just the beginning of the building effort. The place was located about fifty miles northeast of Saigon and it was to be the first of many strategic hamlets. The camp (excuse me, the strategic hamlet) was like a shinning, brand-new Cadillac demonstrator. We had lined up three of our finest Shawnees for the mission. I guess that the people looking over our shoulders were CIA, but there may have been some other security people involved as well. They were all very concerned about the safety of their charges, which included the Secretary, our

Ambassador and ran on down to a flock of full colonels. It included the chief of the MAAG, a couple of three star level officers and civilians and several BGs; U.S. and ARVN. So the security people insisted that our helicopters be lined up near the center of the airbase the night before the flight. They then secured them there with their own set of armed guards.

No one, including the helicopter crews, was to get anywhere near the aircraft until just before the planned take-off time. Trying for any rationality with this bunch was futile, so the crew chiefs finished their inspections and we parked 'em as instructed. In the morning, the security people decided that they should check for any water in the helicopter fuel sumps before we were allowed back into the parking area and they were really upset when they found maybe a fourth of a pint of water in each of them. They were sure it was sabotage. It took a while to convince them that it was just normal overnight condensation and to get rid of it, the sumps were always drained each morning before the first flight. So, the visit started out a little bumpy but it really got tense when we thought that we had lost Mr. McNamara.

We found out, at the last minute as usual, that things had changed. McNamara and one of the other senior people, along with their GVN escort, would fly in a brand new turbine powered French Alouette helicopter that had been acquired by the VNAF. We would only be carrying the remaining VIPs in our CH-21s. There were enough of them to fill up two of our helicopters and we had scheduled a third one to fly along as a spare. It was good that we did too, because when it came time to start back from the strategic hamlet, one of the primary helicopters had a mechanical problem. Naturally, it was the one on which most of the very senior people were scheduled to fly and it quickly became a three ring circus as these individuals began bumping less senior officers out of their seats.

We were busy trying to sort this out, without leaving any U. S. Army colonels on the ground, when the Alouette took off by itself. It took a few minutes to get everyone settled before we could follow. When we arrived at Tan Son Nuht, there was no Alouette and no Secretary in sight. Well, where the hell were they? Many very worried people asked the question, but nobody had the answer. Right about then, I had a vision of the United States Secretary of Defense hunkered down behind some muddy rice paddy dike waiting to be killed or captured by the bad guys.

We immediately began to retrace our steps back to the strategic hamlet. We also radioed the 57th to put all of our flyable helicopters up in a search pattern. The VNAF was just beginning to search as well, when the Alouette touched down on the ramp, about an hour late. Someone had decided to visit another wondrous sight on the way back from the strategic hamlet and they didn't bother to tell anybody. We all breathed an exasperated sigh of relief when we were told that they had landed and that everyone was accounted for. It was no sweat for Mr. McNamara; he and his senior escort just got in their waiting sedans and drove away. They probably never even knew of the anxiety the rest of us had suffered or the hullabaloo they had created. And I've often wondered what might have happened if we had really lost one of the major architects of the Vietnam war that early? Why heck, we might have tucked our tail and run before it had been allowed to get so much worse.

CHAPTER 22

THE POINT OF NO RETURN

The halfway point is when the risk of turning back is equal to the risk of going ahead. In an aircraft, if you haven't turned around yet it is too late to do it now.

For us the halfway point was reached in May. We were no longer on temporary duty (TDY). Our orders had been changed from TDY to a permanent change of station (PCS). We were now assigned to US Army Pacific (USARPAC) with duty station in Vietnam. We had begun our deployment from Fort Lewis on 11 November 1961. Someone had decided that a one year tour was the thing to do, so our year was programmed to be officially up as of 11 November 1962. That being the case, most of us were at least halfway home. It had been recognized that everybody should not rotate at one time, so it was planned to spread the arrival and departure of personnel out over about a three month period. We were already a little short of pilots though, because the TDY guys from Korea were gone, and a few others had drifted off for one reason or another. We did gain several new pilots over the late spring and summer months however. CPT John W. Thomas came in as our new Executive Officer, LT Arthur M. Edquid added to our commissioned ranks and several CWOs came aboard.

Without any records, I have to rely on my old memory to identify the new CWOs that joined us. There was Bobby Bruce who came in with an established reputation as a Fort Rucker standardization pilot. Ken Donley transferred over from the 45th battalion headquarters. Winford Gifford rotated in and soon sported a spectacular handlebar mustache. It didn't ever match the one Bennie Potts grew but hell Giff was just getting started. Red headed Frank Frost arrived but having survived the Korean action was vocally concerned about flying over the jungle. He did it anyway and bitching is good for the soul I guess. It is hard to pin down a particular story related to any one of these guys or the other pilots who came in. They were all professionals and fit right into things.

It was still early enough in this stage of hostilities that John Thomas had been allowed to bring his family with him. He had a little blond daughter and she stood out in a crowd. He told us how the locals would touch her hair in amazement. Some of the MAAG officers and the diplomats still had families in country. He asked, and got permission, to reside with his family downtown, but that didn't last long. He soon learned that, blond hair and smiles notwithstanding, things could be dangerous for them in Saigon. MAAG dependants were beginning to leave and it was not long before John sent his family home and moved onto the base with the rest of us. Once the family situation was solved, he got involved in the flying process with both his front feet. He did not subscribe to the theory that the boss should lead from towards the rear of the flight. He wanted to be in the first helicopter. The XO in most outfits is expected to manage business in the orderly room, but Cherne' couldn't keep him there. Instead, I found myself flying Chalk One with him fairly often.

Art Edquid was older than our other lieutenants. I seem to recall that he had been commissioned through warrant officer ranks. In any event, he was an accomplished pilot and he was absorbed quickly into the job. Art was from the Philippines. He was a short muscular kind of guy who quietly went about his business. Naturally our CWOs called him the Pineapple. One incident sticks in my mind that I always associate with Edquid. A bunch of us were sitting around having our C-rat lunch one afternoon up around Tay Ninh. We were out in the boonies at the time and I had found a small board to sit on. When I finished eating I picked up the board and threw it to Art. At the same time I noticed that under the board was the biggest, blackest, scorpion that anyone ever saw. It must have been nearly a foot long. He was squashed pretty flat by the time I got off of him but he was still able to crank up his tail as we all scattered and he scuttled off into the jungle.

The jungle north of Tay Ninh was different than that to the North and East of Saigon. Although still near sea level, it seemed to be more open under the jungle canopy and although covered in deep elephant grass, it was dryer. The distinguishing geographic feature in the area was an isolated peak named Nui Ba Dinh. The name was translated into the Black Virgin or the Black Widow by U.S. soldiers, depending on their point of view I guess. In either case, the mountain fit the name because it stood out in dark isolation from the highlands which began a short distance to the north. We operated out of Tay Ninh fairly often and we used the Widow as a long distance navigation aid.

Besides the scorpion and the VC, there were other wild creatures we ran into up there by the mountain. The area was spotted with giant termite hills. These were not your everyday, ordinary piles of sand, but were monolithic pillars as tall as a man, and they were baked as hard as concrete. Even so, some of them were nearly concealed in the tall waving grass. Now let me tell you something about those bugs. If you'll think of your normal big black carpenter ant as a pickup, these here were more like semi-trucks. One did not want to get anywhere near those things either on foot or on approach from the air.

The animal that we most often saw, all over the rice paddy Delta, was the domestic water buffalo; a big docile creature that was used by the farmers in their rice fields. Often, as we flew past at low level, we saw young boys riding bareback astride the buffalos. The boys were always nearly naked and they were obviously not a threat to us. Sometimes we would get too close and the buffalo would start in a panic and dump the rider in the rice paddy but otherwise we left them alone. There was one water buffalo incident however that really got my attention. We had volunteer gunners, who for the most part did their job very well, but we had one, no need to name him, who opened up with his machine gun at one of these animals and its rider. The official rule was still to not shoot unless we were shot at. Our company rule was to not shoot at all during a combat assault until the guns were released, first by the flight leader and then by the pilot of each individual helicopter. This guy cut loose with none of the above and he was on my aircraft.

We had seen the alleged target, a boy on a water buffalo, and I immediately yelled for him to cease fire. A bunch of yelling finally worked and fortunately he was a lousy shot. There were water spouts all around the buffalo but he and his passenger just kept walking placidly along. I, however, was somewhat upset by this time. When we returned to the pickup site, I got out of my seat before we had even shut down and I was after that damn gunner. I just wanted to talk to him of course. He must have sensed my unhappiness because he managed to stay out of my reach until he was out the door. Well he made it that far, but I was right behind him and had him by the collar as we leapt from the helicopter. It must have been momentum, or something, that caused him to land on his ass then slide backward under the fuselage and out the other side. That is where we finally had a short discussion and he never manned another gun as long as I was there.

There is, however, a Paul Harvey twist to this story. After I went home the guy was allowed to get back on the gun. The rest of the story centers around a flight that was picking up an ARVN patrol, being closely pursued by the VC, from a small jungle clearing. Breaking contact with the enemy is always a very dangerous exercise and in this case the patrol had stirred up a hornets nest. VC fighters were right behind the patrol as it boarded the helicopters. Our shoot-happy gunner was in the lead helicopter and he was letting them have it until he ran clear out of ammunition, whereupon he grabbed a Browning Automatic Rifle (BAR) from an ARVN soldier near him, and continued to fire. Running out of ammo again, he threw the first BAR down and reached for another one as the flight lifted off. The Bronze Star, that he was subsequently awarded, stated that they would probably have lost some people and some helicopters if he had not taken the action that he did. Well he did good on that one, but I still don't hold with the against-orders-shooting of unarmed kids and water buffalos.

As mentioned before, I didn't do much shooting of my own. I was always too busy trying to fly the helicopter, herding a bunch of them, or both. There was one occasion though, where I might have fired my weapon if I could have figured the situation out and moved fast enough to do it. We had touched down just outside of VC village. As the troops were jumping from the helicopter at the rear cargo door I was looking down at the ground past my feet on the pedals. From my Plexiglas foxhole, sitting about four feet above the surface, I was looking directly into a deep foxhole below me which was just next to our nose gear. There, curled up in the bottom of the hole, was a VC. We stared at each other for what seemed like several minutes, but was probably more like three seconds, before he threw his rifle out of the hole and as far away as he could get it. He was still curled up down there when we pulled pitch and got the hell out of there.

There were many other times when shooting was called for and we didn't hesitate to have our door gunners do it. Going in and going out of assault landing zones, was one place where we always had to be on the lookout for possible threats. Jungle landing areas were bad but at least when we opened up there we were unlikely to hit anything other than the trees or the enemy. We generally gave the jungle edge of our touch-down clearings a good pasting but the Delta was different. Assault targets there were invariably strung along tree lines, outside of, or part of the villages themselves. If the VC had decided to stick around, that is where you would find them. Obviously, the trick was to land close enough to put the troops into the tree line quickly, but we also wanted to be far enough away that the soldiers and our helicopters were not sitting ducks while off-loading. And because of the proximity to villages we tried to withhold firing our weapons.

It was not a unique event, but I remember one time in the Delta, when I was in the lead and we had to fire all the guns we had. We had assaulted into a tree lined field beside another village. A second line of trees was right angled a short distance ahead and directly in front of us. That wasn't all that unusual either, but it just didn't look right to us and we would have to depart right over it; low down and at low speed. We had already ordered the guns released of course. Our gunners were free to shoot if we were to take any fire and I had radioed back for the flight to be aware of the trees to our front. As we lifted off we kept our eyes carefully on those woods and when we caught glimpses of metallic reflection we didn't wait. I kicked pedal hard to put our forward door gunner out to one side and told him to "cut 'em down." Since the rest of the flight had been warned, they all shot up the woods and we managed to leave with only a few holes.

We were running a combat assault one day where Thomas made a decision, partially based on my advice, which got him a personal interview with GEN Harkins. We were staging out of Phouc Vinh, a provincial capital well to the east of Tay Ninh. On the first return trip our "Tail End Charley" maintenance ship suffered an engine failure and was expertly guided into a grass and low jungle covered, opening in the trees. The pilot was the 98th detachment commander, Ken Klippel, who was probably flying with Bob Sword. (That, I'm afraid, is guesswork, but it is reasonable because Bob was assisting with the work in the 98th at the time.) The crew was soon pulled out by another Shawnee, but it was so tight that the only way to reach them was to hover straight down, directly over them. They had to stand on the top of their helicopter to be hauled up, one at a time, into the ship hovering over them. I have no memory of who the rescuing crew was but this was very difficult, precise, work because of the closely surrounding triple canopy jungle and the lower level scrub bush into which the auto-rotation had been made.

The rest of us continued the mission, which required a couple more trips past the downed bird. It was about forty minutes before we could do any more than evacuate the crew, but we soon noticed that vehicle tracks had appeared near the aircraft. The tracks came out from under the jungle canopy and ran straight up to the rear cargo door. It surely looked like a neat opportunity to booby trap a helicopter. Ken told us that the rotors had chopped down enough trees during the auto-rotation that a sudden stoppage of the drive line had occurred. That meant that damn near every moving part on the helicopter would have to be replaced; the engine, three transmissions, six rotor blades for sure and probably everything in between them. So the question was what the hell do we do now?

It was apparent that we would have to get some kind of security around the downed aircraft if it was to be recovered. Troops would have to penetrate deep into the jungle and it would have to be a sizable force. It would take quite a lot of time to get them there. The closest possible landing zone was several miles away. We could try to rappel a force in, as might have been done later in the war, but this was not yet a real possibility, considering the high density altitude and the under-powered Shawnee. Maintenance crews, a few at a time, might be rappelled in from our choppers, but without any ground security that was a poor option. They would have to walk in with the troops. The major aircraft components, the tools, equipment and parts would have to be delivered one ship at a time, and since there was no nearby landing area, they would all have to be slung into the site; heavy stuff, several sling loads, with a vertical decent at the end. To avoid that, a landing area would have to be cleared. Anyway, about the only thing left was a damaged fuselage and every option looked like it would be very time-consuming and dangerous. On top of that, someone would have to determine if explosives had been wired to the helicopter or an ambush had been set up. The whole thing looked very risky.

We described the situation to the ARVN commander, and his U.S. advisor, on the ground. We asked them if they could provide security but their answer was equivocal at best. Ken had told us about the damage to the aircraft and the maintenance situation. There did not appear to be much in the way of useful parts left on the aircraft and it would be a hell of a job getting the remains out of there. John and I stood beside the dirt runway and discussed our alternatives. It didn't look good. Nightfall was near and so was a B-26 WWII light bomber. We decided to have them come in and reduce the downed helicopter to scrap metal. The USAF round-eye didn't hesitate. I'm sure he enjoyed the target practice on a U.S. Army helicopter. The senior American advisor with the ARVN unit had been involved in some of these discussions, but his input had not been helpful. Time was a wasting and we were quickly running out of daylight. We felt that we had to make a decision. Before we got home, there was a phone call from MAAG headquarters, for the senior 57th officer involved to report to GEN Harkin's office immediately.

Well, John had been in charge at the time, so he crawled into his jeep and headed out for what was sure to be a spectacular ass chewing. It turned out that the ARVN III Corps commander had called Harkins and assured him that the ARVN was ready, willing and able to help us recover the helicopter. And he was pissed about it too. The aircraft was still upright so no problem right? Just go in and do the minor repairs and fly it out like we had often done in the past. That was an expensive piece of equipment which, in his view, almost belonged to the GVN and what right did a junior officers have to destroy it? Etc. Etc.

I think it mostly boiled down to the old doctrine that the ground commander was always supposed to be in charge. Many advisors felt that they were in command, so they were supposed to make all the important decisions. In this case, nobody told us that they were all set to help. The advisor didn't understand the full implications of the situation. Nothing would have been possible until the following day, in any case. The ARVN III Corps commander got bad advice from somebody. John, I'm sure, stood at attention for the initial abuse. Then he had to explain the decision rational in detail. He must have done a good job because a new rule was announced on the spot; that the senior Army Aviator on the ground would be responsible to make this kind of decision in the future.

This was another example of how decisions were often made in the Vietnam War; after the fact. Things often boiled up from the bottom; stuff would happen on (or near) the ground; junior leaders or even individual soldiers would take action. Eventually, what had happened would penetrate to higher headquarters where the actions that had been taken would be confirmed or heads would roll. Higher headquarters usually supported such decisions, if they were judged to be appropriate to the circumstances; then the rules would change. This same sort of action / reaction was apparent at the highest levels also, hence "mission creep" and "escalation" which became favored words for most of the war years; until "de-escalation" set in.

Several new aviation units had arrived by May 1962. One outfit, the 57th Medical Detachment, flying the first of the Hueys in Vietnam, was now operating out of Tan Son Nuht. Although numbered the "57th", they were an entirely separate organization. They were the forerunners of the famous "Dust Off" units to follow. They took over most of the med-evac missions that we had formerly been called upon to do in our area. That does not mean that our pilots just laid back, to wait for Dust Off, if they happened to be near the place of need. Med-evacs were not a mission where you could stand on ceremony. That being said, the 57th Dust Off went on to do a spectacular job. The use of helicopters for med-evac has dramatically improved the chance of survival for wounded soldiers ever since.

We were being "reported" in newspapers and magazines regularly now. They normally portrayed the overall situation fairly well, in spite of the "Five O'clock Follies," as they began to call their afternoon briefings from the MACV headquarters staff. The reports, however, were necessarily short on detail and often contained inaccuracies. It is doubtful that most people ever noticed these omissions and mistakes, but they sometimes irritated us when we saw them. A typical report would start with the usual attention getter like: *Red held village taken by South Viet Nam troops* or *'Copter lost south of Saigon.* This would be followed with something like: *Two South Vietnamese companies, supported by US helicopters, attacked a village forty miles south of Saigon last Friday. One helicopter was shot down by the Viet Cong after being hit in the main fuel pipe. Most of the enemy escaped . . .*

You get the idea. The stories were not quite this brief of course. There was always a little more fiber and filler. The stories eventually got quite a bit better as the reporters began to get out of the Caravelle Hotel and into the field more often But still, I never could exactly identify some of their lines like the "*main fuel pipe*" in this example from memory. That description was actually used in one account that I read at the time. What really got to us though, was the routine mention of "U.S. Air Force" helicopters. We could shrug off the rest pretty well. Most of the reporters were young and not well educated on things military; army or helicopter. While sometimes naive, they were not dumb. Even early black-and-white television was not much in evidence then. If Uncle Walt Cronkite was around, I don't remember seeing him. The lack of detail in these early media reports must have been unsatisfactory to the big Army Aviation thinkers back at Fort Rucker, home of the Army Aviation School, because they soon sent one of their own over to try to find out just what we were doing over there.

This visit was the occasion for me to relearn a lesson that I thought I had already gotten down pat back when the Korean War had just gone into stalemate. As I've mentioned before, a large number of officers had found themselves reverted back to enlisted ranks after WWII. Many of these, now NCOs, had been recalled as commissioned officers during the Korean war. Due to this recent experience, the artillery saying at the time was: "don't crap on your gun corporal; he may be your battery commander next week." I thought that I understood that message well enough and besides the Major from Fortress Rucker was already way senior to me. The major's name was Ruffus Lester Leggett and I have good reason to remember all of it. He came out to my operations office at Tan Son Nuht and wanted to know all about what we were doing with our helicopters. I was, as usual, very busy and after a short time I turned him over to Benny Potts and Sal Formica to answer his questions. They were certainly as well qualified as I was to do that, but this didn't satisfy MAJ Leggett. He went away for a day or two, but soon I received a questionnaire from him in distribution from downtown. He had typed out all of his questions for us. These were still the days of paper conservation in the Army, so he had single spaced his questions, filling up both sides of an 8x10 sheet of paper.

The first question was "how much does a CH-21C carry?" Well, that is a question the answer to which, depends on a lot of factors, such as density altitude, take off conditions, take off space available, etc. And there was a lot of variation, in performance, between these old helicopters as well. The next few questions were equally simple sounding when asked, but very difficult to answer simply, and I was still very busy. I took a pilots' handbook on the CH-21C, a technical manual about an inch thick, which is called a Dash 10, stapled the questionnaire to it along with a note that said: "they wrote a book about that and it is attached." Then I sent it back downtown. I never heard from MAJ Leggett after that; while he was in Vietnam. I didn't see him again until I went back to Germany. And it's a good thing that he didn't carry too much of a grudge. That meeting took place in his office when he reported in as my new boss; the 503rd Aviation Battalion Commander.

I can only think of three or four individuals in the 57th who caused me to take the risk of "crapping on my gun corporal." One of them was our water buffalo shootin' cowboy and the other two shall also go nameless. They were defintly an aberration from the rest of our pilots. Their conduct was well known by everyone however, so they might possibly be identified by some of those that flew with us. One of them was so unsure of himself (and rightfully so) and so concerned about his personal welfare, that whenever crew assignments were posted, he would quickly check the board to discover who was to be his pilot (he was always satisfied to be the copilot) he would approach the assigned individual and essentially ask them to take good care of him. And he didn't seem to be at all embarrassed in the process. I made input to the worst efficiency report I ever saw written on anybody. He was forced to leave the Army, but again there is a twist. I heard that he joined his brother running a sand and gravel company in California when he got out. They were enjoying profitable state road contracts so he was said to be worth a mint.

The other one was so active at the mess hall table that you had to be quick to get to any food ahead of him. One of our pilots named him "The Vacuum Cleaner" because he scarfd up the food so fast and because he never left much behind. This was not the major complaint though. He had a tendency to be unpredictable in the cockpit. One day he was flying the left seat of a crew during a combat assault. They were discharging troops in close proximity to what was thought to be a VC stronghold. For some reason, without warning, he reached up and pulled the fluid cut-off switch. That, of course, killed the engine right there in the assault landing area with several helicopters waiting for take off behind him. Rapid action by the other pilot got a restart, so no one got hurt, but we could never figure out what the devil he was thinking. Because we needed him to fill a seat, we kept him flying. One of the pilots that flew with him regularly said that every time they entered the cockpit he told him to "just sit there; keep your feet flat on the floor and don't touch nothin." I seldom flew with him, but when I did, I used the same words. No telling what happened to this inept aviator when our tour ended but I'm happy to say that I never ran into either of these "gun corporals" again.

CHAPTER 23

THE BATTLES AT AP BAC

All pilots take warning when tree lines are near
Let's land those darn choppers one mile to the rear.
Taken from: "In Memory of the Ap Bac Operation"[*1]

I mentioned in the previous chapter that there were at least two LTCs, with whom we had to deal with in Vietnam, who did not appear to us to have their heads screwed on tightly. John Stockton was one of them and Lieutenant Colonel John Paul Vann was the other. The colonels and generals up the chain of command liked Vann for awhile because he appeared to be a real tiger to them. He was forcing action against the VC, in spite of the institutionalized reluctance of the Diem government and the ARVN. And he talked an even better game; promoting himself until his arrogance and big mouth got him in serious trouble. The generals, and both the U.S. and South Vietnamese governments, continued to put the best face on a very bad situation while Vann injudiciously spouted off to the media about the shortcomings.

With all the press attention, he became a well known character during the Vietnam War. The reporters in 1962 liked him because they were able to get closer to the truth about what was going on from him, than they were able to get from the headquarters in Saigon. His portrayal of the situation more closely aligned with their own observations and they stood the test of common sense as well. Neil Sheehan's book ("*A Bright Shinning Lie*" published by Random House in 1988)[*2] tells a comprehensive story of Vann, from his first involment in Vietnam until his death there ten years later. Vann often told the truth, as he saw it, in spite of his bosses' versions up the chain of command. You have got to give him that. But he was another egocentric, lets-go-kill-'em, kind of guy in what was not yet that kind of war. He was constantly upset that he couldn't force the division commander that he was advising into more aggressive action.

We in the 57th also knew Vann in 1962 and we were significantly less impressed with him than were the reporters. There were several reasons for this. He was a small blond man with a high pitched, grating, petulantly demanding voice who, in spite of his slight appearance, was an over-confident, hyper-acting, and arrogant individual. He had a very high opinion of himself. He let us know that he had a superior understanding of the war; that his tactical expertise was perfect and that he could fly a helicopter better than any of us. He also viewed the poor ARVN conduct of the war as a personal challenge. Vann took the reins, as the senior advisor to the 7th ARVN Division, from LTC Frank Clay during March 1962. The ARVN division commander, Col Huyah Van Cao, was the same reluctant warrior as he had always been, but Vann was determined to get him off the dime. In essence, he intended to run that ARVN division himself. This was still the Vietnamese's war. We Americans were still three years away from our half-ass attempt to take the conflict over as our own, but Vann was correct in his view that the ARVN was very unlikely to win any war the way they were going about it.

We didn't disagree with his attempt to energize the division and cause it to fight more aggressively. Our problems with Vann were that he thought that he knew more about flying helicopters than we did and he was heedless of risk to himself or others in planning for our employment. According to Sheehan, he had indeed taken Army Air Corps flight training in 1944 but he had not graduated because of some unauthorized stunt flying as a student.[*3] The stunt flying might have presaged some of his later conduct, but it did not qualify him to fly helicopters nor did it make him an expert in the employment of helicopters.

He first came to my attention when he insisted on kneeling on the cockpit floor between me and the other pilot, in the lead helicopter on a combat assault. He thought that he could run things from there. I explained to him that that was not going to work and that he should take his seat until we landed. We would get him to where he wanted to go. He had to trust us on that. You might question where my boss, MAJ Cherne', was in all this. His method of leadership was to run the company from the headquarters. He had plenty to do there and he normally left the operations of the company to me. And you will remember that I was a junior CPT talking to an LTC. I was polite.

Soon however, our pilots began complaining that Vann wouldn't stay out of the cockpit and that he was interfering with the crew. Both of our Shawnee intercom lines were used; one by the crew chief / gunner at the left rear door and the other by the right forward door gunner. We had no intercom connection to spare for him, but he was always hyper and he never could stop trying to run things. He would kneel in the cockpit between the pilot seats. When he wanted to talk to one of them, he would just reach up to grab a flight helmet pulling a pilot's head over so he could yell at him. I had already talked to him about keeping his seat when we were in the air, but particularly when it was our warrant officers up front. He had no compunction at all to getting in the way in the cockpit. He would jerk their heads around while they were fully engaged in managing the helicopter, and usually, the flight behind them. He was particularly demanding and in the way of the crew during final approach, the most critical part of any flight.

Being a junior captain, I had always tried to be respectful when asking Vann to keep his seat. Maybe I was not so respectful when I told him again that the pilot was in command of his aircraft, regardless of his rank, and that he had to keep his seat while the helicopter was in the air. Just because the pilots were sometimes warrant officers did not change that. It made it even more important that he not try to order them around. I also told him that I had instructed the pilots to not initiate take-off until he sat down and was strapped in and to let me know if he got up during the flight. That is when he told me that he had been an Air Force pilot and that he could fly any goddamn helicopter better than any of us did. He didn't mention that he had been kicked out of Air Force fixed wing flight school and that he had never been to any kind of rotary wing training.

The reason for insisting that he stay seated was not only to keep him from bothering the crew, but also to keep him from trying to direct the rest of the flight. Changes to a carefully planned and briefed flight could always create confusion and without proper handling would cause problems. It was not like a ground commander telling his personal light helicopter pilot to go here or go there; or to go higher or go lower; or to land here or land there. There was always a flight of several helicopters following the lead helicopter in a combat assault and the pilot flying that lead helicopter always had to consider the flight behind him, as well as the helicopter he was helping to fly.

The flight leader had to understand what was happening in the landing zone so he could react to changes in the situation there. He had to be on the lookout for threats to his aircraft and to the rest of the flight. He was in charge of the guns. In addition he had to coordinate with any external participants in the assault such as our O-1 communication and navigation airplane flying above the flight, VNAF/USAF close air support, UH-1 gun ship escorts, medical evacuation requests and maintenance if one went down. He would have to bring in an air cap and begin to arrange for ground security in that case. The flight leader was always in contact with somebody and he was monitoring two radios and the intercom at all times. The necessary coordination with ground force advisors needed to be accomplished before take-off, except in unusual cases. We, of course, also stayed in contact with the ground force advisors *on the ground,* but we had very little time or interest in dealing with one kneeling in the cockpit.

Vann would invariably be embarked in the lead ship. He thought that he could run both the ground operation and the air portion of the assault from the there. The Shawnee was not a Command and Control (C&C) equipped aircraft. It did not have the necessary commo suite to allow command from the air. In addition, later U. S. commanders found that control of ground troops from the air was often very difficult, even when embarked on a C&C equipped helicopter. They could help coordinate things and provide commo assistance, but to actually direct a battle commanders normally had to land and become more directly involved. The good ones landed at or near the action, where they were able to exercise effective command on the ground.

Vann thought that he was following U. S. Army doctrine, which was that the ground commander was always the guy in charge of all elements involved in any operation. If you accepted the fiction that Vann was not just an advisor to the ARVN division commander but was, in fact, the actual division commander himself, you could bite off on that. I didn't. If any change in the threat or mission required that a flight be altered in the air, that change needed to be directed by the flight leader. It was not a spur of the moment thing on combat assaults. Even while conducting so called eagle flights, where the flexibility to land quickly was required, the flight leader had the ultimate responsibility to place the troops on the ground safely and in a tactically sound position. There had to be consultation with the American officer accompanying the troops, before landing of course, but this had become boiled down to a few concise words. It was a practiced and formalized thing. It is my opinion, that Vann's overly aggressive commitment of the ARVN and our helicopters, along with his constant interference in the air during combat assaults, eventually caused us to get one man killed and two Shawnees shot down. This happened on 5 October 1962 near a little village called Ap Bac. There was a famous fight later, in that same area, which became known as the battle of Ap Bac. What is not widely known, is that this was the second battle at Ap Bac involving the 57th and LTC John Paul Vann.

The well known battle happened in January of 1963 and LTC Vann was "in charge" of that fiasco too. Orbiting in an O-1 fixed wing airplane, he was attempting to run the battle from the air while the casualties on the ground mounted. Things did not go as he had planned for various reasons but poor security had to be a major factor. It had seemed to us, in the 57th, that the VC always knew we were coming so the only real question was whether they would run or stay to fight. This time it was fight. As the situation degenerated, the ARVN deviated from the plan. The needed adjustments were ordered by Vann, flying over the battle, but these were stymied on the ground, largely because the ARVN troops and their commanders would not follow his orders (*excuse me; his advise*). The senior ARVN officers on the ground would not move aggressively. They were, in fact, trying to disengage, while Vann was trying to get them to close with and destroy the enemy.

I had rotated home before the second battle of Ap Bac occurred, so this is not an eye-witness account. The best description of the fight, that

I have read, was in Sheehan's book. When it was over, the Government of Vietnam, the ARVN, and MACV headquarters tried to ignore the obviously lost battle and declared victory. You will find no believable account from any official source. Vann raised hell after this botched fight, and placed the blame on anybody and everybody else. After several other debacles and his constant venting to the press he was effectively muzzled. His career was badly damaged and he soon left the Army.

I have talked to some of the aviator participants and read as much as I can find about this 1963 battle at Ap Bac. No, I wasn't there, but my earlier association with Vann leads me to make a few observations about this screwed-up operation. First, in Sheehan's account, Vann admits no mistakes. He accepts no responsibility for over-extending the reluctant ARVN. He knew that the 7th ARVN Division commander and his officers were normally intent on avoiding close contact with the enemy. It was politically damaging for them to accept casualties. It was unrealistic to think that the politician colonel would turn warrior over night. There is no question in my mind that Vann intended to do it himself; that is command the operation, which was equally unrealistic.

I also believe that he incorrectly responded to the changes in the weather and the limited resources available to him. Ground fog delayed the second helicopter lift and he had not been given half enough helicopters for the mission in the first place. There was a competing mission in another area of operations that required helicopter support and it was a mistake to allow both to go at the same time. Close air support was busy covering the other mission. There was an apparent over-reliance on a poorly trained ARVN Armored Personnel Carrier (APC) unit. That unit's ability to even properly negotiate the rice paddies, dikes and obstacles on the way to the fight was questionable. The APCs were newly arrived in the Delta so even with good leadership, which they didn't have, their ability to influence the battle was still unproven. Vann forced the mission through anyway. He knowingly accepted the increased risks that were imposed by these conditions, before the assault even got underway.

In his after action comments, he placed the blame on the pilots and their flight leaders for the loss of several helicopters and their crew members. Sheehan provides no understanding of the aviator's view about that, except to admit that relations between Vann and the helicopter companies had been poor.*[4] Based on my past experience with Vann, I can believe that! He was critical of the attempt to pick up the crews of the first downed helicopters. In his view I guess, the helicopter crews should have fought as infantry, with their .45 caliber pistols, while all around them was turning to crap. According to Vann, he told a subsequent helicopter lift to land 300 yards from the tree line, a distance that he considered to be just out of effective rifle range, but that they chose to ignore him and landed 200 yards from the tree line. That is exactly the opposite of what I would expect. He had always attempted to get us to land right on top of the bad guys; the closer the better. He had stated to me, that until the helicopters did that, they could not be effective; like we were flying armored vehicles instead of aluminum and plexiglas flying machines.

I have a clipping that was sent to me, authored by Peter Arnett, headlined "*Frontal Attacks By 'Copter Seen Key In Viet Nam.*" Unfortunately, the date and the newspaper that printed it were cut off before it was sent, but it had to have been early. (Eventually the papers began to call it Vietnam instead of Viet Nam.) Since Arnett was reporting for the Associated Press it was probably from the Seattle Times and was sent to me by wife or family. The first paragraph of the article sez that U. S. Army advisors believe that the military high command in South Viet Nam must be willing to send U. S. helicopters right into the muzzles of Communist guns if the full effectiveness of helicopter attacks is to be realized.*[5] That sure sounded suspiciously like what Vann had previously said to me. And it still seems idiotic to me, to land troops so close that helicopters are *likely* to get shot down and troops killed while exiting from them. There may be times when this tactic might be called for, but Ap Bac was not, in my opinion, one of them.

In his account, Sheehan does not mention who was leading the helicopters, nor is there any indication that he talked with anyone in charge of that part of the operation. It is almost like they had nothing to do with it, except for being shot down and the attempted rescues. In his book he does not bother to name the 93rd or any individual pilot flying the helicopters. I feel sure that Vann had let him know that he, Lieutenant Colonel John Paul Vann, the big commander, was in charge of everything, except for that which went wrong of course, and Sheehan just seems to accept Vann's word for that being exactly the way it really was. Vann was expert at identifying ARVN weaknesses, but he was also expert at aggrandizing his own importance and expertise. He didn't admit his own mistakes and, like a true fictional hero, he didn't apologize for any of his own shortcomings. I feel sure that he had little compunction about rearranging the truth to make himself look like the hero he wanted to be. I don't know which aviator led that mission, but I'd sure like to get his side of the story.

Vann managed to be awarded a Distinguished Flying Cross (DFC) for orbiting above the fray, in the back seat of an O-1, that day. There were five helicopters shot down, three Americans killed in action, and eight more wounded, along with eighty to one hundred ARVN casualties at the second battle of Ap Bac. In my view, he could just as easily have been convicted in a general court marshal for stupidity and his reckless lack of concern for friendly casualties, than to have received a medal of any kind, let alone a DFC for pitching temper tantrums in the back seat of an observation airplane. It is uncharitable for me to say so, but Vann always came across to me as a kind of sociopath with an outsized ego; not, in my opinion, just what we needed to advise ARVN commanders at that time and it brings up the question for me, of just what the hell we were doing there in 1962. If we couldn't get the South Vietnamese to fight for their own survival, maybe we should have picked up our marbles right then.

I won't go into the January 1963 fight at Ap Bac in any more detail. I wasn't there. Read Sheehan's book, but keep your grain of salt handy. When it comes to those areas where he is taking Vann's statements about the helicopter part of things as the true picture, maybe you better keep the whole bottle close.

I was along however, on the first battle at Ap Bac; the one back in October 1962. This is the one that few ever heard about, but Vann was the major architect of this one too, and he was personally involved with the outcome. At this time I think that Cherne' was back in Washington D. C. representing the 45th Battalion. It had been selected by the Army Aviation Association of America as their Aviation Unit of the Year. That fine recognition for the battalion had been based primarily on Cherne's write-up for 57th accomplishments. CPT John Thomas, our company exec, was now leading missions. He and LT Rod Magie were flying lead on this one. The assault landing area was tight. We had planned two flights, with just enough separation between them, to let the first flight unload its troops and depart before we brought the second flight into the assault area. I was leading the second flight. The first lift had their troops on the ground and the second flight was departing the assault landing area when the shooting started. Each helicopter had been on the ground for only seconds, but the troops were coming under fire by dug-in VC as we took off.

We were low on fuel when we got back to the troop pick-up site at Tan Hiep and we had planned to refuel before the next run. Vann, however, was anxious to get the remainder of the troops out to the fight so he urged us to go without refueling. I recommended against that, saying to Thomas that things will be close for the helicopters without more fuel; we would put them on the red light (the low fuel warning light) and be unable to carry in reserve troops if needed later. Besides, why not let the ARVN, on the ground, fight it out for awhile. The fact that they were in contact *at all* was unusual enough. Why not see if the fight didn't break up soon anyway. John, however, agreed to an immediate return trip.

CPT Ray Hout, our signal detachment commander, was flying top assistance, as he often did, in an O-1 Birddog, that day. His job was to help us navigate and communicate with air support from altitude. For some reason we did not have VNAF fighter cover, or maybe the T-28s had just run low on fuel or ammo and had departed the area at the critical time, as was often the case. Anyway, as we again approached the assault area, Ray could see that there was heavy fighting below, so he decided that he might be able to make the VC keep their heads down by making diving passes at them while rapidly turning his magneto switch on and off. That would make the engine pop loudly. He thought that the VC might mistake the noise as a machine gun firing. That was a very un-wise move. They shot him.

The round came up through the belly of the airplane, passing through Ray's leg just above the ankle; it then clipped off the throttle quadrant before exiting out the windshield. When he called to say that he had been hit and was loosing blood, I turned over the lead of the second flight and went after him. Looking back, I shouldn't have done that, but I knew that CWO Billy J. Williams was in the number two position and that he was very capable of leading the flight. We had been together as a unit for a long time by October 1962. We were all close. Ray was a buddy and I was concerned that he would pass out and crash before we could get to him. Right or wrong, the decision to follow him was made in a matter of seconds.

Vann, as usual, was aboard the lead aircraft. There is little doubt in my mind that since he was on the helicopter he had positioned himself as close as he could get to the cockpit so that he could supervise the landing. Thomas was doing the communicating and navigating. Rod Magie had worked up the mission and was flying the helicopter. Magie remembers that they received a radio call specifying a different landing site than had been planned. Hout had already been hit, so that call must have come from the advisors on the ground, but I would be surprised if Vann did not get involved at this point. Thomas couldn't find the new landing area without maintaining some altitude, so the flight proceeded into the landing from a very vulnerable height. The deck was stacked.

Both pilots were on the controls when they began to receive fire. They had approached to land right in the middle of an intense fire fight. Their helicopter took thirty-six holes while making a 180 degree turn at a hover. The crew was forced to land when it had sustained enough damage that it wouldn't fly anymore. The number two ship could not get down behind the turning hover of number one and flew to the left where it was brought down by heavy fire. Eighteen holes were counted on number two. A third ship dropped its load of troops and then picked up the crew of the lead helicopter. It exited the area without getting hit at all. Another one came in to get the crew of number two, including the dead crew chief. Vann stayed to enjoy the fight. Specialist Five Richard L. K. Ellis, from Honolulu, Hawaii, was killed in this action and was the first such loss for the 57th. He was standing in the door of the helicopter, pointing out where the enemy fire was coming from to the departing troops, when he was hit.

In my mind, Billy J. Williams was the primary hero that day, when he held the second flight off to one side, positioning his troops so as to cause the VC to begin a withdrawal. He then continued in to extract casualties. Although I had missed this part of the action, I could hear that something bad was going on, as I landed behind Hout's Birddog at Tan Hiep. He had managed to put the airplane down with a straight-in, downwind landing, before he passed out. My forward rotor system overlapped his vertical stabilizer before he stopped rolling. Blood coated the underside of his fuselage all the way to the tail wheel. We dragged him out of the O-1 and into our Shawnee and headed for Saigon.

You should know how this botched up mess was reported by Sheehan in his book.*6 Again, there is no indication that he talked with anyone except Vann, so as you might expect, LTC Vann comes out looking like the singular good guy. Sheehan seemed to just take his word on everything. He sure as hell never talked to me, or Thomas, or any of the other 57th pilots that day; or ever, for his book. He reports that Vann flew in with replacements on the critical second lift. I guess he just flapped his wings. No, he rode into trouble with the flight crew that flew in, on the lead helicopter.

Vann later noted in the margin of a news report, one which he had clipped and sent home, that he was "on the one with thirty-one holes", as if that was something of which to be proud. He said that Ellis, the crew chief that had been killed, had been manning the machine gun in the front exit of his helicopter. Not so; Ellis was the crew chief at the back door of the second ship. Vann said that the crew of the lead ship "had lost their heads" and left the helicopter engine running, so that he had had to go back in, under fire, to shut it down.*7 Horse hockey. The rotors of any helicopter will keep turning for a while after everything is shut down. He may have thought he needed to do something, since he knew very little about helicopters, but it sounds to me, like just another effort to make himself look like the intrepid aviator he would have liked to have been. I can see him dodging bullets to go back inside the helicopter, he was that careless, but I doubt that he would even have known how to shut a Shawnee down.

Except for his subsequent venting to the press, that ends Vann's connection with the helicopter piece of the October 1962 battle near Ap Bac, but his part in the January 1963 Ap Bac battle can be better understood when viewed from his conduct in the first one. The official reaction to those helicopters being shot down, with the loss of a helicopter crewman and the wounding and death of several ARVN soldiers in the 1962 screw-up, seemed to be: well that's the breaks and the aviators have to expect some losses. But, it wasn't the flyers that knowingly picked a landing area right on top of the enemy. Vann had already told me that he didn't think helicopters would ever be valuable unless they landed right on top of the enemy's position. He and his team caused us to do precisely that. I will always hold him at least partially accountable for our losses in the Ap Bac before Ap Bac, although, at least officially, no one else did. President Diem was very unhappy about the large number of ARVN casualties though and he let everyone know about it. The division commander almost didn't get his promotion.

I flew four different helicopters and one fixed wing airplane that day and they were some interesting flights. When we picked Ray Hout up we were already low on fuel, but we felt that we had barely enough to get back to Saigon. Ray was stretched out on a row of seats in the cargo compartment; he had lost a lot of blood and was still unconscious. We didn't waste any more time; just headed out at low altitude and high speed. When I looked back into the cargo bay, our crew chief was trying to take the boot off of Ray's injured leg. The round had penetrated his boot just above the ankle. I went back and instead, assisted the crew chief in wrapping the boot even tighter around the ankle while we elevated the leg. Back up front, when we got close enough for radio contact with our base at Tan Son Nuht, I had them go get our new doctor, CPT Arthur Lennon, and described the wound to him.

The proper course of action upon our arrival at Tan Son Nuht would have been to transfer Ray to a USAF airplane for movement to the Army evacuation hospital which had just been established at Nha Trang. They would then make the decision about medical attention in-country or further evacuation if they thought it was needed. Nha Trang is a long distance from Saigon and Doc Lennon felt that, since we would already have Ray on an Air Force medical transport, they might just as well take him directly to the USAF hospital in the

Philippines. Well that violated all kinds of medical rules, so he caught a little hell for recommending that, but Ray was in the Clark AFB hospital just a few hours after he was hit. They saved his leg.

Before we landed in Saigon, Ray had woken up again, so I went back to tell him that we had made arrangements with the USAF to fly him directly to the Philippines. At that, he said "well if you don't come over there to see me, I'm going to kick your ass!" I did take a quick trip there later, to bring him his personal stuff before they sent him back to the states. He didn't, however, manage to kick my ass.

When our Shawnee touched down on the ramp at Tan Son Nhut the crew chief decided to see if we had any gas left at all. He said that he was only able to drain about a cup full out of the helicopter. Rather then wait to refuel we jumped into another one that had just come out of maintenance and headed back down to Tan Hiep and on out to the battle, now crash, site. The fight was barely over but Ken Klippel already had his 98th maintenance crew inspecting damage, plugging holes and making the needed repairs, so that we could get Chalk One out of there.

Thomas had said that it felt like a piece of wet shit when they had to put it down. Bullet holes had been found near some of the critical flight control cables. It was evident that the cables had been hit so they had inspected them carefully. They found them to be okay for a one-time flight. One round had punctured the engine oil tank. The oil tank is not pressurized, so the maintenance team just made an emergency repair by fashioning wooden pegs and driving them into the holes. Other fixes were applied, while I hung around to help fly the helicopter back to Tan Hiep, when Ken decided it could be flown that far. Of course, by the time we fired her up, she was mired deep in the rice paddy. I was on the controls and decided that a full application of power would be needed to get her up out of the mud.

That part worked fine, but then I found that the cyclic stick had been forced back into my crotch. I couldn't move it forward, so the nose of the helicopter just kept coming up. Ken was looking out his side window because he heard that we were being shot at. I was pushing forward on the back of the cyclic stick so hard that I couldn't even get my fingers around to the intercom button. I couldn't depress it to talk to him. When the nose was really high, like we were about to turn turtle, I dropped my hand off the collective stick to get both hands on the cyclic; still trying to move it forward to stop the nose from climbing. The collective was not frictioned into position, so it began to drop when I let loose of it. With that, we began to sink back into the rice paddies, tail first. Ken finally noticed that something was wrong and looked back inside the cockpit. Finally! It seemed like forever but was probably only a matter of seconds. With Ken pushing along and handling the collective, we managed to move the cyclic stick forward and regained some control of the helicopter. I think we both damn near had heart attacks until I had centered the trim wheel back to neutral and things had settled back to normal.

What had happened was that the maintenance people had had to roll the cyclic trim wheel all the way in both directions to thoroughly examine the control cables. It was apparent that the cables had been hit, but they were judged to be not badly enough damaged to prevent a one-time flight. The problem was that they had left the trim wheel in the cockpit, rolled all the way to the rear position. That was an easy thing to overlook and we did. I wasn't strong enough to keep the nose from climbing when we popped out of the mud and I couldn't let go of the controls to reach the trim wheel. Neither Ken nor I noticed the problem until I had yanked the helicopter into the air. After that scary event I didn't need any more excitement, but I picked up another ship at Tan Hiep to ferry a crew out to recover the remaining downed helicopter. I didn't stick around for that one though. Somebody else flew that 18 holer home.

My flying day was not yet over however. Not many of us were fixed wing qualified and checked out in the O-1; I was. Since Houts' throttle quadrant was mangled we arranged to bypass it and fixed it so that I could just push and pull the throttle and mixture rods themselves. The left side of the windshield was shattered, so it was like flying an open cockpit airplane; even worse because the wind was channeled right back into my face, on that night flight back to Saigon.

Upon arrival back at Tan Son Nuht I found that a few of the pilots were so angry that they wanted to fight the guy in charge of this fiasco. The loss of crew chief Richard Ellis had hit us all hard. There was plenty of load talk and fists were in the air. We calmed them down and after a couple of drinks, we all went to bed early.

The 93rd Helicopter Company had provided some of the ships for this mission and after doing it again in January 63, some of their pilots working in an anonymous group, or perhaps a single unsung poet, (I had always heard that it was a group effort, until I read in Ralph Young's book "*Army Aviation in Vietnam 1961-1963,* that 93rd CWO Frank Baldwin had given CWO Pappy Clayton credit) Anyway, they soon came up with the following memorable song. It was to be sung to the tune of "On Top of Old Smoky." It was entitled "*In Memory of the Ap Bac Operation,*" or as reported by Young "*On Top of Old Ap Bac*" and it fits both battles well:

We were called into Tan Hiep
On January Two
We would never have gone there
If only we'd knew

We were supporting the ARVANS
A group without guts
Attacking a village
Of straw covered huts

A ten copter mission
A hundred troop load
Three lifts are now over
A fourth on the road

The VCs start shooting
They fire a big blast
We off load the ARVANS
They sit on their ass

One copter is crippled
Another sits down
Attempting a rescue
Now there are two on the ground

A Huey returns now
    To give them some aid
The VCs are so accurate
    They shoot off a blade

Four pilots are wounded
    Two crewmen are dead
When it's all over
    A good day for the Red

They lay in the paddy
    All covered with slime
A hell of a sun bath
    Eight hours at a time

An armored Battalion
    Just stayed in a trance
One Captain died trying
    To make them advance

The paratroopers landed
    A magnificent sight
There was hand to hand combat
    But no VCs in sight

When the news was reported
    The ARVANS had won
The VCs are laughing
    Over their captured guns

All pilots take warning
    When tree lines are near
Let's land those darn choppers
    One mile to the rear.

This bit of doggerel is, as best as I can judge, an accurate description of the battle and it well illustrates the lack of confidence that we had in the 7th ARVN Division commander and his senior U.S. advisor.

Although I take great issue with how he misused helicopters, Vann's perception of how badly the war was going was, in my view, absolutely correct. After Ap Bac his reports, as I understand them, were right on the money with regard to the ARVN, and when they were ignored and contradicted at the top level, the interviews that he gave to his favorite reporters also painted the true picture of that aspect of the war. This divergence between his opinion and the official MAAG and RVN positions, kept him in trouble until he rotated out at the end of his tour about three months later. If the political generals and the American politicians had adopted his view, even partially, perhaps the war could have been turned around in time. I greatly doubt it though; because we would have had to somehow get the South Vietnamese energized enough to solve their internal problems, so that they could fight for their survival as a nation with enough energy and focus to beat their obviously determined enemy. Instead we just kept trying to do it for them.

There is an old army adage, which is probably true for many large organizations, that goes; "screw up and move up" (sometimes stated in even stronger terms). There is another one which I like, that says "the Army promotes megalomania" so, of course Vann went on to bigger and better positions and that still amazes me. It was not exactly in the U. S. Army though; he realized that he would not be promoted so he retired as an LTC in July 1963. Even that didn't shut him up though, because he continued in his efforts to get his message across and he was listened to by many. Vann believed strongly that America should take over and run the war. He believed that only by doing so could the war be won. I'm sure that he felt that he was just the man to do it too. I never heard his speeches, but they must have fit in perfectly with the thoughts of those who believed that it would be an easy war to win; if the military were just turned loose.

In spite of what Sheehan reports, as considerable opposition from the senior Americans in Vietnam, Vann was back in country by March 1965.[*8] He was assigned as a pacification representative at the province level for the U. S. Agency for International Development (AID). That was a nice euphemism for the civilians that flooded the country to assist in the war effort. The AID organization could not accomplish much "pacification" except by force of arms in Vietnam and it had even less to do with "development," but the neat AID acronym, must have been nicely misinterpreted by many, if not most, American citizens and foreign observers.

By May 1971, Vann had risen to unheard of heights at AID. He had been promoted to the position of Senior Advisor to the ARVN II Corps in the geographical area composed of the highlands and the coastal lowlands centered on the cities of Qui Nhon and Pleiku. It was a huge zone of operations which stretched from Phan Thiet in the south to north of Kontum. Without regard to the fact that he was still an AID employee, he was now the equivalent of a U. S. military three star lieutenant general; in addition to his AID workers, he had now been given authority over all U. S. forces in the area. Obviously he had just charmed the hell out of the big war leaders in Saigon. It boggles my mind.

The history above is again mostly from Sheehan's *A Bright Shinning Lie.* If you strip out my opinions, and make allowance for Vann's distortion of fact, his account seems comprehensive enough and I say again, read the book. What follows is also based on what I have read in Sheehan's book about Vann's death in 1972, but here I want to interpret what he has reported based on my understanding of Vann from 1962, as well as my familiarity with helicopters, the OH-58A Kiowa in particular (I helped develop it), crashes (I have a specific comparison), flying weather (again lots of experience—not all comfortable), low level flying (trained and with hours of it), and my trip to Vietnam in 1969 to introduce the OH-58 helicopter as new equipment.

In 1969 I was the OH-58A Kiowa Project Officer in the office of the Project Manager for Light Observation Helicopters (LOH). I was introducing new deliveries of the OH-58A, by visits made to the first units that would receive them, all over South Vietnam. The LOH office also managed the OH-6A Cayuse, so a secondary purpose of the trip was to try to understand why they were wrecking about twenty-five OH-6A helicopters a month there. I won't go into all of that, but after talking with many of the pilots and their bosses I discovered one likely reason: It had become routine for many an old colonel to "get a little stick time." After a hard day of flying the boss might offer to "take her home" and maybe get a little flight training on the way. From that start it would be easy enough for the pilot to allow the "colonel" to "go ahead and land it" This seemed likely to happen mostly in the small flight detachments, where only one or two helicopters and pilots were assigned. Nobody told me any of this directly but just hinted at it; the pilots a little sheepishly and the bosses kinda proudly.

With this kind of scenario, problems could happen if the old man was on the controls at the bottom of an approach, because as you might expect, crashes usually happen upon contact with the ground. I confirmed my guess with a couple of maintenance companies, that many wrecks were coming in as apparent tail rotor strikes. The OH-6A had an unfortunate characteristic that would cause that kind of accident. If it was set down hard on the rear of the skids, the helicopter would then slap forward and rock back. This would cause the main rotor to flex down excessively and cut off the tail boom. The helicopter would then wrap-up around itself. Fortunately, everyone would usually walk away uninjured from these events; just another combat loss. It seemed to me to be possible that the boss had actually been flying in some of those hard landings.

I have told that story so that you would know that I am quite familiar with the OH-58A and with what I gathered was the rather loose control of helicopters in some small flight detachments in 1969. Vann died in an OH-58A crash in June 1972.*[9] The take-off from Pleiku was recorded at 2100 hours (9 PM for civilians). It was a night flight into the mountains during marginal weather. They were headed for Kontum in the highlands where Vann felt that he had to be present in the morning. Vann reportedly radioed for a weather report at Kontum. You can see where I'm going here. Obviously, he was no longer kneeling in the aisle of the cockpit; he was right up front in a pilot's seat. Knowing Vann's conviction that he was the world's greatest helicopter pilot, and the tendency in Vietnam at the time to sometimes let the boss fly, I find it hard to believe that he was not on the controls. In my opinion, sure as hell he was flying the helicopter. They were reported to have crashed into a grove of trees in a 45 degree dive at full cruising power.

Sheehan records several other things that, without much doubt in my mind, place the total blame for this accident on Vann. I am sure that he died from his own arrogance and stupidity, but officially the cause was placed squarely on the young pilot who died with him. What we had was a young, relatively inexperienced pilot, flying with an aggressive, untrained boss, at night, after an evening of partying, and at low level through the mountains during adverse weather conditions; sounds to me like the perfect recipe for disaster. There was by the way, a slightly longer route that was relatively unobstructed by terrain or weather, but the decision was made to take the short, more dangerous route instead. That sounds like a typical Vann decision to me; a decision that would not have been made by any trained and even half responsible Army pilot.

The weather obscuration at the time of the crash was intermittent, but floating at or near ground level. That is a dangerous situation because you can be caught in the soup without warning. Vertigo can occur very quickly in that case. Even the best of pilots would probably have difficulty trying to maintain visual flight in such weather. Once in the cloud, the only way out without plenty of altitude, would be to very quickly start flying based entirely on what your instruments are telling you. In this case the low lying clouds had moved on within minutes because another helicopter landed at the site while the fire was still burning.

I have witnessed another accident in Germany that was similar to this except that it happened during daylight. In that one, two experienced Army pilots flying a CH-34, had entered a small storm at low level. They were not able to transition to instruments and climb quickly and they got vertigo immediately while trying to fly visually. They flew at high speed into the ground. It was just a small patch of bad weather and another helicopter landed beside the wreckage within fifteen minutes. This sounds to me like what had happened to Vann; not surprising as he was not qualified to fly anything in the first place. These things happen fast. His qualified pilot probably had had only minimum instrument flight training and it is my guess that he wasn't on the controls anyway.

It is interesting to note that his regular pilot was not flying the helicopter. According to Sheehan's account, he had gone AWOL, absent without leave, because he had lost his nerve flying with Vann.

Smart man that; Vann was one scary guy anywhere and in the air, that pilot must have known that his days were numbered, if he kept flying with him. Another interesting fact was that there was also a captain riding along that the pilot was planning to give some informal instruction to on the way back. This indicates the kind of loose control that I had thought existed during my trip to Vietnam a couple of years earlier

This amazing story confirms my poor opinion of him when he was an LTC advisor in 1962. As I have said, Vann was one of two lieutenant colonels we, in the 57th, had to deal directly with. They were two out of many others that were fine leaders and courageous fighters, but these two seemed to me to be way, way, out of bounds; dangerously so. I am also sure, unfortunately, that they were not alone. Senior commanders seemed to love and fear Stockton and Vann and others like them. Through the strength of an abnormal personality and unlimited persistence Vann managed to have his war. He was an early leader into Halberstam's quagmire and also, in my view, he finally managed to kill himself. Even in view of his climb to high position, he apparently never did get his head screwed on tightly.

Was he representative of the poor thinking, high level arrogance and pure ignorance of our national leaders at the time; or the thirst for aggrandizement of some in our military officers then? Over the years I have become to believe it so.

CHAPTER 24

WELL, WE ARE WINNING RIGHT?

"There is no doubt that we are on the winning side"
Chief of MAAG Vietnam, General Paul Harkins
Honolulu July 1962[*1]

In spite of the obvious problems with the ARVN at the October 1962 battle of Ap Bac the official outlook stayed rosy. Funny, because it was pretty clear that there was questionable rationale for that position. The first reason for the official line had to be to not upset President Diem and the ruling South Vietnamese politicians and the second one was, no doubt, for our senior officials to look good up the chain of command, all the way through the political hierarchy at home. American officials all up the line had thrown the family jewels on the table. We had picked a government on the South Vietnamese side that seemed, early on, to be one that we would have to buck up to the task. We Army flyers would understand the problem mostly from the media. We weren't consulted about what we observed in our travels and we were not privy to any official reports, except our own after-mission reports, which didn't dwell on outcomes. Sometimes we felt like the well known mushroom. You know: keep 'em in the dark and feed 'em crap!

But I'm sure our political blindness was not of much concern to anyone, including us. We began to mark our calendars and carve our short timer sticks, while we continued to coordinate with the III Corps advisory headquarters and fly the missions. We were concerned about the poor ARVN security however, and we took some measures to protect ourselves from the leaks that often seemed to go straight to the VC. Sometimes our navigation skill might have seemed weak, when we landed a little short, or a little long, from our planned, and advertised, point of landing. Unlike our friend LTC Vann, we did not think that it was useful to land right on top of them. No one ever mentioned our near misses though; we were usually not that far off and maybe their map reading ability wasn't that good anyway. Operational security being practically nonexistent, this sliding slightly, one way or another, or long or short, seemed to work out quiet well. We caught fewer holes and the troops usually didn't get shot while stepping off of the helicopter.

I will admit that, by this time, we were quite apprehensive about the apparent ability of the VC to always know when we were on the way. I'll give you one example, out of several, where the near miss technique paid off well. This time, on the afternoon preceding the operation, I had been over at III Corps Headquarters picking up the details concerning the combat assault mission we had planned for the next morning. I sometimes wandered upstairs to the ARVN S-3 operations portion of the headquarters. This time, although I couldn't understand a word, I noticed what seemed to me to be some excited phone conversation going on. It was obviously long distance because the phone call was being carried on at a very high volume. "Our" man did not seem to be happy with the responses he was getting from the other end. Heliborne assaults were the only game in town, so one could guess that our morning mission was the topic. I went around downstairs among the advisors asking what all the excitement was about upstairs. They didn't know and they were unconcerned, but it bothered me.

Many of the advisors in the field were also very upset about the lack of security in our heliborne assaults. All of the missions were initiated at division headquarters in the field, then run up the chain of command to III Corp for approval and finally back down. Much of that communication appeared to be through unsecured phone lines; at least twelve hours before the lift could begin. This time I talked privately with the senior advisor at the troop pick-up site; the one who was going out with the troops. I told him that I would probably be landing "a little long" that morning and told him why. He understood. We terminated about 1000 feet beyond where we had planned. We received no holes that morning and the troops were able to exit the helicopters without immediately being brought under enemy fire. They had a little time to form-up into a line of battle before they surprised a bunch of VC that were just leaving the area where we would have landed. This was not the first or last time something like this happened. However, I did not always talk to the US advisors. Some of them could tolerate no input from us aviators. If it were to be just a slight adjustment, I might not mention it to anybody.

The war stories that I have been telling here are just as I remember them. As I've said before, I have very few documents available to draw on. I did follow up on an opportunity to check my memory of the October '62 imbroglio at Ap Bac with Rod Magie, because I was otherwise engaged when those two Shawnees were shot down and during the rescues that followed. I have also talked to other 57th members about their memory of events from time to time. I've even suggested that their stories, about anything, would be interesting and that I might even include some of them in this missive. But the old reticence prevails and response has been slim; one might even say, except for Rod, non-existent. On the other hand, all of our memories must be fairly similar and so our stories might get to be a little repetitious. In a letter, Rod said: "like you, my clearest memories are of the weird kinds of things and people we had to deal with." I'll recount a couple of those.*2

Magie remembers several things that flavored the scene for all of us, from first to last: "Saigon had an unprecedented cold spell while we were still quartered in the unfinished Rex hotel. It got into the low 50s one morning. We were wearing shirts with the sleeves rolled up and the natives were huddled around bonfires set in the streets. Weird!" "Towards the end of the year's tour, I remember walking by myself along a crowded downtown street. I absent mindedly looked down the block and saw a man approaching who looked out of place. It took me a split second to realize that he looked odd because he was a Caucasian and by that time, Oriental looked normal to me. I then realized that I needed to get out of there!" Yeah, didn't we all.

Rod goes on to recount a couple other incidents: "For a month or two, before we got 'permanent' barracks on the airbase, we were allowed to live in town on our own. It was CWO Bob Hoskins, I believe, that jointly rented with me. I remember one morning early, being awoken by machine gun fire which seemed to be right outside. I had visions of a Viet Cong sneak attack in downtown Saigon, and that they were coming to get me! Soon enough, we heard that a rogue South Vietnamese air force pilot was strafing the President's palace.' It turned out that our apartment was on a direct line in front of the strafing position of the T-28. I think our place may have been in as much danger as the palace." I wondered where these two were that morning.

Well, I didn't hear this story on the morning of the palace bombing, but I heard others much like it. Some of our pilots, including young Lieutenant Magie, had been given the morning off, but their platoon leaders knew where they were downtown. They knew to head for Tan Son Nuht as quickly as they could. In a couple of cases however, we didn't know where the pilots were and I had to send people out looking for them; "under fire so to speak." The danger to our people, acerbated by the inability to round up all our crews quickly, were two of the major reasons that Cherne' ordered everyone back to on-base billets as soon as he could do so.

Magie was the youngest pilot in the outfit but he and the other lieutenants stepped up to the job like old professionals. In doing so, Rod managed to get his full share of excitement. Some of our more memorable moments were not directly due to enemy action. Most of us experienced one or more aircraft malfunction that left us unexpectedly on the ground when we really did not want to be there. Magie tells us of one engine failure that he experienced: "Between Ap Bac (early October) and my leaving Saigon in early November, a new CWO and I were coming home from Tay Ninh, about 45 minutes northwest of the airport. As we got about 15 miles from the runway, the engine quit cold turkey. Both of our left arm reflexes were obviously working as we jammed the collective down. A flawless auto-rotation was performed and fortunately we landed in a dry rice paddy. As the dust settled, I glanced to my right. About two hundred yards away I saw 10 to 15 locals running towards us with objects in their hands that looked like weapons to me. Although the engine had died completely, we were extremely motivated to get a restart. Amazingly it restarted at once. We picked it up and flew three feet off the ground, all the way back to base. The next day the crew chief brought me two hands full of metal chunks that he had retrieved out of the (engine) sump. I never got an answer whether that restart and flight on in qualified as a miracle or a reasonably expected consequence." Sounds like some expert Army Aviator flying might have had something to do with it.

Our original pilots were leaving rapidly. CWOs Thomas B. Deason, Blair R. Hileman, Virgil L. Morris, Marion R. Music, Louis J. Oddone, Ronald D. Rodgers, Walter D. Sabey and Granvil (Granny naturally) Thurmond were soon gone. Some of tose names have not come up before in these memoirs, but only because I can't remember the exploits with which they were involved. If any of them ever happens to read this they may even recognize incidents where they were sitting right beside me in the cockpit. They were solid citizens, and like all the rest of the original group, I would recognize them a block away coming down the street today.

We were getting more new pilots in all the time now, and sorry to say, I can't remember many of their names but they had been cut from the same cloth as those that were leaving. They knew how to jerk my chain just like the rest of them. Some of them had been there long enough to play a really dirty trick on me one evening. I had walked over to somebody else's hootch to tell, or ask, somebody something. It was a group of about five CWOs; maybe Don Beachnau, Charley Quann, Duke Youngblood and a couple more. My memory is weak on the names, probably because of what them dirty dogs done to me. They were sitting around on their bunks drinking what they called "little green devils." They said that these were a really great mix of Crème de Menthe and Seven Up or some other kind of nearly tasteless mixer. Someone asked if I would like to try one and another started to fill a glass. It sure tasted fine and I quaffed a water glass full. It wasn't until I tried to stand up and couldn't, that I found out that they had made mine with a mix of Crème de Menthe and vodka. I was cussing as I crawled out the door.

Way back while we were still housed at the Rex, someone in the MAAG had told me about the French sports club named the Cercle Sportif. It was considered an honor by MAAG officers, in what might be called that pre-war time, to be a member of the club. You had to be nominated by a current member, so after a couple of months, and a very few dollars had passed hands, Monsieur le President notified me by a nicely embellished card, that the “Board of Directors has accepted your admission in the club.” That was at the same time that I was attending spoken Vietnamese classes. I thought that I might have time to enjoy both things but it didn’t turn out that way. The classes went on without me and I managed to squeeze in only a few visits to the swimming pool at the Cercle.

There still seemed to be quite a few Frenchmen around. You would see them sitting around at the sidewalk cafes, lounging in the hotel bars and playing tennis at the club. Every once in awhile, I might manage to get an afternoon off so I would gather a small crowd of guests to go swimming, or to sit at the edge of the pool drinking Biere LaRue, while watching the French ladies and their families go by. Saigon, at the time, was relatively peaceful, only interrupted now and then by an explosion here or there, or by an occasional, lively but contained, shooting spree. The Cercle was like a piece of Miami Beach tossed in the middle. Four or five of us would expose our farmer-white skins to the sun and lounge back in the plastic rattan chairs to catch the rays. We called our drink of choice Tiger Beer because it had a tiger represented on the label and it was much, much, smoother than the local Biere 33; the Ba-muoi-Ba that had been cured with Formaldehyde which we would drink downtown. Too much Tiger Biere would only give you a normal hangover not the hair-on-fire one that Ba-muoi-Ba did.

I saw some senior MAAG headquarters officers and visiting dignitaries on the tennis courts at the Cercle. I noticed that visiting generals never seemed to wait long for membership approval to appear there. I remember one conversation with a MG Jablonski who was in country on some kind of fact finding mission. He joined us for a beer and we carefully responded to his questions. He had been all over the country and he did seem to know what he was talking about. I wonder what ever happened to his reports.

I also met the Canadian member of the four party International Control Commission (ICC) on one of his returns from North Vietnam. I think that I also recognized the family of the Polish member of the ICC. I never did figure out what they thought they were accomplishing, running back and forth between North and South Vietnam, but at least they seemed to know where to relax in Saigon. The Canadian was friendly, but he knew that he was just spinning his wheels trying to offset the reports of the three supposedly non-aligned members of the commission (Poland, Hungary and Indonesia). It was fun while it lasted, but I quickly ran out of time and interest. It was a civilized oasis in war time and I visited it again in 1969 just to see if anything had changed. The pool was just as blue, the tennis courts just as manicured, and the Biere LaRue was still just as good then. But the Americans soldiers are gone now, and the ICC has finished its mission, so one has to wonder if there are Russian advisors enjoying their Tiger Biere at the pool's edge and if the French plantation owners and businessmen are still hanging out at the Cercle Sportif.

Early on I had ordered a brand new Akia reel-to-reel tape recorder through some arrangement that the MAAG had set up with a local import company. It was a major expenditure for me since most of my pay had to go home to support my family in Tacoma. So why do I bring this miscellaneous subject up now you ask; because I'm relooping back to a couple of those unimportant things that hang big in my memory. I borrowed every Long Playing record that I could find and bought a few more which I listened to almost every night. I played the Brothers Four, the Kingston Trio, Dave Brubeck, Johnny Mathis, Count Basie, Bill Evens and others until my hutch mates were sometimes ready to throw me and my machine out the door. I was particularly happy with a tape that I had rounded up of old WWII Air Force songs, sung by Oscar Brand; songs like the ones that went: "*Give me Operations out Here in Some Friendly Atoll for I'm too young to die. I just want to go home.*" and "*Throw a Nickel on the Grass, Save a Fighter Pilots Ass.*" I haven't heard those songs in half a century but they hit a friendly chord in me back then and that tape recorder and those seven inch reels filled up most of my hold baggage on the trip home.

The 33rd Transportation Company (Lt Hel) (CH-21C), a sister company from Fort Ord, California, joined us operating mostly north of Saigon in support of the ARVN 5th Division from their base in Bien Hoa. The operations officer was an old friend, CPT Ben Luck, and we ran into the Olsen twins, that we had known from Fort Lewis. They were now in the 33rd. We flew a number of joint missions with them, and as we had done with the USMC and the 93rd, we led them into the first few missions while they got a taste of what the future held for them. I have read a report of the first assault mission that the 33rd flew with us. It was in late September up north and west of Nay Ninh and we were leading. The problem is that I have no memory of the mission, in the way that it was apparently reported back to the home base of the 33rd in Bien Hoa, or the way it was later written. The report was second hand, and the account that I read was written years after the fact, so that explains part of it, but still, it illustrates how far apart people can be when observing or even directly involved in the same situation.

The account begins by saying that the mission started with a briefing from the 57th operations officer, which could have been me; new captains were arriving all the time now so I don't know, but I flew on nearly every combat assault. It goes on to say that the reports back to Bien Hoa were that things were not going well. I would not dispute that; maybe so, but the report goes on to say that three 57th helicopters were lost, including one that had rolled over. There was reportedly after mission talk about tracer rounds and other things that indicated that the adrenaline was still flowing at high rate and maybe the alcohol, back in the hutches at Bien Hoa, was not far behind. I admit that my memory may have faded with the passage of time but there is no way that we lost three or had one roll over. I would remember that. It is more likely that we took holes and had to do some repairs before they could all limp home, but we didn't lose any on that mission. One might guess that this report actually covered things that happened at a slightly later date; maybe even a combination of events. Memories do get old and can get screwed up over time.

It is hard to say that things can get to be fairly routine, even when people are shooting at you, but that is a fact. By this time the shooting had become "normal" and receiving fire during missions was nothing new. Individual incidents are now blurred in my memory by repetition. We flew around with the 33rd for a few weeks before I left, but I can't recall any specifics from those jobs, maybe because I had gotten jaded but also, as I said at the start of this thing, it's mostly the funny things that form a picture in my mind. One such picture was implanted during a mission with the 33rd one day, when I saw the 5th

ARVN Division commander walking along a dike with an American colonel walking single file behind him. Something caused an explosion in the rice paddy next to them, causing water to geyser upward. It was about two rotor discs away from us. A mortar shell, a mine or a booby trap, who knows, nothing hit us, but the American colonel took an immediate swan dive into the flooded rice paddy while the ARVN colonel just kept on walking up the dike like nothing had happened. Well maybe it was just a wing-over, because the American quickly scrambled to his feet and ran to catch up while we were pulling pitch to get the hell out of there.

Things heated up for us in early October with the arrival of the UH-1A equipped Utility Tactical Transport (UTT) Company. This outfit with its rockets, grenades and machine guns had been given a spurious name to confuse, not only the ICC, but also the United States Air Force. I doubt that the presence of an armed helicopter company could be obscured from anyone for very long but the name might have provided a temporary basis for denial. The USAF had been convinced for years that the U.S. Army was trying to horn in on its mission. They argued that providing close air support to ground forces was their business and that anything that delivered violence from the air should belong to them. This was an ongoing interservice squabble. We saw it as another pretty obvious escalation in both fights, the real one with the VC and bullets and the other one with the USAF and words, but we had not been highly impressed with Air Force efforts at close support so far and we were very happy to see the UTT come in with its guns and rockets.

The UTT had arrived from Thailand displacing a platoon at a time. It was trying, with limited success, to keep a low profile. They occupied our old tent city at Tan Son Nhut and began to provide armed escort for us in combat assaults. We were still under orders to wait until we were shot at, before returning fire, but it was nice to not have to rely entirely on surprise in our approach to a target area, or on our crew chief and door gunners when we did fly into trouble. It was seldom that we did not receive enemy fire by October. It was fine to see those tree lines start to light up, when those UH-1A turbine powered helicopters began to snoop fast and low along the tree lines. The VC could no longer slip away as easily as they had previously done because the Hueys were pouring it in. They also took much of the return fire that probably would have formerly been aimed at us. We had taken to sweeping the jungle edges with our door guns on each approach, shot at or not, long before the gunships arrived. We knew that it was very unlikely that there was anyone but bad guys out in the jungle. We had been hesitant however, to fire in populated areas with our old M1918A1 machine guns or hand-held sub-machine guns. Now we could depend on the UTT to get in close, deliver fire much more accurately and with much better stuff.

The first mission that we flew together was kind off entertaining. When we began our approach the air was filled with chatter. Our new escorts kept up a steady conversation as one platoon flew along each side of the troop carriers. The lead CH-21C was supposed to be in charge of the combined assault but with the steady: "blue leader this is red leader we have contact . . . roger blue leader this is red leader coming over . . . negative red leader we got it covered . . . okay blue leader . . ." You get the idea. I could hardly get the mike button depressed to talk to either the escort or the flight behind me. When I finally got a word in edgewise, I asked them to please hold down the radio chatter in case I wanted to talk to somebody. We had bad days and good days but we got very used to having our UTT escort along and soon hated to go without them.

The fact that they were now picking up some of the rounds that would have been aimed at us, in earlier days, was brought home sadly when SGT Jonnie Lee, one of their door gunners, was killed and a pilot, CPT Joel Stein, collected a .30 caliber bullet in the pocket of his armored chest protector. Joe was real proud of that bullet. He planned to frame it and keep it forever. He liked to show it around while describing its arrival to everybody. He was doing that while drinking too much beer one night and unfortunately he lost his bullet as a result.

After three years of flying the CH-21C, I was now flying without having to think too much about it. The helicopter did as it was supposed to do and everything felt natural. I was flying with old man Potts again one day. Bennie was his usual self. He just sat over there and let me fly. After dumping troops all day, we were on another run with a full load. Things had been going fine. I had made the take-off and landings in accordance with the book with everything in the green; no problemo, but I was having to stay focused on the controls. I was getting tired I guess, so I said: "Bennie it's getting a little rough out here why don't you take it for awhile?" He said okay and took hold of the controls with his big Kansas farmer hands and clomped his number twelves on the pedals. I put my arm out the window and watched the rice paddies go by. After a short time Bennie said "Gee, it don't seem too bad to me." I looked over and he had everything trimmed up and wired down. He was sitting there with his hands folded over his big belly and his feet flat on the floor. He wasn't touching nothin' and the helicopter was flying straight and level and smooth as glass. I said "goddamn you Bennie. I'll never learn to fly this helicopter like that." He said "oh you're doing fine" and that was high praise for Bennie but he wasn't finished.

He said "how would you like to see a 2000 RPM approach?" I said okay. Go ahead." Now the school solution was to hold 2400 RPM until near the end of the let-down, increase RPM to 2500, or up to 2700 as needed, and draw in full power early, than terminate at a three foot hover. Bennie dropped the collective and wired it down again. He didn't even touch the cyclic stick while we loped down the approach at 2000 RPM. At the bottom, he reached out, and scooping up all the controls at once, brought us to a perfect three foot hover at 2700 RPM and full power. I cussed him again and he just grinned. I had bursitis in my right shoulder so bad by then that I had to reach over with my left hand to lift my right arm off the window sill and place it back on the cyclic stick, but I didn't ask him to help me fly anymore.

CHAPTER 25

THE MEDIA

Who reads newspapers or magazines much anymore?
Not my kids nor my kids kids.
If it ain't on TV or the I-phone forget about it!
War coverage on television began in The Republic of Vietnam.
Helicopters filled the little screen. But the media was in transition then.
We had mostly print reporters; Newspapers and Magazines

I have mixed emotions about the press in Vietnam and anywhere else for that matter. Hell, my grandfather, a grand uncle, and most of the rest of the senior Knight family, were involved with newspapers somehow. I was even aimed for the School of Journalism at the University of Washington until I discovered that I couldn't spell, didn't know how to punctuate properly and was not particularly good at sentence construction. I was also not interested enough to learn how to do it right. I switched to business administration.

You may have noticed a minor irritation with the media here and there in these pages. I had had some early brushes with reporters in Vietnam, but the unease that I felt really started with that December 1961 report, quoting a "senior officer," who had said that "it was just like WWII out there." How could anyone take such a comment, at that time and place, seriously? Where were the casualties? What was the offsetting opinion of some others who had participated? Where was the common sense that should have been exercised by the reporter? Why didn't he talk to anyone else? Instead, the reporter managed to locate the single worst individual for his quote regarding the activity of that day. And then he and his editors decided to go with the sensational statement rather than trying harder to uncover the factual story. I do have to admit however, that there was probably another side to that coin; maybe nobody else would talk to him, so that the reporter had few actual facts and no rational comments to report. We are talking about the first mission here and we are already leery about talking to the press.

Whatever the case, that incident colored most of my attitude in dealing with reporters for the next year. There had, however, been an even earlier indication that our interaction with the media would have to be like two porcupines making love: you know, awful damn careful. Remember the article in the San Francisco Chronicle that had used unclassified information to reveal where we were headed when we deployed. Our destination was classified secret, and only carefully sanitized confidential orders had been released to us, but a good reporter managed to zero in on the "news." The media has little respect for military secrets. They love to quote the "freedom of the press" and the "public right to know" as justification for whatever they choose to write. That, in spite of the fact that the publication of such information may very well be contrary to our national interest and might even get some of our own killed. Okay; but we ought to be able to expect some discretion in this. None of the following stories will show that any news reporting that first year in Vietnam caused the failure of any actual combat mission or directly caused any U.S. casualties. The information flow from our media, however, which rotated through the U.S. back to Hanoi and south to our enemy forces, combined with the security sieve within the ARVN, sure didn't help any.

The freedom of the press was not one of the things that we were much concerned with in 1962. We had plenty of other things to keep us busy. Besides, we agreed when the reporters attempted to tell the story "as they saw it." For the most part, we applauded the stories that we saw concerning the events of which we had been a part. Nor did the information exposed to our adversaries in Hanoi seem to be much of a problem at the time. We didn't yet grasp the importance of the reporting, or how it would eventually impact the American will to continue the fight. Their reports were rarely "in-depth," but what we read in the papers was better than the feedback we were getting from the ARVN, the MAAG, or any other official source. The reporters often rode to the war on our helicopters, but we only saw their first hand accounts after the stories had been clipped by our wives and rotated back from stateside. I don't know why not, but the Saigon reporters we ferried to the field, rarely spent much time talking to the pilots. Maybe the wary feeling we had was mutual.

Even though we were eager to see the published articles, some of them came across to us as having been reported as seen from afar or well after the fact. We used to tell each other that "the goddamn reporters should get out of the Caravelle and quit reporting the war from the bar on the hotel roof." They could lean on the rail up there and watch the explosions and hear the gunfire echoing across the city and for miles out over the flat Delta rice paddies. Closer observation was probably not required to write some of the stories we had been seeing. I sometimes regretted having those thoughts though, because when they did get wind of something important that was happening, or was about to happen, they were likely to flood my operations office looking for a U.S. Army helicopter ride to the nearest observation point. We did not schedule transportation specifically for them, but we did squeeze them in to wherever we happened to be flying anyway. I've got to say though, when that gang arrived on my doorstep, I often wished that they would just go on back to the hotel bar.

Some of the reporters, in the Vietnam of 1962, were even younger than we pilots and they were usually unfamiliar with military things. Some of them therefore had a tendency to get their reports just not-quite-right. That didn't seem to inhibit the reporting much though. Call it youthful enthusiasm, journalistic confidence, or what you will, but most of them seemed to have no doubt about their ability to understand things or their right to be anywhere, anytime they pleased, and they had no compunction about butting-in to conversations. In the age-old, time-honored tradition of course, writing up the sensational aspect of an event was preferred over simply stating the cold hard facts which were, admittedly, often much more difficult to come up with. Some of them also seemed to feel that they had the right to use as much artistic license as they needed to fill in the blanks. The problem, of course, is that the aggregation of not-quite-right stories, over time, can lead to problems in understanding the true picture.

My initial interaction with the reporters led to a definite reluctance to have much to do with them if I could avoid it. I eventually learned that this was not a good attitude and I got to know several of them fairly well. I enjoyed talking with them and respected much of their work, but in the meantime, I tried to pass off the media queries that Milt Cherne' didn't handle, to Sal Formica who worked well with them, and to Bennie Potts who could cover the technical aspect of things. I couldn't duck one interview with a radio reporter though, while we were still in tent city. You get that? A radio reporter? You remember, before everyone had a TV. Anyway, my answers to his questions were so short and my speech so thoughtfully modulated that when it was broadcast in the Seattle area, my mother listened and said "no that can't be Emmett. It doesn't sound anything like him."

One of the more irritating things to me, was when they misidentified people, organizations, capabilities, service branches or types of equipment; things that should have been easy to get right. Often, to avoid those kinds of mistakes, they would just pass over the subject and settle for generalizations or no names at all. One of the first of these minor mistakes, and one that really pissed-off us Army Aviators, was an article in the December 22, 1961 issue of Time Magazine, that announced our arrival in Saigon, concluding one paragraph with the sentence: "Leaning on the ship's rail were some of the 387 pilots and maintenance men of the *U. S. Air Force*." The article went on to say that the helicopter could carry "a maximum of 21 soldiers and be able to stay aloft three hours without refueling." Well, almost right. The Shawnee sported 21 seats alright, but you couldn't fill them all up if you wanted to get the damn thing off the ground; that is unless they were midgets and carried no equipment. And you could fly for three hours, but on some of our gas eaters you could only do that if you were quite prepared to run out of fuel while on final approach to landing.

Then, just to finish the thing off, the reporter tried a quote from one U.S. pilot: "We have mixed emotions about being here, but our job is to fly the bananas and that's what we'll do."*[1] The quote is okay, except that I never did hear any U.S. Army Aviator call the CH-21C a banana. It was mostly the reporters that did that; a little artistic license to get the proper color I guess. (I will admit that the comparison with a banana was useful in trying to describe the shape of a Shawnee to the uninitiated, and now-a-days, I even find myself using it on occasion.) These kinds of near misses however, continued to be made fairly often for the rest of the war, but after awhile, they usually just gave us a laugh. The reporting, of course, got better as time went by and it occurs to me that maybe I shouldn't be so critical. I'm sure that the old chief warrant officers that I flew with, will pick this account apart too, if they ever read it. Everyone makes mistakes right?

We can attribute most of this near-miss reporting to the early ignorance, which we all shared, about just what was happening here? And some of it could be chalked up to pre-conceived ideas. You know like: American airplanes are flown by U. S. Air Force pilots, right? Or accepted theories like: officers of more senior rank always know much more than lower ranked officers. Or the opposite view, that only the common soldier can put the correct slant on anything. I remember telling reporters in a later assignment, that they were welcome to talk to the "bricklayers" but please come back to hear some words from the "architect" before trying to describe how the building was being constructed.

They used code words to identify how much trust they had in any sources they couldn't name. They would quote "a highly reliable source" or "a usually reliable source." Naturally, they never quoted a "sometimes reliable source" or a "seldom reliable source" but at the bottom of the code was: "it is rumored."

Also, when making these observations, one has to consider the limited communication means which were available to the reporters at the time. They had only so much time in which to get something on the wire and back to the editors at home. The editors then had to chop the copy to fit the page and there they could insert their own ignorance and pre-conceptions into any story. And the rose colored liberal slant was already alive and well in the media then. Sometimes you have to wonder how anything of great accuracy ever got into print, or recorded to view on television, under those constraints.

There is a third leg on this stool and it can only be called pure youthful intellectual arrogance. Most of these young guys were smart as hell. Okay; but a few of them showed obvious distain for the military and anyone in it. It is doubtful that any officer had less education then they did. It should also have been obvious, that any soldier was bound to know more than any of them would ever know, about their individual job, the duties of those around them, and the application of their joint efforts to the total military mission of their unit. A few of them might even have had some idea about the big picture. Sometimes it seemed like the reporters were content to talk only with those who shared their views and could ignore the rest. It was a definite minority, but it was difficult to watch a few of those know-it-all word-smiths pass through my operations office, with their 27 year old noses in the air, whenever they decided to foray out to the war on our helicopters.

I watched one of these arrogant reporters who was observing an operation down in the Delta one day. The 21st ARVN Division was embarking on an unusually large operation. It included a heliborne assault on a VC target south of the Mekong River to be followed by a wide sweep through a highly populated area of villages and rice paddies. The assault had been accomplished and we were standing by at the air-strip pickup site which was also the division "field" command center for the operation. The ARVN colonel in command had been trained by both the U.S. and the French in the efficacy of the map display. The colonel had his plan layed out on a large map board in the shade and was discussing the continuing action with his US Army lieutenant colonel senior advisor. Now, besides the blatant overconfidence in the colorful map display, this operation had some pretty obvious shortcomings. It was unlikely to result in any major victories. It was, however, a great improvement just to see a division sized operation being attempted by this reluctant commander. He was maybe now beginning to respond to LTC Jonathan "Fred" Ladd, our carefully placed and highly competent, U.S. Army senior adviser.

At this point a young reporter, no I don't remember which one it was, crowded up to the map board, grabbed the grease pencil out of that ARVN colonel's hand and with a few deft arrogant strokes, tore his plan to pieces. The ARVN colonel was highly embarrassed and visibly upset. The U.S. Army lieutenant colonel went livid. The reporter, of course, had no idea that this plan was the result of weeks of work by the U.S. advisory team. The plan was made up of a series of compromises as the advisors tried to gain some trust and influence with the division commander and his staff. Nor did he consider that this was the first tactical operation by that division since the advisory team had gotten there. Weeks of work was destroyed in a minute. The reporter was surely ignorant of the fact that the ARVN commander was more of a politician than he was a soldier and he didn't really want to risk any fight in the first place. My memory is that this division sat on its ass for a few weeks before it tried to go out again. I know we didn't fly much with them for quite a while. To top it all off, I got my butt chewed out by LTC Ladd, with whom we normally worked very well, for having brought that expert down with us. Like I had a choice.

Ignorance, arrogance, and preconceived opinion; fortunately only a few of the early Vietnam bunch of news reporters exhibited more than one of them at a time. You have heard about the one bad apple though; you know how it can affect the rest of the barrel, so you can understand how one bad reporter could negatively color our attitude about the rest of them. Even when it is only one bad experience it sticks with you. Again though, our war correspondents got much better at it in a few months. And they were among the first to smell a rat.

There were, of course, many notable exceptions to these observations. There were some reporters that seemed to be especially good from the start. These reporters probably got their educations, and began their careers, back when reporting the news had more to do with facts then the interpretation of the facts. Malcolm Browne, reporting for the Associated Press, didn't sit too high on his horse and he wrote well. He avoided hyperbole, did not attempt to color up the story and tried to be as accurate as the MAAG would allow him to be; his unnamed sources sometimes tripped him up though. One report, in March 1962 for example, told of the decision to change our orders from temporary duty to a permanent change of station. The military had been trying to downplay that change because it could be interpreted as squarely in violation of the 1954 Geneva truce accords and so the reporters had not been given much official information from headquarters and we had heard nothing from them either.

Browne had to gather his stuff from other sources and, as was often the case, he was given incorrect information. He reported a change in the length of tour from six months to eighteen months for key personnel only. We figured that this probably included pilots but the question was who else would be considered key? That question was left wide open. And the report came as a blow to us. We had thought it would only be a year long tour; and what about our mechanics, or the other personnel that we would consider critical, but who would not necessarily be thought so by others? Our families at home were more upset than we were. After all, they had been essentially abandoned in place when we deployed in November. Eventually it became clear that the tour would be one year long for most everybody. The "informed source" in this case either didn't know what the hell he was talking about or he was consciously misleading the AP guy.

Mal Browne went on to write fine stories but we saw less of him as the war expanded with the addition of more aviation companies. The AP reports we read led us to believe that he was out in the field most of the time. Either that or his view from the Caravelle was much better than most. I remember him as one of the best reporters writing about actual missions during our year and he went on to write an excellent book entitled "*The New Face of War*" which was published by Macmillan in 1965 and later revised.*[2] It gives a good picture of things as they stood at that time, but again you have got to be careful in the detail. For example, he identifies two USMC helicopter squadrons in the Delta at the same time. Not so; one of them replaced the other. The USMC was using a six month unit rotation policy at the time.

The reporter that I most admired early on was Francois Sully. From the name, you can guess that he spoke French; as did most of the senior political and military officers of the Republic of South Vietnam. As I said earlier, he had been kicked out of the country once, but he was let back in later. I don't know how long he lasted that time. His problem was simple; when he smelled it, he yelled it. Having reported, from the era of the French Indochina War, he had an excellent background to understand what was happening in a larger context than most. He knew the extent of the imbroglio that we were getting into and US News was not afraid to publish his reports. This was rarely "good news," so President Diem's family troika in the palace had gone out of their way get rid of him. I don't think that he was able to return until they were gone and a new set of caretakers were in place. By then, most of the other reporters had picked up on the true extent of the situation in Vietnam. They could still accept the rational for our being there in the first place, but they were tired of being led down the primrose path by the military and political officials at the top.

Another writer that I remember well was David Halberstam. A big, sort of stoop shouldered guy with a studious look about him; he was personable, quiet and attentive. And he didn't miss nothin.' His first book about Vietnam, "*The Making of a Quagmire*" published by Random House in 1965, accurately portrayed the situation there during the advisory years, and like his previous reporting for the New York Times, it provided a clear warning of the probable outcome of the war that we were, in 1965, about to take over with a large deployment of ground forces.[*3] His book gave the word "quagmire" a connotation that usually is directly associated with the Vietnam War and it is still echoed when we are about to step into it again somewhere else. Halberstam went on to write many books on many subjects and they are all excellent. His reporting on Vietnam, however, gained him a Pulitzer Prize; that and his other books during that era are why he will be remembered. His analysis of the conduct of the war at the highest political levels is a classic. "*The Best and the Brightest*" was published by Random House in 1972 and one cannot get even close to understanding the ultimate failure we experienced in Vietnam without reading it.[*4] What I particularly liked about him in 1962 though, was his friendly, easy going manner. That attitude was apparently easy to disrupt when people started to hand him a load of BS.

Halberstam was in direct contrast to another reporter that used to pass through our flight line. They often seemed to be together because they both liked to fly down to the 7th ARVN Division to talk with the newly assigned senior U.S. advisor there. That was UPI reporter Neil Sheehan and the senior advisor was LTC John Paul Vann. In comparison to Halberstam, Sheehan always seemed to be a little standoffish. Maybe that was because his mind was already occupied in writing his opus based on Vann. That book, "*A Bright Shining Lie,*" was mentioned in the last chapter. Sheehan rightly saw the dichotomy represented by Vann's opinion, freely given, and the official view of how the war was going. We in the 57th saw LTC Vann a little differently than did Sheehan but we have covered that already too.

I have a picture on my wall which was taken by U. S. Army photographer, Master Sergeant Al Chang. It is a flight of our CH-21C helicopters in echelon right. There are two groups of five but only four airplanes are visible in each group. I am not flying any of the ones shown, because Chang was shooting his camera out of the forward cargo door of my helicopter, but it is my favorite picture. Flying helicopters in formation always includes many little adjustments to keep things glued together, but he managed to catch all that movement at just the right time to show us in perfect alignment. Chang took several pictures of the 57th in the early days. They are the best remaining photographic evidence that show that we were ever there. I hope they are still somewhere in the archives at the pentagon.

There were others that I particularly remember. Peter Arnett showed up for the AP in mid year. Norm Sklarewitz put together a nice piece on the 57th, 8th and the 93rd helicopter companies including fine pictures. His "*The Copter's War*" was published in the August 1962 issue of *The Boeing Magazine*.*5 Merton Perry reported for Time Magazine towards the end of the year. Mert particularly liked helicopter pilots and would hang around with us for C-rat lunch under the rotor blades. Most of the reporters eventually became just another part of the group. They were now more seasoned. They didn't seem to be so young and those that went out with the helicopters were seeing things much the same as we did. They were however, anything but convinced, towards the end of 1962, that they were getting the right story from headquarters (in GI lingo: the straight scoop from group) and their reporting had begun to reflect the change.

By the end of that first year their reporting often did not agree with the picture coming out of the MAAG. The military and Washington DC were out of line by consistently painting a rosy picture which slanted the situation in favor of their own performance, while protecting the incompetence of the GVN, and the ARVN. The truth will out. Perhaps a large dose of truth in the beginning would have paid major dividends downstream. It seems to me that in a war, you either have to keep the media totally out by an emergency edict, and that was impossible even then, or you have to very carefully set the ground rules and in any case it is counter productive to try to snow them. In Vietnam, we did most of these things wrong. The reporters were soon not just reporting the story. They were becoming a big part of the story themselves.

CHAPTER 26

TURTLE TIME

He is called a turtle because he always seems to take too long to get there, but when your replacement "turtle" arrives it is time to go home.

We were getting in a herd of turtles by late October and early November. Replacement CWOs began arriving early; they were signing in and quickly going right to work. They paired with the old guys and seamlessly entered into the fray. Soon we got a bunch of captains, almost as a group, and no surprise; many of them were senior to me by date of rank. Taking over as operations officer was CPT Wally McGuire. Wally was okay but he thought that the ops officer belonged in the office putting together missions, not out flying around. He didn't last long in the position because he was soon out-ranked by Dick Bastion who tended to view the job more along the lines that I had. He flew missions. Others that arrived before I left were Dick Freeze, Bill Gardner, Mike Hull, Bob Lawson and Tom (T.C.) West. Our lieutenants were happy to be replaced by the captains and they joined the departing CWOs to get out of there as quickly as they could.

Rather then catch the next big airplane out, I made one of the more questionable decisions of my Army service. Somebody, probably John Thomas or maybe McGuire or Bastion, suggested that I might stick around a few weeks and help show the new guys the ropes. I did that and it was no easy thing. I quickly concluded that the one year tour was probably going to be a difficult way to go. We had learned a lot in our year. The new leaders in the company were going to have to learn it all over again and fast. They were beginning operations from a standing start. Even in a purely support role, if the war went on for very long, this would mean repeated turnover of personnel with the usual difficulty of transitioning to new leaders, the limited time available to form cohesive teams and as Yogi would say: "it's deja-vu all over again."

The detrimental effect of the one year rule was somewhat offset by the repeated tours that we Army Aviators, and many other service members experienced, but there were other problems with the policy. One neat example was how the ARVN took advantage of our short stays to try to mislead the Americans they worked with. I remember sitting at the bar in the Vung Tau officers club on my second tour, when a young lieutenant came in and started bragging that he had gone with an ARVN unit to a place in the Delta that no friendlys had ever gone before. Well I pinned him down on the location and found it to be one where we had often gone about five years before; sorta reminded me of the friendly ranger company that we found in a patch of jungle on our second assault mission in 1962. We were told that no ARVN unit had ever gone there before either.

The one year policy may have been necessary, after all no one likes to be separated from home and family for even that long, but it led to several things that adversely impacted the Army then and probably still does. Ticket punching soon became about the only way to get promoted. Command of a "combat" unit (versus a "combat support" unit) was the most guaranteed way to get ahead. Part of that was to have been awarded the suitable level of awards and decorations. If one had held, for example, a battalion command, where the award of a Silver Star seemed to be fairly common, and did not get that medal, why not?

It became so bad in my view, that commands at nearly all levels, were often limited to six months so that more of our fine officers could get the experience. Good for the individual maybe, but what a way to run a war. Important lessons are missed this way; they have to be repeatedly relearned by the newly assigned leader. (The "newbie" in GI slang) Some things can only be learned by individual experience; as in "damn, I sure as hell ain't going to do that again!" Mistakes are likely to be the old ones, as the wheel is reinvented every year. And maybe we are still relearning those same kinds of lessons year after year today, where the guns are shooting and the explosives exploding.

I digress and it's time to get back to my story. It wasn't the captains in the 57th that were any problem; they were a very capable bunch and picked up on things quickly. The only one that got a little irritated with me was TC West. Tom was ready to take over his outfit which was the platoon that I had inherited when I got kicked downstairs from operations. He was my turtle and could barely wait for me to get out of the way. Well I did that in about a month or so, while he waited impatiently for me to clear post. He was a good guy though and he always managed to keep his sense of humor.

It was the new commander that I got crosswise with from the word go. An Army Aviation Association of America (AAAA) magazine had drifted into the Shawnee Tepee during August or September. In it was a letter to the editor from a recent graduate of the Army Command and General Staff College (C&GSC). The Major was informing the world that he had just graduated from the staff college at Fort Leavenworth and was on orders to command one of the helicopter companies in Vietnam. He said that he was really looking forward to applying all of the tactical and leadership lessons that he had learned at C&GSC. The letter sure sounded like it had been written by a self-satisfied martinet to me and I had thrown it across the room saying "damn, I hope that guy doesn't come here."

How could it be otherwise? MAJ Darwin D. Beauchamp was to be the new boss. I had gone to the Philippines to visit Ray Houts in the hospital and to carry his stuff to him before he was transferred stateside. I was out for only a few days, but Beauchamp had reported in during the time that I was gone. I was flying, back in the gaggle, on a combat assault as soon as I got back. Beauchamp was leading and had formed up the flight in an echelon left, when out near the planned release point, the MAJ gave an order for the flight to "go to a landing trail." Nothing happened. The next command was "now." I nearly fell out of my seat when the pilot I was riding with said that it was the way he always wanted it done; with a preparatory command and a command of execution; just like C&GSC had taught him. Everybody was supposed to move something at once I guess, but that is not how to change a helicopter formation. Each aircraft has to maneuver as needed, and separately, to make it come out right. I would have said something like "okay flight, pick up a staggered trail" and I wouldn't have put them in an echelon formation in the first place. Why do that; just to make it pretty? That set me up for my first black mark with MAJ Beauchamp.

At the operations officer's request, I was still giving advice to flight leaders in the mission planning process and I had been asked to "check out" the captains who would do most of the flight leading. So I was still in the middle of it. The next time I spoke to the group I pointed out that a staggered trail would be their most useful formation because it let each helicopter fly in clean air; avoiding the turbulence from directly following another ship. It also led easily into the right spacing to off-load the ground troops. Assault flights would normally terminate with the helicopters lined up parallel to the tree lined villages and canals.

I went on to say that there was little call for an echelon formation or close formation flying of any kind. We were not subject to enemy air attacks or anti-air artillery fire from the ground. Small arms, up-to an occasional .50 caliber, was all that we had experienced. Close formation flying only increased the risk of pilot error, while the Viet Cong was unlikely to be impressed by such a flying demonstration. We talked a little bit about the need for brevity in radio communications. I guess that I may have hinted at the lack of purpose in preparatory commands and commands of execution in the flying business. In any event, since Beauchamp led few flights while I was there, those quickly went away.

Come to think of it though, that was probably not the first problem the new boss had with me. He was a tall thin guy who habitually stood with his shoulders thrown back and his cap squared in a parade ground manner. His fatigues held a knife edge crease and his boots were highly shined. Unlike Cherne' he didn't carry a swagger stick. He didn't need to; he looked like one. Now me on the other hand, and the other old timers, looked like a collection of unwashed, cast-off laundry. Some of us in stained, scrounged-up air force flight suits; some in hand washed and stone beaten, none-to-clean fatigues;

everybody carrying a variety of weapons in a variety of ways. Any shined boots had long since been scuffed and dulled. And nobody was too careful about what kind of a hat they wore, if any. The contrast was inescapable. Thomas had lost most of the crease in his pants and the shine on his boots by then, so he tried to deflect some of the concern over our lack of parade ground appearance, but obviously Beauchamp felt that the old leadership in the 57th had not been on the ball, and as one of them, I caught the dirty looks and unspoken, but unmistakable, blame from him.

Speaking of dirty looks, I never saw MAJ Beauchamp smile during the few weeks that I knew him. As he went about policing things up, the first thing to go was the Shawnee Teepee evening briefing. Those casual officers' club briefings certainly did not appear to be too professional. It was felt that we no longer needed to let the crews know who was scheduled to fly on the morrow, or who had to stand-by in case of need, or who could relax because they would not be flying. The chain of command was now supposed to work. You know; from the commander to the operations officer, to the platoon and flight leaders, and on down to the individual pilots and crew members. No evening briefing was needed; instead the pilots who were to fly would gather for the early morning mission briefing only. I thought that this procedure left too many pilots and crews out of the loop or standing-by when they didn't need to do so. The rank structure had increased dramatically with the addition of all these captains, so a more formal chain of command was probably inevitable, but I don't know how long this system lasted because the bitching among the pilots was already evident before I departed.

The flight leader of the day would conduct these morning briefings. I would usually have something to add since I would be flying with him. But Beauchamp liked to end them with something similar to a college locker room pep talk before each mission. Because of his height and his shoulders-thrown-back posture, it seemed to me, that whenever Beauchamp talked he was looking down his long patrician nose at us. I found that to be particularly irritating when he was standing over me in a personal conversation, very few of which were pleasant to begin with. Beauchamp was a very doctrinaire officer. He was more closely aligned with Army regulations then I would ever be, and by this time, I was flat tired out. From having pretty much run the flying, to being placed in a position of giving "free advice," was not easy for me. From working like hell to keep things moving, to trying to guide a bunch of new guys, mostly senior to me, along a proven path, was not easy for anybody. And trying to do this with Major Darwin D. Beauchamp breathing down the back of my neck was excruciatingly painful.

I often found that my understanding of how things should be done did not conform to Beauchamp's ideas. That probably should not have come as a surprise because I have never been a military conformist and he obviously was one. My view was to keep it simple and fly the missions to the best of our ability without unnecessarily endangering our people. I paid little attention to military bearing or appearance and I readily accepted comment and criticism from the other pilots. I never stood on ceremony but concentrated on getting the job done. The new major believed in a much higher level of military correctness than I did.

Another example of our early disagreement was when I suggested that commissioned officers should not fly together. I pointed out that the CWOs would invariably have had more cargo helicopter flying experience and that the commissioned officers would normally have other duties to perform besides polishing up on their flying skills. Therefore, it was, in my opinion, a good plan to team warrants with commissioned officers in the cockpit. I had relaxed this rule somewhat towards the end of my tour, and was, myself, flying with the new captains at the time, but it still seemed to me to be a good general rule and a good place for the new pilots to start. Beauchamp let me know right away, that any commissioned officer could fly as well as any warrant officer, and that the captains would be flying together. Well okay boss, but some of the captains had only recently finished transition into the CH-21C and had little time in cargo helicopters of any kind. Some, like Beauchamp himself, had come straight from assignments where they had been barely meeting flight minimums, let alone flying regularly. On more than one occasion, I had had my own ass saved by an old chief's experience. There was no doubt in my mind that putting two commissioned officers in the same cockpit increased the potential for crew mistakes and it had nothing to do with rank.

Soon all of the pilots that had cruised into Vietnam on the USNS Core were gone except for Charley Larkin. Many of the pilots that had joined us during the year were now old hands and had become close friends but it was nice to have one of the original crew still around. Charley was the last one to leave before me and he was the only one of the bunch that had logged a few more flying hours then I had. We didn't get to fly together much at the end though, because we were both too busy working with others. He was checking pilots out at the same time as I was working with the leaders. While I was riding with my fellow captains my procedure was to run the first mission with each; explaining things as we went along. After that, I pretended to be just like our IPs had always been. I wouldn't say much or touch anything unless I was asked to. I might handle the radio, if the work load got heavy enough, and there were a few other times when something was obviously getting out of hand that I might say something.

There was one mission for example, where it was tactically necessary, after the assault landing, to pick-up and turn quickly into a climbing 180 degree turn, exiting back the way we had come. This was necessary, amongst other things, to avoid a VC .50 caliber machine gun emplacement reported to be to our front. The senior captain with whom I was flying was an experienced CH-21C pilot, but he had a tendency to allow his airspeed and rate-of-climb to fall off during climbs. This, of course, would cause the flight to bunch up behind us. The pilots would have to fight their aircraft to even stay in a staggered trail. It would get worse as the problem multiplied further back in the flight; where each helicopter became less able to maintain airspeed or keep their climbs going. They expected chalk one to maintain eighty knots and to climb at 500 feet per minute. With a 180 degree turn during climb-out, this was even more crucial. When our airspeed and rate of climb continued to dip lower, I got on the controls and began to gently increase collective, while at the same time urging the captain to keep his airspeed and rate-of-climb up. This time the captain said "god damn it; you are always trying to tell me how to fly the airplane!" I looked out my side window and back where number seven was just then beginning to loose altitude and fall out of the formation. I said;

"yeah and if you don't pull in some power pretty soon, number seven is going to stop flying completely!"

After a few weeks, I reached the conclusion that the pilots that I had ridden with were pretty much good to go, or at least as good as could be expected, until they got their own bruises. They understood the fundamentals of flight leading and combat assaults. They were generally cool under stress, and when things did get tight, they reacted well. Rarely was any nervousness apparent over the radio. I hated to hear any anxiety voiced by the leader over the radio and what little I had noted soon disappeared. My uncomfortable relationship with Beauchamp however, continued and reached a maximum on one of the last missions that I flew in the 57th. It was mostly based on a misunderstanding but it really poisoned the already foul air between us.

The captain that appeared to be the most ready to go it alone was Dick Freeze. He was an experienced CH-21C pilot and a cool customer in the cockpit. I told the new operations officer that I thought that Dick was ready to lead on his own. The ops officer said "okay but you stay with him on this one. He can lead the next one." Sometime before the flight took off, Beauchamp heard that Freeze was ready. He pulled him aside and gave him the down-the-nose treatment that boiled down to; now you are in charge of this one so you better not screw it up. The operations officer had told me to ride with Dick one more time. The commander had told Freeze that he was in charge and under the gun. Nobody told either of us about what instructions had been given to the other. Again, the deck was stacked.

We had dropped the troops and were on our way back to Vinh Long to stand-by, when we had one go down with a partial engine failure. While it was not under direct, immediate threat, it would be necessary to call in a fighter cap until we could get an ARVN infantry unit spun up to provide security. Freeze had not previously faced this situation. I had been just riding along as usual. When the calls started coming in Freeze rogered the call from the downed aircraft and then hesitated briefly. I called the maintenance ship, tail-end charley, to be sure that they were on it. We landed back at the Vinh Long airstrip and conferred quickly. Freeze said that he would coordinate with the ground unit that was standing-by at the field and get a flight ready to take them out to the site. For some strange reason, we had two standby helicopters parked on the ramp, but Dick and I agreed to just quickly refuel six others to do the job. I stayed on the radio to coordinate the incoming air cover and respond to our people at the downed aircraft. It was possible that the problem involved only a minor fix, so that the helicopter could be flown out soon. In which case we would have to unwrap everything we were just putting together.

Freeze headed out in a hurry to get things going and I stayed in the cockpit on the radios. Since I was no longer involved with the pilot scheduling, I hadn't even realized that MAJ Beauchamp was along on the flight, but after a few minutes he climbed into my helicopter and indicated that I should get off the radio. When I did so, he asked why I had been on the radio. I told him. He said "as of now, you are relieved." I had no idea what the problem was, but things were under control for the moment, so I got up and left the helicopter. As you might well imagine, I was pretty exasperated and wondering just what the hell have I done now? Beauchamp jumped out of the helicopter behind me and stood there with his thumb up his rear looking around.

Soon he noticed that the rotors on the first six helicopters in the flight were beginning to turn. He asked me "where are they going?" I said "to carry out a security platoon." He pointed to the two standbys and asked "why don't you use those?" I said "well, you could use those two and make three lifts to move the platoon, or you could use those six to do it in one." He said "we'll use the standbys; that is what they are for." I turned toward the flight that was turning up and cut a hand across my throat. With that signal they instantly began shutting them down; one, two, three. Dick Freeze came running up yelling "what the hell are you doing?" I just pointed to Beauchamp and said "I don't know; go ask him." Then I went over and sat down on a pile of sand by the runway.

John Thomas told me later that the *commander* had placed Freeze in charge and he had expected him to do everything. Beauchamp was therefore, very upset when he heard me come on the radio instead of Dick. You know, after his bible preacher talk to Freeze, he thought that I was taking over against his direct order! He wasn't even going to let me fly home with Freeze until John convinced him that there must have been some kind of misunderstanding. John dug out the story and explained it to the major after we got home.

Beauchamp crossed my path in the cantonment area that evening, and looking imperiously down at me, he said "I understand that I owe you an apology." I said "don't bother!" I could surely tell, after that short reply, that our poor relationship wasn't going to get better anytime soon. I decided then and there that it was time to for me to gather up my junk and start packing my footlocker. Years later, when Beauchamp was the full colonel Chief of Staff at the Army Aviation Systems Command and I was the lieutenant colonel OH-58A project officer there, he stepped out of his office and hailed me down as I was walking by one day. He stuck out his hand and said "I now know what you were trying to do back then" and he thanked me. I don't remember my answer except that I tried to get away as gracefully and as quickly as possible. I try not to carry grudges, but that took me right back to my less than pleasant last few days with the 57th in Vietnam.

I didn't close my DA Form 759 flight records while I waited for the 45th Battalion to cut my orders. My records indicate that I put in some fixed wing flying in a borrowed U-6 and in the new TL-19D that we had received. I worked at some of my, soon to be required, flight minimums. I was trying to get back to a peacetime flying mode by freshening up on how one flew in the Continental United States of America. For some reason, I also led one more flight of CH-21Cs on a combat assault, flying with CWO Dewey Little, one of our new assistant operations officers.

I was the old guy. I had my orders and was about to get a port call. It was in late November 1962. This would be my last flight in the 57th Trans Co. I went out to that battle weary CH-21C and walked around it with the crew chief at a trail. Stopping by the cargo door, I kicked a tire and said "Okay, will this damn thing fly?" Then I turned to look at the crew chief who I noticed was a bright-stripe PFC. He was in a brace holding a salute and he said "I don't know sir." This was to be his first combat flight. The gunner was just as new, so I decided that we'd better take a closer look and I began to climb the aft pylon while Dewey went around the rest of the preflight again. This was not an auspicious start to the day's flight. Just earlier, at the morning briefing, I had warned the new guys that the dikes were getting hard now, because they were draining off the rice paddies, and if you hit one with any forward motion it would likely strip a landing gear clean off the helicopter. So then I went right out and set the horrible example!

I was leading the flight and Dewey Little was flying the right seat. He was a recently promoted CWO and just new to the country, but he had already shown that he was going to be a good one. He had a couple of ash & trash missions under his belt, but this was to be his first combat assault. We took off for the troop pick-up at Can Tho. Little was flying and I was watching the Delta terrain go by. Everything was going smoothly when we started the approach to an overgrown set of abandoned rice paddies alongside of VC Village. Dewey stayed on the controls with me as I took the aircraft and set our approach for the far end of the landing zone. It's no excuse, but the field was covered with tall weeds and we never even saw the dike we hit. We didn't see it but we sure felt it.

The helicopter was shaking like old Ned, but we were at a hover, and I told the crew chief to go ahead and kick 'em out. Then we took off, not only to get us out of VC Village, but also because we had a flight behind us that was ready to depart the area. After climbing to a couple of hundred feet in forward flight, I called the crew chief and told him to "take a look at the left gear." There was this load rushing noise of wind through his headset when he leaned out the door and he said. "It's gone sir." "Oh shucks" I said (sure that's what I said) and then I wondered about the condition of the other gear, so I told the crew chief to "take a look at the other one." Again there was the rushing sound of wind going by and he came back with "there's one strut hanging down sir." Now it was really oh shucks, and what the hell do we do now? About that time, a friendly voice came on the radio and said in a well modulated, leisurely tone of voice "Chalk One you're on fire." You know, with the rising inflection on the words. "Youuarrea onn fieerrr"

Decisions, decisions. Do you land amongst the Viet Charlies? No; I had always felt it to be preferred, that if you had to crash, you should try doing it in friendly territory. So what then? Should we get some altitude so that we can auto-rotate successfully if the engine quits, or do we stay low, so that we won't have as far to fall if the damn thing blows up? I elected to stay at contour. I put the collective pitch stick up under my armpit, tipped the nose down, and headed for Can Tho as fast as we could go. I figured that one gear was totally stripped and the other one had probably been badly weakened. We were trailing smoke. A gear strut must have punctured the fuel cell because we could see the needle on the gas gauge rotating toward empty as the fuel was being dumped overboard. I called ahead and asked if they could build a cradle of some kind that we could try to land on with damaged landing gear. That was a faint hope. We were streaking toward Can Tho when someone called to say that the smoke was gone. Okay! We were hitting about 150 and I thought maybe we had just blown the damn fire out.

Some further conversation with the crew chief clarified that he had still been looking at the same left gear, during his second report, and that the right gear seemed to be okay. Well that was more relief, but it still left some question open regarding that "strut hanging down" business.

At last we were back at Can Tho. I put old 208 very gently down on the right gear next to a large pile of sand that had been prepositioned for some planned airfield improvement. First, I told the crew chief to get everyone off and to get them as far away from the helicopter as possible. Then I picked it up and edged it over to lean it on the pile of sand. If the right gear was still okay, maybe I could lean the left side against the pile and it would hold us upright. Fat chance! Every time I started down with the collective, the aircraft would begin to keel over into the soft sand. The crew chief had told everyone to get away, but the next thing I saw was a ground-pounding US Army advisor standing just ahead of us trying to guide us down. Well I thought, if this thing rolls, it will fling rotor blades all over hell's half acre and you're dead captain.

I had forgotten about the Time/Life reporter that was with us. It was Mert Perry and he had popped up next to the captain and was taking pictures of us. The fuel gauge needle was no longer moving; it was stuck down on the "you're out of gas" peg. The engine would soon starve. The helicopter would not hold on the soft sand. So I said to Dewey "well I guess we're going to have to find somewhere else to crash" and we went yo-yoing around looking for a hole to put it in. The Vietnamese farmers had fishing ponds in some of the rice paddies and we found one that looked just about CH-21C size. We would again try the leaning-against-the-dike trick.

This time it seemed to hold, but as I lowered the pitch, the rotor blades began to cone down. Before I cut the throttle, I told Dewey that he had better hang on to the cyclic stick real hard, because if those blades hit the water, that stick was going to try to wipe out the cockpit. Dewey had not said a word since we had hit the dike, but now he said "sir, if I hold it any tighter it'll squeeze right out the top!"

Well the blades stopped rotating with the tips about a foot off the water and we sat there in stunned silence. While we regained our composure and waited for someone to come get us, the flood moved up the cargo compartment. It seemed like forever, but eventually someone hovered next door. It did not appear that this crew intended to get their feet wet, so we gathered the guns, swam through the fuselage and lugged everything through the mud to the rescue bird. We took a CH-21C passenger ride back to Tan Son Nhut where John Thomas said that they were going to put me in for a DFC for saving the helicopter. I said no; you don't give anyone a DFC for wrecking a helicopter and that was the end of that. During the evening, someone from battalion told me that they had closed my flight records and that I was on an Air Force flight to the States the following morning. I was ready to go, but I will always remember Dewey Little and his immortal words: "sir, if I hold it any tighter it'll squeeze right out the top".

That should be the end of this tale of woe, but it's not. As Paul Harvey would say "now here's the rest of the story." A combined 57th and 98th maintenance team built a road along the rice paddy dike where they positioned wreaker and lowboy trucks next to the helicopter. They dropped the engine and removed the rotor blades. Then they lifted the fuselage onto the lowboy for transport back to Tan Son Nuht. It was by then, late in the day; not a good time to be on the road in the Delta, so they decided to stay overnight at a hotel in downtown Can Tho. They parked the lowboy on the street outside.

During the night, the VC laid frag and thermite grenades inside the fuselage and blew it to pieces.

And still there is another personal thing to add. Somehow my "hometown" newspaper got the story that I had crashed on my last flight before going home from Vietnam. Courtesy of Mert Perry I guess, but as was often the case, they got the emphasis on the wrong syllable. The article said that I had crashed on my last flight before going home! The impression was that I was not going to make it after all. Needless to say, that created near panic around my house in Tacoma, until I arrived there safely about a week later. Why a week you say. Well the USAF got the last laugh on me. It was Thanksgiving weekend. The crew was stationed at Clark AFB in the Philippines, so when we stopped there for gas, sure enough, the aircraft developed a mechanical problem. They said that the passenger door would not seal. I told them "hell I'll piss on it and it'll seal at altitude" but no, we stayed the long weekend. I lost fifty dollars at the officers club playing blackjack while we waited, but soon my personal exercise in excess of thirty days was about over.

CHAPTER 27

NOTORIETY AND RECOGNITION

The Five Knowledgeable Majors and recognition by the Army Aviation Association of America.

I have two more stories to tell about things that happened during the year following our "in excess of thirty days" deployment. They both relate directly to that tour. My short experience as one of the "five knowledgeable majors," while I was still a captain, was unusual enough to tell and it had, what was for me, a funny twist at the end.

I returned from Vietnam to fill a faculty position at the U.S. Army Transportation School, Fort Eustis, VA. for about six months, while waiting for my TC Officers Advanced Course to start. I instructed aviation subjects to the departing Advanced Course and other classes. Since the TC doctrine on aviation had not been envisioned in the way that we had been employing helicopters in Vietnam, I also rewrote all the aviation subjects to more closely follow what we had been doing there. (Needless to say, when my turn to go to school came, I max'd the aviation part.)

During this time I was also asked to provide a briefing on heliborne assault tactics to a group of high level visitors from Washington DC. The senior official to be briefed was a three star equivalent DA Civilian. I kept no records, but I think it was called the Vidal Committee; named after him. I don't remember his position at the Pentagon, but it had to be important. There were several others of this ilk and shepherding this group was Brigadier General Allen M. Burdett, a well known Army Aviator. They invited all of the early

Vietnam aviation company commanders that were available in the Tidewater Virginia area to be present for the briefing. Included were past commanders, Majors George Aldrich of the 81st, Paul Ewing of the 93rd and Ivan Slavich from the UTT. There was a third former Transportation Corps company commander also. It may have been James Gray from the 93rd or it was one of the other majors that had returned from Vietnam by that time.

I remember Ivan Slavich particularly. His nickname was, of course, "Ivan The Terrible" to us in the 57th, and it was probably spoken only behind his back by the armed helicopter pilots of the UTT. Many of the UTT guys were TC aviators and they all thought highly of Ivan but he was the only non-TC officer present. He was an Infantry officer and was stationed at Fort Monroe. He had sure learned how to gain attention though; he arrived late, soon took a phone call and left early.

I was the only lowly captain in the conference room at the Aviation Laboratories (AVLABS) where the meeting was held. I had been invited to prepare a briefing on combat assault tactics, so I marshaled the resources available at the Transportation School to reproduce some photographs, slides and diagrams describing the first mission flown by the 57th. I also mounted pictures to be displayed on the walls as a kind of story board. Those were the good old days, everything was in black and white; no color. I finished the briefing with some lessons learned and, much to my surprise was invited to take a seat at the table. The visitors began to ask specific questions. Many were directed to me since I had just given the briefing I guess. I answered those to the best of my ability and the others joined in to enlarge on the answers. I escaped some of the questions, of course, when they were asked directly of one of the former commanders.

Each question required some discussion. They had all been well thought out beforehand and most of them were not amenable to simple answers. Although we didn't realize it, the problem started right there. Mr. Vidal, if I have remembered his name correctly, had written his questions out on a 3 by 5 card and he recorded our answers very briefly on the back of each card. The questions ranged all over the board. I don't recall many of them now, but I'll give you an idea of the range of the questions and the problem with the answers that were recorded.

He asked about any need for improved landing surfaces. That sounds fairly simple and it was not of too great importance to us, but we tried to answer by saying things like; it was probably a serious issue for fixed wing operations but not for helicopters; that some kind of stabilization might be useful to keep the dust down in the parking area and that Pierced Steel Planking (PSP) could be used. Even this simple question however, did require some discussion. Our detailed answer was recorded on the back of the card as "PSP."

The discussion got much more energetic when more critical questions were posed. One of those concerned the kind of guns that were needed. We talked a lot about getting proper mounts and sights for our door gunners and we discussed the value of armed helicopter escorts with forward firing weapons. We noted that the escorts needed to have the dash speed capability to take targets enroute, while still being able to catch up to the troop carriers in time to provide suppressive fires in the assault area. We agreed that forward firing guns were not needed on the troop carrying helicopters themselves and we carefully explained the rational for that answer. The back of the card said: "forward firing guns not needed."

The question and answer session lasted for a few hours, at the end of which Mr. Vidal had a stack of 3x5 cards a couple inches thick. Everybody left happy and we locals went back to work. At the time, Combat Development (CD) was a major U. S. Army command with its headquarters in the Washington, DC area. A few days after he returned to the Pentagon, Mr. Vidal reportedly walked into the CD commanding general's office and threw the 3x5 cards on his desk while asking "what are you doing about these general?" That caught the CG unaware, so he called the colonel commanding the Army Aviation CD Agency at Fort Rucker, AL and ordered him to report to headquarters in Washington immediately. After a few choice words by the general perhaps, the 3x5 cards were carried to Fort Rucker by the colonel where they caught everyone flat footed down there as well. Now, there were some highly irritated senior Army Aviators around. They felt that they had been blindsided and that we should have coordinated with them before the meeting.

Remember that all the helicopter companies in the Army at the time were assigned to the Transportation Corps. That included the 45th Battalion and its subordinate units in Vietnam. We had our own TC CD Agency at Fort Eustis. Part of their mission was to deal with transportation helicopter matters. We had told that agency of the conference. The conversion to branch immaterial Assault Helicopter Companies had not yet happened and formation of the Aviation Branch was well into the future. Fort Rucker was the location of the Army Aviation School. They taught Army Aviators to fly and they had an interest in broad aviation developments, but they were not yet in charge of anything else as far as we knew. Maybe we should have known that they were already plotting to take over the business, but we didn't, so we really didn't see any need to talk much to Fort Rucker.

In order to address the situation quickly and correctly, as the CG had requested, the Army Aviation CD Agency called everyone that was, or had been, in command of helicopter units in RVN to hurry to Fort Rucker for a major "come to god" meeting. LTC Robert L. Hoffman had assumed command of the 45th Transportation Battalion at Tan Son Nuht so both he, and LTC Howard Richardson the former commander, were called in, along with company commanders and a few others that had held or were holding responsible positions. We at the Transportation Center, who had been involved with the Vidal briefing, also received orders to report to Fort Rucker and the word was passed that we were in trouble because we had answered his questions without consulting Fort Rucker. LTC Hoffman, a Transportation Corps officer, was placed in charge of the welcoming committee.

LTC Hoffman informed us, first thing, that we were there to defend ourselves because we had our asses' way out on a limb. MAJ Ewing, who had commanded the 93rd, stopped it short right there and said "nobody here has their ass out on a limb Colonel and nobody has to defend themselves about anything!" In a calmer tone of voice we tried to explain the circumstances; that we were invited to present a briefing. We were not told to expect detailed questioning. We had no choice but to answer to the best of our ability. We were assured that Fort Rucker had been notified. Since nobody from down there had showed up, it appeared to us that they must not have been interested.

We felt that it was the Fort Rucker CD Agency that had been caught with their pants down. Much information had been available to them from our RVN periodic reports. I thought that the whole thing was probably some Machiavellian Pentagon maneuver to get priority on some questions they wanted answered.

In any event, we were all gathered in a room where LTC Hoffman had the podium. He would read the question on the front of the 3x5 card and then, with a flourish, he would turn it over and sarcastically start each time by saying: "and the five knowledgeable majors said" Then he would read the severely truncated answer. One of us would try to explain the discussion that took place around each question. Since many of the questions had been directed to me in the first place, I was often the guy that was looked at for the expanded answer. There I was, a junior captain, in a room full of field grade officers, many of them showing some irritation, and me trying to keep my cool.

I remember one question that had to do with the need for helicopter qualified instrument rated pilots. My answer had been recorded as "not needed." What I had really said was that we didn't need instrument rated pilots in Vietnam; what we really needed was pilots that could read a map. That answer was not predicated on anything other than my recent, on the ground and in the air, experience in Vietnam. The weather there was rarely too bad for helicopter operations and too many of the pilots we were getting could not work efficiently with the maps we had. They were not aeronautical charts and they were difficult to work with. We all could have used some "schoolhouse" instruction. The Aviation School, however, was in the process of justifying some major bucks to establish an instrument flying curriculum and I had stepped right in the middle of that effort. A Full Colonel Phillips, (I remember his name with some argument induced clarity) was the driving force behind this effort. He was loud and pissed. No one paid much attention to the implied criticism of the school instruction regarding how to read a map.

We struggled through the rest of the day and into the next, then we all stood to have our pictures taken. I have a copy of that picture, without names I'm afraid, but it is without doubt the most complete photo record of the earliest Army helicopter commanders in Vietnam.

There are some notable omissions though; both MAJ Bob Dillard and Chuck Hardesty of the 8th are missing for example, and several others were not available for the photo. But it reminds me of a memorable experience when I inadvertently stepped on the toes of the military bureaucracy as a junior captain.

Years later, as a fairly senior lieutenant colonel, I was newly assigned to the G-4 of the Eighth United States Army in Korea. I took a brace and saluted the deputy G-4 when I reported for duty. It was Col Robert L. Hoffman. He stood up behind his desk and pointed a finger at my nose, and while waving it up and down there, he said "I remember you. You were one of the five knowledgeable majors." After all those years he was still angry. That turned out to be another great tour of duty.

As any of my former compatriots in the 57th will know, there is a final story to be told. It is the recognition that we received from the Army Aviation Association of America (AAAA). As I have mentioned before, at the 1962 AAAA convention, The 45th Transportation Battalion (Helicopter) was recognized with the Hughes Trophy as the outstanding Army Aviation Unit of the Year. The draft for this award was written by MAJ Cherne.' It was based on the 57th record and was intended for the company. After consultation with the battalion headquarters, it was recognized that all of the early units had met the same stringent requirements and all had responded in an outstanding manner. Appropriate revisions were made forthwith.

That same year, Specialist First Class James C. Dykes was presented with the Aviation Soldier of the Year Award. In spite of the Army rank designation, we didn't call senior "specialist" by that title. We called them sergeants in recognition of the work they were doing and the leadership that they were providing to their teams. Sergeant Dykes and his teams kept our radios working against tremendous odds.

The following year, in 1963, I was picked as the Army Aviator of the Year based upon my work in Vietnam during 1962. I couldn't believe it. I was flabbergasted. It seemed to me that I had been in constant conflict with authority over there. I wasn't even a member of the AAAA at the time. I had been earlier, but they had a flight pay protection insurance program, which we had all signed up for, that had a combat exclusion in it. What the hell, we were being shot at, so what good was that? We remonstrated. We resigned as a group. The AAAA corrected this war time exclusion as quickly as they could, but I had still not returned to the fold. I rejoined quickly and am a lifetime member of this fine organization today.

MAJ Cherne,' again, wrote the primary nomination. MAJ Dillard, CPT Houts, CWO Charley Larkin, and maybe others, added their endorsements or sent separate letters. The Honorable Stephen Ailes, Under Secretary of the Army, presented the Award and I received congratulations from the Army Vice Chief of Staff, GEN Barksdale Hamlett. The award that year was an engraved sterling silver cigarette box. It remains interesting to me, that no certificate was presented and even considering the high ranking Army presenter and occupants of the head table, the award was never made an official part of my personnel record at DA.

This, of course, is the main thing that review boards look at when selecting officers for schools and promotion. The rationale was that the AAAA was not an official part of the Army. Eventually, I told someone that I would at least like something to hang on my "I love me wall" so they did prepare a one-of-a-kind document. Later, I forwarded a copy of that with a request that it be placed in the "unofficial" side of my file. I certainly hope that this bureaucratic nonsense has been revised for current recipients of this, and any other such an award, which has obviously been based on the high level performance of Army duty.

All that being said, it was still a very much appreciated recognition by my bosses, contemporaries and the AAAA. To quote from the Oct-Nov 1963 issue of the Army Aviation magazine: Named Army Aviator of the Year for 1962-63: "for his outstanding performance as Operations Officer of the 57th Aviation Company, (even then they were reluctant to use the correct TC title) Captain Knight's development of new and imaginative techniques for the employment of rotary-wing aircraft in the assault role contributed greatly to the success of helicopter operations in Vietnam."*

Obviously that gives me more credit than I deserve and I would like to conclude this chapter with a portion of my remarks at the award ceremony: "An Operations Officer . . . primarily acts as an agency through which the individual talents and energies of the members of the helicopter company can be directed into action. I would particularly like to thank two groups within that organization. First, the maintenance and enlisted flight personnel. No unit can operate successfully without the outstanding quality which many of us in Army Aviation have come to accept as routine. We had the finest."

I continued: "Secondly, the people I dealt most directly with over there; the warrant officer pilots. These are the individuals within the Transportation Light Helicopter Company who flew the missions. Many of the warrant officers in the 57th logged well over 300 hours of combat support time. They were guaranteed a flight nearly every day for the eleven months we were in operation there. They performed these missions—I don't need to tell you—in an outstanding fashion. The 57th deployed to South Vietnam in November of 1961 as a unit. It was a fine company, and I can only accept this award with the full knowledge that each of the individuals in that company can claim ownership to a large part of it." And I still feel that way about it!

AFTERWORD

Our Combat Losses Remembered

It was a very bad day for all of us in the 57th when we lost our one and only Hawaiian NCO on 5 October 1962. Specialist Fifth Class Ellis was one of our more experienced crew chiefs. He took great pride in his work and his helicopter. He was the picture of a professional soldier; always standing tall and wearing a wide smile. His name is high on the Vietnam Wall. We had opened a chapel just before he was killed We initially named it after him, but with a later decision, our whole home base was designated as the Specialist Five Richard Leialola K. Ellis Compound.

This was not to be the only casualty among our friends of that first year. It happened on 3 January 1963, when a 57th helicopter tumbled-in from flight altitude; a pilots worst fear. They were returning home after dark at a reported 2500 feet. People on the accompanying flight reported seeing only the green and red running lights rotating wildly as the ship went down. It was full dark before they could search, and search they did, but nothing could be found until the wreckage was located the next day. There were no survivors. I have seen it reported that the cause was everything from colliding with a mortar round, to the loss of flight control. The cause was soon narrowed down by an accident investigation to loss of control probably due to mechanical failure.

The wreckage was recovered by the 611th Direct Support Maintenance Company and returned to Vung Tau where the probable cause was further narrowed to either a separated flight control cable, due to corrosion, or to the failure of a control rod among a nest of bell-cranks located in a compartment under the floor of the cockpit. The rods and bell-cranks were there to "mix" pilot input to the rotor system for flight control. Since the bell-cranks were stacked one on top the other and because they had to handle input from each of the pilots, it was a critical, but extremely crowded area; very difficult to inspect or to work on. We called it "The Christmas Tree" and to most of us it just looked like a damn mess. Occasionally the crew chief would have the inspection panel open and ask me if I wanted to inspect it. I would do so, but it scared the hell out of me just to look at it, so I would quickly tell him okay, now button it back up! There is little doubt in my mind that the cause of the loss of that helicopter was located somewhere in that Christmas tree.

The pilots that night were CWO's Lawrence C. Hammond and Raymond C. Wilde. Larry and Ray were among the more experienced and competent of the new officers that had joined us in late 1962. The crew chief was PFC Boyce Lawson. This was the same new crew chief that had ditched old 208 with me during the previous November. The gunner was Sergeant (Specialist 5) James D. McAndrew. Mac had been my operations sergeant for the past year in Vietnam. He was the soldier that I had worked most closely with since taking the Operations Officer job back at Fort Lewis in mid 1960. He was a Spec 5 for pay, but he was a damn fine NCO for me and for the 57th. As if that were not bad enough, four pilots from the 93rd had hitched a ride up to Saigon. They were on their way to catch the big airplane home. Those officers were CPT Don Toth, lLTs Charlie Fitts and Lew Stone. We had worked closely with the 93rd from the time they arrived at Soc Trang. I had planned and flown only a few missions with them but they were all old friends in the way that the dangers of war make old friends fast.

REFERENCES

Chapter 1

1 - John F. Kennedy, *Public Papers of the Presidents of the United States*, 1961 (Washington: U. S. Government Printing Office, 1962), pp. 1-3.

2 - Veterans of Foreign Wars Magazine, *50th Anniversary: First U. S. KIA in Vietnam*, November/December, 2011 p. 8.

Chapter 2

Karl von Clausewitz, *Principles of War*, Stackpole, 1944, *(On War*, Germany 1832).

Chapter 3

U. S. Army Transportation School, *Special Text, ST 55-156, The Transportation Corps in Army Aviation II*, Fort Eustis, VA, July 1961.

Chapter 5

1- U. S. Army Helicopter School, *Hover Bug Pocket Card*, Camp Wolters, TX, undated.

2 - Unknown Seventh Army Pilots, mimeograph *Instructions for Passengers in Army Helicopters*, Germany, undated.

Chapter 6

1 - General Maxwell D. Taylor, U. S Army Retired *The Uncertain Trumpet*, Harper & Brothers Publishers, New York, NY, 1960.

2 - William J. Lederer and Eugene Burdick, *The Ugly American*, W. W. Norton & Company New York, NY, 1958.

3 - Graham Greene, *The Quiet American*, William Heinemann, London, 1955.

Chapter 7

1 - Peter T. White with photographs by W. E. Garrett, *South Viet Nam Fights the Red Tide*, The National Geographic Journal, National Geographic Society, Washington, DC, October1961, pp. 445 – 489.

2 - Bernard B. Fall, *Street Without Joy*, The Stackpole Company, Harrisburg, Pennsylvania, 1961, and 3rd Revised Edition *Insurgency in Indochina 1946 – 1963*.

Chapter 8

1 - James C. Fahey, *The Ships and Aircraft of the United States Fleet – Second War Edition*, Ships and Aircraft, New York, NY, 1944 p. 13.

2 - Herb Caen, *Monday-Go-Round*, San Francisco Chronicle column, Monday 19 November 1961.

Chapter 9

Time, *SOUTH VIET NAM – Yes, We Have Bananas*, December 22, 1961 p. 25.

Chapter 10

U. S. Army Transportation School, *Special Text, ST 55-156, The Transportation Corps in Army Aviation II,* Fort Eustis, VA, July 1961.

Chapter 11

Rudyard Kipling, *The Ballad of East and West,* 1889, from *Barrack-Room Ballads, Poems 1886 – 1920*, Doubleday Doran, New York, NY, 1930, p. 177.

Chapter 14

Chinese Zodiac, Placemat from the Peacock Restaurant, Saigon, South Vietnam 1962.

Chapter 15

Jack Foisie, *'Combat' in Vietnam - Chronicle Man's Report on U. S. Copter Missions* San Francisco Chronicle, San Francisco, CA, March 26, 1962.

Chapter 17

David Halberstam, *The Coldest Winter – America and the Korean War,* Hyperion, New York, NY, 2007.

Chapter 18

1 - Dickey Chapelle, *Helicopter War in South Viet Nam,* National Geographic Journal, National Geographic Society, Washington, DC, pp. 722 – 754.

2 - Richard Tregaskis, *Guadalcanal Diary,* Random House, New York, NY, 1943.

3 - Richard Tregaskis, *Vietnam Dairy,* Holt, Rinehart, Winston, New York, NY 1963, p 173.

4 - Behind The Scenes at the National Geographic Society, *An Angel Gets His Wings Back,* National Geographic Journal, National Geographic Society, Washington, DC, March 2004.

Chapter 21

1 - William Shakespeare, *Julius Caesar,* The Easton Press Complete Works, Norwalk, CN The Tragedies pp. 481 - 554, 1980.

2 - David Halberstam, *The Making of a Quagmire,* Random House, New York, NY 1965.

3 - Colonel Charles A. Beckwith U. S. Army, Retired and Donald Knox, *Delta Force,* Harcourt, Brace, Jovanovich Publishers, New York, NY, 1983

Chapter 23

1 - Ralph B. Young, *Army Aviation in Vietnam 1961 – 1963,* The Huey Company, Ramsey, NJ, p 113, 1999.

2 - Neil Sheehan, *A Bright Shinning Lie – John Paul Vann and America in Vietnam,* Random House, New York, NY 1988.

3 - bid., not graduated from USAF flight school, p.429.

4 - Ibid., relations with helicopter companies poor, p. 214.

APPENDIX 1

HEADQUARTERS FORT LEWIS
Fort Lewis, Washington

AMNLE-GCT-P&O 8 November 1961

SUBJECT: Movement Order Number 3
Movement of 57th Transportation Company (Lt Hel)(H21) and 98th TC Detachment (CHFM) from Fort Lewis, Washington to Overseas Exercise Area

THRU: Commanding General
4th Infantry Division
Fort Lewis, Washington

TO: Commanders Indicated in Distribution

1. Prepare for foreign service and move personnel and equipment of the following units from Fort Lewis, Washington to Overseas Exercise Area through Oakland Army Terminal, TCS:

UNIT	TOE	SHIPMENT NR.	AUTH STRENGTH
57th Trans Co (Lt Hel)(H-21)	55-57D	2080-A	147
98th Trans Det (CHFM)	55-500R	2080-B	56

2. Movement Instructions. a. This is a temporary Change of Station (TCS) for period in excess of 30 days. Detachment remains as presently assigned until embarkation, at which time it will be attached to Overseas Commander for period of TDY.

b. Provisions of Chapter 3, less paragraph 6b, AR 220-10 (POM) apply.

c. Provisions of AR 612-35, as changed, do NOT apply in the selection of personnel for participation except that immunization requirements will be met and the following personnel will NOT participate:

(1) Personnel with an ETS prior to 30 May 1962.

FOR OFFICIAL USE ONLY

M. O. NR. 3, Headquarters Fort Lewis, Ft Lewis, Wash (Cont'd),
8 Nov 61

(2) Separate instructions will be published on messing, upon determination of mode of travel.

b. Class II and IV.

(1) C&E will be as prescribed in paragraph 5, DA Message 579839.

(2) Uniform for embarkation and debarkation will be prescribed by overseas area commander.

(3) All WABTOC items listed in TOE will accompany units.

(4) Individual weapons will be shipped in accordance with paragraph 40f, AR 220-10 (Yellow Disk).

(5) Protective masks will be taken.

(6) Station (PCS) property will not be taken.

(7) OVM equipment, excluding radios and that not required for maintenance, will be removed from wheeled vehicles and packaged.

(8) Wheeled vehicles will be processed for active storage to provide for exercising in accordance with TB 9-300-2/1.

(9) Aircraft will be shipped in accordance with oral instructions.

(10) STRAC basic load of expendables will be taken

(11) Items, other than Yellow Disk TAT shipped from home station, will be addressed to appropriate terminal marked: 2080-LTR.

(12) Equipment, other than Yellow Disk TAT, will be tactically loaded in organic transportation in accordance with the unit loading plan and paragraph 75, AR 220-10.

(13) Level of protection for vehicles should be level "C" to extent possible within time available.

(14) Yellow Disk TAT equipment shipped from home station will be addressed to appropriate terminal and marked: 2080-LTR-TAT.

3

FOR OFFICIAL USE ONLY

M.O. NR. 3, Headquarters Fort Lewis, Ft Lewis, Wash (Cont'd), 8 Nov 61

(15) Prescribed load Class IV repair parts (1st and 2d echelon) will be shipped. Supplies will include insect repellent, halazone tablets, and oral penicillin.

c. Class III.

(1) Gasoline and fuel will not be taken. Cleaning and preserving materials will be packed separately, and identified by notation "FLAMMABLE" as outlined in paragraph 36, AR 220-10. All fuel containers will be drained and flushed and appropriate certificates attached to the crate or package in which they are packed.

(2) Fifteen-day basic load of special aircraft lubricants will be shipped.

(3) Vehicles will be loaded aboard vessels with fuel tanks 3/4 full. Vehicles which move by rail/commercial carrier will be loaded with fuel tanks 3/4 full. OVM and extra containers will not be filled.

(4) Acetylene and oxygen bottles will be removed from vehicles and will be boxed, marked, and crated to permit stowage on deck.

(5) Gross weight will be chalked on the inside of vehicles on the dashboard and on the outside tailgate of the trailers.

d. Class V. Basic load Class V will be taken.

e. Medical.

(1) Evacuation enroute will be to the nearest Army, Navy, Air Force, or other US Government hospital. Medical attendance at other than US Government hospitals will be afforded under the provisions of AR 40-101 and AR 40-103.

(2) Immunizations for overseas area will be as prescribed by AR 40-562. Provisions of paragraph 25, AR 220-10, apply.

f. Movement will be by commercial, government, or organic transportation on schedule established by the Post Transportation Officer.

4

FOR OFFICIAL USE ONLY

M.O. NR. 3, Headquarters Fort Lewis, Ft Lewis, Wash (Cont'd),
8 Nov 61

5. FUNDS TDY TDN. 2122020 56-1211 P2000-21 2100 (M14-02) S4S-016 2040.1520 (8-7618)

2122020 56-1211 P2000-22-25 (M14-33) S45-016 2040.1520 (8-7618).

6. Reports.

a. Morning Report entries will be made in accordance with AR 335-60.

b. Multiple addressee telegraphic reports of arrival and departure will be submitted in accordance with paragraphs 55 and 65, AR 220-10.

7. Authority. a. DA Movement Directive, Message 579839, 7 November 1961, as amended by DA Message 580140, 8 Nov 1961.

b. Sixth US Army Movement Directive, Message AMGCT-T M-29, 8 November 1961.

c. Port Call, Message TCPTC MOVP 11293, USATTCP, Ft Mason, California, 8 November 1961.

FOR THE COMMANDER:

WILLIAM K. LOFTUS
1st Lt, AGC
Asst AG

DISTRIBUTION:
A, Plus 10 to (9)(39)
Plus 50 to (110)(111)
Plus 10 ea indiv

SPECIAL DISTRIBUTION:
20 - TAG-AGAO-O, Wash 25, D.C.
5 - COFT, DA, Wash.
5 - CG, USCONARC
5 - CG, Sixth Army, Sfran, Calif.
5 - CG, USARTTCA, New Orleans, La.
5 - CT, USARTTCP, Ft Mason, Calif.
5 - CO, USATTA, Seattle, Wash.
5 - CO, OART, Oakland, Calif.
5 - CO, USAPC, OART, Oakland, Calif.
5 - CO, Alameda Naval Air Stn, Calif.

5

FOR OFFICIAL USE ONLY

APPENDIX 2

HEADQUARTERS
US ARMY PERSONNEL CENTER
Oakland 14, California

SPECIAL ORDERS
NUMBER 325

21 November 1961

E X T R A C T

52. FNO & EM, having reptd this sta for trans to OS destn. WP o/a 21 Nov 61 to port TBGAA and/or coml trans to OS destn aboard USNS CORE, Off & EM are asg 57th Trans Co (Lt Hel)(H-21). (APO number for mailing address will be furnished by overseas command). Shpmt Nr: 2080-A. Bag alws SR 55-160-1. as amended. TDN 212220 56-1211 P2000-21 2100 (M 14-02) S45-016 2040.1520 (8-7618). TDN 212202 56-1211 P2000-22-25 (M 14-33) S45-016 2040.1520 (8-7618). (DESTN: EXERCISE AREA) USNS CORE departs Alameda, Calif 21 Nov 61.

1. DILLARD ROBERT J 0-00058881 MAJ
2. KNIGHT EMMETT F 0-00081469 CPT
3. WEBB, IVAN R 0-01885150 CPT
4. BRETHOUR WILLIAM 0-05505887 1LT
5. FORMICA SALVATORE 0-05006414 1LT
6. HINDS WILLIAM H 0-05203982 1LT
7. SMITH JOHN W. 0-04069591 1LT
8. BAILEY RODGER P 0-05213378 2LT
9. GARNER, JOHN L 0-05409608 2LT
10. MAGIE RODERICK 0-05309584 2LT
11. POTTS BENNIE B W-02146519 CW3
12. BISHOP, JERRY N. W-02207702 CW2
13. CAREY, JACK J. W-02203877 CW2
14. CAUSSEAUX, ALLEN B. W-02207703 CW2
15. DUNBAR, QUINTIN R. W-02206537 CW2
16. DEASON, THOMAS B. W-02206536 CW2
17. EAKINS, JAMES R. W-02150389 CW2
18. EASTLAND, ROBERT L. W-02207681 CW2
19. HENDRICKSON, CHARLES W-02206109 CW2
20. HERMAN, DONALD E. W-03150227 CW2
21. HOSKING, ROBERT S. W-03150755 CW2
22. HILEMAN, BLAIR R. W-02207685 CW2
23. JESKA, RAMON S. W-03150632 CW2
24. LAMKIN, ULYSES W-02207668 CW2
25. LARKIN, CHARLES E. W-02206468 CW2
26. MC ANERNEY, WALTER RW-02208014CW2
27. MORRIS, VIRGIL L. W-02207741 CW2
28. MUSIC, MARION R. W-02206487 CW2
29. NELSON, HUEY R. W-02205535 CW2
30. ODDONE, LOUIS J. W-02206114 CW2
31. PARSONS, RICHARD W. W-02205787 CW2
32. ROBERTS, EDISON I. W-02207720 CW2
33. RODGERS, RONALD D. W-03150744 CW2
34. SABEY, WALTER D. W-02205864 CW2
35. SAYLOR, DAVID R. W-02205172 CW2
36. SWORD, ROBERT P. W-02206104 CW2
37. THURMOND, GRANVIL W-03150545 CW2
38. WILLIAMS, BILLY J. W-02205457 CW2
39. WILLIAMS, WILLIAM W-02207637 CW2
40. WILSON, LEONARD R. W-02207625 CW2
41. ZEIGLER, ROBERT M. RW-03150257 CW2
42. BARMORE THOMAS B. RA18315461 SSG6
43. BARLOW JAMES C RA18316064 SFC6
44. GREEN CARL R RA54089944 SP6
45. HARMS MELVIN H RA16331777 SFC6
46. HAYNES ANDREW R RA18245488 SP6
47. LEISER ALVIN R RA19259183 SFC6

48.	MOODY FRANK P	RA33734903	SFC6
49.	POWERS CHARLES A	RA38602464	SP6
50.	REED LEROY F	RA38692621	SP6
51.	SCHULTZ WILLIAM D	RA16232229	SSG6
52.	THOMPSON ARTHUR J	RA16472338	SP6
53.	YATES ROBERT L	RA16243516	SP6
54.	AGUILAR FRANK	RA13548442	SP4
55.	ALDAMRONDO-SANTIA	RA30405992	SP4
56.	AMARAL REGINALD L	RA10109658	SGT5
57.	ANDERSON, JOHN T	RA19665630	PFC3
58.	BANNER WILLIAM K	US55695271	PFC3
59.	BLAND DONNEL	RA56051158	SGT5
60.	BOYLES RAY E	RA34607276	SGT5
61.	BROCK NORRIS G	RA16500484	SP5
62.	BURCHER,ALVIE E	RA19292958	SP5
63.	CARRILLO MOISES	US54221916	PFC3
64.	CAPPS JAMES R	RA15542397	PFC3
65.	CADDELL DAVID	RA12605688	PFC3
66.	CAMPBELL JAMES L	RA19506133	SP5
67.	CALHOUN CHARLES R	RA19679956	PFC3
68.	CLINE DONALD W	RA19361171	SP6
69.	COFFEY CHARLIE R	RA14346169	CPL4
70.	COLOMBETTE ANTHO	RA12626360	PVT2
71.	CRAFT FLOYD L	RA23510634	SP5
72.	CURL VINCIENT R	RA14276951	SP5
73.	CYR IVAN E	RA11333620	SP4
74.	DE VOE DOUGLAS E	RA16657799	PFC3
75.	DEHNKE MELVIN H	US56617935	PFC3
76.	DUVALL PAT	RA15380036	SP5
77.	DUNCAN DAVID L	RA16670115	PFC3
78.	EDINGER JAMES	RA13674661	PFC3
79.	ELLIS RICHARD L K	RA10106902	SP5
80.	FALZONE THEODORE	RA17588709	PFC3
81.	FRANKLIN LESLIE D	RA18560119	PFC3
82.	GIBSON SAM E	RA14704789	PFC3
83.	GODBER CHARLES A	RA14730097	PFC3
84.	GONZALES ALFONSO	US56294647	PFC3
85.	GRIGGS ADRIAN A	RA19336121	SP4
86.	HANSEN LARRY L	RA56332495	PFC3
87.	HAYDON JOHN H.	RA13256691	SGT5
88.	HENLEY ODIS D	RA18401919	SP5
89.	HINTON WILBERT D	RA17513843	SP4
90.	HINZ ROBERT L	RA17455104	PFC3
91.	HOWELL JOHN D	US54218038	PFC3
92.	IACOBELLIS VINCEN	RA19674282	PFC3
93.	JASPER ROGER G	US51464583	PFC3
94.	JOHNSON RONALD E	US56333666	PFC3
95.	JONES RICHARD E.	RA17469666	PFC3
96.	KACKMEISTER DONAL	RA17402191	SP5
97.	KIRKPATRICK DONAL	US53340659	PFC3
98.	KLOCKE LAVERNE M	RA17581531	PFC3
99.	KNOX BILL H	RA19099781	SGT5
100.	LA MARRE OLIVER W	RA11189010	SP5
101.	LESTER CHARLES M	US56321607	PFC3
102.	LIESURE JAMES M	RA18602835	PFC3
103.	LIBBY CHESTER E	US53320157	PFC3
104.	LINNE CHARLES D	RA15252272	SP4
105.	LINDE CLARENCE M	RA19657692	PFC3
106.	LONG FOY C	RA34899703	SGT5
107.	MAHLER RALPH C	RA55680098	PFC3

Para 52 SO 325 Hq USA Pers Cen Oakland 14, Calif dtd 21 Nov 61 (Cont'd)

108.	MARTIN WILLIAM A	RA13671140	SP4
109.	MC CLENDON JACK W	RA19645420	SP4
110.	MC DONALD VERNON	RA35838819	SGT5
111.	MC ANDREW JAMES D.	RA19539885	PFC3
112.	MERGHART JERRY	RA19645778	PFC3
113.	NALL JAMES T.	RA14733214	PFC3
114.	O'NEILL ROBERT F.	RA57156664	SP5
115.	PALOMBO JOHN A	RA11365485	PFC3
116.	PAYNTER WILLIAM A	RA19331349	SP5
117.	PETERS ROBERT W	RA35677339	SP5
118.	PIEPER ROBERT T	RA17562613	PFC3
119.	PITTMAN RAYMOND D	RA19657813	PFC3
120.	POORBAUGH CHARLES	US54234946	PFC3
121.	ROBERTS WARREN J	RA06968731	1SG8
122.	SLOBADZIAN WILLIAM	RA35781242	SP4
123.	SMITH DONALD A.	RA13272683	PFC3
124.	SNYDER RICHARD J.	RA19238573	SP4
125.	STUTEVILLE JAMES	RA19489651	SP4
126.	TALLEY LEON B	RA17362450	SP5
127.	TAYLOR CHARLES P	RA18506805	SP4
128.	TABOR RONALD D.	RA16677139	PFC3
129.	THORSGORG CHRISTIAN	RA19649752	SP4
130.	TUNNELL ARTHUR	RA19623676	SP4
131.	ULERICK LOVEN D.	US55688652	PFC3
132.	VANDEVENDER JAMES	RA14301894	SP5
133.	VEACH DOYLE G.	RA19670179	PFC3
134.	VISCAINO MICHAEL	RA19473188	SP5
135.	VOSS BENJAMIN E.	RA14749328	PFC3
136.	WARD DAVID R	RA53324146	PFC3
137.	WASHINGTON ARTHUR	RA51225970	SP5
138.	WELCH JERALD J.	RA28760598	SP4
139.	WOOD FRED W	RA14455647	SP5

FOR THE COMMANDER:

OFFICIAL

MARY E MURPHY
CAPT WAC
ADJUTANT

A TRUE COPY

Kenneth G. Donley
KENNETH G. DONLEY
CWO, W-2, USA

Significant others that closed us out at Fort Lewis, and then flew on to Saigon as our advanced party, thereby missing our Pacific cruise, were: CPT (P) Milton P. Cherne', 57th Executive Officer; CPT Kenneth L. Klippel, CHFM Commander; CPT William C. Rudd, 57th Maintenance Officer; CWO-2 Perry D. Leonard, Unit Supply and Property Book Officer; and SGT Watt.

APPENDIX 3

AIRCRAFT CLEARANCE
(DELIVER DUPLICATE TO BASE OPERATIONS AT DESTINATION)

DATE: 9 Nov 61

A. OPERATIONS OFFICE: STEAD AIR FORCE BASE, NEVADA

AIRCRAFT SERIAL NO.: 554149

B. OCCUPANTS (State whether crew or passenger. List additional passengers on separate sheet and attach.)

DUTY	NAME AND INITIALS		GRADE	SERVICE NO.	ORGANIZATION	HOME STATION
PILOT IN COMMAND	DILLARD, R.J.		MAJ	056881	57th TRANS. Co	GRF
FLIGHT	562055	554208				
	562056	554219				
	562058	554220				
	562059	562047				
	562071	562048				
	562060	562049				
	562061	562050				
	562064	562062				
	562019	562065				
	554217					

C. FLIGHT PLAN

RADIO CALL: 554148 FLT of 20
AIRCRAFT TYPE: H-21-C
POINT OF DEPARTURE: STEAD AFB, NEVADA
BASE NAME OF DESTINATION: STOCKTON AAF

ROUTE TO BE FLOWN

IFR	VFR	ALTITUDE	ROUTE	TO
	✓	1000' ABVE TERR	DIR	STOCKTON AAF

MILEAGE: 120 NAUT. ETD: 0015
EST TRUE A/S: 80 KTS. ETE: 01+40
ALTERNATE: — ETE TO ALTERNATE: —
TRANS. FREQ. HF( ) VHF( ) UHF(All)HG
PILOT'S LAST NAME: DILLARD
FUEL ON BOARD: 03 HRS. 30 MIN.

INSTRUMENT RATING

NAVY	AIR FORCE	ARMY
SPECIAL PILOT —	PILOT RATING —	PILOT RATING 3
STANDARD PILOT —	INST RATING —	INST RATING 3

DD FORM 365F FILED AT: 57th OPNS — DATE FILED: 15 Aug 61
HIGHEST RANK ON BOARD: CODE# NAME N/A REQ

LETDOWN EQUIPMENT ABOARD AIRCRAFT: ILS VOR ✓ ADF RADIO RANGE TACAN
LETDOWN AVAILABLE AT DESTINATION: ILS VOR ✓ ADF GCA RADIO RANGE TACAN
NOTAMS CHECKED: ✓ YES NO

REMARKS
PRES ALT 4930 T/O ROLL
RWY TEMP +14°C

Robert J. Dillard (SIGNATURE OF PILOT)

D. WEATHER

EXISTING: DESTINATION — TIME OF OBS; ALTERNATE — TIME OF OBS

FORECAST: DESTINATION (ETA) ±1 SCK CLEAR 3H LYV AS 29.90; ALTERNATE (ETE) — AS

ROUTE FORECAST: MIN CIG — AT —; MAX CLD TOPS — FT MSL; THUNDERSTORMS —; TURBC LGT OVR MTS; HAIL —
MIN VIS FLT LVL 15+; DUST OR HAZE —; SMOKE —; RAIN —; FOG —
MIN FRZ LVL 12000 FT MSL; ICING —; FRZ PCPN —; SNOW —; BRIEFING VOID AFTER 0115Z
WINDS RAA - SCK 10M 270/10/+5
SIGNATURE: /s/ W. R. Grimes

E. FLIGHT CLEARANCE AUTHORIZATION

SUBMITTED TO: ARTCC FLT SVC TIME BY
INSTRUCTIONS AND APPROVAL TRANS. TO TOWER OR PILOT BY: ALERT TWR
ACTUAL T.O. TIME
STATION ARRIVED AT TIME NAME GRADE OR POSITION
SIGNATURE OF CLEARING AUTHORITY: FOR THE COMMANDER: J. Moore

DD FORM 1 OCT 56 175

APPENDIX 4

THE FIVE KNOWLEDGABLE MAJORS
AND VIETNAM COMMANDERS
Gathered at Fort Rucker early in 1963
To discuss the brief answers recorded by Mr. Vidal

Not all of them are pictured here, but this may be the best group photograph available of the earliest helicopter company commanders that served in Vietnam, during the 1961 – 1963 "advisory" period of the war. With three or four exceptions, all are Transportation Corps aviators. This is a U. S. Army photo, but the names are from memory.

Front Row left to right:
MAJ Charles H. (Hooker) Amos, XO 8th Trans Co, unknown CPT, MAJ Morgan H. Mathews, CO 1st Aviation Co (Caribou) and then 45th Bn XO, LTC Robert L. Hoffman, second CO 45th Trans Bn, (Temporarily returned from Vietnam; he conducted this meeting; the author of the sarcastic term "The Five Knowledgeable Major's") LTC Howard Richardson, first CO 45th Trans Bn, COL "Ace" Phillips (best guess) Aviation School Fort Rucker (interested in establishing instrument training for helicopter pilots), LTC Kenneth D. Mertel, Infantry, Inspector General, Vietnam Support Command; author of the "Vietnam Reports") not yet in position, but destined to be the third and last CO 45th Trans Bn and first CO when it was redesignated as the 145th Aviation Bn, MAJ Ivan L. Slavich, second CO of the UTT, in that position for the majority of the time in 1962/63, MAJ George W. Aldridge, CO 81st Trans Co, CPT Emmett F. Knight, Ops O 57th Trans Co.

Second Row:
MAJ Milton P. Cherne, second CO 57th Trans Co, in that position for the majority of time in 1962, MAJ Darwin D. Beauchamp, third CO 57th Trans Co, MAJ Paul R. Ewing, CO 93rd Trans Co, MAJ John W. Martin, 45th Bn Liaison Officer at ARVN III Corps HQ, Two unknown majors, (probably CO of the 18th Otter Co and another early unit – the faces are familiar but I can't place the names)

Some early commanders not present:
MAJ Robert J. Dillard, first CO 57th Trans Co, (soon promoted to LTC), MAJ Charles D. Hardesty, first CO 8th Trans Co. (soon retired), MAJ James E. Gray first CO 93rd Trans Co, MAJ Joseph E. Henderson, first CO 33rd Trans Co, MAJ Robert E. Runkle, first CO of the UTT

About the Author

Colonel Emmett Knight received an Infantry commission in 1953. He commanded an Infantry platoon before pinning on his Army Aviator wings in 1954. He then joined a 280 mm atomic cannon outfit, in Germany. After three years flying there, he was transferred to the Transportation Corps and preceded through helicopter transition to join the 57th Helicopter Company at Fort Lewis WA. Upon promotion to Captain he assumed duties as the Operations Officer and deployed with the unit to Vietnam; arriving on 11 December 1961. As the operations officer he planned, and on 23 December, led thirty helicopters in the first heliborne combat assault of the war. His pioneering work in the development of helicopter tactics during the next year led to his being recognized as the Army Aviator of the Year in 1963. During the next thirteen years, he completed two more trips to the combat zone, and was often involved in other jobs supporting the war effort. This included Army management of the development and initial Vietnam deployment of the new OH-58 helicopter and then service as a Department of the Army staff officer. His thirty year career included commands from platoon, to battalion level and assignments from Korea to Iran. He is a graduate of the Canadian Land Forces Command and Staff College. A Master Aviator, his decorations include, among others, the Legion of Merit, two Distinguished Flying Crosses (one for that first mission), two Bronze Stars, twenty-one Air Medals and the Vietnam Service Medal with three battle stars. Colonel Knight's last assignment was as the Director of the Aviation Applied Technology Directorate, a laboratory assigned to the U.S. Army Aviation Research and Development Command. He retired from that position in January 1984 and now lives with his wife Margie in Williamsburg, Virginia.

GLOSSARY

Military Slang, Terms, Abbreviations & Acronyms

AAF: Army Airfield.

ABC: nickname for CWO Allen B. Causseaux.

Able, Baker, Charley, Dog:

Army phonetic alphabet - first four letters. Used during the brown shoe Army of WWII and Korea - these code w'ords were followed by Easy, Fox, George, How, Item, Jig. King, Love, Mike, Nan, Oboe, Peter, Queen, Roger, Sugar, Tare, Uncle, Victor, William, Xray, Yoke and Zebra.
(Alfa, Bravo, Charlie, Delta are the code words now used, followed by Echo, Foxtrot, Golf, Hotel India, Juliet, Kilo, Lima, Mike, November, Oscar, Papa, Quebec, Romeo, Sierra, Tango, Uniform, Victor, Whiskey, Xray, Yankee and Zulu.)

AD-6 and A-l: Older USAF propeller driven attack aircraft replacing the T-28 and they were a great improvement in that role.

ADS: Aircraft Direct Support. Army 3rd Echelon maintenance companies. The 611th and 56th ADS companies provided back-up for the field maintenance teams assigned with each helicopter company for those aircraft which did not require 4th echelon or depot level work. A major additional job was to rig downed aircraft for field recovery by medium lift helicopters.

AFC: Automatic Flight Control - nicknamed “Charley” in Army helicopter lingo at the time.

Agent Orange: Defoliant used to kill jungle vegetation - exposure believed to cause cancer.

Airborne Brigade: Headquarters for subordinate parachute delivered battalions.

ALOC: Air Line of Communication - planned to use army aircraft to carry cargo and personnel within an operational area.

AOC: Air Operations Center.

AR: Army Regulation.

ARVN: Army of the Republic of Vietnam (South Vietnam).

Auto-rotation: landing without power. The residual lift of the rotating rotor blades alone is used to control the decent and make the touch down, hopefully without further damage.

AVGAS: Aviation fuel.

B-26: WWII Douglas twin engined medium bomber - redesignated and presumably rearmed as an A-26 and used in Vietnam for a while as a ground attack plane.

BAR: Browning Automatic Rifle. This was a heavy, bi-pod fired, .30 Caliber infantry' weapon. It was possible, but difficult, to shoulder fire. It had good range and a rapid fire capability to supplement the lighter infantry rifles.

Battalion: Headquarters for subordinate company sized units.

BNMT: Beginning Nautical Morning Twilight (Oh Dark Hundred in soldier language).

BG: Brigadier General, one star, senior to Colonels and junior MG an LTG.

C: Combat - the type of flying to be entered on pilot flight records during war.

C&C: Command and Control: Helicopters equipped with separate radios and desk arrangements in the passenger compartment to allow commanders and some staff to ride herd on ground operations.

C-l 23: USAF Twin engined, high wing troop and cargo carrier with a rear loading door - operating as in Vietnam as “Mule-Train” during late 1962.

C-l 30: Lockheed Hercules - four turbo-prop engined high wing heavy transport aircraft.

Ca Mau: The biggest town with a runway way down in the Mekong Delta. We used it to stage operations in that area and to service Father Hoa's forces.

Camp Alpha: Replacement center billets for incoming enlisted personnel, referred to as a replacement center or “repo depot” located centrally at the Tan Son Nuht airbase.

Caribou: de Havilland CV-1 or CV-2 aircraft. The Army designation for the Caribou changed rapidly from its' first production in 1960. We first encountered it in Vietnam when we called it a CV-1 (Cargo-VTOL) aircraft. These very early models were redesignated and joined new production aircraft as CV-2 during early 1962.

CH-21C: Cargo Helicopter, Army assigned number 21, third major design change, i.e. C model. Tandem rotor Piasccki produced helicopter. Army name Shawnee.

CH-34: Cargo Helicopter, Army assigned number 34 - single main rotor Sikorsky produced helicopter. Army name Choctaw.

Chalk: A number assigned to each helicopter to indicate it's position in a formation.

CHFM: Cargo Helicopter Field Maintenance. A detachment assigned with each helicopter company.

Colonel: Senior to Lieutenant Colonels but junior to all General Officers. They are sometimes called Bull Colonels or, due to their eagle insignia, Bird Colonels or Chicken Colonels depending on the point of view of the beholder I guess.

Comm / Rccon: Communication Reconnaissance. Units with a primary mission of detecting and monitoring enemy radios.

CONEX Containers: Large steel boxes made for commercial packing and multi-mode shipping.

Collective: Helicopter control stick to change the angle of attack of all rotor blades simultaneously for climb or descent. This stick also incorporates a twist throttle to control engine power.

Commissioned Officers: swom-in officers with ranks from Lieutenant to General.

Combat Arms: Infantry, Armor and Artillery branches of the Army in 1962.

Commo: an abbreviation for communications.

Corps: Headquarters commanding Divisions assigned to it. The ARVN I Corps was the farthest north next to the so called demilitarized zone between North and South Vietnam. II Corps was next toward the south operating in the central highlands with III Corps covering about one half of the country from well north of Saigon and south to the end of the Mekong Delta. IV Corps was established eventually in the lower half of that area.

CD: Combat Developments - Once a major separate command in the Army but now incorporated in each branch and at the Training and Doctrine Command.

CPT: The Army rank of Captain (senior to Lieutenants and junior to Majors).

CG: Commanding General. The boss at each organizational level headed by a General Officer.

CS: Combat Support - the type of flying which was temporarily entered on pilot flight records at the beginning of the Vietnam War.

CV-2: de Havilland of Canada, Cargo VTOL (Vertical Takeoff and Landing) medium transport aircraft, can lift 32 troops or 3 tons of cargo from short, rough fields. Does not takeoff vertically so should have been called STOL (Short field Takeoff and Landing), Army name: Caribou.

CWO: Chief Warrant Officer. A series of grades starting from Warrant Officer One and proceeding through CW-2 & CW-3 (The grades now go up to CW-5); a category officer category for those performing duties requiring special skills, in this case Army pilots. The warrant grades are ranked between non-commissioned and commissioned officers. They are formally addressed as Mister or informally as Chief.

Cyclic: Helicopter control stick which allows angle of attack change of individual blades in a rotor disc; used to make turns and to change fuselage attitude for climb, descent or level flight.

DA Form 759: Individual Flight Record.

Dai Uy: Vietnamese captain. Pronounced “Die We” phonetically.

Dead Man’s Curve: where both helicopter airspeed and altitude are too low to allow a successful autorotation. The term is derived from a chart contained in the pilots Dash 10 handbook. The condition will always be encountered, but usually only briefly, during approach to landing. A pilot may find himself inside the curve for a longer period in some situations - for example a long vertical decent due to terrain restrictions.

Density Altitude: The theoretical density of the air. Air density changes as temperature and humidity conditions change - changes are measured against an established set-point of sea level on a standard temperature and humidity day. Higher density altitude reduces the power available in a reciprocating engine just as an actual increase in altitude does.

DFC: Distinguished Flying Cross - ranked as the forth highest decoration after the Silver Star and may be awarded in either war or peacetime. It sometimes even went to other than flight crew members in Vietnam which often did not seem appropriate to us.

Dust Off: The Army Call Sign for medical evacuation helicopters. The 57th Medical Evacuation Detachment (helicopter Ambulance) that arrived in Vietnam during 1962 adopted this radio call sign as the name for the unit. It has subsequently become rightfully famous and is used as a well earned title to identify all medical evacuation helicopters.

Eighth United States Army: major headquarters for US Army troops in Korea.

Fifty-one and one-half inches of manifold pressure: The maximum power, or “Red Line.” Pilots would avoid exceeding this because too much manifold pressure would be likely to damage the engine in the CH-21C.

Five O’clock Follies: The slightly derogatory name that the news reporters put on the evening briefings presented for them by the MAAG and later by MACV. The name indicates the confidence they had in what was covered in these briefings.

Fulda Gap: main avenue of enemy approach from East Germany to West Germany during the Cold War.

GPM: Gallons Per Minute.

Helibome: Carried by helicopter - helibome assaults: troops carried by helicopter into contact with the enemy.

Hibachi: a small charcoal burning cooking devise, usually placed directly on the ground and attended by one or more squatting cooks.

HMM-362: Helicopter Marine Medium followed by numbers 362 indicating the specific identity of the unit. HMM-163 was the second Marine helicopter company to arrive in Vietnam.

Hotel Three: Main helipad at Tan Son Nuht Airfield. The "H" for helicopter. Where the "Three" came from I don't know but perhaps from a number one at MAAG HQ and a number two at the MAAG flight detachment. (That's a guess).

Hover: Stabilized flight low to the ground, generally with about 3 feet of air under the low point in a Ch- 21C, with no movement over the ground except for limited distances or when intended as the mode of flight. A high hover can be maintained under specific conditions and by more powerful helicopters.

Howze Board: General Hamilton H. Howze headed up a study beginning in late 1962 which charted the future for Army Aviation. It was staffed by senior officers, including Army Aviators and is now recognized for creating the foundation for airmobile operations.

HQ: Headquarters.

Huey: Commonly used nickname for the Bell UH-1 Iroquois. This helicopter was originally designated by the Army as HU-1 so the soldier version of that quickly became "Huey" and it stuck.

International Control Commission: Established after the end of hostilities in the French Indo-China War to monitor violations of the treaty that ended it. Obviously they couldn't control anything and violations by the North Vietnamese started to happen quickly and repeatedly. American violations seemed to start with our entry in 1961; at least we were still trying to hide the helicopters.

ID: Infantry Division - composed of Brigades, Battalions & support units - the major operational organization in the Army assigned to Corps, Field Armies or in independent operations.

Idiot Circle: The rectangular traffic pattern prescribed at air fields - close-in, almost circular, turning from cross wind to downwind to base leg and into the final approach to land. Repeated circles in training can get boring so helicopter pilots thought that anyone who had to stay in the pattern multiple times for training was an idiot, hence the humorous name calling - truth be known, we all spent lots of time in the idiot circle.

IFF: Identification Friend or Foe - aircraft electronic equipment which interacted with air control radar to enhance the signature on the operator's radar scope - Air Force types often called it a "parrot.'"

IG: Inspector General.

IP: Instructor Pilot - designated on orders for a particular type aircraft.

L-19: Cessna, single engine, light observation aircraft later called an 0-1. It was normally assigned to artillery outfits for fire adjustment and to other elements of the Army for command & control. It flew many other missions as well. Army name: Birddog.

L-20: A de Havilland of Canada, Single engine light utility aircraft originally designed as a bush plane to be used in Canada and Alaska. Army name: Beaver, later called a U-6.

LT: The Army rank of Lieutenant (newly commissioned officers are Second Lieutenants
(2LT). They are sometimes uncharitably called other things like Two Johns or Shave Tails, etc.
First Lieutenants (1LT) are never called anything like that. They are junior to Captains.

LTC: Lieutenant Colonel, senior to Majors but junior to full Colonels.

LT Hel: Light Helicopter; the CH-21C was designated as a Light Helicopter since the Army had helicopters able to lift bigger loads. Medium and Heavy Categories also existed.

MAAG: Military Assistance Advisory Group.

MACV: The U.S. Army Military Assistance Command - Vietnam. Replaced the Military Assistance Advisory' Group as the war progressed.

MAJ: The Army, Air Force and Marine rank of Major. A Field Grade officer; junior to Lieutenant Colonels but senior to Captains nd everyone else in a Helicopter Company where he is called Sir.

MG: Major General - Two Stars - senior to Brigadier Generals but junior to Lieutenant Generals.

Manifold Pressure: Engine power measured in inches of mercury.

Mekong Delta: that area of South Vietnam which is dominated and fed by the Mekong River and its' tributaries.

MOS: Military Occupational Specialty.

NCO: Non-commissioned officers - Corporals and Sergeants.

Newbie: Slang for any newr arrival in Vietnam.

Nuc raaum: phonetic spelling for a vile smelling (to us) fish sauce used as a flavoring addition to many local dishes.

NVA: North Vietnamese Army. Regular army personnel and organizations moving into South Vietnam with comparatively well trained and equipped combat troops. The NVA came with recent experience fighting the French in the Indochina war of the 1950s.

0-1: Cessna, previously designated L-19 (see that entry) observation aircraft. Used by the Artillery for fire adjustment, Army name: Birddog.

OH-6: Hughes turbine powered light helicopter that performed scout duties in Vietnam. It was a small agile and versatile helicopter still seen, in later configurations today, both civilian and military.

OH-23: Hiller light observation helicopter. Used for pilot training, observation and command & control. Some were employed later with Army Divisions in Vietnam. Army name: Raven.

OCS: Officers Candidate Schools - Internal Army training, a source of commissioned officers.

Olio struts: CH-21 landing gear struts using a type of oil internal to the struts to absorb landing forces.

OV-1: Grumman twin turbo prop observation airplanes. These were low wing fairly high performance airplanes that employed sophisticated equipment including cameras, side looking radar (SLAR) and other means of surveilling the battlefield. They also mounted guns until the USAF really took exception.

Over-boost: Too much manifold pressure - over red line power.

Paul Harvey: Some may be too young to remember this very popular radio and newspaper personality. He told unusual stories and always with a "twist," usually a humorous twist, at the end which he would start by saying "now here is the rest of the story."

PCS: Permanent Change of Station. Never "permanent" but used for longer term assignments where a person would not be returning to the former station. The term was also used to transfer individuals between organizations on the same post.

Pentomic Division: A more flexible arrangement with five battle groups rather than the triangular organization ("two up and one back") that had been used in WWII and Korea. It offered better dispersion to handle the tactical nuclear threat of the 1960s.

PFC: Private First Class. New' recruits were know as "Buck" Privates and carried no stripes. The new' PFC had earned one bright yellow' stripe. His next promotion would be to Corporal or Specialist Fourth Class.

Plain of Reeds: a large area spreading west from Saigon to the Cambodian border where only low level cane like vegetation covered the ground.

Plexiglas foxhole: The two pilots sit in the nose of a CH-21C which is almost entirely made of clear Plexiglas, including the chin bubbles fitted under the directional control pedals. The slang term however w'ould fit about any Army helicopter.

POL: Petroleum, Oil & Lubricants.

Porcelain Pony: Soldier slang for a normal, western style toilet.

PSP: Pierced Steel Planking - sections joined together to form hasty runways and aircraft parking Areas. The troops naturally found other great uses for PSP.

PX: Post Exchange on an Army base. Small store selling clothing and general merchandise. Overseas soldiers often refer to the LInited States as "The Land of the Big PX." They are mostly referring to our civilian shopping centers and department stores.

QCA: Quick Change Assembly - where the basic engine has sub-components attached and is ready for immediate installation in the helicopter.

R-1820 dash 103: the 103fd derivative of the R-1820 reciprocating aircraft engine.

Red Line: instrument marking to indicate the maximum allowable, or "do not exceed," limit for that system being measured by the instrument.

ROTC: Reserve Officer Training Corps - at colleges and universities, a source of commissioned officers.

RP: Release Point - where individual helicopters are free to maneuver for landing.

RPM: Revolutions Per Minute: A single instrument which displays both engine and rotor RPM for pilot control in a reciprocating engine equipped helicopter.

Runway 25: airport runway designated by directional heading - this one is 250 degrees and would be called the west runway.

RVN: Republic of Viet Nam.

S-2: Intelligence Officer on a Special Staff at Battalion and higher. The others are: S-l Administration, S-3 Operations & S-4 Supply.

S-58: Marine identification of their version of the Army CH-34.

SD: Self Defense: RVN citizen-army units organized by region for self defense under the control of the province chief!

Shawnee: US Army name for the CH-21C helicopter.

Sixth United States Army: major headquarters for the Western US part of the US Army located at the Presidio in San Francisco, CA

SOP: Standard Operating Procedure: often a written document but also unwritten for normal procedure.

Spec: abbreviation for Specialist: ranks that run parallel to non-commissioned officer ranks, but are assigned to soldiers that have jobs which do not require the command of troops. For example, a Spec-4 is at the same level and pay grade as a Corporal and our helicopter tech inspectors positions were Spec-6, level with Sergeant First Class NCOs. Crew Chief positions were manned by Spec-5 or 6 when we could get 'em.

STRAC: Strategic Army Corps: Units so designated were to maintain a high level of readiness to deploy. (Roman numeral, as in STRAC II, indicates a high priority in deployment.)

STRAP: Strategic Army Force: Identified but with lower level of required readiness to deploy. (Roman numerals, as in STRAF VIII, indicates a lower priority for deployment)

T-28: USAF single engine airplane being used to train VNAF pilots and because it was all they had to offer at the time they also provided the only available air to ground support during 1962.

Tan Son Nhut: main military / commercial airport at Saigon.

TC: Transportation Corps: support branch of the Army.

TDY: Temporary Duty: usually used to indicate a short duty assignment as opposed to a PCS (Permanent Change of Station) and authorizes payment of a small amount to offset costs for the additional expenses incurred while away from home station.

TO&E: Table of Organization & Equipment. Army published document listing all personnel and equipment authorized for a particular type unit.

U-l: Utility Airplane: de Havilland of Canada ten passenger or 2500 pound cargo "bush" type aircraft. Army name: Otter.

U-6: Utility Airplane: de Havilland of Canada 6 passenger light "bush" type aircraft. Formerly called an L-20. Army name: Beaver.

U-8: Army executive transporter: Beech twin engined passenger aircraft generally used to take senior officials over longer distances. Army name: Seminole.

UH-1: Utility Helicopter: The Bell "Huey" a single rotor, turbine powered, utility helicopter; used in Vietnam for troop carry, medical evacuation and as an armed gunship (The Huey nickname stems from the original Army designation of "Helicopter Utility." That changed but the nickname stuck). Army name Iroquois.

UHF: Ultra High Frequency - USAF air-to air radios operated only in this frequency range during the first year of the Vietnam War and probably longer - unable to communicate directly with Army aircraft.

USARPAC: U.S. Army Pacific; the major headquarters in Hawaii overseeing Army operations in the Pacific Theater.

USARYIS: U.S. Army Ryukus Islands; the Army headquarters in Okinawa subordinate to USARPAC to which some units in

Vietnam were temporarily assigned.

U. S. MAAG-V: United States Military Assistance Advisory Group - Vietnam.

USNS: United States Naval Vessel (manned by merchant seaman rather than US Navy sailors).

UTT: Utility Tactical Transport Company - a funny name to try to conceal the capability and mission of this armed helicopter company.

VC: Viet Cong short for Vietnamese Communist / National Liberation Front.

VC Village: Generic slang used to describe any small town of unknown or unpronounceable name but known to be used by the Viet Cong. Often the target village near helibome assaults.

VHF: Very High Frequency: Army helicopters operated only on frequencies in this range for air-to-air during the first year of the Vietnam War and maybe longer - unable to communicate directly with US Air Force airplanes.

VNAF: South Vietnamese Air Force.

VTOL: Vertical Take-off and Landing fixed wing aircraft. This probably stems from experiments with convert-a-planes that could do both such as the USMC V-22 today. The category' was later changed to more exactly portray their capability as STOL or VSTOL (Vertical/Short Field Takeoff and Landing) but the "V" designation did not change for a number of years.

Walter Cronkite: Some may not remember this famous news anchor on CBS television. He was called "Uncle Walter' by his fans and 'The most trusted news voice in America." This was in the days of one half hour reports of only news stories with little commentary. Cronkite broke the code when he said that the war was not going to be successfully concluded or words to that effect. That broadcast is said to have led to President Johnson's decision to not run for further office.

Warrant Officer: The mid-grade between NCO & Commissioned Officers. Specially warranted for a career long specialty; in this case as an Army Aviator. Pay scale shadows commissioned officer pay. In the 1960s a CW-3 pay about equaled that of a major. Now the allowable grades have been increased to CW-5 and the pay has continued to parallel commissioned officer pay scale so that a senior CW-5 can serve with about the same remuneration as a colonel and with comparable retirement benefits.

WOJG: Warrant Officer Junior Grade, WO-1; new warrant officers. They are sometimes less than charitably called other things like Wobbly Ones, Wojjee Bears, etc. They are junior to all CWO.

XC: an abbreviation for cross-country.

XO: Company Executive Officer (2nd in command).